The Fuller Court

ABC-CLIO SUPREME COURT HANDBOOKS

The Burger Court, Tinsley E. Yarbrough
The Fuller Court, James W. Ely, Jr.
The Hughes Court, Michael E. Parrish
The Stone Court, Peter G. Renstrom
The Taft Court, Peter G. Renstrom
The Taney Court, Timothy S. Huebner
The Waite Court, Donald Grier Stephenson
The Warren Court, Melvin I. Urofsky

Forthcoming:
The Chase Court, Jonathan Lurie
The Jay/Ellsworth Court, Matthew P. Harrington
The Marshall Court, Robert L. Clinton
The Rehnquist Court, Thomas R. Hensley
The Vinson Court, Michal R. Belknap
The White Court, Rebecca S. Shoemaker

Peter G. Renstrom, Series Editor

ABC-CLIO SUPREME COURT HANDBOOKS

The Fuller Court

Justices, Rulings, and Legacy

James W. Ely, Jr.
Vanderbilt University Law School

ABC-CLIO

Santa Barbara, California • Denver, Colorado • Oxford, England

Library of Congress Cataloging-in-Publication Data

Ely, James W., Jr., 1938–
   The Fuller court: justices, rulings, and legacy / by James W. Ely, Jr.
      p. cm. — (ABC-CLIO Supreme Court handbooks)
Includes bibliographical references and index.
  ISBN 1-57607-714-4 (hardcover : alk. paper); ISBN 1-57607-715-2 (e-book)
 1. United States. Supreme Court—History. 2. Fuller, Melville Weston, 1833–1910.
 3. Constitutional history—United States. I. Title. II. Series
  KF8742.E45 2003
  347.73'26'09—dc21

                                 2003012951

07 06 05 04 03 10 9 8 7 6 5 4 3 2 1

ABC-CLIO, Inc.
130 Cremona Drive, P.O. Box 1911
Santa Barbara, California 93116-1911

This book is printed on acid-free paper ∞ .
Manufactured in the United States of America

For Mickey

Contents

Series Foreword

T here is an extensive literature on the U.S. Supreme Court, but it contains discussion familiar largely to the academic community and the legal profession. The ABC-CLIO Supreme Court series is designed to have value to the academic and legal communities also, but each volume is intended as well for the general reader who does not possess an extensive background on the Court or American constitutional law. The series is intended to effectively represent each of fourteen periods in the history of the Supreme Court with each of these fourteen eras defined by the chief justice beginning with John Jay in 1789. Each Court confronted constitutional and statutory questions that were of major importance to and influenced by the historical period. The Court's decisions were also influenced by the values of each of the individual justices sitting at the time. The issues, the historical period, the justices, and the Supreme Court's decisions in the most significant cases will be examined in the volumes of this series.

ABC-CLIO's Supreme Court series provides scholarly examinations of the Court as it functioned in different historical periods and with different justices. Each volume contains information necessary to understand each particular Court and an interpretative analysis by the author of each Court's record and legacy. In addition to representing the major decisions of each Court, institutional linkages are examined as well—the political connections among the Court, Congress, and the president. These relationships are important for several reasons. Although the Court retains some institutional autonomy, all the Court's justices are selected by a process that involves the other two branches. Many of the significant decisions of the Court involve the review of actions of Congress or the president. In addition, the Court frequently depends on the other two branches to secure compliance with its rulings.

The authors of the volumes in the ABC-CLIO series were selected with great care. Each author has worked extensively with the Court, the period, and the personalities about which he or she has written. ABC-CLIO wanted each of the volumes to examine several common themes, and each author agreed to work within certain guidelines. Each author was free, however, to develop the content of each volume, and many of the volumes advance new or distinctive conclusions about the Court under examination.

Each volume will contain four substantive chapters. The first chapter will introduce the Court and the historical period in which it served. The second chapter will examine each of the justices who sat on the particular Court. The third chapter will represent the most significant decisions rendered by the particular Court. Among other things, the impact of the historical period and the value orientations of the individual justices will be developed. A fourth and final chapter will address the impact of each particular Court on American constitutional law—its doctrinal legacy.

Each volume will contain several features designed to make the volume more valuable to those whose previous exposure to the Supreme Court and American constitutional law is limited. Each volume will have a reference section that will contain brief entries on some of the people, statutes, events, and concepts introduced in the four substantive chapters. Entries in this section are arranged alphabetically. Each volume will also contain a glossary of selected legal terms used in the text. Following each of the four chapters, a list of sources used in the chapter and suggestions for further reading will appear. Each volume will also have a comprehensive annotated bibliography. A listing of Internet sources is presented at the end of the bibliography. Finally, there will be a comprehensive subject index and a list of cases (with citation numbers) discussed in each volume. ABC-CLIO is delighted with the quality of scholarship represented in each volume and is proud to offer this series to the reading public.

Permit me to conclude with a personal note. This project has been an extraordinarily rewarding undertaking for me as series editor. Misgivings about serving in this capacity were plentiful at the outset of the project. After tending to some administrative business pertaining to the series, securing authors for each volume was the first major task. I developed a list of possible authors after reviewing previous work and obtaining valuable counsel from several recognized experts in American constitutional history. In virtually every instance, the first person on my list agreed to participate in the project. The high quality of the series was assured and enhanced as each author signed on. I could not have been more pleased. My interactions with each author have been most pleasant, and the excellence of their work will be immediately apparent to the reader. I sincerely thank each author.

Finally, a word about ABC-CLIO and its staff. ABC-CLIO was enthusiastic about the project from the beginning and has done everything necessary to make this series successful. I am very appreciative of the level of support I have received from ABC-CLIO. Alicia Merritt, senior acquisitions editor, deserves special recognition. She has held my hand throughout the project. She has facilitated making this project a reality in every conceivable way. She has encouraged me from the beginning, provided invaluable counsel, and given me latitude to operate as I wished while keeping me on track at the same time. This project would not have gotten off the ground without Alicia, and I cannot thank her enough.

—*Peter G. Renstrom*

Preface

The Supreme Court under Chief Justice Melville W. Fuller largely mirrored the attitudes and values of Americans at the close of the nineteenth and the beginning of the twentieth centuries. It was a time when sweeping changes in the economy and public life transformed American society. It was a time of conflict between traditional values and the forces of innovation. The Progressive Movement, which emerged after 1900, sought to utilize the powers of government in novel ways to address some of the social issues arising from urbanization and industrialization. The Fuller Court, like other organs of both federal and state government, was confronted with new and vexing legal conflicts, and the justices became increasingly active in exercising judicial review of legislation.

Although dominated by economic conservatives, the Fuller Court was never the servant of corporate special interests pictured by its Progressive critics. Rather, the justices sought to vindicate time-honored principles of limited government and economic freedom in a society undergoing rapid change. Drawing upon Jacksonian principles, they looked with disfavor upon laws favoring any class or group of citizens. This libertarian impulse, moreover, was reinforced by a strong desire to safeguard investment capital and to foster the growth of a national economy. The private law doctrines fashioned by the Fuller Court were generally consistent with developments in constitutional law, and also pointed toward encouragement of interstate business enterprise.

Still Fuller and his colleagues, again reflecting tensions inherent in the polity, were often torn between respect for state sovereignty and the need for federal judicial intervention to vindicate the constitutional rights of property owners. Consequently, they usually deferred to state governance of social issues and criminal justice, and upheld most state health and safety regulations as valid exercises of the police power. Aside from the just compensation requirement in the takings clause of the Fifth Amendment, the Fuller Court justices declined to extend the Bill of Rights guarantees to the states by means of the Due Process Clause of the Fourteenth Amendment. They were, however, deeply suspicious of legislation that was redistributionist in nature or that impeded the workings of the national market. Like the framers of the Constitution and Bill of Rights, members of the Fuller Court linked respect for property rights with the preservation of individual liberty.

The Fuller Court rarely wandered outside the contours of dominant public opinion. To be sure, Populists and Progressives were often critical of the work of the Court, but they did not reflect majority sentiment. This was an era of Republican Party ascendancy in national political life. The only Democrat to reach the White House in these years, Grover Cleveland, shared many of the conservative economic views of the Republican presidents. Not surprisingly, the Fuller Court justices generally took positions congruent with the prevailing societal attitudes. In an age of pervasive racism, this helps to explain why the Court was indifferent to the claims of racial minorities.

The unique place of the Fuller Court in history was shaped by its robust defense of economic liberties in the face of growing governmental regulation. To some extent, the Fuller era justices were just following in the footsteps of their predecessors. The federal courts early assumed the role of protecting property and contractual rights through the enforcement of both constitutional provisions and common law rights. Indeed, protection of property rights was a central theme in American jurisprudence from the Marshall Court until the so-called constitutional revolution of 1937. At that point, in a sharp departure from the past, the Supreme Court created a dichotomy between property rights and other personal liberties, and afforded a lesser degree of constitutional protection to economic liberty. The Fuller Court was therefore operating well within the main currents of American constitutionalism before the New Deal. What set the Fuller Court apart was its willingness to wield forcefully judicial review and to articulate novel constitutional doctrines designed to protect economic liberty.

The Fuller Court and the justices who served on it, with the conspicuous exceptions of Stephen J. Field, John M. Harlan, and Oliver Wendell Holmes, Jr., have been unaccountably neglected by historians. For too long scholars have simply ratified the assessments of Populists and Progressives, and adopted a dismissive tone toward the work of the Fuller Court. Such an approach, however, oversimplifies a more complex story. I hope in this volume to convince readers that the Fuller era was a time of rich constitutional jurisprudence. The justices of the Fuller Court tackled fundamental questions concerning the role of government in American life, and rendered decisions that had a lasting impact. Indeed, the themes of federalism and property rights, which bulked so large in Fuller Court jurisprudence, are once again lively subjects of constitutional dialogue.

Over the past few years I have written an earlier book and published a number of articles dealing with the Supreme Court under Chief Justice Fuller. I welcomed this opportunity provided by ABC-CLIO to revisit this important topic and to incorporate the fruits of additional research as well as more recent scholarly literature.

Readers should bear in mind some features of this volume. An alphabetically arranged reference section gives information about selected people, legislative acts, and signal events to augment the discussion found in the first four chapters. At the end of the reference section is a chronology of the period 1888–1910, which presents the dates of key Fuller Court decisions, major legislative enactments, personnel changes in the Court, and other important developments. A glossary of legal terms follows the reference section. There are also three appendices. The first contains Fuller's 1889 address to Congress to commemorate George Washington's inauguration as president. The second provides excerpts from a speech by Justice David J. Brewer in 1898 discussing the decisions by the Fuller Court invalidating the 1894 income tax. The third gives the full text of the important and controversial decision of the Fuller Court in *Lochner v. New York* (1905). Lastly, there is an extensive annotated bibliography on the Fuller era.

A number of people contributed to the publication of this book. I wish to give special thanks to my colleague, Jon W. Bruce, who read large portions of this manuscript and offered helpful comments. My colleague Donald J. Hall made astute observations about the section on criminal law. The series editor, Peter G. Renstrom, convinced me to undertake this project and provided encouragement at every turn. The reference staff of the Massey Law Library of Vanderbilt University furnished outstanding support service and helped me track down obscure sources. I, of course, accept full responsibility for any errors. Finally, many thanks to my wife Mickey for her love and support.

James W. Ely, Jr.

The Fuller Court

PART ONE

Justices, Rulings, and Legacy

The Fuller Court and the Period

T he Fuller Court spanned the end of the nineteenth and the first decade of the twentieth centuries. It coincided with a pivotal era in American history, marked by far-reaching economic changes and the emergence of the United States as a world power. Under the leadership of Chief Justice Melville W. Fuller, the U.S. Supreme Court addressed a host of novel legal issues arising from the transformation of the United States into an industrialized nation. The Fuller Court rendered many important and well-known decisions that defined economic and social institutions for decades, and it left a lasting imprint on American law. The Fuller era represents one of the most bold and creative chapters in the history of the Supreme Court.

Fuller was nominated as chief justice of the nation's highest court by President Grover Cleveland on April 30, 1888, to replace Morrison R. Waite, who died in March of that year. After some delay, the U.S. Senate confirmed Fuller's appointment in July. Fuller took the oath of office in October and was the first person to be formally commissioned with the title Chief Justice of the United States. In this new role he immediately presided over the first session of the Fuller Court. Fuller served as chief justice for nearly twenty-two years (1888–1910), a period longer than any other chief justice except John Marshall (1801–1835) and Roger B. Taney (1836–1864). He died on July 4, 1910, and was succeeded by Edward D. White, one of the associate justices who had been on the Court with Fuller.

Fuller and his colleagues believed that individual liberty and property rights were interdependent. The Fuller Court was therefore dedicated to economic liberty as the preeminent constitutional value. The jurisprudence of the Fuller era was characterized by the principles of limited government, state autonomy, and respect for the rights of property owners. Consequently, the Fuller Court assumed the desirability of private economic ordering and looked skeptically at measures that infringed upon the workings of the free market. Cases involving economic rights certainly did not entirely define the Fuller Court; in other areas of law the justices generally upheld governmental authority. Hence, the historical reputation of the Fuller Court is closely linked with the defense of property rights.

No court functions in a vacuum. Much of the work of the Fuller Court was molded by social, economic, and intellectual currents of late-nineteenth-century America. To understand the historical context of the Fuller Court one must bear in mind the often conflicting forces that shaped the polity of America during the Gilded Age. This chapter canvasses, albeit briefly, the historical milieu in which the Fuller Court operated. In so doing, I will identify the major factors that influenced the Supreme Court's pattern of decision. I will also introduce the associate justices who sat on the Fuller Court, as well as the circumstances surrounding their nominations. And finally, in wrapping up this introduction, I will describe the aggregate personality of the Fuller Court, ending with a discussion of Fuller's leadership style as chief justice.

Gilded-Age America

When Fuller became chief justice in 1888 the United States was in the midst of profound economic and social change. The most significant change was the dramatic growth of industry and large-scale corporate enterprise. Manufacturing replaced agriculture as the primary source of national wealth. Indeed, by 1900 the United States had become the foremost industrial country in the world. Railroads, America's first big business, created a national market for goods, linked farming communities and small towns to urban centers, and pulled farmers into the market economy. Private investment capital was essential to finance this spectacular economic spurt.

Industrialization altered American society in fundamental ways. People continuously migrated from farm to city, causing explosive urban growth. There they joined recent immigrants in the search for greater economic opportunities. The percentage of the American population living in urban areas increased steadily during the late nineteenth century. This rapid growth in the nation's cities led to overcrowded housing and public health problems, often overwhelming local officials. The physical proximity of commercial operations to residential areas posed safety and health concerns. Congested living conditions meant that one owner's use of land had a direct impact on his neighbor's quality of life. This in turn led to fledgling attempts to control land use.

Another concern was the distribution of wealth created by the new industrial order. Many Americans prospered during the Gilded Age, and property ownership became widespread. Still, there were fears about an increasing economic disparity within society. The federal government relied almost entirely on excise taxes and customs duties for revenue. Some commentators and political figures promoted a federal income tax as a means of reducing the tariff and redistributing wealth, a view that proved highly controversial.

Employment relationships were fundamentally changed by the rise of large business enterprises. Employees increasingly worked in an impersonal environment and had little ability to improve working conditions. Not many employees were members of labor unions, and employers as a practical matter could determine wages and other conditions of employment. A ten-hour workday was common. Workplace safety was also a vexing issue. Early factories were frequently dangerous, and many workers were hurt on the job. Railroad work was especially hazardous. Determining responsibility for workplace accidents proved a challenge for the legal system. The victims of industrial accidents brought many lawsuits for negligence, but common law doctrines restricted employer liability. As a result, injured employees frequently received no compensation.

Patent law was also affected by changes in the economy. The Gilded Age produced an extraordinary outpouring of inventive activity. The number of patents grew steadily, giving rise to complex litigation. The Supreme Court under Fuller heard a steady stream of appeals involving the validity and enforcement of patents.

In addition to the problems associated with industrialization and urbanization, many Americans grew increasingly apprehensive about massive immigration in the late nineteenth century. As more and more immigrants came from Southern and Eastern Europe, critics blamed crime, political radicalism, and a variety of social ills on the traditional policy of open immigration. Unions argued that immigrants competed for jobs and reduced wage scales. Pressures for exclusion mounted, and Congress gradually tightened the laws governing immigration. Still, employers continued to need labor, and not until the 1920s would the United States abandon the open-door policy.

Immigrants from China and Japan aroused especially intense resentment. There was continuous agitation to stop further Chinese immigration and to restrict those Chinese already in the country. Starting in 1882, Congress passed a series of Chinese exclusion acts. Congress also established procedures to deport resident Chinese laborers unless they obtained special certificates. Similar limitations were directed against Japanese immigrants.

Although the bitter feeling aroused by the Civil War gradually faded, the defeated South remained a singular region. There were a number of problems associated with that impoverished region during the Gilded Age. Most conspicuous was the successful drive to restore white rule. As northerners turned away from Reconstruction, white supremacist sentiments gained ascendancy in southern politics. Southern Democrats curtailed black suffrage, instituted a one-party political system, and imposed formal racial segregation on many social institutions. Perceived challenges to the racial order triggered a wave of lynchings of blacks throughout the South in the 1890s, a testament to the climate of intense racial hostility. Racist social views were widely shared in America at the end of the nineteenth century, but the South was unique with its demand for legalized segregation.

Southerners were not of one mind with respect to national economic development. On the one hand, champions of the New South sought to encourage industrial growth and lured northern investors with tax exemptions and subsidies. Indeed, industrial activity in the region expanded, and railroad mileage increased considerably. On the other hand, most southerners were still engaged in agriculture, and a system of tenant farming spread widely. Many poor farmers felt trapped by crop-lien laws, whereby crops were pledged as security for supplies advanced for planting. The crop-lien laws tended to augment the power of large landowners and merchants. Further, some southern political leaders were skeptical about northern control of the southern regional economy. These attitudes would fuel populist attacks on railroad companies and federal courts during the 1890s. Despite attempts to foster economic growth, the South as a whole stayed well behind the rest of the nation in industrialization and personal income.

Another bitterly contested issue in the South was debt repudiation. After Reconstruction many debt-ridden southern states and localities repudiated or scaled back their large bonded indebtedness. Vast sums were at stake, and northern investors turned to the federal courts to compel states and localities to pay their obligations. The upshot was protracted litigation, renewed sectional tensions, and impaired future credit for southern governmental units.

As a result of the Spanish-American War in 1898 the United States acquired the overseas territories of the Philippines and Puerto Rico. This put the United States in the awkward position of holding colonial possessions, triggering a debate over whether colonialism was fundamentally inconsistent with American constitutionalism. The constitutional status of these annexed lands raised novel questions. In a number of cases, the Fuller Court was called upon to decide whether, in the language of the day, the Constitution followed the flag or whether the United States could rule these territories without regard to constitutional guarantees.

The dominant political attitudes of the day generally favored a laissez-faire approach to economic questions. There was little expectation that the federal government should play a large part in governing American society. Still, there was apprehension about control of the economy by large corporations. This prompted a few tentative steps by Congress to police business activity. In 1887 Congress passed the Interstate Commerce Act, the first major affirmative use of federal regulatory authority, creating the Interstate Commerce Commission to supervise railroad operations. Some businesses sought to stabilize volatile markets through a variety of contractual or trust arrangements. These practices aroused public hostility because they were seen as limiting competition and raising prices. The Sherman Anti-Trust Act of 1890 outlawed combinations in restraint of trade and sought to preserve the notion of competition and free markets. These measures were difficult to enforce and had only modest impact until after 1900.

Absent a sustained assertion of federal power, the political structure of the country remained largely decentralized. The states continued to exercise primary regulatory authority over economic activities. There was an outpouring of state laws designed to harness the new economic forces. In particular, the states took the lead in enacting laws to safeguard public health, safety, and morals. Yet such state statutes inevitably curtailed the use of private property and contractual freedom, and they threatened to interfere with interstate commerce.

Economic and social changes proceeded hand in glove with new patterns in constitutional thought. The leading constitutional theorists of the Gilded Age decried governmental intervention in the economy and had a broad conception of property rights. These new intellectual currents focused on the provision of the Fourteenth Amendment to the U.S. Constitution that no state should "deprive any person of life, liberty, or property without due process of law." There was similar language in many state constitutions. The due process norm has deep roots in Anglo-American history. Although due process was commonly associated with procedural guarantees, state courts in the antebellum era wrestled with the notion that due process also encompassed substantive restraints on government. Substantive due process was grounded on the premise that there were certain fundamental liberties, beyond those mentioned in the Constitution, that government could not arbitrarily infringe. In other words, due process imposed substantive constraints on legislative power. Business enterprises increasingly turned to the Fourteenth Amendment as a federal guarantee against what they perceived as unreasonable interference with their economic rights.

Following the Civil War, influential treatise writers, such as Thomas M. Cooley and Christopher G. Tiedeman, insisted that due process went beyond mere procedure and safeguarded the economic rights of individuals. Linking the Jacksonian heritage of equal rights and hostility to special privileges with due process protection, Cooley assailed class legislation that conferred special benefits on individuals or groups. Lawmakers, he reasoned, could not legitimately advance the condition of one group at the expense of others. Tiedeman underscored Cooley's ideas and urged a narrow understanding of state regulatory authority. He was especially concerned that courts protect the freedom of private parties to make contracts without legislative infringement.

Initially the Supreme Court, despite forceful dissents by Justice Stephen J. Field, was reluctant to accept a broad construction of the Fourteenth Amendment. But judicial attitudes began to shift in the 1880s, and the Court was more receptive to the contention that the Due Process Clause of the Fourteenth Amendment limited state police power over economic life. In *Mugler v. Kansas* (1887), for instance, the justices moved toward a substantive interpretation of the Due Process Clause to uphold the rights of property owners. The Supreme Court sustained the constitutionality of a Kansas prohibition statute but stressed that courts could scrutinize the purpose behind state regulation and need not presume the validity of statutes. With

Mugler, the Supreme Court served notice that laws ostensibly designed to protect public health, safety, or morals might be deemed in actuality to constitute unreasonable deprivations of property without due process. Fuller's appointment as chief justice came at a crucial time in the evolution of substantive due process. Shortly after Fuller assumed the center chair, the Supreme Court began to affirm a wide-ranging federal judicial supervision of state economic legislation and to strike down state laws on due process grounds.

Voices of Discontent

Americans struggled to come to terms with the rapid and unsettling changes of the late nineteenth century. Although a growing urban middle class prospered, an economic transformation of such magnitude inevitably caused social dislocation. In particular, many farmers and industrial workers felt vulnerable in a society dominated by large corporations. Their misgivings sparked political protests and led to calls for a radical new notion of law as a vehicle to curb private economic power and to aid the disaffected.

The early 1890s was an especially difficult period for agriculture. Facing declining crop prices and drought, western and southern farmers were sinking into debt. Feeling victimized by an unstable agricultural market, discontented farmers lashed out at the new economic order. They urged steps to inflate the currency, a demand that increasingly took the form of calls for the unlimited coinage of silver. Many farm groups also took special aim at railroads, the most conspicuous symbol of industrialization. Feeling at the mercy of railroads, farmers complained about excessive transportation charges that allegedly consumed their profits. Although the allegations of railroad abuse were overblown, the anger of southern and western farmers toward the carriers contributed to a mood of political radicalism.

As unrest among farmers grew, their discontent found expression in the formation of a new third political party, the People's Party, better known as the Populists. The Populist movement reflected deep agrarian disenchantment with the economic changes sweeping the nation. In essence, Populists hoped to reshape governmental policy for the benefit of agriculture in the face of an industrializing economy. They rejected the dominant laissez-faire philosophy and the existing political system. Viewing economic issues in a moralistic light, Populists attributed agricultural distress to large corporations and concentrated wealth.

The People's Party platform of 1892 spoke in dire terms of "a nation brought to the verge of moral, political, and material ruin." Departing sharply from laissez-faire norms, Populists insisted that the powers of government should be expanded to assist the disadvantaged. Specifically, they demanded government ownership of the railroads, a graduated income tax, currency policies to benefit debtors, limits on immigration, and reduced working hours. Many of these ideas had been around for years, and there is reason to question whether any of them adequately addressed the root causes of agrarian distress. Still, the Populist movement was the first important political movement in American history to maintain that the government should affirmatively check private economic power. Conservatives assailed the Populists' proposals as class legislation and predicted they would lead to the confiscation of private property.

Although the People's Party never prevailed in a national election, some Populist proposals were adopted by the major political parties and became law at the federal or state levels. But the Populist program ran directly counter to the Fuller Court's attachment to market arrangements and private property rights. Populist leaders watched with dismay as the Fuller Court struck down the income tax, curtailed the reach of antitrust laws, and rendered a line of decisions sympathetic to railroads. The direction of the Supreme Court under Fuller became an issue in the 1896 presidential election. The Democratic Party platform, reflecting strong Populist influence, denounced the income tax ruling as well as other decisions by Fuller and his colleagues. These Populist-inspired complaints were to no immediate avail. The election of Republican William McKinley as president in 1896 temporarily halted the anti-Court agitation.

Not typically drawn to the rural-based Populist movement, industrial workers nonetheless had their own concerns about the new industrial order. Periodic economic downturns left much of the workforce unemployed. Strikes, commonly triggered by employer moves to cut wages, increased in frequency and violence during the late nineteenth century. Major strikes occurred in coal mines, steel plants, and the railroad industry. The bitter Homestead strike by Pennsylvania steelworkers in 1892 witnessed violent clashes between troops and laborers. The Pullman strike of 1894 in Chicago disrupted the national railroad system and generated destructive riots. President Grover Cleveland dispatched federal troops to restore order.

Unions were not a vital force in American life at the end of the nineteenth century. The American Federation of Labor, organized by craft unions in 1886, urged legal recognition of unions and collective bargaining. But less than 10 percent of the industrial workforce was unionized during the Gilded Age. Labor law was largely fashioned at the state level. Legislators responded to changing labor conditions in contradictory ways. On the one hand, states sought to eliminate grievances arising from industrialization. Some enacted laws, for example, imposing methods of wage payment and regulating working conditions. Similarly, a number of states restricted the use of child labor. On the other hand, states passed legislation that outlawed boycotts and curtailed picketing.

An important reform movement, known as Progressivism, gained strength in the first decade of the twentieth century. The objectives of the Progressives were diverse and even contradictory. Although they borrowed ideas from Populists and labor unions, Progressives were largely middle class in background and had centralist political views. Progressives were interested in electoral reforms to make the political system more responsive to the public. Their primary concern, however, was the imbalance of power associated with the new economic order. They accepted private property and market ordering as the basis for the economy but attempted to mitigate the abuses and harshness of industrialization. To achieve such goals Progressives insisted on more active involvement by the state and federal governments in the economy to control corporate enterprise and to improve conditions in the industrial workplace. They championed a broad reading of state police power to provide a constitutional basis for their legislative program. President Theodore Roosevelt, the former vice president under McKinley, who was reelected in 1900 and then assassinated in 1901, embodied much of the Progressive spirit.

Progressives were confident about the ability of social science to resolve social and economic problems. They urged the creation of administrative agencies, staffed by nonpolitical experts, to regulate aspects of the economy. As Progressives saw it, such agencies had the benefit of expertise and flexibility and offered a rational means of managing business activity free from political manipulation. The Progressives' faith in administrative regulation seems misplaced to modern eyes. In practice, agency decisions on economic issues could seldom be separated from political considerations. Nor did administrative bodies prove to be any panacea for economic problems.

Whatever their limitations, Populists, labor unions, and Progressives helped to shape national political life and challenged the prevailing constitutional norms that stressed limited government and entrepreneurial liberty. Although not doctrinaire adherents of laissez-faire, Fuller and his colleagues looked askance at laws impinging the rights of property owners or the flow of trade among the states. The stage was therefore set for a series of clashes that pitted the property-minded Fuller Court against those who were calling for increased governmental regulation.

Assembling the Fuller Court

When Fuller took the oath as chief justice on October 8, 1888, he faced the daunting task of gaining the confidence of the sitting justices. Fuller had only limited experience in public life and, although he had argued before the Supreme Court, was largely unknown to his new colleagues. Indeed, several of the associate justices had urged that one of their number, Stephen J. Field, be named chief justice. To this point in American history, however, every chief justice had been selected from outside the

The Fuller Court from 1888 to 1889: (front row—left to right) Joseph P. Bradley, Samuel F. Miller, Melville W. Fuller, Stephen J. Field, Lucious Q. C. Lamar; (back row—left to right) Stanley Matthews, Horace Gray, John Marshall Harlan, Samuel Blatchford (C. M. Bell, Collection of the Supreme Court of the United States)

existing Court membership. President Grover Cleveland wished to follow this practice, and he looked for a conservative Democrat who shared the president's commitment to sound money and his aversion to governmental paternalism.

Cleveland's decision to nominate Fuller was guided by a number of political considerations. A presidential election, widely expected to be close, was only months away when the vacancy was created by the death of Chief Justice Morrison R. Waite in March 1888. Cleveland needed to move quickly or possibly lose the chance to make an appointment. With the Senate under narrow Republican control, it was necessary to name a person who could attract a degree of bipartisan support.

There were, moreover, compelling reasons to select a nominee from Illinois. When not sitting in Washington, Supreme Court justices were still obligated by the Judiciary Act of 1789 to conduct judicial business in the circuit courts, which at that time were the principal federal courts of general jurisdiction. Circuit duty necessitated considerable travel and became ever more burdensome as the nation expanded. By tradition presidents picked justices so that the Court would include one from each of the various circuits. Yet the Seventh Circuit (which included Illinois) did not have a representative on the Court. Cleveland may also have reasoned that by selecting an Illinois nominee he would aid his chance of carrying that state in his bid for reelection.

After considering other names, Cleveland settled on Fuller, who was then a lawyer in private practice in Chicago. A lifelong Democrat, Fuller was a strong supporter of the Cleveland administration and agreed with the president's conservative economic views. The two corresponded regularly, and the president sought Fuller's advice with respect to political patronage in Illinois. Impressed with Fuller's abilities, Cleveland offered him a number of important posts, including chairman of the Civil Service Commission and solicitor general. Disinclined to leave Chicago, Fuller repeatedly declined the president's requests.

Clearly Fuller did not seek the chief justiceship and was, in fact, hesitant to accept the nomination. Fuller was genuinely concerned about disrupting his large family by a move to Washington, but he was doubtless also aware of the financial implications of service on the Supreme Court. Fuller would suffer a severe loss of professional income, since the salary of the chief justice was a modest $10,500. Still, the call to the nation's highest court proved too strong to resist, and so Fuller allowed his name to go forward.

Fuller's nomination was well received in Illinois, but the reaction elsewhere was more cautious. Approval of Fuller's designation by the Senate was delayed for several months, largely for partisan reasons. Senator George F. Edmunds of Vermont vigorously opposed Fuller's appointment and stalled consideration by the Judiciary Committee. Two objections were raised in opposition to confirmation. The first concern was Fuller's political activities during the Civil War. As a state legislator, Fuller had been sharply critical of Abraham Lincoln's administration and had denounced the Emancipation Proclamation, which freed the slaves. Opponents pictured him as a Copperhead, a northern sympathizer with the Confederacy. The second issue pertained to shadowy charges of professional misconduct brought by disappointed litigants. Fuller's backers, however, successfully refuted the allegations of wartime disloyalty. Nor was any credible evidence presented of impropriety by Fuller. Even so, the Judiciary Committee took no action on Fuller's nomination, apparently hoping to delay any report until after the November presidential election.

Republican senators favorable to Fuller eventually insisted that the committee send the nomination to the full Senate. On July 20, 1888, the Senate debated Fuller's appointment in an executive session. Critics argued that Fuller could not be trusted to interpret the Reconstruction amendments, but the Senate confirmed Fuller's appointment by a vote of 41–20.

Fuller was understandably apprehensive about establishing a relationship with the current members of the Supreme Court, among whom were several imposing figures. "No rising sun for me," he reflected in 1890, "with these old luminaries blazing away with all their ancient fires" (quoted in Ely 1995, 25). Fuller's efforts to win the friendship and support of his associates was made more difficult by frequent changes in the composition of the Court. The early 1890s was a period of exceptionally heavy turnover among Court members. Five of the justices on the bench when Fuller became chief died by 1893. Eleven new justices appointed by five presidents joined the Court during Fuller's period of service. Despite this high turnover rate, the Fuller Court contained a number of distinguished jurists. There were, of course, other justices who were not particularly strong and left little mark on American law.

Given the large number of justices who served with Fuller, it is perhaps surprising that more of the appointments to the Court during this era did not stir controversy. Contested appointments were most likely when the president was a member of one political party and the Senate was under the control of the other party. Partisan, patronage, and geographic concerns, not judicial philosophy, were behind confirmation battles. Indeed, it was not the practice in the nineteenth century for Supreme Court nominees to make a personal appearance before the Senate Judiciary Committee or to answer questions about their views.

Samuel F. Miller was the most senior justice when Fuller became chief. Miller's appointment to the bench was prompted in part by an overhaul of the circuit courts to take account of the newer western states. At the outbreak of the Civil War, Congress adjusted the judicial circuits and created a new circuit encompassing four states west of the Mississippi River. The seat of the deceased Justice Peter V. Daniel had been vacant for more than two years. President Lincoln was determined to select a Supreme Court justice who resided in the new circuit and shared the president's antislavery convictions. Active in Iowa Republican politics and a strong supporter of Lincoln, Miller was one of the most prominent attorneys in the trans-Mississippi West. Lincoln did not know Miller personally, but key political figures in western states aggressively promoted his candidacy. Nominated by Lincoln on July 16, 1862, Miller was unanimously confirmed by the Senate that same day.

Miller was generally an apostle of judicial restraint. He is best known for decisions that influenced the initial understanding of the Fourteenth Amendment. Miller authored the majority opinion in the famous *Slaughterhouse Cases* (1873), holding that the Privileges and Immunities Clause of the Fourteenth Amendment did not enlarge the constitutionally protected rights of citizens or bring about a fundamental change in the authority of the national government over the states. In line with this narrow view of the Fourteenth Amendment, Miller supported a wide latitude for the states to regulate business. Miller died in October 1890, having served only two years with Fuller. His contribution to American law, therefore, largely predated the Fuller era. Miller did little to shape the record of the Fuller Court.

In contrast, another Lincoln appointee, Stephen J. Field, became the most influential jurist of the Gilded Age and made a major contribution to the jurisprudence of the Fuller Court. Like Miller, Field owed his nomination to changes in the structure of the federal judiciary. In 1863 Congress temporarily increased the number of Supreme Court justices from nine to ten and created a new Tenth Circuit consisting of California and Oregon. Lincoln wanted a justice from the new circuit who was a strong Unionist. He turned to Field, a Democrat, who at the time was the chief justice of the California Supreme Court. Field had been an outspoken defender of the Union cause. Field's candidacy was urged by his brother, David Dudley Field, a leading law reformer with ties to the Lincoln administration. This was an early instance of a president filling a Supreme Court vacancy with a candidate from another political party. Lincoln sent Field's name to the Senate on March 7, 1863, and he was unanimously confirmed four days later.

As Lincoln hoped, Field sustained the president's course in litigation arising from the Civil War. Thereafter, during his long service on the Court, Field was a forceful champion of the rights of property owners. To Field, economic liberty was among the most important constitutional rights. He pioneered an expansive reading of the Due Process Clause of the Fourteenth Amendment to guard private property and business enterprise from state regulation. Over time Field saw the dissenting opinions of his early years adopted by the Fuller Court.

Justice Joseph P. Bradley, nominated to the Supreme Court by President Ulysses S. Grant in 1870, was on the bench less than four years while Fuller was chief. A leading New Jersey attorney, Bradley represented railroad companies and had argued several cases before the Supreme Court. Like Fuller and Miller, Bradley had no previous judicial experience. The retirement of Justice Robert C. Grier created a vacancy on the Supreme Court. Geographic considerations dictated that Grier's successor should come from the same judicial circuit, which included New Jersey. A strong Republican and a Grant supporter, Bradley was an obvious choice for the President.

Bradley's nomination was caught up in the controversy surrounding the *Legal Tender Cases* (1870). Briefly stated, those cases involved the validity of the Civil War legal tender legislation under which the federal government had issued large amounts of paper money. In *Hepburn v. Griswold* (1870), one of the *Legal Tender Cases*, the Supreme Court, by a margin of 4–3, struck down the legal tender act as applied to contracts made before its enactment. On the day *Hepburn* was decided Grant named Bradley and William Strong to fill vacancies on the Supreme Court. It was widely believed that the two appointees would vote to overrule *Hepburn* and sustain the legal tender laws. Grant's action prompted allegations that Bradley and Strong had been selected to pack the Court. Bradley, who had consistently favored legal tender laws, did indeed vote to overturn *Hepburn*. Although most historians reject the court-packing charge leveled at Grant, the controversy over the *Legal Tender Cases* jeopardized the Court's reputation for political independence.

Nominated by Grant on February 7, Bradley faced opposition from some Republican senators who regarded him as sympathetic to soft money. Yet all the Democrats supported him. Senate consideration of the appointment was delayed for six weeks, when Bradley was finally confirmed by a vote of 46–9.

On the bench Bradley took a restrictive view of civil rights protection under the Fourteenth Amendment. His record on issues pertaining to economic regulation was mixed. Dissenting in the *Slaughterhouse Cases* (1873), Bradley insisted that the Fourteenth Amendment safeguarded the right to pursue lawful occupations. Yet he generally upheld the power of states to regulate railroads and other businesses that had acquired a public character. Bradley authored some important decisions dealing with the repudiation of bonded debt while on the Fuller Court, but he is best remembered for work before Fuller took the center chair.

John Marshall Harlan, nominated by President Rutherford B. Hayes, was the only sitting justice who went on to serve for the entire period of the Fuller Court. A Kentucky native, Harlan became a Republican after the Civil War and twice unsuccessfully ran for governor. He was a leader among Kentucky Republicans and was instrumental in switching Kentucky's votes to Hayes at the 1876 Republican national convention. When Hayes finally prevailed in the disputed presidential election of that year, he decided to send a commission to Louisiana to help resolve a conflict over which claimant was the governor of that state. Harlan agreed to serve on the commission, a vexing task that earned him the gratitude of the president. When Justice David Davis of Illinois resigned in 1877 to accept a Senate seat, Hayes spent months deciding upon a successor. Geographic considerations pointed toward a candidate from the same circuit as the departing Davis. Nonetheless, Hayes nominated Harlan, who made no secret of his aspirations for a seat on the Supreme Court, on October 16, 1877. The president acted in part to encourage sectional reconciliation by naming a border-state moderate acceptable to the South.

The initial reaction to Harlan's nomination was cool, and opposition soon gathered. One point of opposition was predicated on circuit grounds. With Harlan's confirmation, the Seventh Circuit, which included Illinois, would lose a representative on the Court. A number of prominent Chicago attorneys, including Fuller, assailed Harlan's nomination and called for the selection of a justice from within the Seventh Circuit. Fuller called the Harlan nomination "a disagreeable surprise" and added that it "accomplished nothing except to reward a Louisiana Commissioner, a personal and secondary consideration. I hope the nomination will fail of confirmation" (quoted in Ely 1995, 28). Another line of attack questioned Harlan's commitment to the Republican Party and his initial criticism of the Emancipation Proclamation and the Reconstruction amendments. Finally, Republican senators associated with the stalwart faction opposed Harlan simply as a way to undercut President Hayes. In turn, Harlan defended his dedication to the program of the Republican Party. The opposition to Harlan gradually melted away, and he was confirmed by voice vote on November 29, about six weeks after the nomination.

Harlan was an important, if somewhat enigmatic, figure on the Fuller Court. Celebrated among modern scholars for eloquent dissenting opinions in civil rights cases, Harlan compiled a complex and even contradictory record while on the bench. In some respects he stood apart from the mainstream of Fuller Court jurisprudence. Harlan was often sympathetic to the equal rights claims of blacks, favored an income tax as a vehicle to shift the tax burden to the wealthy, and took a dark view of the unchecked power of large corporations. Yet he voted with his colleagues to affirm contractual freedom, to establish that the Due Process Clause of the Fourteenth Amendment guaranteed substantive rights, and to hold that the Due Process Clause required states to pay just compensation when private property was taken for public use. Although a frequent dissenter, Harlan also authored a number of leading opinions for the Fuller Court. The career of this individualist continues to fascinate historians.

In January 1881 Justice Noah H. Swayne resigned. This resignation brought the lame-duck President Hayes another opportunity to name a member of the Supreme Court. Late that month Hayes nominated Stanley Matthews of Ohio, a Kenyon College classmate and lifelong friend. Matthews had served with Hayes in the Ohio Volunteer Infantry during the Civil War. Moreover, Matthews had skillfully represented the Hays-Republican presidential electors before the election commission of 1876–1877. The Matthews nomination, however, ran into stiff opposition based in large part on Matthews's representation of the controversial financier Jay Gould. The Senate took no action, and the Matthews nomination seemed to be dead.

Incoming president James A. Garfield (elected 1880, assassinated 1881) surprised many by renominating Matthews. This step may have been due to the political influence of Gould. In any event, the renomination of Matthews triggered two months of bitter debate. Once again opponents focused on Matthews's ties to railroad interests. Some critics also stressed that, as the U.S. attorney for the southern district of Ohio, Matthews had enforced the Fugitive Slave Act in the late 1850s despite his anti-slavery convictions. He was finally confirmed on May 12, 1881, by a vote of 24–23. Matthews remains the only justice to reach the Court by a one-vote margin.

Dying in March 1889, Matthews was on the Court just six months during Fuller's chief justiceship. He was ill when Fuller took the oath and never sat on the bench with Fuller. Under these circumstances, Matthews played no role in developing the Fuller's Court legacy.

President Chester A. Arthur, who succeeded Garfield and served until 1885, appointed two justices who performed ably on the Fuller Court. The death of Justice Nathan Clifford in early 1881 created a vacancy that Arthur filled with Horace Gray of Massachusetts. Gray, the chief justice of the Supreme Judicial Court of Massachusetts at the time, was strongly recommended to Arthur by the Massachusetts congressional delegation. The nomination enjoyed wide support both in Congress and on the Court itself. Gray was confirmed by a vote of 51–5 on December 20, one day after his name was submitted to the Senate.

A hard-working and scholarly jurist, Gray was an authority on legal history. He wrote frequently for the Court, particularly on private law issues, and rarely authored dissenting opinions. Gray's opinions tended to take the form of lengthy excursions into legal history and searches for precedents. He was not entirely in harmony with the economic liberty themes of the Fuller era. Instead, Gray was inclined to allow the states ample power to control economic activity absent a contrary federal statute and to resist the development of substantive due process.

President Arthur's second appointment to the Supreme Court, made to fill a vacancy created by the resignation of Justice Ward Hunt, went to Samuel Blatchford of New York. Blatchford received the nod only after President Arthur's first choice, Senator Roscoe Conkling of New York, declined to serve on the Court following his confirmation. A Republican with links to the New York business community, Blatchford was a judge on the Circuit Court for the Second Circuit. An expert on admiralty law, the colorless Blatchford was not a controversial choice. Arthur nominated Blatchford on March 13, 1882, and the Senate confirmed the appointment by voice vote later that month.

Blatchford attracted little notice from either contemporaries or historians. A moderate, Blatchford was known as a consensus-builder rather than an innovator. He voted with the majority on most issues and wrote only two dissenting opinions. But the contributions of Blatchford to the Fuller Court should not be overlooked. An industrious jurist, he was already regarded as the workhorse of the Court when Fuller became chief. In the early years of the Fuller Court Blatchford wrote more opinions than any other justice, and he made his mark in admiralty and patent cases. In his most famous opinion Blatchford interpreted the Due Process Clause of the Fourteenth Amendment to require that state-imposed railroad rates must be reasonable, this being the first application of substantive due process by the Supreme Court.

During his first term (1885–1889), President Cleveland appointed two justices to the Supreme Court. Fuller was nominated and confirmed in 1888. The death of Justice William B. Woods in May 1887, however, had presented Cleveland with his first chance to name a justice, and the president turned to his secretary of the interior, Lucius Q.C. Lamar. This proved to be a controversial move.

A native of Georgia, Lamar had moved to Mississippi and supported secession. He served the Confederacy in both military and diplomatic posts and was subsequently elected to Congress as a Democrat. Lamar was the first Southerner appointed to the Supreme Court since the Civil War. Indeed, President Cleveland acted in part to reward the strong political support he had received in the South and to underscore his desire for sectional reconciliation. He also shared Lamar's tendency to construe strictly the powers of the national government.

Even before Cleveland formally nominated Lamar in December 1887, Republican leaders began to attack the appointment. Some of the criticism was based on Lamar's relatively advanced age (sixty-two at the time of nomination) and his lack of sustained legal experience. More serious were charges that Lamar was tainted by treason and opposed the Reconstruction amendments. The Senate Judiciary Committee gave a negative recommendation concerning the nomination. By a vote of 32–28, however, Lamar squeezed out confirmation by the full Senate in January 1888.

The bruising confirmation struggle demonstrated lingering sectional tension in the Gilded Age. It also left a mark on Lamar. He expressed feelings of inadequacy about membership on the Supreme Court and almost always voted with the majority headed by Fuller. Lamar was on the Court only a few months before Fuller was appointed, and he developed a close relationship with the new chief justice. Plagued by ill health, Lamar never became a major force on the Fuller Court. Most of his opinions dealt with such private law matters as patents, land claims, torts, and municipal bonds.

President Benjamin Harrison, who defeated the incumbent Cleveland in the closely contested election of 1888, named four justices to the Supreme Court. Several had a major impact on the Fuller years. Harrison generally sought Republicans who had judicial or legal experience and who agreed with his conservative economic philosophy.

The president's first nominee, and in many respects the most important, was David J. Brewer, who was selected to replace the deceased Justice Stanley Matthews. Educated at Yale University and Albany Law School, Brewer moved to Kansas in the late 1850s. A staunch Republican, he served with distinction on the Supreme Court of Kansas from 1870 to 1884 and the federal Circuit Court for the Eighth Circuit from 1884 to 1889. A number of Brewer's opinions as a federal judge gained national attention, and he demonstrated misgivings about governmental regulation of business activity. Brewer was a nephew of Justice Stephen J. Field, whose views he largely embraced.

Brewer was recommended to Harrison by leading Republicans and prominent members of the bar. Justice Samuel F. Miller spoke warmly of Brewer's ability. Harrison deliberated for months and considered a number of candidates before nominating Brewer on December 4, 1889. The Republican-controlled Senate confirmed the appointment later that month by a vote of 53–11. Interestingly, much of the opposition to Brewer was generated by prohibitionists. While on the federal circuit court Brewer had ruled that a ban on the manufacture and sale of alcoholic beverages could be seen as a taking of property, which necessitated the payment of compensation. Any payment to the owners of breweries and distilleries was, of course, anathema to prohibitionists, and this led some senators to oppose the appointment on this ground. Other critics questioned Brewer's alleged favoritism to railroads.

One of the best-known justices of his time, Brewer was an intellectual leader of the Fuller Court. Brewer did not always vote with the majority, but even in dissent he did much to set the terms of debate. Historians have commonly depicted Brewer as a champion of laissez-faire and a doctrinaire opponent of economic regulations. To be sure, he often stressed the vital importance of private property to a free society. But Brewer's overall record on the Court was in fact balanced. Far from an uncritical defender of business interests, Brewer frequently upheld state regulatory authority and was sympathetic to antitrust prosecutions. He was also a passionate defender of Chinese immigrants against discriminatory treatment.

Justice Samuel F. Miller died ten months after the confirmation of Brewer, giving President Harrison his second opportunity to fill a Court vacancy. He settled upon Henry Billings Brown of Michigan. Then a federal district court judge in Michigan, Brown had built a national reputation for his admiralty decisions. Brown had long been active in Republican politics and was a Yale classmate of Brewer's. He actively sought appointment to the Supreme Court, and to this end he secured the endorsement of Circuit Judge Howell E. Jackson (later a member of the Court himself). Nominated by President Harrison on December 23, 1890, Brown was confirmed by voice vote of the Senate within a few days.

Although his service on the Fuller Court was overshadowed by more forceful colleagues, Brown was a capable and diligent jurist. Brown was generally protective of the rights of property owners, but he sanctioned a good deal of legislation that regulated the marketplace. Brown is best remembered today as the author of *Plessy v. Ferguson* (1896), which upheld state laws mandating racial separation in railroad cars. That opinion has been vilified by modern observers, but it is important to bear in mind that Brown's ruling reflected the racial assumptions of the Gilded Age.

Harrison's third Supreme Court nominee, George Shiras, Jr., of Pennsylvania, was a replacement for the deceased Justice Joseph P. Bradley. The president determined to name a Pennsylvanian so that the Third Circuit would continue to have a representative on the Court. The search for a suitable candidate was complicated, however, by a patronage dispute between Harrison and Senator Matthew S. Quay, Republican leader of Pennsylvania. Shiras, a little-known but successful Pittsburgh attorney, had developed a wide-ranging corporate practice representing railroads and steel interests. Independent of Quay's machine, Shiras was recommended to Harrison by such imposing figures as Secretary of State James G. Blaine and steel magnate Andrew Carnegie.

Although Shiras had no political or judicial experience, Harrison appointed him to the Court on July 19, 1892. Quay and the other Republican senator from Pennsylvania, feeling affronted, attempted to block confirmation. But their efforts floundered, and the Judiciary Committee reported the nomination without recommendation. Apparently to save face, Quay then moved for confirmation, and the Senate unanimously concurred.

On the Court, Shiras steered a moderately conservative course. He had a high regard for Fuller and sided with the chief on most issues. Shiras sometimes approved state police power to regulate business, but he endorsed the freedom of contract doctrine and voted to invalidate the 1894 income tax. A tireless worker, Shiras nonetheless did not exercise much influence over his colleagues.

President Harrison's fourth appointee to the Fuller Court was Howell E. Jackson of Tennessee. Justice Lamar died in January of 1893. At this point Harrison was a lameduck president, having been defeated by Grover Cleveland in the November 1892 election. Harrison realized that under the circumstances the Democratic-controlled Senate would not confirm a Republican nominee. Moreover, he preferred to name a Southerner to replace Lamar. Harrison had become friends with Jackson, a moderate Democrat, when they served together in the Senate. In 1887 Cleveland had appointed Jackson to the federal Sixth Circuit Court, where he proved an able judge. Justice Henry Billings Brown played a key role in recommending Jackson to the president.

On February 2, 1893, Harrison nominated Jackson to the Supreme Court. Jackson was the first Democrat named by a Republican president since Lincoln selected Stephen J. Field in 1863. Jackson was readily confirmed by the Senate in less than three weeks. Suffering from ill health, Jackson served only two and a half years on the Fuller Court, and he was unable to participate in some of the leading constitutional cases of the day. Jackson often joined with the majority to safeguard property rights, but his brief tenure prevented him from assuming a leadership position on the Court. In the most dramatic episode of his short Supreme Court career, Jackson left a Nashville sickbed in May 1895 to go to Washington for the reargument of *Pollock v. Farmer's Loan and Trust Co.*, the income tax case. Jackson voted to uphold the constitutionality of the levy, but his courageous effort was in vain because the Court majority struck down the income tax. He died a few months later.

President Cleveland's second term (1893–1897) afforded him two opportunities to appoint justices to the Fuller Court. He experienced considerable frustration in finding a successor to Samuel Blatchford, who died in July of 1893. Two of his nominees were defeated in the Senate as a consequence of a patronage dispute with Democratic senator David B. Hill of New York. An angry Cleveland then selected a member of the Senate, Edward Douglass White of Louisiana. Several factors influenced the president to pick White. The Democratic majority leader, White was generally a Cleveland loyalist and agreed with the president's economic views. No member of the Supreme Court had ever come from Louisiana. Moreover, the designation of White was partly an attempt by Cleveland to regain favor with the Senate. It has also been suggested that Cleveland hoped to remove White from the Senate because White was a champion of a protective tariff on sugar and opposed the president's tariff reform proposals. Whatever Cleveland's motives, his nomination of White was well regarded. The appointment was unanimously confirmed by the Senate on February 19, 1894, the same day that it was received.

Conservative by instinct, White did not follow a consistent pattern in cases dealing with governmental regulation of the economy. He sought to curtail national authority over commerce in order to preserve states' rights. White played a significant role in determining the constitutional status of the overseas possessions acquired after the Spanish-American War. His most important legal contribution, however, involved statutory construction of the Sherman Anti-Trust Act. Rejecting a literal interpretation of the act, White developed the rule of reason and insisted that only unreasonable restraints of trade were outlawed. White was an industrious justice who maintained a high level of productivity in writing opinions.

The death of Justice Howell E. Jackson in August of 1895 presented President Cleveland with yet another vacancy to fill. This time Cleveland made peace with Senator Hill and resolved to designate a nominee from the Empire State. His choice, Rufus W. Peckham, had been a successful corporate lawyer and a close political ally of the president. Peckham was a member of the New York Court of Appeals, the state's highest tribunal, when he was tapped by Cleveland for the U.S. Supreme Court. Appointed on December 3, 1895, Peckham was readily confirmed by the Senate only a few days later.

On the Fuller Court, Peckham consistently demonstrated his economic and social conservatism. Deeply suspicious of governmental intervention in the economy, Peckham vigorously wielded the liberty of contract doctrine as a means to test the validity of state regulations. For example, he authored the majority opinion in *Lochner v. New York* (1905). One of the most famous and controversial decisions ever rendered by the Supreme Court, the *Lochner* opinion struck down a state law limiting the hours of work in bakeries as a violation of the liberty of contract protected by the Fourteenth Amendment. Moreover, Peckham often dissented without opinion when the Fuller Court sustained state health and safety laws. Yet Peckham also wrote opinions strengthening the power of government to enforce antitrust laws, an indication that he was genuinely committed to economic liberty and not simply defending big business. In the area of criminal law, Peckham maintained that the procedural guarantees of the Bill of Rights (the first ten amendments to the U.S. Constitution of 1787) did not apply to the states.

President William McKinley had just one chance to nominate a Supreme Court justice, whereas his two predecessors had selected eight between them. McKinley turned to Joseph McKenna of California. McKenna's path to the Court was complicated by intricate maneuvering to persuade Justice Field to retire. Field's declining mental state was a source of concern to Fuller and the other justices. After 1895 the chief stopped giving Field opinions to prepare (one of the responsibilities of the chief justice is to assign the writing of opinions when he is in the majority), and in early 1897 Fuller and Justice Brewer renewed their effort to obtain Field's resignation. As part of these negotiations Field requested some assurance that his replacement

The Fuller Court from 1895 to 1902: (front row—left to right) David J. Brewer, John Marshall Harlan, Melville W. Fuller, Horace Gray, Henry B. Brown; (back row—left to right) Rufus W. Peckham, George Shiras, Jr., Edward D. White, Joseph McKenna (C. M. Bell, Collection of the Supreme Court of the United States)

would come from California. President-elect McKinley informally promised that he would appoint McKenna, thus satisfying Field's desire. Field's resignation, effective December 1, 1897, paved the way for McKinley to designate McKenna.

A stalwart Republican, McKenna served several terms in the U.S. House of Representatives. There he and McKinley became close friends. In 1892 President Harrison had named McKenna to the Court of Appeals for the Ninth Circuit. McKenna's performance on the court, however, was undistinguished. Nonetheless, President McKinley appointed his friend McKenna as U.S. attorney general in March of 1897. McKenna held that post for nine months, until Field's resignation.

McKinley promptly nominated McKenna to the Supreme Court. Aside from personal friendship, the nominee's religious faith may also have been a factor in the president's decision. McKenna was a Roman Catholic, and McKinley hoped that his selection would set to rest fears that the president harbored anti-Catholic sentiment. The nomination of McKenna was not greeted with enthusiasm. Fuller, for instance, received several letters from federal judges claiming that McKenna was a mediocre judge who lacked the qualifications for a spot on the Supreme Court. After investigating the matter, Fuller raised these concerns with McKinley in hopes of stopping the appointment. The president, however, stood by McKenna and sent his name to the Senate on December 16, 1897.

The Republican-controlled Senate did not wish to embarrass McKinley, yet confirmation was delayed for several weeks. Senators expressed concern about McKenna's modest legal attainments and his ties to the Southern Pacific Railroad. There is also some evidence of lingering anti-Catholic attitudes within the chamber. Despite this opposition, the McKenna nomination was confirmed without a formal vote.

McKenna served twenty-six years on the Supreme Court, and his tenure lasted well beyond the close of the Fuller era. Although honest and conscientious, McKenna never gained the confidence of his colleagues. Revealingly, Fuller tended to assign McKenna pedestrian cases in which to write opinions. McKenna never developed a consistent outlook with respect to economic regulatory measures, but he generally favored a broad construction of federal power under the Commerce Clause. It is hardly surprising that McKenna failed to become a strong influence on the Fuller Court.

The assassination of McKinley in 1901 elevated Vice President Theodore Roosevelt to the presidency. Roosevelt articulated views associated with the Progressive movement and promoted a more activist exercise of governmental power to achieve social reforms. Specifically, Roosevelt reinvigorated antitrust enforcement, favored stricter railroad regulations, and urged the passage of social legislation such as the Pure Food and Drug Act of 1906. Much of Roosevelt's program was centralizing and raised again the long-standing tension between federal authority and state autonomy. Roosevelt was resolved to fill Supreme Court vacancies only with persons who shared his Progressive outlook and would sustain the regulatory power of government. He also expressly rejected the geographic and circuit-court considerations that played so large a role in judicial selection process during the nineteenth century. The president would have three opportunities to achieve his goals for the Supreme Court.

Roosevelt first nominated Oliver Wendell Holmes Jr. of Massachusetts to replace the ailing Justice Horace Gray. In July of 1902 Gray resigned contingent upon the appointment of a successor. A renowned legal scholar, Holmes was the author of the acclaimed book *The Common Law*, published in 1881. This pioneering volume urged an instrumental understanding of law as a vehicle to achieve desired ends. Holmes had also served for twenty years on the Supreme Judicial Court of Massachusetts. On that court Holmes generally deferred to legislative policymaking. He expressed support for the right of unions to organize and picket peacefully. Senator Henry Cabot Lodge recommended Holmes to the president. Holmes was very anxious to secure a Supreme Court nomination and even met privately with Roosevelt to answer questions about his views. Being reassured about Holmes's supposed Progressive inclinations, Roosevelt appointed him to the Supreme Court on August 11, 1902. On December 2 the president formally submitted the nomination, and the Senate unanimously confirmed Holmes a few days later.

Fuller was delighted with the selection of Holmes, and the two soon formed a close relationship. This was remarkable because Holmes had few friendships among his associates on the Supreme Court. Despite differences in age, temperament, and outlook, Fuller and Holmes each found things to admire in the other. Holmes saw Fuller as an effective judicial administrator and seemed at times to relish Fuller's sense of restraint. For his part, Fuller regarded with pleasure Holmes's literary style and appreciated his prompt preparation of opinions. Yet Fuller was also concerned that Holmes's eagerness to write opinions and his aloof attitude were often irritating to other justices. Fuller sought to harness Holmes's zeal in order to preserve harmony and enhance the collective work of the Court.

Holmes had a long and distinguished career on the Supreme Court. His towering reputation, however, rests largely on opinions rendered after the Fuller period. Holmes authored a number of forceful dissents in landmark cases but rarely dissented while Fuller was chief. The fact was that Holmes commonly voted with Fuller in the disposition of cases during their period of common service on the Court. Although Holmes was a darling of the Progressives because he was usually deferential to legislative decisions, Holmes was an intellectual elitist who had no personal commitment to any reform agenda. In particular, Holmes was highly skeptical about the economic wisdom of the Sherman Anti-Trust Act, which Roosevelt was seeking to enforce. The president was bitterly disappointed when Holmes dissented in the celebrated *Northern Securities* antitrust case in 1904. Roosevelt supposedly quipped: "I could carve out of a banana a judge with more backbone than that" (quoted in Fiss 1993, 137–138). In retrospect, Roosevelt seems to have misunderstood Holmes's judicial philosophy and exaggerated his Progressive leanings.

William R. Day of Ohio joined the Fuller Court a year after Holmes, filling the vacancy created by the retirement of Justice George Shiras Jr. Day had studied law at the University of Michigan and developed a successful law practice in Canton, Ohio. A Republican loyalist, Day became a close friend of William McKinley. In 1897 McKinley, as the president, named Day as assistant secretary of state, and a year later he elevated Day to the post of secretary of state. Day resigned to represent the United States at the negotiations to end the Spanish-American War. McKinley then appointed his friend to the Sixth Circuit Court of Appeals in 1899. While an assistant secretary of the Navy in McKinley's administration, Roosevelt had worked closely with Day. Roosevelt selected Day for the Supreme Court in part to shore up his support with the McKinley wing of the Republican Party. Nominated by Roosevelt on February 19, 1903, Day was confirmed four days later without a formal vote.

Overshadowed by more prominent justices, Day compiled a mixed record with

The Fuller Court from 1906 to 1909: (front row—left to right) Edward D. White, John Marshall Harlan, Melville W. Fuller, David J. Brewer, Rufus W. Peckham; (back row—left to right) William R. Day, Joseph McKenna, Oliver Wendell Holmes, Jr., William H. Moody (C. M. Bell, Collection of the Supreme Court of the United States)

respect to the social legislation of the Progressive era. He was generally receptive to the exercise of the police power by states to regulate the economy and promote public health and safety. Yet Day was more cautious with respect to federal regulatory authority. He readily sanctioned federal power to prosecute trusts and to control interstate railroads, but he did not recognize plenary federal authority over all aspects of the economy. As with other justices appointed late in Fuller's tenure, Day had slight impact on the Fuller Court and is best remembered for his contribution to subsequent periods of the Supreme Court's history.

Roosevelt's final chance at a nomination came when Justice Henry Billings Brown resigned in 1906, effective at the end of the Court's term. After approaching several other candidates who declined, the president turned to his attorney general, William H. Moody of Massachusetts. Moody had developed a legal career in Essex County, Massachusetts, and served as a prosecutor. He was elected to several terms in the U.S. House of Representatives as a Republican. Moody became friends with Roosevelt, and the president first brought him into the cabinet in 1902 as secretary of the Navy. Two years later, Roosevelt designated Moody to be U.S. attorney general. In that capacity, Moody aggressively carried out Roosevelt's antitrust policy, assailed railroad rebates, and challenged peonage in the South. Although Moody was the second Massachusetts nominee in four years, Roosevelt sent his name to the Senate on December 3, 1906. Confirmation of Moody came quickly by voice vote.

On the bench Moody proved amenable to a broad use of governmental power. He adopted an expansive reading of congressional authority under the Commerce Clause. But he also supported state autonomy in the field of criminal justice, holding that the Fifth Amendment privilege against self-incrimination did not bind the states. Moody fulfilled Roosevelt's expectations, but his judicial career was cut short by crippling rheumatism in 1908. He was unable to attend Court sessions in 1909, and he resigned the following year.

When Fuller administered the oath of office to President William Howard Taft in March of 1909, the chief was suffering from ill health and had little more than a year to live. The last member to join the Fuller Court, Horace H. Lurton of Tennessee, was nominated by Taft on December 14, 1909, as a replacement for the deceased Rufus W. Peckham. A veteran of the Confederate Army, Lurton practiced law until he was elected to the Tennessee Supreme Court in 1886. President Grover Cleveland had appointed Lurton to the federal Court of Appeals for the Sixth Circuit in 1893. On that court Lurton gained the esteem of Taft, a fellow judge. As president, Taft carefully considered his choices for the Supreme Court. He gave little regard, however, to political affiliation. Taft resolved to name his friend Lurton, a Democrat, despite the latter's relatively advanced age. At sixty-six, Lurton was the oldest person yet named to the Court. Confirmed easily without a roll call vote, Lurton served only six months on the Fuller Court. He wrote no major opinions while Fuller was chief and left little imprint on the Fuller era.

The Fuller Court: An Aggregate Profile

The lodestar of the Fuller Court was a commitment to individual liberty. This guiding spirit permeated the work of the Court and was shared to some degree by every justice who served during the Fuller period. American constitutionalism had traditionally aimed to safeguard liberty by restricting the reach of government. The Framers of the U.S. Constitution felt that the acquisition and enjoyment of property was among the most vital of all liberty interests. Moreover, constitutional thought had long emphasized that the security of private property was preservative of other individual rights.

Of course, defense of property rights was scarcely a novel theme in Supreme Court history. From even before the tenure of Chief Justice John Marshall, the protection of economic rights had been a central concern of the Court. In this sense there was a clear continuity between the jurisprudence of the Fuller years and earlier constitutional developments. The advent of the Fuller Court, in other words, did not mark an abrupt turning point in constitutional history. But the Fuller Court, faced with increased governmental intervention in the economy, pursued with heightened zeal the long-standing judicial dedication to property, free-market ordering, and limited government. The Fuller Court's hearty embrace of economic liberty, coupled with its willingness to use judicial review aggressively, made this period a distinct chapter in the evolution of the Supreme Court.

Historians have sometimes employed the phrase *laissez-faire constitutionalism* to describe the work of the Fuller Court. Although such a characterization contains an element of truth, it is also potentially misleading. Certainly the Supreme Court under Fuller generally preferred market approaches over government control of economic resources. It was especially loathe to interfere in freely made contractual bargains. These baseline assumptions tended to protect economic liberty by restraining the reach of government. But at no time did the Fuller Court espouse a total laissez-faire philosophy, and it readily sustained a number of regulations that curtailed market freedom in order to safeguard public health, safety, and morals.

As this suggests, one must be careful not to exaggerate the activism of the Fuller Court. It bears emphasis that the Supreme Court under Fuller upheld far more economic regulations than it struck down. Moreover, the Fuller Court took account of other constitutional values than the rights of property owners. Foremost among these was a strong regard for the states in the federal system. In line with their dedication to a limited federal government, Fuller and his colleagues recognized a large measure of autonomy for the states. The Fuller Court, for instance, tended to defer to state governance of criminal justice, race relations, and public morals. Nor did the Court foreclose any supervision of economic matters by the states. The conflicting pull of support for property rights and a high regard for federalism caused some ambivalence and inconsistency as the Court grappled with novel questions posed by state-imposed regulations.

The work of the Fuller Court was by no means confined to weighty issues of constitutional law. Unlike the current docket of the Supreme Court, the Court in Fuller's day continued its historic function as a common law tribunal. Much of its docket was filled with cases that raised issues of admiralty, contracts, property, and torts. Many of these cases reached the Court under diversity of citizenship jurisdiction. In effect, the Fuller Court was the chief umpire of private law disputes as well as an interpreter of the Constitution and federal statutes.

In sharp contrast to an increasingly fragmented Supreme Court after 1941, members of the Fuller Court generally adhered to the norm of acquiescence. Stressing the importance of maintaining a united front to the public, notwithstanding private disagreements, chief justices had long attempted to discourage dissenting opinions. As a result, there was no culture of dissent on the Supreme Court in the nineteenth century. Like his predecessors, Fuller sought to limit the public expression of dissent. Leading by example, Fuller authored just thirty dissenting opinions during his twenty-two years in the center chair, and overall he maintained a low dissent rate of less than 3 percent.

By today's standards Fuller was highly successful in achieving unanimity in the work of the Court. The dissent rate during the Fuller years, although higher than that of the preceding Waite Court, was consistently low, never exceeding 20 percent in any year. During some terms there were only a handful of dissenting opinions. Nonetheless, Fuller was unable to achieve unanimity in some major constitutional cases. Under Fuller there were seventy-one decisions rendered by a 5–4 or 4–3 vote of the Court. By way of comparison, in the late 1990s and early 2000s the number of 5–4 rulings by the Supreme Court increased to unprecedented levels.

The most frequent dissenter during Fuller's tenure was Justice Harlan, who was more liberal than his colleagues on some issues. Brewer and Brown were also inclined to express their separate views, and Brewer often dissented without opinion. Individual dissent rates of Fuller Court justices appear in Table 1.1.

Table 1.2 presents the proportion of each justice voting with Fuller in cases in which the Court divided. Note that Justices Lamar, Blatchford, Holmes, and Gray were most likely to agree with Fuller; Justices White, Harlan, and Miller most often parted company with the chief.

In addition to a low dissent rate, the Fuller Court was characterized by an absence of recognizable voting alignments. Patterns of bloc voting did not emerge during Fuller's tenure. Nor did the justices divide along the lines of political affiliation. Justices appointed by Republican and Democratic presidents commonly voted together. The historian Charles Warren noted that "the slight importance . . . which was to be attached to the party designations of the Judges upon the Court was never better illustrated than during Fuller's Chief Justiceship" (Warren 1926, II, 721). As this suggests, it is not easy to pigeonhole individual justices into neat categories. For instance, the property-conscious Brewer wrote several opinions sympathetic to Chinese immigrants. Notwithstanding his liberal views on race relations and the income tax, Harlan strictly scrutinized state railroad rate regulations and helped to formulate the liberty of contract doctrine. Few members of the Fuller Court developed a comprehensive philosophy that consistently determined their vote on a variety of matters.

Fuller as Leader

The leadership of the chief justice is a key factor in the operation of the Supreme Court. Fuller has universally received high marks as a judicial administrator. Despite frequent changes in the composition of the Court, Fuller maintained good working relations with the justices. Blessed with easy manners and a genial temperament,

Table 1.1 Individual Justice Dissent Rates (in percent), 1888–1910

Blatchford	0.0	Fuller	2.9
Lurton	0.6	Miller	2.9
Bradley	1.0	Field	3.3
Lamar	1.0	Brown	3.8
Gray	1.7	White	4.7
Holmes	2.3	Brewer	4.8
Day	2.4	Peckham	4.9
Jackson	2.5	McKenna	5.0
Shiras	2.6	Harlan	6.0
Moody	2.8		

SOURCE: Goldman, Sheldon. *Constitutional Law: Cases and Essays*. 2nd ed. New York: HarperCollins, 1991, p. 87.

Table 1.2 Justices Agreeing with Fuller on Divided Courts

	Number of Joint Participations in Nonunanimous Cases	Agreement Rate (in percent)
Fuller-Lamar	107	86.9
Fuller-Blatchford	116	84.5
Fuller-Holmes	304	76.3
Fuller-Gray	441	74.4
Fuller-Bradley	75	72.0
Fuller-Jackson	75	72.0
Fuller-Day	282	71.6
Fuller-Shiras	379	71.5
Fuller-Lurton	20	70.0
Fuller-Moody	91	68.1
Fuller-Field	263	67.6
Fuller-Peckham	533	65.9
Fuller-Brown	579	64.9
Fuller-Brewer	732	63.9
Fuller-McKenna	482	62.4
Fuller-White	624	59.9
Fuller-Harlan	747	57.0
Fuller-Miller	38	44.7

SOURCE: Goldman, Sheldon. *Constitutional Law: Cases and Essays*. 2nd ed. New York: HarperCollins, 1991, p. 88.

Fuller was a masterful social leader of the Court. He orchestrated the talents of his independent-minded associates and prevented destructive personal feuds from disrupting a collegial working environment. To this end, Fuller inaugurated the practice of requiring each justice to shake hands with the other justices before each conference.

Fuller's task was eased by the fact that the justices of his court were appointed during the era of Republican ascendancy in the late nineteenth and early twentieth centuries. The only Democrat to reach the White House in these decades, the conservative Grover Cleveland, agreed with many of the economic views of his Republican rivals. Thus, the members of the Fuller Court largely shared the same fundamental outlook. There were differences in emphasis, of course, but they were not sharply ideological. This made it much easier for Fuller to forge a consensus and downplay conflicts.

Yet even like-minded justices do not automatically pull together. The Supreme Court under Chief Justice Harlan Fiske Stone (1941–1946), although composed almost entirely of liberal activists appointed by President Franklin D. Roosevelt, was notoriously fragmented and torn by personal quarrels. It takes a special talent for a chief justice to achieve harmony. Fuller may have lacked intellectual brilliance, but it is questionable that any other justice of the era could have handled the Court as well as he did.

As chief justice, Fuller was responsible for assigning the writing of opinions when he was in the majority. Since Fuller almost always voted with the majority, he assigned most of the opinions during his tenure on the Court. Historically, many chief justices have elected to write the opinions in cases of greatest interest. Early in his service Fuller personally authored such major opinions as *Pollock v. Farmers' Loan and Trust Co.* (1895) and *United States v. E. C. Knight Co.* (1895). Subsequently, he regularly assigned leading cases to others. Fuller did not use his power of assignment to reward or punish colleagues for their votes. Any such approach would have been contrary to his desire to foster goodwill among the justices. Assignments were guided by a justice's dispatch in writing opinions and his expertise in particular areas of law.

Still, Fuller was able to shape the law by skillful exercise of the power to assign opinions. He frequently turned to Brewer and Peckham to write for the Court in important constitutional cases. They authored many of the decisions that gave the Fuller Court its place in history.

A tireless worker, Fuller undertook far more than his share of the opinion-writing burden. He authored 840 majority opinions, speaking for the Court more often than any other justice during his tenure on the bench. It has been estimated that he was the fifth most productive opinion writer in the Court's history. Because he assigned most of the important cases to others, Fuller usually wrote unglamorous opinions concerned with jurisdictional and procedural matters or commercial transactions. Such cases do not provide the basis for a lasting reputation. Moreover, Fuller's style of writing opinions was verbose and lacked clarity of expression.

When Fuller became chief justice he inherited an antiquated federal court structure ill-equipped to handle a steadily increasing workload. The Supreme Court had a heavy backlog of cases and was three years behind in the disposition of appeals. Moreover, under the Judiciary Act of 1789, members of the Supreme Court were required to conduct circuit court in their respective circuits. This necessitated lengthy travel away from Washington. Between 1889 and 1891, for instance, Fuller spent much of each summer presiding over trials and adjudicating largely routine private law matters at the circuit-court level.

Fuller had long favored the establishment of intermediate courts of appeal to ease the burden of the Supreme Court. As chief justice he was instrumental in winning passage by Congress of the Evarts Act of 1891. This measure created new circuit courts of appeals and limited appeals to the Supreme Court in private law matters. Under the Evarts Act the justices of the Court, in a gesture to tradition, were designated judges of the new circuit courts of appeals. Fuller took part in a number of cases heard by the Fourth and Seventh Circuit Courts of Appeals.

Fuller's most significant ruling as circuit justice grew out of the national controversy over opening the 1893 World's Columbian Exposition in Chicago on Sundays. Congress had appropriated funds to help underwrite the costs of the fair on the express condition that the exhibition not be open on that day. Yet in a period when a six-day workweek was common, many workers could not attend the fair except on Sundays. When the fair directors decided to open on Sundays, the federal government sought to enjoin such operations as a breach of the condition. The government secured an injunction from the trial court, and the issue was appealed to the Seventh Circuit Court of Appeals, where Fuller was temporarily presiding. In June he delivered an opinion reversing the trial court and denying the requested injunction. Framed in terms of traditional equitable principles, Fuller's opinion stressed that there was no showing of irreparable harm to the government or allegation that the remedy at law was inadequate. His decision allowed the directors to open the fair on Sundays. The ruling indicated Fuller's personal lack of sympathy with Sunday closing laws and can also be seen as a move toward a new understanding about the place of religion in a more diverse society.

Most historians agree that Fuller was an administrative leader of the Court rather than a dominant intellectual force. "In the realm of ideas, he was just one more vote" (Fiss 1993, 27). But Fuller's contributions should not be slighted. Behind the scenes he did much to mold a cohesive majority supportive of economic liberty, and he guided the Court toward a more active role in American society.

References

Abraham, Henry J. *Justices, Presidents, and Senators: A History of the U.S. Supreme Court Appointments from Washington to Clinton.* Lanham, MD: Rowman and Littlefield, 1999.

Ely, James W., Jr. *The Chief Justiceship of Melville W. Fuller, 1888–1910.* Columbia: University of South Carolina Press, 1995.

Fiss, Owen M. *History of the Supreme Court of the United States, Volume 8: Troubled Beginnings of the Modern State, 1888–1910.* New York: Macmillan, 1993.

Goldman, Sheldon. *Constitutional Law: Cases and Essays.* 2nd ed. New York: HarperCollins, 1991.

Hall, Kermit L., ed. *The Oxford Companion to the Supreme Court.* New York: Oxford University Press, 1992.

Keller, Morton. *Affairs of State: Public Life in Nineteenth Century America.* Cambridge, MA: Harvard University Press, 1977.

King, Willard L. *Melville Weston Fuller: Chief Justice of the United States, 1888–1910.* New York: Macmillan, 1950; rpt. Chicago: University of Chicago Press, 1967.

Ross, Michael A. "Justice for Iowa: Samuel Freeman Miller's Appointment to the United States Supreme Court During the Civil War." *Annals of Iowa* 60 (2001): 111–138.

Urofsky, Melvin I., ed. *The Supreme Court Justices: A Biographical Dictionary.* New York: Garland, 1994.

Warren, Charles. *The Supreme Court in United States History.* 2 vols. Rev. ed. Boston: Little, Brown, 1926.

White, G. Edward. *Justice Oliver Wendell Holmes: Law and the Inner Self.* New York: Oxford University Press, 1993.

2

The Justices

Melville W. Fuller was chief justice for twenty-two years, a period longer than any other chief in American history except John Marshall and Roger B. Taney. During that time nineteen justices, aside from Fuller, served on the Supreme Court. Chief Justice Fuller, for whom the period is named, was nominated by President Grover Cleveland in 1888. The Fuller era was marked by frequent changes in the composition of the Court. The nineteen associate justices were appointed by ten different presidents, spanning American history from Abraham Lincoln to William Howard Taft. Only John M. Harlan served with Fuller for the entire period.

The Fuller Court justices are discussed individually in the remainder of this chapter, ordered by date of appointment to the Supreme Court. Table 2.1 presents each justice's birth date, date of appointment, nominating president, age at appointment, and justice being replaced.

The Lincoln Appointments

Samuel F. Miller

Congress reorganized the federal judicial circuits in 1862 in order to reduce the South's disproportionate representation on the Supreme Court. As a part of this scheme Congress created a new circuit that included states west of the Mississippi River. President Abraham Lincoln then selected Samuel F. Miller of Iowa, who resided in one of the states in the new circuit, to serve on the Supreme Court. Promptly confirmed by the Senate, Miller served on the Court for twenty-eight years until his death in 1890. Blunt and outspoken, Miller's forceful manner sometimes vexed his colleagues on the bench. Miller was the most senior justice when Fuller became chief. Most of his contribution to jurisprudence, therefore, predated the formation of the Fuller Court.

The son of a farmer, Miller initially decided upon a career in medicine. He graduated from the medical school of Transylvania University and became a prosperous

Table 2.1 Fuller Court Justices

	Birth Year	Appointment Year	Appointing President	Appointment Age	Replaced
Blatchford	1820	1882	Arthur	62	Hunt
Bradley	1813	1870	Grant	56	Grier
Brewer	1837	1889	Harrison	52	Matthews
Brown	1836	1890	Harrison	54	Miller
Day	1849	1903	T. Roosevelt	53	Shiras
Field	1816	1863	Lincoln	46	New Seat
Fuller	1833	1888	Cleveland	55	Waite
Gray	1828	1881	Arthur	53	Clifford
Harlan	1833	1877	Hayes	44	Davis
Holmes	1841	1902	T. Roosevelt	61	Gray
Jackson	1832	1893	Harrison	60	Lamar
Lamar	1825	1887	Cleveland	62	Woods
Lurton	1844	1909	Taft	65	Peckham
Matthews	1824	1881	Garfield	56	Swayne
McKenna	1843	1897	McKinley	54	Field
Miller	1816	1862	Lincoln	46	Daniel
Moody	1853	1906	T. Roosevelt	52	Brown
Peckham	1838	1894	Cleveland	57	Jackson
Shiras	1832	1892	Harrison	60	Bradley
White	1845	1894	Cleveland	48	Blatchford

SOURCE: Hall, Kermit L., ed. *The Oxford Companion to the Supreme Court.* New York: Oxford University Press, 1992.

doctor in Kentucky. Increasingly dissatisfied with his medical career, Miller began to teach himself law and was admitted to the Kentucky bar in 1846. Active in the Whig Party, Miller gradually came to oppose slavery. Unhappy with his economic prospects and upset about growing proslavery sentiment in Kentucky, Miller moved with his family to Iowa in 1850. There he quickly became a prominent attorney, joined the Republican Party, and backed Lincoln's presidential bid in 1860. He handled a number of cases in which Iowa towns sought to escape liability for default on bonds issued to finance railroad construction. As a result of this sour experience with railroad bonds, Miller developed a deep hostility to eastern bondholders that marked his years on the bench.

On the Supreme Court Miller proved to be a consistent supporter of Lincoln's Civil War policies. He voted to sustain the constitutionality of loyalty oaths for former Confederates seeking to hold office and to uphold the validity of legal tender notes issued to finance the war effort. Yet he did not manifest a dedication to racial equality and felt that the federal government had no authority to attack private discrimination.

Miller also harbored antibusiness sentiments and did not believe that the Fourteenth Amendment fundamentally altered the federal system. These views coalesced in Miller's important majority opinion for the Court in the *Slaughterhouse Cases* (1873). Rejecting a challenge to the exclusive privileges granted a new slaughter-

Samuel F. Miller (Handy Studios, Collection of the Supreme Court of the United States)

house in New Orleans, Miller narrowly interpreted the Privileges and Immunities Clause of the Fourteenth Amendment. He asserted that the Amendment was designed to safeguard former slaves, not to constitute the Supreme Court "a perpetual censor upon all legislation of the States" (*Slaughterhouse*, 78). Miller thus sought to affirm the power of the states to enact economic regulations. One effect of the *Slaughterhouse Cases*, however, was to curtail the authority of federal government to enforce equal rights in the South.

Miller compiled a mixed record with respect to economic issues. He regularly dissented in municipal bond cases, expressing resentment that the Supreme Court frequently enforced the claims of bondholders. He took the position that the states had ample authority to control business. Yet Miller also recognized the need for national uniformity in commercial matters, holding in *Wabash, St. Louis, and Pacific Railway v. Illinois* (1886) that state regulation of interstate railroad rates invaded federal authority under the Commerce Clause. Moreover, Miller authored a seminal opinion strengthening the rights of property owners whose land was physically invaded by governmental action. In *Pumpelly v. Green Bay Co.* (1871) he ruled, for the Court, that flooding destroyed the usefulness of land and constituted a taking of property even though title remained in the owner.

Perhaps Miller's most important opinion for the Fuller Court was *In re Neagle* (1890). Speaking for a divided Court, he broadly interpreted the term *law* in a federal statute to encompass actions done under the authority of the United States. This ruling allowed federal courts to issue writs of habeas corpus to remove federal officials from state criminal jurisdiction. In addition, Miller wrote a thoughtful concurring opinion in *Chicago, Milwaukee, and St. Paul Railway v. Minnesota* (1890), maintaining that states could not fix transportation charges so low as to amount to a confiscation of property.

Remaining vitally interested in politics while on the Court, Miller served with five other justices on the special electoral commission that tallied the electoral votes in the disputed Hayes-Tilden presidential election of 1876. He also had presidential aspirations and in the 1880s was considered for nomination by some Republican Party leaders. When the chief justiceship became vacant in 1873 upon the death of Salmon P. Chase, Miller felt that he was entitled to the position. Miffed when President Ulysses S. Grant turned instead to Morrison R. Waite, Miller was hostile to Waite and disparaged his talents. Fuller, however, managed to win Miller's friendship during their brief period of joint service on the Court.

Stephen J. Field

President Abraham Lincoln named Stephen J. Field in 1863 to fill a new tenth seat on the Supreme Court. Creation of this seat was part of a move by Congress to revamp

Stephen J. Field (Handy Studios, Collection of the Supreme Court of the United States)

the federal judiciary and to provide a place on the Court for a justice who would have responsibility for the isolated Pacific Coast federal judicial circuit. Anxious to name a Californian for political and geographic reasons, Lincoln tapped Field in part to strengthen California's attachment to the Union cause. The Senate confirmed the appointment of Field on March 10, 1863, and he served as a justice until his resignation on December 1, 1897. With thirty-four years on the Court, Field ranks second among justices for longevity of service.

Field was born in Haddam, Connecticut, on November 4, 1816. His father, a Congregationalist minister, moved his large family to Stockbridge, Massachusetts, where the young Field grew up. After spending several years in Turkey and Greece with an older sister, Field entered Williams College, graduating in 1837. He studied law in the New York office of his brother, David Dudley Field, who was rapidly becoming one of the nation's most prominent lawyers. Field then practiced law with his brother before departing for California during the 1849 Gold Rush. Unlike so many others, Field was not interested in mining. Instead, he worked to establish a legal practice, was elected *alcalde* (mayor) of Marysville, and grew wealthy through land speculation. In 1850 Field was elected to the California assembly, where he served one term and successfully urged adoption of new codes of civil and criminal procedure. Field was elected as a Democrat to the California Supreme Court in 1857, becoming chief justice two years later. He built a reputation for his handling of land claims and mining disputes and supported the Union cause at the outbreak of the Civil War. Field was therefore a logical choice for a Supreme Court appointment.

During Field's long tenure on the Court, Americans were grappling with sweeping changes brought about by the Civil War and industrialization. Field early emerged as an outspoken champion of individual liberty, and much of his judicial career can be understood as an effort to define and preserve liberty. In *Cummings v. Missouri* (1867) and *Ex Parte Garland* (1867), for instance, Field authored majority opinions that struck down Civil War–era loyalty oaths as unconstitutional ex post facto laws. Although not fully consistent in his handling of cases involving Chinese immigrants, Field gained a reputation as a defender of the Chinese against discrimination. The most famous case involved the San Francisco queue ordinance. In 1879, while he was performing circuit-court duties in California, Field invalidated this ordinance, which directed jailers to cut the hair of any persons in jail. He reasoned that it constituted discrimination against Chinese immigrants who commonly wore a braided queue.

But Field was usually unsympathetic to the civil rights claims of blacks. In particular, he insisted that discrimination by private parties did not run afoul of the Equal Protection Clause of the Fourteenth Amendment.

A bedrock principle for Field was that liberty was best safeguarded by confining the reach of government. He articulated this view in a number of opinions that championed entrepreneurial liberty and asserted that the Due Process Clause of the

Fourteenth Amendment protected substantive rights. In his dissenting opinion in the *Slaughterhouse Cases* (1873) Field maintained that the Constitution safeguarded the right to pursue a lawful occupation and that this right was infringed by a state-conferred monopoly. He enlarged his argument in a powerful dissent in *Munn v. Illinois* (1877). Field declared that the rights of property owners were entitled to the same level of constitutional protection as liberty, and he argued that owners were entitled to determine the compensation charged the public for use of their property. Although these positions were originally advanced in dissenting opinions, Field's ideas gained currency during the 1880s. To be sure, Field recognized that states could exercise their police power to promote public health, safety, and morals. But police power could not legitimately be used to interfere in the market and adjust economic power. Moreover, Field reserved for the courts the crucial inquiry of whether a statute was within the boundaries of the police power.

Although a supporter of economic liberty, Field was not a handmaiden for business interests. Rather, his jurisprudence derived from the Jacksonian precepts of equal rights and hostility to special economic privileges. As Morton Keller has rightly explained, "Field adhered to old American values of private right and individual freedom that led him to be as ill at ease with corporate power as he was with legislative activism" (Keller 1977, 367). Hence, Field opposed the conferral by government of special advantages or monopoly status on business enterprise. He regularly sustained statutes that required business enterprises to meet safety standards. Field was also sympathetic with the claims of injured employees and inclined to find industrial employers liable for workplace accidents. In Field's mind, his jurisprudence was designed to give "the under fellow a show in this life" (quoted in McCurdy 1975, 979).

Like a number of other Supreme Court justices over the course of time, Field had presidential ambitions. In 1880 he actively sought the Democratic Party nomination. It has been suggested that Field's stress on states' rights in civil rights cases was calculated in part to boost his support in the South.

The implications of Field's economic liberty jurisprudence came to fruition after Fuller became chief justice. Ironically, Field authored few major opinions for the Supreme Court during the Fuller era. One exception was *Davis v. Beason* (1890). Reflecting the widespread disapproval of the Mormon practice of polygamy, Field upheld an Idaho territorial statute that denied the suffrage to any person who was a polygamist or a member of any association that encouraged polygamy. Field vigorously denounced polygamy as degrading and distinguished between religious belief and conduct. One was free to adopt any religious doctrine, he ruled, but behavior was outside the scope of the First Amendment and could be sanctioned.

As his mental powers waned in the 1890s Field grew increasingly irascible and erratic. Fuller ceased assigning Field opinions in 1896. Perhaps Field's most famous opinion in the Fuller period was his concurrence in the income tax case, *Pollock v.*

Farmers' Loan and Trust Co. (1895). "The present assault upon capital," he darkly warned, "is but the beginning. It will be but the stepping-stone to others, larger and more sweeping, till our political contests will become a war of the poor against the rich" (*Pollock* I, 607). If he wrote less in the 1890s, Field nonetheless had provided the intellectual basis for much of the jurisprudence of the Fuller Court. He had pioneered federal judicial acceptance of substantive due process and strengthened private property rights. Field's spirit influenced the direction of the Supreme Court long after his retirement.

The Grant Appointment

Joseph P. Bradley

President Ulysses S. Grant appointed Joseph P. Bradley of New Jersey to the U.S. Supreme Court in 1870. Although his nomination was shrouded by the larger controversy over the validity of the Legal Tender Act and allegations of court-packing, Bradley was easily confirmed. He remained on the Court until his death in 1892, serving just over three years under Fuller.

The son of a farmer, Bradley was born into a large family. He exemplified the self-made man, attaining success through hard work. Bradley largely educated himself before he entered Rutgers College in 1833. After graduation Bradley studied law on his own and was admitted to the New Jersey bar in 1839. He practiced law in Newark for the next thirty years and became a prominent attorney, representing railroad and business interests. He served as counsel for the Camden and Amboy Railroad, a monopoly that exercised a great deal of political influence in antebellum New Jersey politics. A Republican, Bradley unsuccessfully ran for the House of Representatives in 1862. He favored the elimination of slavery, but stopped short of endorsing equal rights for freed persons.

On the Supreme Court, Bradley generally followed a moderate course. He wrote the historic opinion in the *Civil Rights Cases* (1883), holding that the Fourteenth Amendment applied only to state action and did not reach private discrimination. Asserting that racial antipathy could not be halted by law, Bradley maintained that newly freed slaves must cease "to be the special favorites of the law" (25). This decision restricted the power of Congress to safeguard blacks from discriminatory treatment. Bradley was more protective of civil liberties. In *Boyd v. United States* (1886), for instance, he adopted a broad interpretation of the Fourth Amendment. Bradley declared that the compulsory production of a person's private papers to be used in a criminal prosecution of that person constituted an unreasonable search and seizure.

Joseph P. Bradley (Vic Boswell, National Geographhic, Collection of the Supreme Court of the United States)

Bradley held traditional views concerning gender roles in society. In *Bradwell v. Illinois* (1873) the Supreme Court held that a decision by Illinois excluding a woman from the practice of law did not abridge the Privileges and Immunities Clause of the Fourteenth Amendment. Concurring, Bradley asserted that the law "has always recognized a wide difference in the respective spheres and destinies of man and woman." In a bow to Victorian values, he added: "The paramount destiny and mission of woman are to fulfill the noble and benign office of wife and mother. This is the law of the Creator" (*Bradwell*, 141).

In terms of economic liberty, Bradley pursued a somewhat inconsistent course. He dissented in the *Slaughterhouse Cases*, arguing that a state law that prohibited persons from pursuing lawful employment deprived them of liberty and property without due process in violation of the Fourteenth Amendment. But he also joined the Court majority in *Munn v. Illinois* (1877) and voted that states could regulate the charges of business enterprises "clothed with a public interest."

Bradley played only a secondary role in shaping the jurisprudence of the Fuller Court. He dissented in the important case of *Chicago, Milwaukee, and St. Paul Railway v. Minnesota* (1890), which established federal judicial review of state-imposed railroad rates. Bradley adhered to the position that the determination of reasonable charges was a legislative matter and that regulation did not infringe property rights. The vexing issue of southern states' attempts to repudiate their bonded indebtedness raised a number of cases for the Fuller Court. Writing for a unanimous bench, Bradley sided with the creditors in *McGahey v. Virginia* (1890). He ruled that a Virginia statute that undercut the validity of tax-receivable bond coupons was so onerous as to impair the obligation of contract. In the landmark case of *Hans v. Louisiana* (1890), Bradley took a different tack. He determined that states, under sovereign immunity, could not be sued by their own citizens in the federal courts. The upshot of this decision was that the Fuller Court closed the doors of federal courts to many bondholder lawsuits and thus left creditors without an effective remedy.

As part of the national campaign to stamp out polygamy, Congress in 1887 abrogated the charter of the Mormon Church and directed legal proceedings to confiscate the property of the church. Bradley, speaking for the Court majority in *Late Corporation of the Church of Jesus Christ of Latter-Day Saints v. United States* (1890), upheld the legislation. Comparing polygamy to barbarism, Bradley dismissed claims of religious freedom and stressed the plenary power of Congress to legislate for the territories.

Aside from Bradley's judicial career, mention should also be made of his service on the electoral commission named to resolve the disputed presidential election of 1876. On the closely divided commission Bradley consistently voted with the Republicans and was thus instrumental in the selection of Rutherford B. Hayes as president.

The Hayes Appointment

John Marshall Harlan

When Justice David Davis resigned effective in March of 1877, President Rutherford B. Hayes moved carefully in selecting a successor. He eventually settled on John Marshall Harlan of Kentucky. A member of a prominent slave-owning family, Harlan graduated from Centre College and received his legal education at Transylvania University. He was admitted to the Kentucky bar in 1853 and practiced for a time with his father in Frankfort before moving to Louisville. Active in the Whig Party, Harlan always upheld the Whig belief in a strong national government. When the Whig Party collapsed in the 1850s Harlan searched for a new political home. An opponent of secession, Harlan joined the Union Army as a colonel in 1861 and served for nearly two years. Harlan joined the Republican Party in 1868, and in 1871 and again in 1875 he ran unsuccessfully for governor of Kentucky on the Republican ticket. In these political contests Harlan repudiated his early support of slavery and defended the civil rights program enacted during Reconstruction. Harlan's rising political visibility, his bipartisan support in the South, and his ties to President Hays helped to convince Hays that Harlan was the best choice to replace Davis in 1877.

Harlan's understanding of judicial office was shaped in part by his deep religious convictions. There was a religious basis to much of his legal thought. Justice Brewer once remarked that "Harlan goes to bed every night with one hand on the Constitution and the other on the Bible, and so sleeps the sweet sleep of justice and righteousness" (quoted in Przybyszyewski 1999, 54). A believer in a literal interpretation of the Bible, Harlan employed the same formalistic approach to reading the Constitution. Judges, in Harlan's view, did not make law but simply applied correct legal principles to changing situations.

As a consequence of his strong convictions, Harlan developed a highly personal and result-oriented jurisprudence. As G. Edward White explained, "Harlan's theory of judging was primarily designed to implement his individual convictions. It placed a premium on arriving at desirable results, not on internal consistency" (White 1988, 130). In other words, Harlan was inclined to decide cases according to his personal values and was little concerned with developing a coherent judicial philosophy. Seen as unpredictable and something of a maverick, Harlan was certainly not an intellectual leader of the Fuller Court. Indeed, on many issues he was isolated from his colleagues. By the same token, Harlan's colleagues on the bench had slight impact on his individualized style of decisionmaking.

Harlan's historical reputation has fluctuated over time. He was largely ignored for decades after his death, and as late as 1947 Justice Felix Frankfurter dismissed Harlan as an "eccentric exception" (*Adamson v. California*, 332 U.S. 46, 62 [1947]).

John Marshall Harlan (Matthew Brady, Collection of the Supreme Court of the United States)

The post–World War II civil rights movement renewed interest in the then obscure Harlan. He was rapidly elevated to heroic status because of his defense of civil rights and broad federal regulatory authority. But Harlan's overall record on the Supreme Court remains puzzling to historians. One must be wary of efforts to portray Harlan as a forerunner of the New Deal or a prophet of the modern civil rights movement. He cast a number of votes difficult to reconcile with these pleasing if simplistic images.

Briefly stated, there were strains of Harlan's thinking that pulled him in different directions. A strong sense of nationalism lead him to favor an expansive reading of the equal protection guarantees in the Reconstruction amendments. Dissenting in the *Civil Rights Cases* (1883), Harlan insisted that Congress had the power under the Thirteenth Amendment to prevent denial of equal access to public accommodations. Likewise, he dissented in *Plessy v. Ferguson* (1896), which upheld racial segregation on railroads. In a famous phrase Harlan asserted that "the Constitution is color-blind, and neither knows nor tolerates classes among citizens" (*Plessy*, 559). Yet Harlan seemingly drew a line between public accommodations and the more intimate associations of marriage and education. In *Cummings v. Richmond County Board of Education* (1899), Harlan, speaking for the Court, stressed that public education was a state matter and failed to enforce the equal component of the separate but equal standard. He allowed a county to close its only black high school while subsidizing private high schools for white students. Nor did Harlan display any sympathy for the plight of Chinese immigrants who faced harsh legal restrictions in the late nineteenth century.

Harlan was an early proponent of the view that the Fourteenth Amendment's Due Process Clause incorporates the Bill of Rights (the first ten amendments to the U.S. Constitution of 1787) and applies them to the states. For example, he asserted in dissent in *Hurtado v. California* (1884) that the Fourteenth Amendment imposed criminal procedure guarantees on the states. Harlan's colleagues on the Fuller Court generally resisted this argument, holding that the Bill of Rights did not extend to the states. Harlan, however, was able to establish one major exception to this rule. Writing for the Court in the seminal case of *Chicago, Burlington, and Quincy Railroad Co. v. Chicago* (1897), he ruled that just compensation for private property taken for public use was an essential element of due process and thus binding on the states by virtue of the Fourteenth Amendment. This reflected Harlan's support of private property against state interference.

In cases involving economic rights Harlan compiled a mixed record. Consistent with his nationalist outlook, he favored broad federal regulatory authority and looked skeptically at state legislation that threatened the national market or the sanctity of contracts. Thus, he favored vigorous enforcement of the Contract Clause and restricted state efforts at rate regulation. Harlan fashioned the so-called fair-value rule in *Smyth v. Ames* (1898) to protect railroad and utility investors from the imposition of confiscatory state rates. He also espoused the liberty of contract doctrine to strike down state labor laws designed to protect unions, and he sought to enlarge federal court diversity of citizenship jurisdiction. Yet at the same time Harlan, often in dissent, supported a generous understanding of congressional power to address perceived economic abuses. He voted to affirm the regulatory authority of the Interstate Commerce Commission and to expand the reach of the Sherman Anti-Trust Act. Moreover, Harlan did not close the door on any state regulation. He frequently upheld the exercise of state police power to safeguard the safety, health, and morals of the public. This was exemplified by his dissenting opinion in *Lochner v. New York* (1905), favoring the regulation of hours of work for bakers. It was also shown by Harlan's decision for the Court in *Mugler v. Kansas* (1887), in which he sustained a state prohibition law as a valid exercise of the state police power to protect health and morals. Similarly, in *Hennington v. Georgia* (1896), Harlan upheld application of state Sunday laws to railroad operations despite the adverse impact on interstate commerce.

Like many contemporaries, Harlan had difficulty coming to terms with the new industrial economy based on large-scale business enterprise. He harbored simplistic theories of corruption and monopoly power and voiced concern that concentrated wealth threatened republican government. This attitude found expression in Harlan's dissenting opinion in *Pollock v. Farmers' Loan and Trust Co.* (1895), in which he defended the constitutionality of an income tax and insisted that such a levy was an equitable means of allocating the financial burdens of government. Likewise, he felt that vigorous enforcement of antitrust laws would curb the power of large corporations. In *Northern Securities Co. v. United States* (1904), for example, he advocated a literal application of the Sherman Anti-Trust Act to prohibit any restraints of trade. Harlan was deeply upset when the Supreme Court, just after the end of the Fuller era, adopted a judicial "rule of reason" under which only unreasonable restraints were deemed unlawful. Although lionized by Progressives for his antitrust opinions, Harlan was no seer about the future direction of antitrust policy.

The elusive nature of Harlan's jurisprudence has made him especially difficult to label. Tensions within Harlan's thought about the role of government were not easily reconciled, and they help to explain his uneven pattern of decisions. In the last analysis, Harlan relied more on his individual convictions than on any theory of judicial behavior.

The Garfield Appointment

Stanley Matthews

During the waning months of his presidency, President Hayes, in early 1881, named Stanley Matthews to replace retiring Justice Noah H. Swayne. The nomination proved

Stanley Matthews (Matthew Brady, Collection of the Supreme Court of the United States)

controversial, and the Senate took no action. However, Matthews was promptly renominated by Hayes's successor, President James A. Garfield. Matthews was narrowly confirmed in May of 1881 after months of intense debate.

A graduate of Kenyon College, Matthews formed a lasting friendship with Hayes, a fellow student. Matthews studied law in Cincinnati. After practicing law for a few years in Tennessee, he returned to Ohio and became active in the antislavery movement and an ally of Salmon P. Chase. During the 1850s Matthews served briefly as a judge of the Court of Common Pleas and as an Ohio state senator. In 1858 President James Buchanan named Matthews as U.S. attorney for the southern district of Ohio, in which position he prosecuted a case for aiding in the escape of fugitive slaves. This incident haunted Matthews during his later political and judicial careers. He was an officer in the Union Army for two years and resigned in 1863 upon his election to the state bench. Returning to private practice after a few years as judge, Matthews became one of the leading railroad and corporate attorneys in Ohio. In 1876 Matthews vigorously supported the presidential bid of his friend Hayes and represented the Hayes electors before the electoral commission. Matthews was also elected to the U.S. Senate in 1877 to fill an unexpired two-year term.

Matthews served less than eight years on the Supreme Court, and nearly all of his tenure occurred before Fuller became chief justice. Pragmatic and nondoctrinaire, Matthews authored more than 200 opinions for the Court. In his most famous opinion, *Yick Wo v. Hopkins* (1886), Matthews held that a San Francisco ordinance regulating laundries, neutral on its face, was applied in a discriminatory manner against Chinese laundry owners and constituted a denial of equal protection of law in violation of the Fourteenth Amendment. The full implications of this landmark decision as a safeguard for racial minorities was not realized until the late twentieth century. In addition, Matthews wrote a number of important decisions dealing with economic rights. In the *Virginia Coupon Cases* (1885) he ruled that a Virginia statute that prevented the coupons of state bonds from being received in payment of state taxes impaired the obligation of contract in violation of the Contracts Clause. Speaking for the Court in *Bowman v. Chicago Northwestern Railway Co.* (1888), Matthews found that an Iowa law forbidding common carriers from transporting liquor into the state unconstitutionally interfered with interstate commerce. With regard to criminal procedure, Matthews insisted in *Hurtado v. California* (1884) that the specific guarantees of the Fifth Amendment were not incorporated into the Due Process Clause of the Fourteenth Amendment. He maintained that any legal proceeding that preserved fundamental justice satisfied due process norms.

Becoming ill in the fall of 1888, Matthews was unable to attend the Court while Fuller was chief. Matthews died in March of 1889 and thus made no contribution to the jurisprudence of the Fuller Court.

The Arthur Appointments

Horace Gray

Born in Boston and a graduate of Harvard College, Gray also studied law at Harvard. He was admitted to the bar in Massachusetts in 1851. After a brief period in private practice, Gray became the court reporter for the Supreme Judicial Court of Massachusetts. In 1864 he was appointed to that bench and became its chief justice nine years later. Gray built a solid reputation as an erudite scholar and as a prodigious worker. A Republican with conservative political instincts, Gray was nonetheless willing to uphold some governmental regulation of the economy. President Chester A. Arthur's nomination of Gray to the Supreme Court in December of 1881 was widely applauded, and Gray was quickly confirmed by the Senate with no controversy.

Gray, who served on the Supreme Court for more than twenty years, was a prolific author, writing more than 450 opinions. He rarely dissented. In preparing opinions Gray often relied on historical examples and investigations of English common law. Perhaps because of this emphasis on history, Gray's opinions, in the words of one historian, "lack any distinctive perspective or judicial position" (Fiss 1993, 30). Gray's lengthy and citation-laden opinions, moreover, often appear tedious to modern readers.

Gray proved a property-conscious jurist who joined in most of the leading economic rights opinions of the Supreme Court under Fuller. Thus, he united with his colleagues to affirm the liberty of contract doctrine in *Allgeyer v. Louisiana* (1897) and to uphold the use of labor injunctions in *In re Debs* (1895). Gray voted with the majority in *Pollock v. Farmers' Loan and Trust Co.* (1895) to invalidate the 1894 income tax as an unconstitutional direct tax. He also sided with a unanimous bench in *Smyth v. Ames* (1897) to insist that regulated industries, such as railroads, must receive a "fair return" upon their capital investment and were constitutionally entitled to charge reasonable rates. The effect of the *Smyth* ruling was to curtail states' rate-making authority with respect to railroads. Speaking for a unanimous Court in *Missouri Pacific Railway Co. v. Nebraska* (1896), Gray held that a state law taking the land of a railroad for private use by others constituted a deprivation of property without due process in violation of the Fourteenth Amendment. It is perhaps noteworthy, however, that Gray did not write any of the most important opinions of the Fuller era.

Early in his tenure on the Supreme Court Gray manifested nationalist sentiments and gave a broad reading to the powers of Congress. For example, in *Juilliard v. Greenman* (1884) he ruled that Congress had the constitutional authority to make notes of U.S. legal tender in payment of private debts in time of peace as well as war. Writing for the Court in *Fong Yue Ting v. United States* (1893), Gray maintained that

Horace Gray (Harris & Ewing, Collection of the Supreme Court of the United States)

aliens resided in this country subject to the arbitrary power of Congress to expel them whenever it thought their removal necessary. Such authority, he reasoned, was the inherent right of a sovereign nation. But Gray later joined with Fuller in *United States v. E. C. Knight Co.* (1895) to hold that federal commerce power did not encompass manufacturing, a decision that limited the reach of federal antitrust laws.

If generally supportive of national authority, Gray was prepared to allow the states selective latitude to act in the absence of congressional legislation. He was skeptical about the Fuller Court's frequent invocation of the dormant commerce power (which foreclosed state laws that unduly hampered commerce among the states) to invalidate state laws that infringed upon interstate commerce. Gray dissented when the Court majority insisted that alcoholic beverages were articles of commerce and could be transported from state to state despite state prohibition laws. Similarly, in *Gladson v. Minnesota* (1897), Gray, speaking for the Court, upheld a state law requiring intrastate passenger trains to stop at all county seats in their course, holding that such a provision was not an interference with interstate commerce. Nor did Gray see the Due Process Clause of the Fourteenth Amendment as a barrier to state health and safety regulations. In *St. Louis and San Francisco Railway Co. v. Mathews* (1897) Gray sustained a state statute that made railroads strictly liable for damages caused by fire communicated from a locomotive. Brushing aside an argument that such a law deprived the carrier of property without due process, Gray ruled that the measure was a valid exercise of the state police power to protect property against loss caused by the use of locomotives. He also voted with the majority in *Holden v. Hardy* (1898) to validate a state law limiting the hours of work in underground mines as a health measure.

Like most of his colleagues on the Supreme Court in the late nineteenth century, Gray was little concerned about racial minorities. Thus, he joined in a number of opinions, most notably *Plessy v. Ferguson* (1896), upholding racial segregation. On occasion, however, Gray adopted positions helpful to minorities. He articulated the widely shared ethnocentric view of Indians, describing them as "a weak and dependent people, who have no written language and are wholly unfamiliar with all the forms of legal expression" (*Jones v. Meehan* 1899, 11). Yet this attitude led Gray to insist in *Jones* that ambiguous provisions in treaties between the United States and Indian tribes should be construed in favor of the Indians. Striking a blow in favor of beleaguered Chinese immigrants, Gray maintained that a person born in the United States of Chinese descent was a citizen of the United States. Speaking for the Court in *United States v. Wong Kim Ark* (1898), Gray undertook an extensive historical review of the concept of nationality, concluding that the Fourteenth Amendment affirmed the principle of citizenship by birth in the United States. It followed that the government could not deport the defendant under the Chinese Exclusion Acts.

Late in his career on the Supreme Court Gray took a major step toward the recognition of customary international law by courts of the United States. In *The Paquete Habana* (1900), a case arising out of the maritime seizure of a Spanish fishing vessel during the Spanish-American War, he declared that "international law is part of our law" and that to ascertain international law absent a treaty "resort must be had to the customs and usages of civilized nations" (*Pacquete Habana*, 700). After an exhaustive review of the historical evidence, Gray concluded for the Court majority that under established international law coastal fishing vessels were exempt from capture.

Although Gray was by temperament a meticulous scholar rather than a trail-blazer, he was also a generally dependable member of the Fuller Court's conservative bloc on economic issues. Further, Gray did initiate one important innovation in the life of the Supreme Court. He was the first justice to employ recent law school graduates as law clerks, a practice eventually followed by all his colleagues.

Samuel Blatchford

President Arthur turned to Samuel Blatchford of New York in 1882 to fill a vacant seat on the Court. Arthur's nominee was selected for his legal attainments and Republican political affiliation, as well as for geographic considerations. Born in New York City in 1820, Blatchford graduated from Columbia University. He studied law in the office of William H. Seward and entered the private practice of law in New York City. Thereafter Blatchford practiced law with Seward in Auburn, New York, for several years before returning to the metropolitan area and forming his own law firm. He built a distinguished reputation in the field of admiralty law and served as a reporter of the decisions of the U.S. Circuit Court for the Second Circuit. In 1867 President Andrew Johnson named Blatchford a federal district judge for the southern district of New York. President Rutherford B. Hayes appointed him to the circuit court in 1878.

To replace retiring Justice Ward Hunt, President Arthur sought a nominee from the states composing the second judicial circuit. After Senator Roscoe Conkling of New York declined to serve on the Court, Arthur looked to Blatchford, who had fifteen years of experience on the federal bench and was an acknowledged admiralty law expert. A noncontroversial choice, Blatchford was easily confirmed by the Senate. Although Blatchford is not well known today, he was a prodigious worker who authored 430 majority opinions during his eleven years as a justice. Blatchford almost always voted with the majority, writing just two dissenting opinions. Many of Blatchford's majority opinions dealt with issues of admiralty, patents, and bankruptcy. These are, of course, important topics but rarely provide the basis for a lasting reputation. Blatchford served for five years with Fuller as chief justice and continued to demonstrate "industry rather than brilliance" (King 1950, 134).

In his most significant decision for the Fuller Court, *Chicago, Milwaukee, and*

Samuel Blatchford (Handy Studios, Collection of the Supreme Court of the United States)

St. Paul Railway Co. v. Minnesota (1890), Blatchford accepted the premise that the Due Process Clause of the Fourteenth Amendment curtailed state regulatory authority to interfere with property rights. Specifically, Blatchford declared that a state law regulating railroad charges was unconstitutional because it failed to provide for a hearing or for judicial review of the fairness of rates imposed by state law. He insisted that a railroad was entitled to charge reasonable rates for the use of its property and suggested that the reasonableness of a rate was a matter for independent court review. This landmark decision seemingly overruled *Munn v. Illinois* (1877), which held that rate-setting was solely a legislative function. Coming at the start of the Fuller era, Blatchford's opinion in *Chicago, Milwaukee, and St. Paul* was a harbinger of future developments. It signaled that property ownership encompassed usage for economic gain and that the Court under Fuller would become more active in defending economic liberty in the face of increased regulation. One historian has argued that Fuller tapped Blatchford to write this opinion because he was a consensus-builder who could forge a majority for a major constitutional innovation (Semonche 1978, 19).

Yet only two years later the sometimes puzzling Blatchford authored an opinion in *Budd v. New York* (1892), upholding a New York law fixing the charges for grain elevators. Brushing aside the argument that this regulation constituted a deprivation of property without due process, he unconvincingly attempted to distinguish *Chicago, Milwaukee, and St. Paul* by asserting that rates set directly by the legislature itself, as in *Budd*, were not subject to judicial review, whereas rates fixed by a state commission could be reviewed. This distinction made little sense. It focused on the regulatory technique used in a particular case rather than on the reasonableness of an imposed rate. In any event, the Fuller Court soon moved away from *Budd*.

Blatchford's record in other areas of law was similarly checkered. Speaking for the Court in *Counselman v. Hitchcock* (1892), he adopted an expansive reading of the Fifth Amendment privilege against self-incrimination. He insisted that the privilege not only applied to criminal trials but also extended to inquiries in any official proceeding. Blatchford, however, shared the reluctance of the Fuller Court to apply the procedural guarantees of the Bill of Rights to state criminal proceedings. Thus, in *O'Neil v. Vermont* (1892) he held that the Eighth Amendment prohibition against cruel and unusual punishment was not binding on the states. Although Blatchford joined in several opinions, notably *Yick Wo v. Hopkins* (1886), which sought to protect Chinese immigrants, he voted in the *Civil Rights Cases* (1883) to invalidate a congressional ban on racial discrimination in privately owned public accommodations.

A diligent worker with a moderate outlook, Blatchford was not a major force in influencing the early years of the Fuller Court. He never developed a distinctive judicial philosophy and was generally content to go along with his colleagues.

The Cleveland Appointments

Lucius Q. C. Lamar

Grover Cleveland was the first Democratic candidate to be elected president since the Civil War. No Democrat had been named to the Supreme Court since Stephen J. Field in 1863. During his two nonconsecutive terms as president Cleveland consistently looked to appoint Democrats who shared his conservative economic views. He was remarkably successful in this endeavor, and in the process he selected several of the key justices of the Fuller era.

By the late 1880s there was no member of the Supreme Court who had been born in any of the states that composed the Confederacy. Southern political leaders strenuously argued that in fairness there should be at least one justice from their region. Moreover, Cleveland had received overwhelming political backing from the South. Not surprisingly, therefore, Cleveland named a southerner, Lucius Q.C. Lamar of Mississippi, as his first pick for the Supreme Court.

Lamar was born in Georgia and graduated from Emory College in 1845. He studied law for two years in Macon but practiced law thereafter only from time to time. As a young man Lamar moved between Georgia and Mississippi. Disappointed with his meager law practice and poor political prospects in Georgia, Lamar permanently settled in Mississippi in 1855. Campaigning as an advocate for southern interests, he was twice elected to the House of Representatives in the late 1850s. In 1861 Lamar helped to draft the Mississippi secession ordinance and resigned from the U.S. Congress. Upon the outbreak of the Civil War Lamar served the Confederacy in various posts—as a military officer, diplomat, and judge advocate in military courts. At the end of the hostilities Lamar became professor of law at the University of Mississippi, but he also developed a part-time private practice. In 1872 Lamar was again elected to the House of Representatives and reentered public life as a champion of sectional reconciliation. Elected to the U.S. Senate in 1876, Lamar demonstrated a commitment to sound money and built a national reputation as a former Confederate now loyal to the Union.

The election of Cleveland as president opened new doors for Lamar. Needing representation from the South in his cabinet, Cleveland appointed Lamar as secretary of the interior. Lamar favored assimilation of the Indians and supported passage of the Dawes Act to allot reservation lands to individuals. The death of Justice William B. Woods, a native of Ohio who settled in Atlanta after the Civil War, in May 1887 gave Cleveland his first Court vacancy to fill. The choice of Lamar, who shared Cleveland's view of the limited role of the federal government, made good sense as a symbol of reconciliation. The appointment aroused heated criticism, much of it stemming from Lamar's Confederate background and limited legal practice. He was narrowly con-

Lucius Q. C. Lamar (Matthew Brady Handy Studios, Collection of the Supreme Court of the United States)

firmed by the Senate after a bruising struggle, and the episode underscored persistent sectional tensions in the late nineteenth century.

Lamar's five-year tenure on the Supreme Court was marked by his perception of inadequacy growing out of the confirmation battle, as well as by his recurring poor health. Fuller was named chief justice only months after Lamar joined the Court, and the two Democrats became friends. Lamar tended to side with Fuller on most issues. Like Justice Blatchford, Lamar rarely dissented. Most of Lamar's opinions for the Court dealt with private law matters, such as land disputes, torts, and patents. Lamar wrote no opinions after May 1892 but remained on the bench until his death in January 1893. As this record suggests, Lamar was not a particularly influential justice on the Fuller Court.

The central theme of Lamar's judicial philosophy was a dedication to a limited national government and to the separation of powers. This was demonstrated in his most noteworthy ruling, *Kidd v. Pearson* (1888), decided at the very start of the Fuller era. Upholding an Iowa law that prohibited the manufacture of alcoholic beverages within the state even for purposes of export, Lamar distinguished between manufacturing and commerce. The power of Congress, he declared, extended to transportation but did not include productive industries or agriculture. It followed that the states retained broad control over economic activity within their borders. The *Kidd* decision anticipated Fuller's famous opinion in *United States v. E. C. Knight Co.* (1895), which restricted the reach of congressional power over the economy.

Similarly, Lamar's dissenting opinion in *In re Neagle* (1890) assailed an expansion of federal executive power without a positive enactment by Congress. Lamar insisted that a federal marshal, who acted as a bodyguard for Justice Field without explicit statutory authority, was not in the discharge of his official duties when he killed a man and was therefore not entitled to a writ of habeas corpus from the federal courts. Since there was no national law governing this matter, Lamar concluded that the state courts had jurisdiction. The *Neagle* dissent is a classic statement rejecting the doctrine that the president could exercise implied powers.

Lamar was also dubious about the expansion of federal judicial authority over the states. Splitting with Fuller, he resisted early moves by the Court to interpret the Due Process Clause of the Fourteenth Amendment as a shield against unreasonable state regulations. For instance, Lamar dissented in *Chicago, Milwaukee, and St. Paul Railway Co. v. Minnesota* (1890), asserting that the state legislature, not the federal judiciary, was the final arbiter in the regulation of railroad rates.

Aside from interstate transportation, where he accepted an expanded federal role, Lamar tended to construe national statutes strictly and to defend state autonomy. His judicial career reflected the states' rights creed formed during his years in political life.

Melville W. Fuller

Melville W. Fuller, whose name is associated with a distinctive chapter in Supreme Court history, was President Cleveland's second and most reluctant nominee. When Chief Justice Morrison R. Waite died in March 1888, Cleveland swiftly turned to Fuller as his choice for the center chair. The nomination generated opposition from some Republican senators, and they delayed confirmation for nearly three months. In the end, however, Fuller was confirmed by a comfortable margin with support from both political parties.

Born in Augusta, Maine, on February 11, 1833, Fuller was raised in the home of his maternal grandfather, Judge Nathan Weston of the Supreme Judicial Court of Maine. Judge Weston was an ardent Democrat who stressed the virtues of Jacksonian policies and limited government. Under his tutelage Fuller acquired a lifelong commitment to the Democratic Party and a love of literature. Fuller graduated from Bowdoin College in 1853, where he was a member of Phi Beta Kappa, and began to study law in the Bangor office of his uncle. In the fall of 1854 Fuller entered Harvard Law School and attended lectures for six months. Admitted to the Maine bar in 1855, Fuller started to practice law and dabbled in local politics. Despite his ties to Maine, Fuller, like so many other New Englanders of his generation, soon gravitated westward.

Settling in Chicago, Fuller over time built a thriving law practice that focused on appellate advocacy. He regularly appeared before the Illinois Supreme Court and handled a number of appeals to the U.S. Supreme Court. He increasingly represented banks, railroads, and members of the Chicago business elite such as Marshall Field. Yet Fuller valued professional independence. He continued to represent individuals and municipal bodies, and he refused to become the regular counsel for any enterprise. Fuller's far-ranging practice reached many fields of law, including real property, torts, commercial law, and state taxation.

Fuller also became active in Democratic Party affairs and was a supporter of Stephen A. Douglas. He made brief excursions into active political life, serving as a delegate to the Illinois constitutional convention in 1862 and as an Illinois legislator for a single term in the mid-1860s. During the Civil War Fuller supported military action to defeat secession, but he also criticized the policies of the Lincoln administration and denounced the Emancipation Proclamation as unconstitutional. Fuller attended several Democratic Party national conventions, and he enthusiastically backed Cleveland's presidential bid in 1884. In time Fuller and the new president formed a close friendship. The two corresponded frequently, and Cleveland consulted Fuller on the distribution of political patronage in Illinois.

Impressed with Fuller's character and skills, Cleveland repeatedly asked him to serve in important governmental posts, including that of solicitor general, the nation's representative in cases before the U.S. Supreme Court. Fuller consistently rejected

Melville W. Fuller (Harris & Ewing, Collection of the Supreme Court of the United States)

these overtures, citing family concerns. Advised that the president had determined to nominate him as chief justice in April 1888, Fuller requested time to consider. Cleveland, however, declined to wait and formally sent Fuller's name to the Senate. A few days later Fuller accepted the appointment, "trusting that the country will never have cause to regret your calling me to it, and earnestly hoping that God will give me strength equal to the exalted responsibilities imposed" (quoted in Ely 1995, 19).

Two observations elucidate Fuller's tenure as chief justice. First, Fuller excelled in establishing harmonious personal relations with persons of diverse legal and political views. He possessed a genial nature, a keen sense of humor, and unflagging courtesy. Moreover, Fuller combined a scholarly manner and sharp mind with generous impulses. These winning personal characteristics helped Fuller gain the support of his colleagues and direct their talents. An excellent social leader, he prevented destructive personal feuds from damaging the work of the Court. To further this goal, Fuller introduced the custom of requiring each justice to shake hands with other justices each morning before conferences. This practice continues to the present. Henry J. Abraham aptly described Fuller as "a superb manager and executive" who "is generally regarded as one of the two or three best presiding officers in the Court's history" (Abraham 1999, 108). An outstanding Court administrator, Fuller was less interested in leaving a personal stamp on constitutional thought.

Second, the constitutional jurisprudence espoused by Fuller had deep roots in Jacksonian Democracy, with its emphasis on equal rights and its aversion to class legislation. Jurists in the late nineteenth century drew upon Jacksonian tenets as they attempted to protect economic liberty and distinguish between appropriate regulations for the public welfare and illegitimate special-interest laws. The importance of Jacksonian thought in molding constitutional law applied with special force to Fuller. A commitment to minimal governmental intervention and support of economic individualism were hallmarks of his philosophy. "Paternalism," Fuller declared in 1880, years before he became chief justice, "with its constant intermeddling with individual freedom, has no place in a system which rests for its strength upon the self-reliance energies of the people" (quoted in Ely 1995, 14).

Further indications of Fuller's constitutional outlook can be found in his 1889 address on George Washington. To mark the 100th anniversary of Washington's inauguration as president, Congress invited Fuller to deliver a speech before a joint session. The president and much of official Washington attended this high-visibility event. Fuller's speech was a great success and enhanced his status with his new colleagues on the bench. The justices published Fuller's remarks in the United States Reports. Indeed, Fuller's speech and Washington's famous farewell address have been reprinted together as vehicles that shed light on American law and society in the nineteenth century (Kosma and Davies 1999, 9–72).

In addition to presenting a thoughtful assessment of Washington, Fuller discussed in general terms some of the leading constitutional issues of the day. One of these was the balance between the states and the federal government. Fuller recognized the increased power of the federal government, but emphasized the continuing importance of the states within the constitutional system. The Civil War, according to Fuller, preserved the Union "without the loss of distinct and individual existence or of the right of self-government by the States." (Fuller 1889, 728). Fuller also considered the role of property rights in the constitutional order. He guardedly affirmed legislative moves to alleviate inequality of conditions, but expressed concern that "when man allows his beliefs, his family, his property, his labor, each of his acts, to be subjected to the omnipotence of the State, or is unmindful of the fact that it is the duty of the people to support the government and not of the government to support the people, such a surrender of independence involves the cessation of such progress in its largest sense." (Fuller 1889, 732). This comment underscores Fuller's dedication to limited government. He next explored the relationship between the rights of property owners and the regulatory authority of government, declaring that

> while the rights to life, to use one's faculties in all lawful ways, and to acquire and enjoy property are morally fundamental rights antecedent to constitutions, which do not create, but secure and protect them, yet it is within the power of the State to promote the health, peace, morals, education, and good order of the people by legislation to that end, and to regulate the use of property in which the public has such an interest as to be entitled to assert control. (Fuller 1889, 732)

Moreover, Fuller praised the provisions of the Constitution, "which inhibit the subversion of individual freedom, the impairment of the obligation of contracts, and the confiscation of property." (Fuller 1889, 732).

This language provides a window into Fuller's constitutional values. The chief justice clearly stressed the important place of states' rights and private property in his conception of the constitutional system. Following John Locke and natural law theorists, Fuller believed that personal rights, including the right to obtain property, existed before the creation of political authority. It was the function of government to protect these already existing rights. Still, Fuller was not a doctrinaire adherent of laissez-faire philosophy. He expressly recognized that government could control the use of property to foster the health, safety, and morals of the public.

Fuller never dominated the Supreme Court intellectually, but under his leadership the Court almost at once began to more forcefully review marketplace regulations and to champion economic freedom. The chief justice did not author many of the famous opinions of the age, but he usually voted with the majority and was a successful coalition-builder. The general direction of the Court was clearly in harmony with his personal views. During Fuller's tenure the Court was less inclined to defer to economic regulation initiatives by legislators and assumed a more active role in governance.

If Fuller was solicitous of the rights of property owners, he was influenced by other constitutional values as well. Consistent with his belief in limited federal government, Fuller sought to maintain a large measure of autonomy for states as vital components of the federal system. Thus, Fuller was prepared to give states almost free reign in governing criminal justice, race relations, and public morals. Even in the economic area, Fuller favored an important role for the states. The tension inherent in safeguarding property rights while respecting state authority was evident in a number of Fuller's opinions.

One of Fuller's most significant opinions was *United States v. E. C. Knight Co.* (1895), the first antitrust prosecution under the Sherman Anti-Trust Act to reach the Supreme Court. The government charged that the American Sugar Refining Company, through various contracts, controlled virtually all sugar refining in the United States and constituted a combination in restraint of trade. Speaking for a majority of eight justices, Fuller held that congressional power over interstate commerce extended only to trade among the states and did not encompass manufacturing. In one of his most quoted sentences, Fuller famously declared: "Commerce succeeds to manufacture, and is not a part of it" (*E. C. Knight*, 12). It followed that Congress could not suppress an alleged monopoly in manufacturing. Scholars have sometimes overlooked the states' rights theme in *E. C. Knight*. Fuller revealingly explained: "Slight reflection will show that if the national power extends to all contracts and combinations of manufacture, agriculture, mining, and other productive industries, whose ultimate result may affect external commerce, comparatively little of business operations and affairs would be left for state control" (*E. C. Knight*, 16). To Fuller's mind, the prospect of plenary federal control over commerce threatened the autonomy of the states in the constitutional system and was more menacing than the supposed danger of business consolidations.

Fuller, however, was prepared to enforce the Sherman Act when the authority of Congress was clear. In *United States v. Trans-Missouri Freight Association* (1897) he voted with the majority to apply the act to railroads and thereby invalidate a pooling arrangement between competing lines for the purpose of fixing charges. Late in his tenure as chief justice, moreover, Fuller, writing for a unanimous Court in *Loewe v. Lawlor* (1908), held that the Sherman Act reached a nationwide secondary boycott by a union. He reasoned that the boycott threatened to obstruct the free flow of commerce among the states.

Sometimes Fuller's commitment to federalism reinforced his desire to protect the rights of property owners. For example, in *Pollock v. Farmers' Loan and Trust Co.* (1895) Fuller, writing two opinions for the Court, struck down the 1894 income tax. He reasoned that the income tax was a "direct tax" that was not apportioned among the states according to population, as required by the Constitution. Fuller viewed the Direct Tax Clause as a vital limit on congressional taxing power. The purpose of this provision, according to Fuller, was "to restrain the exercise of the power of direct taxation to extraordinary emergencies, and to prevent an attack upon accumulated property by mere force of numbers." If this "rule of protection could be frittered away," he warned, "one of the great landmarks defining the boundary between the Nation and the States of which it is composed, would have disappeared, and with it one of the bulwarks of private rights and private property" (*Pollock* I, 583). In *Pollock*, his most well-known and controversial decision, Fuller insisted that the Direct Tax Clause protected both the places of the states in the federal union as well as the rights of individual property owners. He correctly perceived that the income tax would open the door for an expansion of federal power and a fundamental alteration of federal-state relations.

Despite Fuller's attachment to a large role for the states in governing much of public life, he recognized federal supremacy in certain areas. Fuller was determined to wield the dormant commerce power to prevent state restrictions on interstate commerce. In *Leisy v. Hardin* (1890) Fuller held that states could not ban the transportation of liquor, an object of commerce, because the regulation of interstate commerce was reserved for Congress. Drawing upon Chief Justice John Marshall's original package rule articulated in *Brown v. Maryland* (1827) with respect to state taxing authority, Fuller maintained that an importer had the right to engage in the interstate shipment and sale of commodities in their original package. The *Leisy* opinion set the stage for a number of subsequent Fuller Court decisions invalidating state prohibition laws as infringements of congressional control of interstate commerce. It also signaled the Fuller Court's repeated invocation of the dormant commerce power to safeguard the national market against state encroachments. Freedom of commerce among the states was a consistent theme in Fuller's jurisprudence. For instance, he dissented in *Hennington v. Georgia* (1896), in which the Court majority sustained the application of state Sunday laws to interstate rail transportation. Fuller argued that rail travel between states was a national matter and that state laws preventing such commerce one day a week were unconstitutional.

Of course, not all state laws that incidentally impacted interstate commerce were invalidated. Fuller certainly agreed that states could protect public health and safety. Still, Fuller and his colleagues tended to closely scrutinize whether a challenged state regulation unreasonably burdened commerce among the states.

Another important vehicle by which the Fuller Court vindicated property and contractual rights was the Due Process Clause of the Fourteenth Amendment. Although Fuller did not write any of the leading opinions that treated the due process norm as the basis for federal judicial review of state economic regulations, he consistently sided with the majority in fashioning a muscular Due Process Clause. Starting with *Chicago, Milwaukee, and St. Paul Railway Co. v. Minnesota* (1890), Fuller voted in a line of cases to establish federal judicial oversight of state railroad rate regulations and to insist that railroads, via due process, were constitutionally entitled to a reasonable return on their capital investment. Likewise, Fuller agreed that liberty, as protected by the Fourteenth Amendment, encompassed the right to pursue any lawful calling and to enter contracts. He joined in the most prominent liberty of contract rulings of the era, including *Allgeyer v. Louisiana* (1897), *Lochner v. New York* (1905), and *Adair v. United States* (1908).

Committed to economic individualism as a support for political liberty, Fuller favored minimal government interference with the rights of property owners. Still, he struggled to keep a balance between the traditional legislative authority of the states, on the one hand, and judicial protection of property and contractual rights, on the other. He supported no blanket displacement of state regulations and, in fact, sustained a wide variety of state economic controls. For example, in *New York and New England Railroad Co. v. Bristol* (1894) Fuller upheld the validity of a state statute compelling the removal of a railroad-grade crossing annually, at the sole expense of the company, as a proper exercise of police power. As this suggests, Fuller was never a single-minded champion of business interests, and his approach to economic issues did not fit into a neat pattern.

It is fair to conclude that Fuller, like most Americans of the Gilded Age, was relatively unconcerned about claims for better treatment by racial and religious minorities. As suggested by his record during the Civil War, he was not emotionally or intellectually inclined to attack racial segregation. Not surprisingly, Fuller repeatedly voted to uphold state segregation laws and joined in such well-known opinions as *Plessy v. Ferguson* (1896) and *Cumming v. Richmond County Board of Education* (1899). Likewise, he regularly deferred to congressional policy with respect to Indians and control over tribal lands.

Yet Fuller was sometimes sympathetic to the plight of outsiders. He forcefully dissented in *Fong Yue Ting v. United States* (1893) when the Court majority held that Congress had absolute authority to summarily deport resident aliens. Dissenting in *Late Corporation of the Church of Jesus Christ of Latter-Day Saints v. United States* (1890), Fuller protested the confiscation of Mormon Church property by Congress as part of the campaign to stamp out polygamy. He was also concerned about the legal status of the residents of the overseas territories acquired by the United States following the Spanish-American War. In *Downes v. Bidwell* (1901), the most important of the so-called *Insular Cases*, Fuller, again in dissent, insisted that Congress could not treat the new overseas territories by different rules than those prevailing in the United States. He argued that the Constitution followed the flag and that the power of Congress over U.S. territories was therefore restricted by the Constitution.

The Supreme Court under Fuller is best known for its vigorous defense of economic liberty against legislative infringement, but it bears emphasis that during this era the justices had a heavy docket of private law disputes. In this connection, Fuller wrote a number of important opinions dealing with commercial practices, corporate governance, and bankruptcy. He sustained a pioneering use of equity railroad receiverships, a technique fashioned to keep insolvent carriers in operation pending reorganization. The corporate reorganization provisions of modern bankruptcy law can be traced directly to the evolution of these equity receiverships.

Fuller also made a mark with several leading opinions dealing with enterprise liability. Speaking for the Court in *Johnson v. Southern Pacific Co.* (1904), he gave a broad reading to the Safety Appliance Act, a measure designed to safeguard rail employees and travelers by requiring safety devices on trains. Fuller adopted a common-sense approach to statutory interpretation, emphasizing the remedial purposes of Congress rather than a technical construction of the statute. In the same vein, he was uncomfortable with strict application of the fellow-servant rule to defeat the claims of injured employees, and he sought to restrict its application. He maintained, for example, that the fellow-servant rule and the assumption of the risk doctrine did not excuse the failure of an employer to provide a safe workplace. "The general rule," Fuller commented in *Union Pacific Railway Co. v. O'Brien* (1896, 457), "undoubtedly is that a railroad company is bound to provide suitable and safe materials and structures in the construction of its roads and appurtenances."

Edward D. White

During his second term as president, Grover Cleveland named two additional justices who were a major influence on the work of the Fuller Court. Frustrated when two candidates from New York were defeated in the Senate as the result of a squabble over patronage, he turned to Edward Douglass White, a senator from Louisiana. Born into a wealthy sugar-planting family, White was raised a Roman Catholic. He was educated in Jesuit schools and attended Georgetown University until the outbreak of the Civil War. White joined the Confederate Army as a private and was captured by the Union after less than two years of military service. Following the war he studied law in the office of a prominent New Orleans attorney. White became active in Louisiana Democratic Party politics and served in the state senate and briefly on the Louisiana Supreme Court. In the meantime he built a thriving law practice.

In 1891 White was elected to the U.S. Senate by the Louisiana legislature. As senator White was generally a loyal supporter of Cleveland, backing the president's call for sound money and repeal of the Sherman Silver Purchase Act. His overriding concern, however, was to safeguard Louisiana sugar interests. He even delayed resigning from the Senate after his confirmation as justice to successfully defend tariff protection for domestic sugar in the Wilson-Gorman Tariff Act of 1894.

Although White was a prolific author of opinions, it is not easy to assess his constitutional ideology. He wrote few landmark constitutional law decisions for the

Edward D. White (Harris & Ewing, Collection of the Supreme Court of the United States)

Court while Fuller was chief. Usually conservative in outlook, White was nonetheless unpredictable. He did not follow a consistent approach to the issues arising out of assertions of federal government power to regulate the economy. White joined Fuller's opinion in *United States v. E. C. Knight Co.* (1895), which held that congressional power over commerce did not extend to manufacturing. Yet in *McCray v. United States* (1904) White, speaking for the Court, insisted that Congress could use the taxing power to regulate or prohibit economic activity. The *McCray* decision seemingly allowed Congress to regulate indirectly all aspects of the economy and was clearly at odds with *E. C. Knight Co.*

White's attitude toward state economic regulations is similarly uneven. He sided with the Court majority in a number of cases, culminating in *Smyth v. Ames* (1898), which held that railroads, under the Due Process Clause of the Fourteenth Amendment, were constitutionally entitled to a reasonable return on their investment. These decisions limited state regulatory authority over railroads. White also espoused the liberty of contract doctrine in such decisions as *Allgeyer v. Louisiana* (1897) and *Adair v. United States* (1908). Yet White did not interpret the Due Process Clause to bar all state regulation of the industrial workplace. He voted in *Holden v. Hardy* (1898) to uphold a Utah statute that limited the hours of work in mines, and he likewise sustained a maximum hours law for women in *Muller v. Oregon* (1908). White dissented in *Lochner v. New York* (1905), which struck down a state measure curtailing the working hours in bakeries. Seemingly searching for a middle ground in due process cases, he was willing to recognize a degree of state regulatory authority.

Perhaps White's most striking action was his dissent in both of the *Pollock* opinions. Given his concern for states' rights and the rights of property owners, one might have expected White to join with Fuller in voiding the 1894 income tax. Yet White disagreed. Pointing to earlier authority that sustained an income tax, he emphasized the binding authority of stare decisis as a constraint on the judiciary. White further complained that the majority "takes invested wealth and reads it into the Constitution as a favored and protected class of property" (*Pollock* II, 712). The sectional dimension of the income tax debate helps to explain White's vote. The income tax found much of its support in the southern states with low per capita wealth, and most of the justices who voted to uphold the levy came from that region. Moreover, the income tax was enacted as part of the Wilson-Gorman Tariff Act, a measure that White had strongly backed while in the Senate.

Not surprisingly for a justice from the Deep South in the late nineteenth century, White consistently endorsed racial segregation. He joined the majority in *Plessy v. Ferguson* (1896) and a string of other decisions upholding segregation laws and devices to disenfranchise black voters. Nor did he demonstrate interest in vindicating the equal rights claims of Chinese immigrants and Indians. Speaking for a unanimous Court in the leading case of *Lone Wolf v. Hitchcock* (1908), White ruled that

Congress had plenary authority over Indian affairs and could exercise complete control over the allocation of Indian lands.

One of White's most significant contributions to constitutional law was his articulation of the doctrine of incorporation in the *Insular Cases*. Concurring in *Downes v. Biddle* (1901), he maintained that constitutional guarantees applied to the inhabitants of a territory only after the territory had been incorporated by Congress into the political community of the United States. Although it was unclear how such incorporation was to be achieved, the Supreme Court majority adopted White's theory in *Dorr v. United States* (1904). By taking the position that the Constitution did not extend by its own force to the new overseas possessions, White confirmed broad congressional authority over U.S. territories. Historians have speculated that White's position in the *Insular Cases* was a factor in his later selection as chief justice by President William Howard Taft.

White also made a lasting mark on American jurisprudence in the area of statutory construction. He repeatedly insisted that the Sherman Anti-Trust Act should not be read literally to bar any restraint of trade. Instead, drawing upon common law principles, he proposed that the statute be interpreted to outlaw only unreasonable restraints of trade. White's famous "rule of reason" was never adopted during Fuller's tenure, but in 1911 the rule of reason was accepted by the Court as the correct standard for determining Sherman Act violations. Henceforth only unreasonable restraints were prohibited. The rule of reason necessitated a case-by-case factual inquiry and gave great discretion to the courts to decide what was reasonable. It also signaled the Court's realization that large-scale enterprise had become a permanent feature of the American economy.

Upon Fuller's death in 1910 President Taft named White as chief justice. This was the first time that an associate justice had been elevated to the center chair. Aside from developing the rule of reason in antitrust cases, White left few jurisprudential landmarks from his years as chief justice. He gingerly accepted much of the growth of federal governmental power during the Progressive era and World War I. Thus, he sustained the Adamson Act setting an eight-hour workday for railroad operating employees in *Wilson v. New* (1917), as well as the military draft as an exercise of congressional power to raise an army. But White continued to be concerned about the autonomy of the states within the federal system. He sided with the majority in *Hammer v. Dagenhart* (1918), which ruled that Congress could not use its power over interstate commerce to bar products manufactured by child labor. White's continuing solicitude for property rights was demonstrated by joining the dissent in *Block v. Hirsh* (1921), protesting that rent control laws were unconstitutional. If generally conservative, White was also something of an enigma.

Rufus W. Peckham

President Cleveland's last appointee to the Supreme Court, Rufus W. Peckham of New York, was destined to be a major influence on the Fuller Court; Peckham authored many of its most famous decisions. Born in Albany, New York, in 1838, Peckham was part of a prominent family of lawyers and judges. He was educated locally and studied law for two years in his father's office. Joining the family law firm, Peckham built a successful practice representing railroads and real estate magnates. He became active in Democratic Party affairs and served as district attorney for Albany County between 1869 and 1872. Thereafter Peckham was named corporation counsel for the city of Albany. Peckham developed a close friendship with Grover Cleveland and actively supported Cleveland's rise in New York political life. In 1883 Peckham was elected to the New York Supreme Court, which despite the name is in fact that state's trial court. Three years later, then–President Cleveland helped to engineer Peckham's election to the New York Court of Appeals, the court of last resort.

On the appellate bench Peckham proved to be an able judge, one who rejected party influence by adopting a nonpartisan attitude. Significantly, he demonstrated skepticism about governmental regulation of the economy, an aversion to class legislation, and a willingness to define liberty as encompassing economic freedom. Peckham's philosophy found its most revealing expression in his dissenting opinion in *People v. Budd* (1889). At issue was the constitutionality of a New York law regulating the rates of grain elevators. The Court majority sustained the measure, but Peckham vigorously disagreed. To his mind the statute departed from the general law of trade and interfered with "the most sacred rights of property and the individual liberty of contract." Peckham warned that laws of this type opened the door to class warfare:

> To uphold legislation of this character is to provide the most frequent opportunity for arraying class against class; and, in addition to the ordinary competition that exists throughout all industries, a new competition will be introduced, that of competition for the possession of the government, so that legislative aid may be given to the class in possession thereof in its contests with rival classes or interests in all sections and corners of the industrial world. . . . (*Budd*, 68–70)

He dramatically concluded that the law "is not only vicious in its nature, communistic in its tendency, and, in my belief, wholly inefficient to permanently obtain the result aimed at, but, . . . it is an illegal effort to interfere with the lawful privilege of the individual to seek and obtain such compensation as he can for the use of his own property" (*Budd*, 68–70).

Peckham carried with him to the Supreme Court this deep-seated commitment to economic liberty and limited government. Having at last resolved his patronage

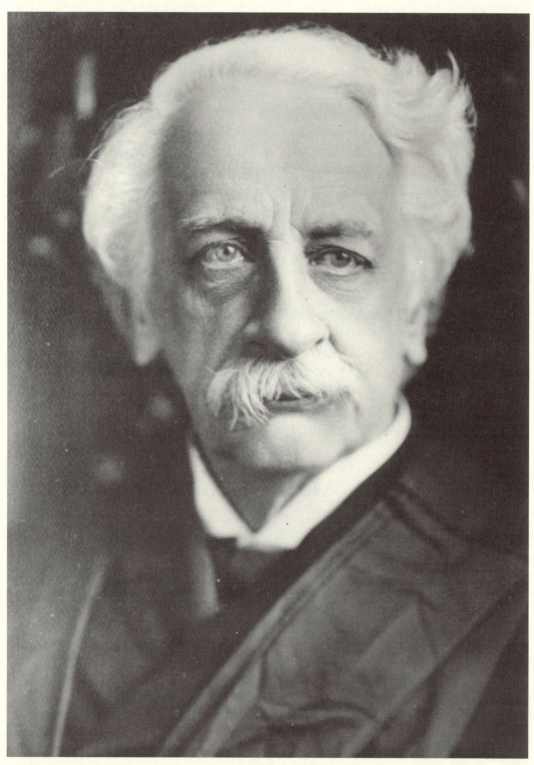

Rufus W. Peckham (Harris & Ewing, Collection of the Supreme Court of the United States)

dispute with Senator David Hill, President Cleveland named his close friend Peckham as his final appointee to the Court in December of 1895. When Peckham joined the Fuller Court his views were already gaining ascendancy. Consequently, he usually voted with the majority. Fuller repeatedly looked to Peckham to author major opinions. Indeed, Owen M. Fiss has pointed out that Peckham and David J. Brewer were intellectual leaders of the Fuller Court, "influential within the dominant coalition and the source of the ideas that gave the Court its sweep and direction" (Fiss 1993, 33).

While on the Court Peckham wrote several well-known opinions invoking his notion that the Due Process Clause of the Fourteenth Amendment safeguarded an individual's right to enter contracts. Speaking for a unanimous Court in *Allgeyer v. Louisiana* (1897), he struck down a state law that prohibited individuals from obtaining property insurance from out-of-state companies. So intense was Peckham's commitment to freedom of contract that he dissented, albeit without opinion, in *Holden v. Hardy* (1898), in which the Fuller Court majority upheld a Utah statute limiting the hours of work in underground mines; and in *Knoxville Iron Co. v. Harbison* (1901), in which the Court sustained a state law banning payment of employees in script.

In *Lochner v. New York* (1905) Peckham authored his most famous and controversial opinion, invalidating a New York statute restricting the hours of work in bakeries as a deprivation of liberty without due process. He reasoned that the baking trade was not unhealthy and that "the real object and purpose" of the measure was to regulate labor relations, not health. Peckham stressed that the mere assertion by the legislature of a link between law and public health did not render an enactment valid. Since he viewed the freedom of contract as a fundamental constitutional value, he in effect required the legislature to justify any infringement of this right. Finding no plausible health rationale, Peckham concluded that the legislation interfered with the right of employees to make their own judgment about the terms of employment. One of the most significant opinions ever rendered by the Supreme Court, *Lochner* has remained at the heart of the debate over the appropriate role of the judiciary in American society. It poses the basic question of whether the concept of due process provides a foundation for courts to enforce fundamental substantive rights beyond the explicit language of the Constitution.

Despite his stalwart defense of the liberty of contract, Peckham cannot fairly be caricatured as a champion of unbridled laissez-faire. When business associations interfered with interstate commerce, he had no hesitation in applying the Sherman Anti-Trust Act. In *United States v. Trans-Missouri Freight Association* (1897) and *United States v. Joint Traffic Association* (1898) Peckham held that an agreement among railroad companies to maintain reasonable rates was an illegal combination in restraint of trade. In reaching this conclusion he made two vital points: (1) The act prohibited all restraints of trade, not just those deemed unreasonable; and (2) the act covered railroads notwithstanding the fact that they were already governed by the Interstate Commerce Act.

In *Addyston Pipe and Steel Co. v. United States* (1899) Peckham again demonstrated his willingness to uphold antitrust restrictions. At issue in this case was a suit to enjoin an express agreement by cast-iron pipe manufacturers to divide territorial markets among themselves and control prices. Speaking for a unanimous Court, Peckham ruled that Congress had the power to prohibit private contracts that directly affected interstate commerce. He stressed that the power of Congress to regulate commerce could limit the right of individuals to enter contracts.

The Supreme Court, as we have seen, would eventually move away from Peckham's literal reading of the Sherman Anti-Trust Act and adopt the rule of reason. But his opinions applying the Sherman Act against business combinations, in circumstances that directly impacted interstate commerce, coupled with his criticism of concentrated economic power, indicate that Peckham was primarily concerned with economic liberty, not the protection of large-scale enterprise.

Like most of his fellow justices, Peckham stopped well short of recognizing a general power in Congress to govern the entire economy. In *Hopkins v. United States* (1897) he held that an association of merchants buying and selling livestock on commission was local in nature and thus not within the purview of interstate commerce. It followed that the rules of the association governing the business activities of members were not covered by the antitrust laws. Conversely, Peckham was a strong proponent of the view that the Commerce Clause by itself was designed to safeguard the national market from state infringement. He wrote numerous opinions invoking the dormant commerce power, especially with respect to rail transportation across state lines, to invalidate state laws as a burden on interstate commerce. For example, in *Mississippi Railroad Commission v. Illinois Central Railroad Co.* (1906) he struck down a state commission order that certain interstate trains stop at a local station.

The prolonged controversy over state regulation of railroad rates gave Peckham the opportunity to author a seminal opinion dealing with federal judicial power over state officials. The Eleventh Amendment denied the federal courts jurisdiction over suits against states by the citizens of other states. Yet in *Ex Parte Young* (1908) Peckham ruled that the Eleventh Amendment did not bar suits against state officials alleged to be acting unconstitutionally. He reasoned that an officer enforcing an unconstitutional statute "is in that case stripped of his official or representative character and is subjected in his person to the consequences of his individual conduct" (*Young*, 160). By means of this legal fiction Peckham circumvented the Eleventh Amendment and enlarged the power of the federal courts to enjoin state officials from violating federal law. This innovative decision provided a direct access to the federal courts, and it opened the door for railroads to seek federal judicial protection of their substantive right to a reasonable return on capital.

Peckham also contributed to the growth of jurisprudence under the Takings Clause of the Fifth Amendment. He joined the landmark decision in *Chicago, Burlington, and Quincy Railroad Co. v. Chicago* (1897), which determined that the payment of just compensation when private property was taken by a state for public use was an essential element of due process as guaranteed by the Fourteenth Amendment. But Peckham also adopted a generous definition of what constitutes "public use" for the purpose of acquiring property by eminent domain. In two leading opinions for the Court he broadly deferred to congressional or state determinations as to whether an appropriation of property should be deemed for public use. This was demonstrated by *United States v. Gettysburg Electric Railway* (1896), in which Peckham held that congressional legislation authorizing acquisition of the battleground at Gettysburg was for a public use within the meaning of the Takings Clause. More important, Peckham was prepared to sustain the use of eminent domain by the states even when the taking was largely for private advantage. In *Fallbrook Irrigation District v. Bradley* (1896) he upheld a California irrigation law that only benefited certain landowners and observed: "It is not essential that the entire community or even any considerable portion thereof should directly enjoy or participate in an improvement in order to constitute a public use" (*Fallbrook*, 161–162). Contrary to his image as a single-minded champion of the rights of property owners, Peckham left legislators with wide discretion to exercise the power of eminent domain as they saw fit.

Along with most other members of the Fuller Court, Peckham displayed little interest in racial minorities or criminal defendants. He sided with the Court majority in *Plessy v. Ferguson* (1896) and in other decisions that placed the judicial imprimatur on racial segregation in the South. To Peckham the states remained the primary guarantors of most individual rights. Thus, he insisted that the procedural protections of the Bill of Rights were not binding on the states. Brushing aside the contention in *Maxwell v. Dow* (1900) that a criminal defendant's conviction based on information rather than grand jury indictment was defective, Peckham revealingly declared that "there can be no just fear that the liberties of the citizen will not be carefully protected by the States respectively" (*Maxwell*, 605).

The Harrison Appointments

David J. Brewer

Although he served only a single term, President Benjamin Harrison named four justices to the Supreme Court. President Harrison's first appointee, David J. Brewer, wrote a number of prominent opinions and was a pivotal force in shaping the jurisprudence of the Fuller years. Brewer was born to Christian missionary parents

David J. Brewer (Collection of the Supreme Court of the United States)

in Smyrna, in Asia Minor, in 1837. From them he developed deep religious convictions that influenced his personal life as well as his public life. Brewer spent his early years in Connecticut and graduated high in his class from Yale College. He began to study law in the office of his uncle, David Dudley Field, a prominent legal reformer, then completed his legal education at Albany Law School. At the same time, Brewer became active in antislavery and Republican Party affairs. Soon after his graduation from Albany Law School in 1858 Brewer moved west, eventually settling in Kansas. Brewer slowly built a law practice in Leavenworth and was elected a probate judge in 1862 and a district judge a few years later.

In 1870 Brewer was elected handily to the Kansas Supreme Court and was twice reelected. As a member of the Kansas Supreme Court Brewer upheld railroad fencing laws and questioned the validity of the common practice of local-government subsidies for railroad construction. He disliked the use of public funds for private purpose, but he usually sustained broad state taxing power. Brewer's dedication to the rights of property owners was clearly expressed in an 1883 case interpreting the Kansas prohibition laws. Although Brewer sustained the constitutionality of such measures, he suggested that the laws effectuated a taking of property by denying beer manufacturers the intended use of their property. This was an early articulation of the view that severe regulation that rendered property almost worthless constituted a taking that required the payment of compensation. In addition, Brewer was generally supportive of equal rights for women, especially with respect to property ownership.

President Chester A. Arthur appointed Brewer to the Eighth Circuit Court in 1884. While on that court Brewer heard many railroad cases and issued a path-breaking injunction in 1888 temporarily preventing sharp reductions in freight rates ordered by Iowa's railroad commission. The Brewer injunction, which gained national attention, anticipated moves by the Supreme Court to establish judicial review of the reasonableness of state-imposed charges. He also reiterated his view that a state prohibition law in effect deprived a brewery owner of property without compensation, and he held a Kansas prohibition statute unconstitutional in violation of the Fourteenth Amendment. Prohibitionists were dismayed and later opposed Brewer's elevation to the Supreme Court.

Appointed by Harrison to the Supreme Court in 1889, Brewer was easily confirmed despite opposition from prohibitionists and some Grangers. The jovial Brewer soon established a close friendship with Fuller. A nephew of the aging Justice Stephen J. Field, Brewer shared much of his uncle's ideology. Yet Brewer and Field sometimes disagreed, and certainly the independent-minded Brewer was never the total disciple of Field that historians have often pictured. Brewer was strongly committed to individual liberty and suspicious of governmental intervention in the economy. "The paternal theory of government is to me odious," he explained in a dissenting opinion in *Budd v. New York* (1892). "The utmost possible liberty to the individual, and the fullest possible protection to him and his property, is both the limitation and duty of government" (*Budd*, 551).

On cases pertaining to economic rights, Brewer almost always voted with the Fuller Court majority to defend the rights of property owners and contractual freedom. In *Reagan v. Farmers' Loan and Trust Co.* (1894) Brewer, writing for a unanimous bench, voided a Texas railroad rate regulation as a deprivation of property without due process. He concluded that the regulation did not provide for a reasonable return to investors. This was the first Supreme Court ruling to strike down a rate schedule as confiscatory. Not surprisingly, he joined in *Smyth v. Ames* (1898) to insist that regulated industries were constitutionally entitled to a fair return. Brewer sided with the majority in the leading freedom of contract cases, such as *Allgeyer v. Louisiana* (1897), *Lochner v. New York* (1905), and *Adair v. United States* (1908). Likewise, he voted with Fuller and the majority in *Pollock* to invalidate the 1894 federal income tax. In extrajudicial remarks Brewer later asserted that a federal income tax would greatly enlarge the power of the central government and undercut state autonomy as a vital aspect of the federal system of government.

In his most famous opinion, *In re Debs* (1895), Brewer, speaking for a unanimous Court, sustained an injunction preventing the Pullman strikers from blocking the movement of trains operating in interstate commerce. Upholding the equity power of the federal courts to halt unlawful interference with commerce among the states, he ruled that judges could use the contempt power to compel obedience to their injunctions. Brewer's opinion in *Debs* encouraged the growing use of injunctions in labor disputes.

Brewer also wrote several important opinions dealing with the constitutional protection of property rights under the Takings Clause of the Fifth Amendment. In *Monongahela Navigation Co. v. United States* (1893) he explained that the just compensation principle expressed in the Takings Clause "prevents the public from loading upon one individual more than his just share of the burdens of government" (*Monongahela Navigation*, 325). Brewer then expansively defined "just compensation" to encompass the profitableness of land. Furthermore, he argued forcefully in dissenting opinions that laws requiring owners to change existing structures in order to comply with health or safety regulations should be deemed a taking of property for public use. Also significant was Brewer's continued assertion that onerous land-use regulations might effectuate a taking of property for which compensation was constitutionally required. In a well-known 1891 public address he remarked: "Property is as certainly destroyed when the use of that which is the subject of the property is taken away, as if the thing itself was appropriated, for that which gives value to property is its capacity for use" (Brewer 1891, 102). Brewer can fairly be seen as a pioneer of the modern regulatory takings doctrine.

Although Brewer certainly stressed individual property rights as a core constitutional value, he was not a champion of big business or an apostle of unbridled laissez-faire. He frequently voiced concern about concentrated economic power in private hands, and he did not hesitate to apply the Sherman Anti-Trust Act to enterprises clearly in interstate commerce. He joined with the majority in *United States v. Trans-Missouri Freight Association* (1897), and he cast the crucial concurring vote to invalidate the railroad combination in *Northern Securities Co. v. United States* (1904). In his separate opinion Brewer adhered to the rule of reason, which, as we have seen, would soon thereafter be embraced by the Supreme Court.

Moreover, Brewer was receptive to state laws that sought to safeguard the health and safety of the disadvantaged. Although he believed that the liberty of contract doctrine restricted the states' power over employment relationships, he nonetheless sustained in *Muller v. Oregon* (1908) an Oregon law limiting the working hours of women in factories. The paternalistic assumptions behind the Progressive era legislation to protect women and Brewer's *Muller* opinion appear suspect to modern eyes, but the decision makes clear that Brewer and the Fuller Court would uphold workplace regulations when the state could demonstrate their reasonableness. Brewer also soon became the Court's foremost defender of the rights of Chinese immigrants. He frequently dissented in cases arising under the Chinese Exclusion Acts and often expressed sympathy for Chinese immigrants. Dissenting in *Fong Yue Ting v. United States* (1893), he bitterly observed: "In view of this enactment of the highest legislative body of the foremost Christian nation, may not the thoughtful Chinese disciple of Confucius fairly ask, Why do they send missionaries here?" (*Fong Yue Ting*, 744).

But Brewer's solicitude for the Chinese did not extend to blacks. He generally adopted a narrow reading of the Fourteenth Amendment and was skeptical about increasing federal authority over the states. In Brewer's mind the states were free to decide the status of persons. In *Louisville, New Orleans, and Texas Railway Co. v. Mississippi* (1890) he upheld a state separate-car law for intrastate travel, rejecting the argument that the law interfered with interstate commerce. Brewer did not participate in *Plessy v. Ferguson* (1896), but he was prepared to validate segregated educational facilities. Speaking for the Court in *Berea College v. Kentucky* (1908), Brewer sustained a Kentucky statute that prevented a private college from conducting classes in which white and black students were instructed together. This is striking given Brewer's defense of the rights of private property owners in other settings.

Brewer's deep religious values clearly impacted his judicial behavior. He felt that American constitutionalism and Protestant Christianity were closely intertwined, and he invoked express references to Christianity in resolving legal issues. Not surprisingly, Brewer allowed the states wide latitude to regulate public morals. He saw the banning of lotteries, prostitution, polygamy, and the conduct of business on Sundays as legitimate exercises of the state police power. In *Church of the Holy*

Trinity v. United States (1892), a case involving the construction of a congressional statute outlawing contract labor by aliens, Brewer asserted that the United States was "a Christian nation" (*Holy Trinity*, 471). Brewer sensibly interpreted the statute as inapplicable to religious bodies, but he intimated that American laws were to be understood in the context of Christianity.

Modern historians, in a more secular-minded age, have found it difficult to come to grips with the religious dimension of Brewer's legal thought. Only recently have scholars begun to provide a more balanced assessment of this key member of the Fuller Court. As Joseph Gordon Hylton has cogently pointed out: "Depending upon one's definition, Brewer may or may not have been the most conservative Justice of the Fuller Court, but he has certainly been its most misunderstood member" (Hylton 1994, 58).

Henry Billings Brown

President Harrison's second Court appointee, Henry Billings Brown, was born to an affluent Massachusetts family in 1836. Educated at Yale College, Brown studied law in an attorney's office and attended the law schools at both Yale and Harvard. Moving to Detroit, he was admitted to the Michigan bar in 1860. Brown soon became a deputy U.S. marshal, and in 1863 President Lincoln named him an assistant U.S. attorney. He also developed a private practice, concentrating on admiralty cases. After a brief stint as a Wayne County circuit court judge, Brown became a partner in a prominent admiralty firm.

Brown was an active participant in Republican Party politics and a close personal friend of David J. Brewer. In 1875 President Ulysses S. Grant appointed him as a federal district judge in Michigan. On the bench Brown built a favorable reputation as an admiralty law expert. Brown's active lobbying for a Supreme Court appointment was successful in December of 1890. Quickly confirmed, Brown served on the Court until his retirement in 1906. Overshadowed by other justices of the Fuller era, Brown, in the words of one historian, "ranks as one of the most forgotten men who ever sat on the United States Supreme Court" (Glennon 1973, 553).

Generally protective of property rights, Brown voted with the Fuller Court majority on most economic issues. He joined the Court majority in such leading cases as *United States v. E. C. Knight Co.* (1895), *In re Debs* (1895), and *Lochner v. New York* (1905) and stressed the importance of private property in extrajudicial speeches. Brown also frequently invoked the dormant commerce power to strike down state regulations that burdened interstate commerce. Yet he voiced concern about the growth of monopolies, and he sustained a broad exercise of the state police power to safeguard public health and safety. For example, in *Holden v. Hardy* (1898) Brown, writing for the Court, rejected a freedom on contract argument and upheld a state law limiting the hours of work in underground mines.

Henry Billings Brown (Harris & Ewing, Collection of the Supreme Court of the United States)

Even more striking was Brown's strident dissenting opinion in *Pollock v. Farmers' Loan and Trust Co.* (1895), which invalidated the 1894 income tax. Given his opposition to the redistribution of wealth, Brown might well have been expected to vote with the majority. Instead, Brown criticized the majority for allegedly not following precedent construing the Direct Tax Clause of the Constitution and expressed support for the policy of income taxation. He concluded that the "decision involves nothing less than a surrender of the taxing power to the moneyed class" (*Pollock* II, 695). As this dissent demonstrates, Brown never took the position that government could not impinge on the sanctity of private property under any circumstances.

Brown is best known today as the author of the Court's opinion in *Plessy v. Ferguson* (1898), affirming the constitutionality of state laws requiring racial segregation in railroad passenger cars. His opinion largely reflected the racial and social assumptions of the age. Brown observed that segregation laws were a valid exercise of the state police power to promote public peace. He maintained that state legislatures were free to act with reference to public customs and usages. Central to Brown's thinking was the proposition that laws could not eliminate deeply felt racial distinctions. Distinguishing between social and legal equality, he revealingly commented: "Legislation is powerless to eradicate racial instincts or to abolish distinctions based upon physical differences, and the attempt to do so can only result in accentuating the difficulties of the present situation. . . . If one race be inferior to the other socially, the Constitution of the United States cannot put them upon the same plane" (*Plessy*, 551–552). Brown has sometimes been vilified by historians for the opinion in *Plessy*, but it is only fair to point out that the decision aroused little controversy at the time.

Similarly, Brown looked with disfavor on an expansive reading of civil liberties. He adhered to the traditional view that the Bill of Rights limited only the federal government. In *Downes v. Bidwell* (1901), moreover, Brown held that the Constitution did not automatically apply to the overseas territories acquired following the war with Spain. Congress in his opinion could exercise wide authority over the ceded territories but must respect certain natural rights of personal liberty and private property ownership.

Although Brown never developed a comprehensive judicial philosophy, he was temperamentally disinclined to challenge prevailing sentiments. An amiable and modest man, Brown was well liked by his colleagues. Still, he was not a key intellectual force on the Fuller Court. It should be noted that Brown, like other justices, handled his share of the Court's more routine cases. With his background in admiralty law, Brown was often called upon to write opinions regarding shipping. He also spoke for the Court in a decision upholding the grant of a patent for barbed wire. Plagued by poor health and failing eyesight, Brown resigned from the Court in 1906 at the age of seventy.

George Shiras, Jr.

For his third appointment to the Court President Harrison turned to George Shiras, Jr., a native of Pennsylvania. Born into a prosperous family, Shiras graduated from Yale College in 1853. After a brief stint at Yale Law School he studied law in a Pittsburgh attorney's office and was admitted to the bar in 1855. Shiras built a thriving law practice in Pittsburgh, representing railroads, banks, and steel firms. Although a lifelong Republican, he was removed from active partisan politics and in 1881 declined election to the Senate by the state legislature. Unlike Justice Brewer, Shiras was not a religious person. When a Supreme Court vacancy occurred in 1892, Shiras was commended to Harrison as a representative of the Third Circuit who was independent of the Republican political machine of Senator Matthew Quay.

Shiras largely shared the conservative outlook of the Fuller Court majority. He was skeptical about the exercise of federal regulatory power over the economy. Thus, Shiras voted to restrict application of the Sherman Anti-Trust Act in *United States v. E. C. Knight Co.* (1895) and to adopt a narrow reading of the authority of the Interstate Commerce Commission. He authored the important opinion in *ICC v. Alabama Midland Railway Co.* (1897), which undercut enforcement of the ban on long-haul/short-haul rate differentials by requiring that the existence of competition must be considered. Similarly, he was part of the Court majority in *Pollock* that voided the 1894 income tax as an unconstitutional direct tax. Yet as shown by his support of *In re Debs* (1895), Shiras sustained the power of the federal government to protect the instruments of interstate commerce against violent disruption.

Shiras compiled a mixed record with respect to state regulations. He frequently invoked the dormant commerce power to void state laws that burdened the flow of goods across state lines. He declared in 1898 that "freedom of trade and commerce . . . is one of the most important purposes of our Federal system" (*Vance v. W. A. Vandercook Company* [1898], 468). Shiras also adhered to the freedom of contract doctrine, voting to invalidate state regulation of out-of-state insurance contracts in *Allgeyer v. Louisiana* (1897) and to strike down a statute limiting the hours of work in *Lochner v. New York* (1905). He joined the opinion in *Smyth v. Ames* (1898), which imposed limits on state authority to set railroad and utility rates. Yet Shiras certainly did not foreclose any room for appropriate state regulatory activity. In *Brass v. North Dakota* (1894) he upheld the power of a state to regulate grain elevators. Writing for the Court in *Knoxville Iron Co. v. Harbison* (1901), Shiras sustained a state law that required employers who paid employees in scrip to redeem the scrip in money.

Like most of his colleagues, Shiras demonstrated little interest in racial minorities. For example, he regularly joined the majority to uphold state racial segregation laws, and he voted to validate the use of literacy tests to restrict black voting in *Williams v. Mississippi* (1898). In the *Insular Cases* (1901–1904) Shiras consistently

George Shiras, Jr. (Vix Boswell, National Geographic, Collection of the Supreme Court of the United States)

took the view that Congress was free to administer the new overseas acquisitions and that the constitutional provisions only applied after Congress had incorporated a territory. But Shiras struck one important blow for civil liberties. At issue in *Wong Wing v. United States* (1896) was a federal statute that empowered a U.S. commissioner to sentence illegal Chinese aliens to imprisonment at hard labor for a year before their deportation. Shiras, writing for a unanimous Court, held that the Fifth Amendment guarantee of a trial by jury applied to aliens and hence the statute was unconstitutional.

Amiable and diligent, Shiras was well regarded by Fuller and his other associates on the Court. His work on the bench was solid if not uniquely striking. Henry J. Abraham has aptly observed that Shiras "was workmanlike and predictably conservative, but not as inflexible as his colleagues Field, Fuller, Brewer, and Peckham on governmental regulatory questions" (Abraham 1999, 114). In addition to constitutional law, Shiras frequently wrote opinions dealing with property law, rights of navigation, and procedural matters. He resigned from the Court in 1903 while still in good health.

Howell E. Jackson

Howell E. Jackson of Tennessee was President Harrison's final choice for the Supreme Court. Jackson was born in Paris, Tennessee, in 1832 and proved a studious child. He graduated from West Tennessee College and undertook an additional two years of study at the University of Virginia. Jackson read law with a relative, Judge A.W.O. Totten of the Tennessee Supreme Court. He then earned a law degree from Cumberland Law School in 1856. Jackson began the practice of law in the City of Jackson, but in 1858 he moved to Memphis. There he formed a short-lived partnership with another attorney. Although he opposed secession, Jackson accepted appointment as receiver of confiscated property for West Tennessee under the Confederate Sequestration Act. Following the Civil War Jackson shifted his political affiliation from Whig to Democrat, and he resumed the practice of law in Memphis. He handled primarily corporate and railroad matters.

In 1875 Jackson was named to the provisional Court of Arbitration for West Tennessee, a tribunal created to assist in hearing the huge backlog of appeals. After an unsuccessful bid to win a spot on the Tennessee Supreme Court, he was elected to the state's House of Representatives in 1880. A year later the state legislature selected Jackson as U.S. senator. Jackson won a positive reputation as a hard-working and conscientious senator. Equally vital for his future, Jackson became friends with President Grover Cleveland and Benjamin Harrison, who was then a Republican senator from Indiana. In 1887 Cleveland appointed Jackson as a judge on the Sixth Judicial Circuit. As a member of that court he was heavily involved with patent and contract litigation, and he wrote two opinions invalidating state laws as violative of the Con-

Howell E. Jackson (Landy Cincinnati, Collection of the Supreme Court of the United States)

tracts Clause of the U.S. Constitution. In 1892, moreover, Jackson limited application of the Sherman Anti-Trust Act to traffic between states, anticipating the Supreme Court's reasoning in *E. C. Knight*. When a Court vacancy occurred late in Harrison's presidency, Justice Henry Billings Brown warmly endorsed Jackson to the president. Political circumstances dictated the choice of a southern Democrat, and so Harrison turned to his old friend from his Senate days.

Due to failing health Jackson served on the Supreme Court for just two and a half years, and he actually spent no more than fifteen months actively at work. He wrote only forty-six opinions for the Court, few of which dealt with constitutional issues. Jackson was generally sympathetic to the rights of property owners. In *Mobile and Ohio Railroad Co. v. Tennessee* (1894), for instance, he ruled that attempted state taxation of a railroad violated a tax-exemption clause in the corporate charter and thus ran afoul of the Contract Clause. His tuberculosis condition prevented Jackson from participating in some of the most contested decisions of his brief tenure. Jackson did, however, author a number of patent decisions for the Court.

Jackson is best remembered for his role in *Pollock v. Farmers' Loan and Trust Co.* (1895), the decision that found the 1894 income tax unconstitutional. He missed the first argument because of illness. Chief Justice Fuller held that a federal tax on income from state and local bonds violated the principle of state sovereignty. Next he determined that a tax on the income from real property was in effect a direct tax on property, which had to be apportioned according to population. Fuller announced that the Court was equally divided as to whether a levy on personal and corporate income was also a direct tax. From his sickbed in Nashville, Jackson had predicted that the income tax "would be partially sustained and partially declared unconstitutional" (quoted in King 1950, 210–211). Thereafter he indicated a willingness to come to Washington for a reargument. As was widely expected, on the reargument in May of 1895 the frail Jackson voted to uphold the remaining sections of the income tax. The Court majority, however, now struck down the entire levy. Jackson was so ill that he had difficulty delivering his verbal dissent, but he concluded that the majority opinion was "the most disastrous blow ever struck at the constitutional power of Congress" (*Pollock* II, 704). Thereafter Jackson's health deteriorated rapidly, and he died in Nashville in August.

The McKinley Appointment

Joseph McKenna

President William McKinley's sole appointment to the Supreme Court was Joseph McKenna of California. Born in Philadelphia to Irish immigrant parents, McKenna

Joseph McKenna (Harris & Ewing, Collection of the Supreme Court of the United States)

moved with his family to California at the age of twelve. Educated in Catholic schools, he helped to support the family after his father's death. Following a year of law study McKenna was admitted to the California bar in 1865. He soon found politics more attractive than the private practice of law.

Joining the Republican Party, McKenna was elected in 1865 district attorney of Solano County and served two terms in that post. In 1875 he was elected to the state legislature and built a reputation as a party leader. Defeated in his initial campaigns to win a seat in Congress, McKenna was elected to the U.S. House of Representatives in 1885, serving four terms. A faithful Republican, McKenna regularly favored a high tariff and sound money and was supportive of railroads. He also became a political ally of then–Congressman William McKinley and Senator Leland Stanford of California. President Harrison, upon the recommendation of Stanford, appointed McKenna to the Ninth Circuit Court of Appeals in 1892. On that Court he pursued a moderate if undistinguished course. In an important case he blocked a move by California's railroad commission to reduce rail charges, reasoning that a carrier was constitutionally entitled to a reasonable return on invested capital. In 1897 President McKinley named his friend McKenna U.S. attorney general, then within months appointed him to replace the retiring Justice Stephen J. Field. The nomination was not well regarded, but the Senate was reluctant to embarrass McKinley, and so McKenna was confirmed.

McKenna did not make a significant mark on the jurisprudence of the Fuller Court. Most of his experience had been in political life, not law. Not only did McKenna lack a coherent legal philosophy, but his written opinions were not conspicuous for their originality or depth of thought. Fuller was skeptical about McKenna's ability and tried to avoid assigning him important or challenging opinions. Historians have commonly pictured McKenna as confused and inconsistent in his decisionmaking. Still, he wrote 273 opinions for the Court while Fuller was chief.

Although McKenna joined the Court majority in *Lochner v. New York* (1905), he was not a doctrinaire proponent of liberty of contract and recognized a broad legislative discretion to regulate workplace conditions. McKenna voted to uphold a state law restricting the working hours of women in *Muller v. Oregon* (1908), and, dissenting in *Adair v. United States* (1908), he asserted that Congress could encourage collective bargaining on railroads by abolishing yellow-dog contracts as a condition of employment. He was consistently sympathetic to the claims of injured industrial workers, and he voted in several cases to curtail application of the fellow-servant rule.

McKenna's views on property rights are difficult to encapsulate. He sometimes declared that property rights were grounded in natural law, but he felt that property was subject to the taxing and regulatory authority of government. Writing for the Court in *Magoun v. Illinois Trust and Savings Bank* (1898), McKenna upheld the constitutionality of a state inheritance tax that imposed higher rates on legacies to non–family members. Yet he also joined in several opinions that strengthened the protection afforded property owners under the Takings Clause. In *Muhlker v. New York and Harlem Railroad Co.* (1905), for example, McKenna held that previously recognized easements were property interests that could not be eliminated by subsequent state court decisions without the payment of compensation.

He generally favored a broad reading of congressional power under the Commerce Clause. McKenna joined the majority opinion in *Champion v. Ames* (1903), which held that the federal commerce power encompassed the authority to ban interstate shipment of lottery tickets and, in effect, recognized a de facto federal police power. Shortly after the Fuller era, McKenna, speaking for a unanimous Court in *Hipolite Egg Co. v. United States* (1911), relied on *Ames* to uphold the constitutionality of the Pure Food and Drug Act. This measure banned the shipment of impure food in interstate commerce. Starting with *Northern Securities Co. v. United States* (1904), McKenna also favored a broad construction of the Sherman Anti-Trust Act to eliminate restraints of trade. Consistent with his belief in extensive federal power over interstate commerce, McKenna looked askance at state regulations that burdened the channels of trade among the states.

During Fuller's tenure as chief, McKenna had little occasion to address issues pertaining to civil rights and criminal justice. His only significant opinion for the Court in this regard was *Weems v. United States* (1910). In that case McKenna ruled that the Eighth Amendment ban on cruel and unusual punishments meant that punishments must be proportioned to the severity of the offense. He maintained that the Eighth Amendment "is not fastened to the obsolete but may acquire meaning as public opinion becomes enlightened by a humane justice" (*Weems*, 378).

McKenna remained as a justice of the Supreme Court for fifteen years after the close of the Fuller era. This later period of his career will only be briefly sketched here. Despite rhetoric about the sanctity of property rights, McKenna readily upheld early land-use regulations. In *Hadacheck v. Sebastian* (1915) he determined that an ordinance that outlawed a brickyard operation, causing a drastic diminution in land value, was a valid exercise of the state police power to protect public health. Yet McKenna strongly dissented from the Court's opinion in *Block v. Hirsh* (1921), which sustained rent control, forcefully arguing that the regulation of rents constituted an unconstitutional taking of property in violation of the Fifth Amendment. Shortly before his retirement McKenna joined the majority in striking down minimum-wage legislation in *Adkins v. Children's Hospital* (1923) as an interference with the freedom of contract. This brought him once again close to the reasoning he endorsed in *Lochner.* Moreover, he consistently supported the authority of the government to curtail freedom of speech during World War I. In short, McKenna's voting pattern continued to defy easy generalization.

The Roosevelt Appointments

Oliver Wendell Holmes Jr.

President Theodore Roosevelt's first appointee to the Supreme Court, Oliver Wendell Holmes Jr. of Massachusetts, is among the most prominent and influential justices in the history of the Court. There is voluminous literature examining every facet of his career and judicial philosophy. No attempt will be made here to provide a comprehensive treatment of Holmes's judicial service and legacy. Rather, the focus is on the years that Holmes was on the Court with Chief Justice Fuller. It is important to bear in mind that much of Holmes's reputation is based on opinions he wrote after the Fuller period ended. "His appointment was to have great significance for the work of the Court over time," Owen M. Fiss has pointed out, "but his immediate impact—and this cannot be stressed too strongly—was not great" (Fiss 1993, 35). Some dissenting opinions by Holmes set the stage for future developments, but in the main he tended to agree with Fuller in the deposition of cases during the years they served together.

Born into a Boston family of comfortable circumstances, Holmes was reared in a privileged environment. His father was a physician who gained widespread popularity as a writer of essays and poetry. Educated at private schools, Holmes graduated from Harvard College in 1861. In July of that year he joined the Union Army and was commissioned a second lieutenant. He served on active duty for three years and fought in several major battles. Wounded three times, Holmes experienced the danger and horror of war. He left the army before the end of the Civil War, but the military experience profoundly influenced Holmes's thinking and eventual jurisprudence. Rejecting a belief in moral values, Holmes developed a detached and skeptical outlook on life. He was influenced by the tenets of social Darwinism, and the concept of life as a struggle permeated both Holmes's judicial opinions and extrajudicial writings. Holmes observed privately that he came "devilish near to believing that might makes right" (quoted in Howe 1963, 46 n. 41). As Albert W. Alschuler has noted, "Holmes had a brutal worldview and was indifferent to the welfare of others" (Alshuler 2000, 10).

Holmes earned a law degree in 1866 after two years of study at Harvard Law School. Admitted to the Massachusetts bar, Holmes spent the next years alternating between the practice of law and legal scholarship. In 1881 he published *The Common Law*, a landmark in American legal scholarship. Holmes insisted that law evolved and must be adapted to changing circumstances. In often quoted language he observed:

> The life of the law has not been logic: it has been experience. The felt necessities of the time, the prevalent moral and political theories, institutions of public policy, avowed or unconscious, even the prejudices that judges share with their fellow-men, have had a good deal more to do than the syllogism in determining the rules by which men should be governed. (quoted in Keller 1977, 346)

Oliver Wendell Holmes Jr. (Harris & Ewing, Collection of the Supreme Court of the United States)

There is a scholarly debate over the extent to which Holmes's views helped to transform our understanding of law, but *The Common Law* did much to create his high esteem among intellectuals.

After a brief stint on the Harvard Law School faculty, Holmes was appointed to the Supreme Judicial Court of Massachusetts. He served on that bench for twenty years, becoming chief justice in 1899. Most of the cases before the Massachusetts court raised private law issues, such as accidents arising from the industrial workplace. In these cases Holmes usually adhered to precedent and avoided policy analysis. Interestingly in view of the later formulation of the doctrine of regulatory takings, Holmes in several cases suggested that regulations on the use of property might be so severe as to constitute an unconstitutional taking of property. On constitutional questions, however, he usually deferred to legislative judgments. Although Holmes had no personal sympathy with labor unions, his commitment to the idea of struggle led him to back the right of employees to organize and picket to advance their interests. In part because of these labor opinions and his tendency to permit regulation of economic activity, Holmes was mistakenly seen as a Progressive. Much of the work on the Supreme Judicial Court of Massachusetts was mundane, and Holmes was eager for a new challenge when chance events opened the door to the U.S. Supreme Court. Persuaded that Holmes would support his political agenda as well as congressional authority over U.S. territories overseas, President Roosevelt named the sixty-one-year-old jurist to the Court in August of 1902.

Holmes's record on the Fuller Court made clear his skepticism about constitutional rights claims. He was more deferential than most of his colleagues to the states and the other branches of the federal government. Construing the due process guarantee of the Fourteenth Amendment narrowly, Holmes rejected the view that liberty of contract was a protected right. Dissenting in *Lochner v. New York* (1905), he accused the majority—on scant evidence—of deciding the case based on precepts of social Darwinism, and he lectured that "a constitution is not intended to embody a particular economic theory. . . . It is made for people of fundamental differing views" (*Lochner*, 75–76). The famous Holmes dissent in *Lochner* was hailed by Progressive critics of the Fuller Court's defense of economic rights, but it is significant that no other justice joined his opinion. His dissenting opinion is best understood as an expression of the ideology of judicial restraint, not as an endorsement of social legislation. Holmes similarly dissented in *Adair v. United States* (1908), arguing that Congress could encourage the formation of labor unions by outlawing yellow-dog contracts.

Yet in many areas of constitutional law Holmes voted with the Fuller Court majority. He showed no interest in the constitutional claims of racial minorities or aliens. In *Giles v. Harris* (1903), for example, he spoke for the Court in denying a challenge to policies that effectively disfranchised black voters. Holmes likewise joined his associates in *Lone Wolf v. Hitchcock* (1903), which recognized plenary congressional authority over relations with Indian tribes; and he concurred in *Berea College v. Kentucky* (1908), a case that upheld a state law forbidding interracial education at a private institution. Nor was Holmes receptive to allegations that civil liberties were violated. In *Patterson v. Colorado* (1907), the leading freedom of expression case decided during Fuller's tenure, Holmes adopted a restrictive conception of free speech. Upholding the contempt conviction of a newspaper editor, he declined to decide whether the Fourteenth Amendment safeguarded the freedoms of speech and of press against infringement by the states. Holmes further maintained that the purpose of the First Amendment was to prevent prior restraint of publication, not to bar subsequent punishment. In contrast, the economic conservative Justice Brewer dissented on grounds that the editor's claim of a federally protected right should have been considered. The *Patterson* opinion gave no hint that Holmes, a decade later, would advance a more expansive theory of free speech. Holmes also joined the majority in *Ex Parte Young* (1908), which assured access to the federal courts for regulated industries challenging the validity of state-imposed rates.

The same picture emerges with respect to Holmes's handling of nonconstitutional issues. Although Holmes was inclined to uphold regulatory legislation, he could at the same time construe the reach of such measures narrowly. A good illustration was his dissenting opinion in the highly visible antitrust case *Northern Securities Co. v. United States* (1904). In private writings Holmes consistently expressed his antipathy toward the antitrust laws. He tellingly observed in 1910: "I don't disguise my belief that the Sherman Act is a humbug based on economic ignorance and incompetence" (*Holmes-Pollock Letters* 1961, 163). Starting with his dissent in *Northern Securities*, Holmes often sought to cabin the reach of the Sherman Act. He asserted in that case that Congress had not intended to ban the formation of holding companies even for the purpose of elimination of competition between railroad companies. Holmes's opinion infuriated President Roosevelt, who saw antitrust prosecutions as the cornerstone of his effort to curb the perceived abuses of large-scale corporate enterprise. To be sure, Holmes was sometimes supportive of antitrust policy. Yet his abiding disdain for antitrust laws did much to shape Holmes's mixed record in this area.

Likewise, Holmes manifested no inclination while Fuller was chief to protect labor unions or injured industrial workers. In *Loewe v. Lawlor* (1907) Holmes joined an opinion by Fuller that found that a union-instigated boycott of nonunion shops constituted a violation of the Sherman Anti-Trust Act. This action—applying the Sherman Act to unions—dispelled any notion that Holmes was a partisan of the labor movement. In tort cases he regularly invoked the assumption of the risk doctrine to deny recovery to injured parties. Moreover, Holmes was distrustful of juries and sought to fashion clear standards of conduct that would curtail their role in negligence cases.

At the death of Fuller in 1910 Holmes had yet to emerge as the highly distinguished jurist known to later generations. Although more willing to uphold economic regulation and social legislation than some of his colleagues, Holmes on many issues proved quite conservative and well within the Fuller Court mainstream. The subsequent accolades bestowed upon Holmes by scholars seem to rest upon the convergence of two jurisprudential threads. First, in a series of cases during the era of World War I, Holmes articulated a new and enlarged interpretation of the First Amendment's guarantee of free speech. Thus, Holmes has rightly been viewed as a pioneer of modern First Amendment jurisprudence. Second, intellectuals associated with the Progressive movement lionized Holmes because his philosophy of deference to legislative judgments was congenial to their call for a more active governmental role in regulating the economy and meeting social needs. They mistakenly claimed that Holmes was sympathetic to their political agenda. Ironically, by the time of his retirement in 1932 Holmes came to be portrayed as a liberal, a conclusion strikingly at odds with his record during the Fuller years. The continuing debate over the legacy of Holmes is outside the scope of this study, but one should be wary of efforts to canonize this complex and contradictory jurist.

William R. Day

A year after he appointed Holmes, President Roosevelt tapped William R. Day of Ohio for a vacant seat on the Supreme Court. Born in Ravenna, Ohio, in 1849, Day was educated at the University of Michigan. After studying law with an attorney and for a year at Michigan Law School, he was admitted to the Ohio bar in 1872. Day soon formed a partnership with a leading attorney in Canton, Ohio. Aside from brief service on the Ohio Court of Common Pleas, he engaged in the active practice of law between 1872 and 1897. During these years Day was involved in Republican Party politics and became a good friend of William McKinley, later congressman and president.

When McKinley was elected president he named Day as assistant secretary of state. In May of 1898 Day became secretary of state, but he resigned after a few months to serve on the commission that negotiated a treaty to end the Spanish-American War. McKinley appointed Day as a judge of the U.S. Court of Appeals for the Sixth Circuit in 1899, where he joined Horace Lurton and William Howard Taft, both future members of the Supreme Court. Roosevelt named Day to the Supreme Court in 1903, a move calculated in part to attract political support for the president from McKinley's friends in the Republican Party.

Day served only seven years with Fuller as chief, and much of his contribution to the work of the Court belongs to subsequent chapters of the Court's history. He was a swing voter on issues pertaining to economic regulations. Day was generally receptive to the exercise of police power by the states to regulate the economy and

William R. Day (Harris & Ewing, Collection of the Supreme Court of the United States)

promote public health and safety. He dissented in *Lochner v. New York* (1905), where the Court invalidated a statute limiting the working hours of bakers. In *McLean v. Arkansas* (1909) Day wrote for the Court in sustaining a state law that governed the method of calculating wages owed to miners. He also voted in *Jacobson v. Massachusetts* (1905) to validate a state compulsory vaccination statute, rejecting the contention that such a law infringed upon individual liberty. Although inclined to recognize broad state power, Day on occasion enforced constitutional limits on the states. In *City of Minneapolis v. Minneapolis Street Railway Co.* (1910), for example, Day, speaking for the Court, struck down a municipal streetcar rate law as an impairment of contract in violation of the Contracts Clause.

Committed to federalism and state autonomy, Day was more cautious with respect to national regulatory authority. He endorsed vigorous enforcement of the Sherman Anti-Trust Act, and he backed the government's position in the 1904 *Northern Securities* case that the railroad holding company was a combination in restraint of trade. Day also joined the Court majority in *Ex Parte Young* (1908), which strengthened federal judicial power over state officials who attempted to enforce unconstitutional laws. But there were limits to Day's nationalism. He fully supported congressional steps to regulate trade among the states, but, like Fuller, he insisted that the Commerce Clause did not give Congress unqualified authority over all aspects of commerce. In perhaps his most famous opinion, *Hammer v. Dagenhart* (1918), written after the close of the Fuller era, Day asserted that a federal statute banning from interstate commerce goods produced in a factory that employed child labor invaded state jurisdiction over manufacturing in violation of the Tenth Amendment.

Day emerged as a key voice on the Fuller Court in determining the constitutional status of the overseas U.S. territories acquired after the war with Spain. Not surprisingly, he broadly affirmed congressional authority. In *Dorr v. United States* (1904) Day, speaking for the Court, adopted the incorporation theory whereby Congress could determine the political status of the island possessions and was not obligated to provide trial by jury in the Philippines. Under Day's theory the Constitution did not follow the flag, and hence the overseas possessions could be treated differently by Congress.

Two important opinions by Day delivered after Fuller's death also deserve mention. Day formulated the federal exclusionary rule in *Weeks v. United States* (1914), holding that the use of illegally seized evidence in federal courts violated the Fourth Amendment guarantee against unreasonable searches. Furthermore, in *Buchanan v. Warley* (1917) Day wrote for a unanimous Court, ruling that local residential segregation ordinances constituted a deprivation of property without due process of law. In this case an expansive understanding of property as encompassing the right to use and alienate land was instrumental in producing a key victory against racial discrimination.

William H. Moody

President Roosevelt's final choice for a seat on the Supreme Court was William H. Moody, who was his attorney general. Moody was born in Newbury, Massachusetts, in 1853 to an old New England family and was educated at Phillips Andover Academy. He graduated from Harvard College in 1876, but he studied law at Harvard for only a few months. After further study in a Boston law office Moody was admitted to the Massachusetts bar. He began to practice law in Haverhill and served both as city solicitor and as district attorney. In the latter capacity he participated in the famous but unsuccessful 1893 murder prosecution of Lizzie Borden. In 1895 Moody was elected to the U.S. House of Representatives as a Republican, serving for seven years in that body.

Moody met Roosevelt through their mutual friend Henry Cabot Lodge. He and Roosevelt shared a love of outdoor life and a commitment to Progressive reforms. Moody also favored the growth of naval power, and in 1902 Roosevelt named him secretary of the Navy. Two years later Roosevelt switched Moody to the position of attorney general. As attorney general Moody energetically implemented the president's antitrust policy and argued numerous cases before the Supreme Court. He also challenged the ugly practice of lynching. Moody initiated contempt charges against a Tennessee sheriff who allowed the lynching of a black prisoner in disregard of a Supreme Court order staying his execution pending an appeal. This action culminated in the landmark case *United States v. Shipp* (1906, 1909), in which the Court found the sheriff and several members of the lynch mob in contempt. Just appointed to the Court when the case was first argued, Moody did not participate in the deliberations concerning this matter.

Even more than Holmes and Day, Moody appeared to support the reformist and nationalist agenda of President Roosevelt. He was a logical choice for the Court. Confirmed by the Senate in December of 1906, Moody's promising judicial career was prematurely brought to a close by crippling rheumatism. Moody fell ill almost as soon as he joined the Court, and by 1909 he was entirely incapacitated. Writing just sixty-four opinions and five dissents, Moody did not make an enduring mark on the last years of the Fuller Court. He favored a broad construction of congressional power over commerce, stressing that the Commerce Clause was adaptable to meet changing conditions and new technology. But Moody also sought to preserve the rights of the states within the federal system. In his best-known opinion, *Twining v. New Jersey* (1908), he held that the privilege against self-incrimination was not an essential element of liberty binding on the states by virtue of the Due Process Clause of the Fourteenth Amendment. He asserted that the states could be counted on to protect individual liberties. Overruled in 1964, *Twining* was a well-crafted opinion that determined the law on this subject for many years. Moody resigned in November of 1910, a few months after Fuller's death.

William H. Moody (Harris & Ewing, Collection of the Supreme Court of the United States)

The Taft Appointment

Horace H. Lurton

The last justice to join the Fuller Court was Horace H. Lurton of Tennessee. Born in northern Kentucky in 1844, Lurton moved with his family while a child to Clarksville, Tennessee. The outbreak of the Civil War interrupted his study at Douglas University in Chicago. A zealous Confederate, Lurton promptly enlisted in the army and was twice captured by Union forces. With the end of hostilities he studied law at Cumberland Law School, graduating in 1867. Lurton successfully practiced law in Clarksville and served as trial judge between 1875 and 1878. He was elected as a Democrat to the Tennessee Supreme Court in 1886, and in 1893 he became chief justice. Lurton resigned a few months later when President Grover Cleveland named him to the U.S. Court of Appeals for the Sixth Circuit. While a circuit judge he taught law part-time at Vanderbilt University Law School, where he became dean in 1904. Lurton served on the Sixth Circuit with future justices William R. Day and William Howard Taft. Taft was impressed with Lurton's integrity and ability, as well as his general adherence to conservative legal principles. President Roosevelt, at Taft's recommendation, had considered appointing Lurton to the Supreme Court in 1906, but the choice went to Moody instead. As president, Taft was now free to advance his old friend to the Court.

Taking his seat in January 1910, Lurton served less than seven months with Fuller as chief. He authored only a handful of opinions for the Fuller Court, none of which were groundbreaking.

Lurton continued on the Court until his death in 1914, but his record was not especially noteworthy. He pursued a moderately conservative course, characterized by adhering to the precepts of judicial self-restraint. Generally sympathetic to federal economic regulations, Lurton wrote several opinions enforcing the antitrust laws. He also voted to extend the authority of Congress to encompass regulation of intrastate railroad rates where necessary to protect interstate traffic. Lurton was disinclined, however, to favor federal protection of civil rights for blacks.

References

Abraham, Henry J. *Justices, Presidents, and Senators: A History of the U.S. Supreme Court Appointments from Washington to Clinton.* Lanham, MD: Rowman and Littlefield, 1999.

Alschuler, Albert W. *Law Without Values: The Life, Work, and Legacy of Justice Holmes.* Chicago: University of Chicago Press, 2000.

Horace H. Lurton (Harris & Ewing, Collection of the Supreme Court of the United States)

Baker, Liva. *The Justice from Beacon Hill: The Life and Times of Oliver Wendell Holmes.* New York: Harper Collins, 1991.

Bergan, Francis. "Mr. Justice Brewer: Perspective of a Century." *Albany Law Review* 25 (1961): 191–202.

Beth, Loren P. *John Marshall Harlan: The Last Whig Justice.* Lexington: University Press of Kentucky, 1992.

Brewer, David J. "Protection to Private Property from Public Attack." *New Englander and Yale Review* 55 (1891): 97–110.

Brodhead, Michael J. *David J. Brewer: The Life of a Supreme Court Justice, 1837–1910.* Carbondale: Southern Illinois University Press, 1994.

Calvani, Terry. "The Early Professional Career of Howell Jackson." *Vanderbilt Law Review* 30 (1977): 39–72.

Duker, William F. "Mr. Justice Rufus W. Peckham: The Police Power and the Individual in a Changing World." *Brigham Young University Law Review* (1980): 47–67.

Ely, James W. Jr. *The Chief Justiceship of Melville W. Fuller, 1888–1910.* Columbia: University of South Carolina Press, 1995.

Fairman, Charles. *Mr. Justice Miller and the Supreme Court, 1862–1890.* Cambridge, MA: Harvard University Press, 1939.

———. "What Makes A Great Justice? Mr. Justice Bradley and the Supreme Court, 1870–1892." *Boston University Law Review* 30 (1950): 49–102.

Fiss, Owen M. *History of the Supreme Court of the United States, Volume 8: Troubled Beginnings of the Modern State, 1888–1910.* New York: Macmillan, 1993.

Glennon, Robert J. Jr. "Justice Henry Billings Brown: Values in Tension." *University of Colorado Law Review* 44 (1973): 553–604.

Highsaw, Robert B. *Edward Douglass White: Defender of the Conservative Faith.* Baton Rouge: Louisiana State University Press, 1981.

Howe, Mark de Wolfe. *Justice Oliver Wendell Holmes: The Proving Years, 1870–1882.* Cambridge, MA: Harvard University Press, 1963.

———, ed. *Holmes-Pollock Letters: The Correspondence of Mr. Justice Holmes and Sir Frederick Pollock, 1874–1932.* 2nd ed. Vol. 1. Cambridge, MA: Harvard University Press, 1961.

Hylton, Joseph Gordon. "David Josiah Brewer: A Conservative Justice Reconsidered." *Journal of Supreme Court History* (1994): 45–64.

Keller, Morton. *Affairs of State: Public Life in Late Nineteenth Century America.* Cambridge, MA: Harvard University Press, 1977.

Kens, Paul. *Justice Stephen Field: Shaping Liberty from the Gold Rush to the Gilded Age.* Lawrence: University Press of Kansas, 1997.

King, Willard L. *Melville Weston Fuller: Chief Justice of the United States, 1888–1910.* New York: Macmillan, 1950; rpt. Chicago: University of Chicago Press, 1967.

Kosma, Montgomery N., and Ross E. Davies. *Fuller and Washington at Centuries' Ends.* Washington, DC: Green Bay Press, 1999.

McCurdy, Charles W. "Justice Field and the Jurisprudence of Government-Business Relations: Some Parameters of Laissez-Faire Constitutionalism, 1863–1897." *Journal of American History* 61 (1975): 970–1005.

McDevitt, Matthew. *Joseph McKenna: Associate Justice of the United States.* Washington, DC: Catholic University of America Press, 1946; rpt. New York: DeCapo Press, 1974.

McLean, Joseph E. *William Rufus Day: Supreme Court Justice from Ohio.* Baltimore: Johns Hopkins University Press, 1946.

Murphy, James B. *L.Q.C. Lamar: Pragmatic Patriot.* Baton Rouge: Louisiana State University Press, 1973.

Pratt, Walter F. Jr. *The Supreme Court Under Edward Douglass White, 1910–1921.* Columbia: University of South Carolina Press, 1999.

Przybyszewski, Linda. *The Republic According to John Marshall Harlan.* Chapel Hill: University of North Carolina Press, 1999.

———. "The Religion of a Jurist: Justice David J. Brewer and the Christian Nation." *Journal of Supreme Court History* 25 (2001): 228–242.

Ross, Michael A. "Cases of Shattered Dreams: Justice Samuel Freeman Miller and the Rise and Fall of a Mississippi River Town." *Annals of Iowa* 57 (1998): 201–239.

Semonche, John E. *Charting the Future: The Supreme Court Responds to a Changing Society, 1890–1920.* Westport, CT: Greenwood Press, 1978.

Shiras, George III. *Justice George Shiras Jr. of Pittsburgh.* Pittsburgh, PA: University of Pittsburgh Press, 1953.

Spector, Robert M. "Legal Historian on the United States Supreme Court: Justice Horace Gray, Jr. and the Historical Method." *American Journal of Legal History* 12 (1968): 181–210.

Swisher, Carl Brent. *Stephen J. Field: Craftsman of the Law.* Washington, DC: Brookings Institution, 1930; rpt. Chicago: University of Chicago Press, 1969.

Tucker, David M. "Justice Horace Harmon Lurton: The Shaping of a National Progressive." *American Journal of Legal History* 13 (1969): 223–232.

Urofsky, Melvin I., ed. *The Supreme Court Justices: A Biographical Dictionary.* New York: Garland Publishers, 1994.

White, G. Edward. *Justice Oliver Wendell Holmes: Law and the Inner Self.* New York: Oxford University Press, 1993.

———. *The American Judicial Tradition: Profiles of Leading American Judges.* Expanded ed. New York: Oxford University Press, 1988.

3

Significant Decisions

Although appointed by ten different presidents, the members of the Fuller Court shared a number of core constitutional values. Foremost among these were individual liberty and the idea of limited government. The Fuller Court championed the rights of property owners in part as a means to restrict the reach of government. Like the Framers of the Constitution, the justices of the Fuller Court believed that property and other individual rights were interdependent. As Stephen J. Field explained in 1890: "It should never be forgotten that protection to property and to persons cannot be separated. Where property is insecure, the rights of persons are unsafe" ("The Centenary of the Supreme Court," 134 U.S. at 745). Despite this common outlook, the members of the Fuller Court certainly differed in their handling of the novel and complex issues of the day. But in the leading cases of the era the Court majority stressed the economic liberties associated with a market economy, and the justices looked askance at enlarged governmental power and new types of legislation.

Several categories of constitutional issues play a large part in the jurisprudence of the Fuller Court. First, the justices became extensively involved with defending the rights of property owners in the face of increased regulation and taxation. For example, the Fuller Court expansively read the Due Process Clause of the Fourteenth Amendment and put new teeth into the Takings Clause of the Fifth Amendment. It also struck down the first peacetime income tax. The Court sustained many economic and social regulations, but it always assigned a high standing to property rights and contractual freedom.

Second, the Fuller Court had to resolve difficult questions about the division of power between the states and the federal government with respect to the economy. One group of cases raised issues pertaining to the scope of congressional authority over commerce among the states. The Fuller Court adhered to the long-standing view that federal power extended only to interstate traffic and did not encompass all economic activity. Another group of cases involved state regulations, which threatened to burden interstate commerce and undercut the national market. Fuller and his colleagues frequently invoked the dormant commerce power (which foreclosed state actions that unduly hampered commerce among the states) to invalidate state regulations that impeded the movement of goods across state lines.

Cases pertaining to civil rights and civil liberties did not occupy as prominent a place on the docket of the Fuller Court as they would for later courts in the post–World War II era. There were a few issues concerning free speech and the regulation of public morals. The Fuller Court consistently declined to extend the procedural guarantees of the Bill of Rights to state criminal proceedings, and thus it permitted states wide latitude over criminal prosecutions. The Fuller Court, however, addressed some pivotal issues dealing with the status of blacks and Indians.

As suggested by its handling of criminal and racial issues, another major theme of the Fuller Court was a commitment to federalism. Consistent with its goal of limiting national power the Court under Fuller sought to preserve a large measure of autonomy for the states. Indeed, federalism was at times a countervalue to the Court's tendency to fashion constitutional norms protective of economic rights. It helps to explain why the Fuller Court upheld a wide variety of state health and safety laws that impinged the rights of property owners.

Some of the issues raised during the Fuller years, such as state regulation of railroad rates and race relations, were a continuation of matters addressed by the Court under the preceding chief justice, Morrison R. Waite. But many of the questions presented to Fuller and his associates differed from those in prior eras. Congress made new uses of its power to enact antitrust and income tax laws, and it created the Interstate Commerce Commission to police railroads nationwide. State legislatures became more active in regulating workplace conditions and imposing prohibition of alcoholic beverages. The Spanish-American War of 1898 and the subsequent acquisition of overseas territories posed novel and fundamental questions about the nature of the American union. Thus, the Fuller Court was often writing on a fresh constitutional slate, with only general principles for guidance.

Constitutional cases gave the Fuller era its distinctive place in history, but, unlike the jurists on the modern Supreme Court, Fuller and his associates also heard a large number of private law disputes. Litigation involving common law doctrines like torts, property, and contracts reached the justices under diversity of citizenship jurisdiction. Moreover, the Fuller Court addressed important patent and copyright issues, construed federal safety and bankruptcy statutes, and pioneered the use of equity receiverships to operate insolvent railroads. The private law decisions of the Fuller Court, in harmony with its constitutional outlook, tended to encourage economic growth and to strengthen federal judicial authority.

The following discussion seeks to analyze the Fuller Court's response to the legal issues raised by a fast-changing society at the turn of the twentieth century.

Economic Rights

Due Process of Law

The Fourteenth Amendment forbids the states from depriving any person of life, liberty, or property without due process of law. An identical prohibition is placed on the federal government by the Due Process Clause of the Fifth Amendment. Derived from Magna Carta, the due process norm was incorporated into most of the initial state constitutions. In essence, the two clauses on due process were intended to prevent arbitrary interference by federal or state government with the rights of individuals. As generally understood, due process encompassed *procedural safeguards* as well as *substantive limits* on the authority of government to abridge certain basic rights even if not specifically mentioned in the Constitution. The Supreme Court had little opportunity to define the scope of due process until the adoption of the Fourteenth Amendment in 1868. The Waite Court embraced a narrow reading of the amendment, including the Due Process Clause, and thus left most rights under the control of state law. In *Munn v. Illinois* (1877), for example, the Waite Court rejected the argument that the Due Process Clause curtailed the authority of the states to regulate the charges of railroads and allied enterprises.

Under Fuller's leadership, however, the Supreme Court began to construe the Due Process Clause expansively as a check on state legislative authority. Reflecting traditional skepticism, the Court reasoned that unreasonable regulations deprived parties of their property without due process of law. This meant that the justices would not accept state laws at face value but instead would independently assess whether the statutes bore any relationship to their ostensible purpose. They insisted that state regulation of private economic rights must bear a *substantial relationship* to public health, safety, morals, or welfare. The Fuller Court first employed due process to review the state regulation of railroad charges and then turned its attention to a variety of other regulations.

This use of due process by the Fuller Court, and by state judges, has often been labeled *substantive due process*, a phrase that is misleading in several respects. Courts and commentators did not differentiate between the procedural and substantive components of due process until the 1940s. At that time, the label was fashioned as a pejorative description applied only to economic-rights decisions. In any event, the phrase *substantive due process* is anachronistic when used to describe decisions rendered during the nineteenth and early twentieth centuries (White 2000, 243–245).

One of the most highly visible and contested issues of the Fuller era was the extent to which state or federal governments could control operations of privately owned railroad companies. As the principal artery of interstate commerce and travel, railroads occupied a unique spot in American life during the Gilded Age. Railroading was a capital-intensive enterprise that required a continuous flow of funds to establish new routes and make necessary improvements. Shippers and farmers perceived the railroads as wielding monopoly power and charging excessive rates. Responding to a clamor for public control, in the 1870s western and southern states enacted so-called Granger laws, under which commissions regulated the prices charged by railroads for the transportation of passengers and freight. At the same time, railroad officials feared that legislators would seek to help shippers and farmers at the expense of the carriers by mandating unreasonably low rates. Rate regulation could open the door for state legislators to indirectly deprive railroad owners of the value of their property, because such regulations fixed the return on investment. Thus, there rose the fear that state-imposed rates could, in effect, confiscate property. There was an allied concern that rate regulation would jeopardize the long-term economic health of the railroads by discouraging investment.

Although troubled by the redistributionist potential implicit in state rate regulation, the Fuller Court accepted the basic premise that railroads, as common carriers, were subject to a degree of public control. Still, in a line of cases during the 1890s Fuller and his associates moved to curtail the power of the states to set rates. The decision in *Chicago, Milwaukee, and St. Paul Railway Co. v. Minnesota* (1890) was a turning point in the Court's handling of rate regulations. At issue was a Minnesota railroad commission order to reduce the charge for carrying milk on certain routes within the state. By a 6–3 vote the justices struck down the Minnesota rate law. Speaking for the Court, Justice Samuel Blatchford found a procedural infirmity because the statutes did not provide for a hearing before the commission or for judicial review of rates set by the agency. Blatchford then moved beyond this procedural objection and asserted judicial authority to review the fairness of rates imposed by state law. He observed that "if the company is deprived of the power of charging reasonable rates for the use of its property, and such deprivation takes place in the absence of an investigation by judicial machinery, it is deprived of the lawful use of its property, and thus, in substance and effect, of the property itself, without due process of law and in violation of the Constitution of the United States" (*Chicago, Milwaukee*, 458).

There were several noteworthy aspects to this ruling. First, it signaled the Fuller Court's acceptance of the Due Process Clause as a substantive restriction on state legislative authority. Second, it contradicted a fundamental principle of *Munn* that rate-setting was solely a legislative function. Once the justices came to realize that unfettered power to regulate might be used to destroy the value of railroad property, judicial supervision of rates followed logically. Otherwise regulated industries would have only those property rights that legislators chose to recognize. Third, the ruling expanded the range of property interests secured by the Constitution. The Court implicitly took the position that property ownership went beyond title and possession and encompassed the right to use property for economic gain.

In *Reagan v. Farmers' Loan and Trust Co.* (1894) the Fuller Court served notice that it would inquire into the reasonableness of state-imposed rates and would restrain any regulation that operated to divest a property owner of rights. To assess the reasonableness of rates prescribed by the Texas railroad commission, the Court undertook a review of the railroad's earnings, operating costs, and financial condition. Justice David J. Brewer, who spoke for a unanimous bench, noted the importance of investment capital for the achievement of economic growth. "Would any investment ever be made of private capital in railroad enterprise," he asked, "with such an insufficient return as was provided by the Texas rate?" He also invoked "the spirit of common justice" to deny "that one class should by law be compelled to suffer loss that others may make gain" (*Reagan*, 412, 410).

Railroads were not the only business to claim the Supreme Court's protection against confiscatory rates. In *Covington and Lexington Turnpike Road Co. v. Sandford* (1896) the justices unanimously held that legislative control of the tolls on a privately owned turnpike road was also subject to constitutional limitations. The turnpike company alleged that a Kentucky statute would sharply reduce the toll allowed and thereby diminish the income of the company so that it could not meet ordinary expenses or pay any dividend. Such allegations were found to constitute a prima facie case of deprivation of property without due process.

The culmination of this trend came in *Smyth v. Ames* (1898). In 1893 the Nebraska legislature, under Populist influence, established a maximum rate schedule for railroads operating in the state. The effect of the law was to compel an average 30 percent reduction in charges for intrastate freight. Writing for a unanimous Court, Justice John M. Harlan addressed the complex question of how courts should ascertain what compensation a railroad was entitled to receive. He first concluded that the reasonableness of a charge for intrastate transportation must be determined without reference to the return earned by the railroad on its interstate business. Otherwise, Harlan feared, low local rates would constitute a subsidy for state business at the expense of interstate shipping. He then spelled out a standard to guide judicial review of rates, ruling that a railroad was constitutionally entitled to a "fair return" upon the "fair value" of its property.

The so-called fair-value rule as articulated by Harlan was full of ambiguity. He set forth a cluster of inconsistent factors to ascertain the value of a rail enterprise with no indication as to the relative weight to be assigned to each item. Over time, however, courts defined fair value primarily in terms of current or replacement value of a company's assets rather than the actual or original cost.

The upshot of *Smyth v. Ames* was to place constitutional limits on the rate-making process of regulatory bodies. The Supreme Court became in effect the final arbiter of the reasonableness of imposed rates. By promulgating the fair-value rule, the Fuller Court sought both to protect investors and regulated industries against confiscatory rates and to safeguard the interests of consumers. Yet over time the fair-value rule proved difficult to administer. In order to establish a rate base the federal courts had to make an intricate assessment of the current value of a company. This necessitated a substantial commitment of judicial resources to the review of rate-making. Still, *Smyth* created a standard that would increasingly bind state regulatory authority in the years after Fuller's death. A rising level of prices in the early twentieth century meant a steady increase in the worth of assets. Under these circumstances, state agencies found it hard to impose meaningful limits on rates. Progressives began to view the *Smyth* ruling as hampering regulatory bodies and unduly favoring the railroads and utilities.

Scholars have not generally been kind to *Smyth*. The *Smyth* ruling, however, should not be dismissed too quickly. Despite the shortcomings of the fair-value rule, the justices of the Fuller Court followed sound instincts. They were concerned that the regulatory process was often skewed by political manipulation that operated to the unfair disadvantage of railroads and utilities. Politicians seeking to curry favor would be tempted to use the rate-making process as a means of redistributing wealth. Such an outcome would at once infringe on the property rights of regulated industries and discourage capital investment. The fair-value rule of *Smyth* was meant to serve a protective function and not leave railroads to the unrestrained rate-making of state agencies. The hopes of the Court were only partially realized, but *Smyth* did provide a barrier against confiscatory rates.

Notwithstanding its determination to review the reasonableness of imposed rates, the Fuller Court was by no means uniformly hostile to state regulation of railroads. In many cases it recognized broad state authority to control the rates for intrastate travel. Under the Due Process Clause railroads could assert protection only against rates so low as to have a confiscatory effect. Charges fixed by a state regulatory process were presumed to be reasonable, and the burden of proof was placed on the carriers to show the contrary. In practice the Court reviewed state rate decisions on a case-by-case basis, and many regulations were sustained.

In fact, the Fuller Court could be criticized for giving inadequate attention to the adverse impact of state rate regulations on the national railroad system. Regulation of intrastate charges in effect compelled adjustments in interstate rates. It is striking that the Fuller Court did not intervene more forcefully in the state rate-setting process in order to protect the economic health of the roads. This failure may be explained in terms of the Court's commitment to preserving an important role for the states in the federal union. But the Fuller Court's willingness to allow the states regulatory authority over aspects of the national rail network contradicts the older Progressive view of the Fuller Court as a one-sided champion of railroads.

In addition to establishing that the Due Process Clause mandated a reasonable return on investment capital for regulated industries, the Fuller Court espoused the liberty of contract doctrine that limited governmental interference with private economic arrangements. The idea of voluntary contract played a central role in shaping American law during the nineteenth century. Influenced by the antislavery movement, many came to see the right to make contracts as the most conspicuous element of liberty. Contracts were viewed as a vehicle by which individuals could make arrangements to govern their own economic status. Contractual freedom found frequent and varied expression in the nineteenth century. For example, the Civil Rights Act of 1866 enumerated the right to enter contracts as a basic aspect of freedom for the newly emancipated slaves. Moreover, states gradually eliminated the common law limitations on the contractual rights of married women. The prominent historian James Willard Hurst described the nineteenth century as "above all else, the years of contract in our law" (Hurst 1956, 18). Not surprisingly, state and federal courts in the 1880s began to adopt the proposition that the right to make contracts was constitutionally protected.

In the landmark case of *Allgeyer v. Louisiana* (1897) the Fuller Court held that contractual freedom was protected by the concept of due process. At issue was a state law that prohibited persons from obtaining insurance from a company that was not qualified to do business in Louisiana. Declaring the statute unconstitutional, Justice Rufus W. Peckham, speaking for a unanimous Court, broadly defined liberty as guaranteed by the Fourteenth Amendment:

> The liberty mentioned in that amendment means not only the right of the citizen to be free from the mere physical restraint of his person, as by incarceration, but the term is deemed to embrace the right of the citizen to be free in the enjoyment of all his faculties; to be free to use them in all lawful ways; to live and work where he will; to earn his livelihood by any lawful calling; to pursue any livelihood or avocation and for that purpose to enter into all contracts which may be proper, necessary and essential to his carrying out to a successful conclusion the purposes above mentioned. (*Allgeyer*, 589)

It followed that Louisiana could not abridge the constitutionally protected right to make insurance contracts with out-of-state companies.

Although the Fuller Court adopted the liberty of contract doctrine in *Allgeyer*, it never took the position that contractual freedom was absolute. States might seek to justify regulations that outlawed certain contracts as an exercise of the police power to protect the health, safety, and morals of the public. Thus, the Fuller Court sustained a number of workplace regulations where it was convinced that the measures were related to genuine health and safety concerns. Stressing that underground mining was unhealthy, the Court in *Holden v. Hardy* (1898) upheld a Utah law that restricted work in mines to eight hours a day. Likewise, the justices in *Knoxville Iron Co. v. Harbison* (1901) validated a Tennessee law that required employers who paid their workers in scrip to redeem the same in money upon request. Fuller and his colleagues were also disinclined to apply the liberty of contract doctrine in cases involving commercial transactions. In *Otis v. Parker* (1903), for example, the Court brushed aside a liberty of contract argument and sustained a provision of the California constitution that banned contracts for the sale of corporate stock on margin for future deliveries. As this record suggests, the Fuller Court was sparing in its application of the liberty of contract principle.

Nonetheless, the Supreme Court under Fuller treated contractual freedom as a paramount constitutional norm, and insisted that the states demonstrate a good reason for laws that restricted this right. The liberty to make individual contracts, including the right to determine the conditions of one's employment, could be curtailed only to safeguard health, safety, and morals. In other words, the scope of the police power was not unlimited. Laws that sought to redistribute wealth or power, or to confer special advantages upon particular groups, were not seen as legitimate objects of government and were thus particularly suspect. The liberty of contract doctrine, which restricted legislative authority, stood in sharp contrast to the tenets of the Progressive movement, which called for a more active governmental role in regulating the economy and addressing social problems. The Progressives especially urged a more expansive reading of the police power to support legislation designed to correct perceived imbalances of economic power associated with the new industrial order.

The clash between the liberty of contract doctrine and Progressive-era protective legislation came to a head in the famous and much-maligned case of *Lochner v. New York* (1905). At issue was a state law that restricted work in bakeries to ten hours a day or sixty hours a week. Writing for a 5–4 majority of the Court, Justice Peckham invalidated the law as an abridgement of the liberty of contract. He emphasized that states could inspect bakeries and enact measures to improve workplace conditions. But Peckham drew the line at maximum-hours regulations. He was not convinced that the baking trade was unhealthy, and he could find no direct relationship between the hours of work and the health of bakers. Peckham therefore concluded that the "real object and purpose" of the statute was to govern labor relations, not the purported goal of safeguarding health. Asserting that bakers were capable of protecting their own interests, he described maximum-hours statutes "as mere meddlesome interferences with the rights of the individual" (*Lochner*, 61). It followed that the statute exceeded the bounds of the state police power. Moreover, Peckham broadly condemned labor protective laws. "It is impossible for us to shut our eyes," he stated, "to the fact that many of the laws of this character, while passed under what is claimed to be the police power for the purpose of protecting the public health or welfare, are, in reality, passed from other motives" (*Lochner*, 64).

There were two dissenting opinions in *Lochner*. Justice Harlan, speaking for three justices, endorsed the liberty of contract principle and agreed that courts could inquire into whether a challenged statute had a real relationship to the protection of health. He differed with the majority only over the application of the doctrine on the facts presented in this case. Pointing to evidence that prolonged work in bakeries endangered an employee's health, Harlan concluded that the legislature acted reasonably.

Justice Oliver Wendell Holmes Jr., in one of his most famous dissents, went further and rejected the liberty of contract doctrine. He rather unfairly charged that the case "was decided upon an economic theory" and quipped that the Fourteenth Amendment did not enact the views of social Darwinist Herbert Spencer. The majority, of course, made no such claim, and there is no evidence that the majority justices were influenced by Spencer. More significantly, Holmes articulated a philosophy of judicial restraint under which courts should defer to "the right of a majority to embody their opinions in law" (*Lochner*, 75). The legislative branch, in Holmes's view, was free to determine economic policy without judicial oversight.

Although the *Lochner* ruling initially aroused little controversy, Progressives began to see the decision as a setback for their program of legislative reform of workplace and social conditions. To liberal critics, *Lochner* became a term of rebuke, an emotionally freighted symbol of improper judicial activism. This negative image continues to influence most accounts of *Lochner*, but it has been challenged in recent years by revisionist scholarship, which maintains that *Lochner* vindicated the free labor system and reflected long-standing judicial hostility to class legislation. In fact, *Lochner* had deep roots in the Anglo-American political economy. It reflected both the view that individuals could best make decisions regarding their own well-being as well as confidence in the private ordering of the economy.

The *Lochner* decision remains at the heart of a continuing debate about the role of the judiciary in the American polity. To what extent are courts free to review legislative determinations? How does the energetic record of the Fuller Court compare to the activism of the Warren Court? Is there a principled distinction between activism on behalf of economic freedom and limited government and activism to promote equality? These questions cannot be resolved here, but they have spawned a vast literature and underscore the extent to which the contested legacy of *Lochner* hovers over modern constitutional jurisprudence.

The Fuller Court considered the liberty of contract in several important cases following *Lochner*. In *Adair v. United States* (1908) the justices invalidated a congressional statute that banned so-called yellow dog contracts in the rail industry. Such contracts made it a condition of employment that workers not belong to a labor union. Writing for the Court, Justice Harlan affirmed "the general proposition that there is a liberty of contract which cannot be unreasonably interfered with by legislation" and declared that the statute was an arbitrary interference with the right of employers and employees to set the terms of employment.

Yet the Fuller Court did uphold workplace regulations to protect persons who were not deemed capable of fending for themselves in the marketplace. At issue in *Muller v. Oregon* (1908) was a state law restricting working hours for women in factories and laundries to ten hours a day. Stressing the special health needs of women, their maternal function, and their dependent status, Justice Brewer, speaking for a unanimous bench, upheld the regulation as a reasonable exercise of the police power. The *Muller* case is noteworthy because the Court relied in part on social-science data contained in the brief of Louis D. Brandeis as a factual basis justifying different legal treatment of women. It is important to recognize, however, that the *Muller* decision accepted the liberty of contract premise of *Lochner* but found an exception for women. It bears emphasis that the paternalistic assumptions behind Progressive-era laws to safeguard women and the *Muller* opinion appear dubious to modern eyes. To some women the law may well have operated more as a restriction than a protection, effectively pigeonholing them in certain occupations. Judges and legislators had long viewed women as requiring special protection, and the *Muller* opinion was consistent with this line of authority as well as the prevailing attitudes regarding a woman's appropriate role in society. In *Muller*, then, the Fuller Court simply affirmed the dominant belief about the different social functions of men and women.

One must be careful not to exaggerate the impact of the liberty of contract doctrine. The Fuller Court invoked the doctrine infrequently and sustained most regulatory measures against due process challenge. Still, the liberty of contract doctrine significantly shaped constitutional jurisprudence for decades. It was a testament to the Fuller Court's dedication to limited government and to the view that government did not have complete dominion over economic life. Moreover, the doctrine was a potential check on arbitrary government action and reserved for the Court the authority to determine when legislators exceeded the bounds of the police power.

In addition to litigation involving state-fixed rates and the right to enter contracts, the Fuller Court heard a number of other cases alleging that state regulations arbitrarily interfered with the rights of private enterprise in violation of due process. The Court evaluated these regulations against a reasonableness standard. Safety regulations were invariably sustained. For example, in *St. Louis and San Francisco Railway Co. v. Mathews* (1897) the justices upheld a Missouri statute that imposed absolute liability on railroads for damage caused by fire spread from locomotives.

Takings Clause

Although the work of the Fuller Court in giving broader effect to the due process guarantee has done much to mold its historical reputation, the Court also made important and lasting contributions to jurisprudence under the Takings Clause of the Fifth Amendment. That amendment provides in part: "nor shall private property be taken for public use, without just compensation." The Fifth Amendment does not proscribe the taking of property by government; it just bans taking property without compensation. In practice the Takings Clause did not figure prominently in the decisions of the Supreme Court before Fuller became chief justice. In *Barron v. Baltimore* (1833) the Court under Chief Justice John Marshall ruled that the Bill of Rights, including the Fifth Amendment, restrained only the federal government and was inapplicable to the states. During much of the nineteenth century the federal government rarely utilized eminent domain to acquire private property, and so the Supreme Court had little opportunity to pass upon the scope of the Takings Clause. By the Fuller era, however, both federal and state governments began to appropriate land and enact fledgling land-use controls. Much of this activity was dictated by a desire to improve the urban environment and to encourage economic growth. The Fuller Court was the first to come to grips in a sustained way with the takings issue, and it established the basis for later developments in this field.

The relationship between the Takings Clause and the Due Process Clauses was somewhat elusive. On occasion the Fuller Court conflated taking of property with deprivation of property without due process under the Fourteenth Amendment. In theory these are distinct constitutional guarantees. The Takings Clause does not bar governmental appropriation of property, but it does mandate the payment of compensation. But the due process norm prevents the arbitrary deprivation of property or liberty. In practice, however, the norm that government could not seize property without compensation shaped the Fuller Court's thinking about due process rights. As a result, the Fuller Court analyzed some cases under the due process framework that today would probably be treated as a takings problem.

In the leading case of *Monongahela Navigation Co. v. United States* (1893) Justice Brewer, speaking for a unanimous Court, stressed that the Takings Clause was an integral part of the Bill of Rights. In a classic formulation, he observed that the compensation principle "prevents the public from loading upon one individual more than his just share of the burdens of government, and says that when he surrenders to the public something more and different from that which is exacted from other members of the public, a full and just equivalent shall be returned to him" (*Monongahela*, 325). As this suggests, the Takings Clause addresses a fundamental issue for a free society: Should individual owners or the general public bear the expense of providing social goods? In other words, to what extent can society single out individuals to contribute a disproportionate amount toward particular governmental programs? The Supreme Court repeatedly grappled with this question during Fuller's tenure as chief justice.

There are three critical components to takings jurisprudence. The initial inquiry is whether property has been "taken" by the government. A baffling problem is the extent to which governmental action, short of outright acquisition of title by eminent domain, effectuates a taking for which compensation must be paid. The Court revealingly commented in *Scranton v. Wheeler* (1900) that "what is a taking of private property for public use, is not always easy to determine" (*Scranton*, 153). In the often cited case of *United States v. Welch* (1910) the Fuller Court reaffirmed the principle that a permanent flooding of land that rendered it valueless constitutes a taking of property. Such a physical invasion amounted to the practical equivalent of outright appropriation. The Fuller Court, however, was less sympathetic when riparian owners suffered damage as a consequence of federal river and harbor improvements. Declaring that riparian owners were subject to a navigational servitude in favor of the government, the Court, speaking through Fuller in *Gibson v. United States* (1897), ruled that an owner's loss of access to a river did not effectuate a taking of property. In a subsequent line of cases the Fuller Court seemed more concerned to facilitate government control over navigable rivers than to safeguard the property rights of individuals.

In an age before comprehensive zoning, the Fuller Court also dealt with early land-use controls. It heard a number of challenges to legislation compelling owners to incur expenses in order to comply with safety and welfare regulations, as well as challenges to laws limiting the use of land. The justices generally allowed localities to impose structural changes on buildings in order to serve public health and safety. Thus, in *Tenement House Department of New York v. Moeschen* (1905) the Court, in a per curiam opinion (i.e., written by the entire Court, not one justice), upheld a state law requiring tenement owners to install windows and modern sanitary facilities. Some restrictions on the use of land similarly passed constitutional muster. Concerned that tall structures added to urban congestion and deprived adjacent buildings of light and air, many communities enacted height limitations on buildings. In *Welch v. Swasey* (1909) the Fuller Court unanimously rejected the contention that any regulation that deprived a person of profitable use of his property constituted a taking. It held that Boston's height restriction law was a valid exercise of the police power to reduce the danger of fire in residential districts.

Perhaps the most discussed aspect of takings jurisprudence today is the doctrine of regulatory taking. The Fuller Court never squarely addressed the question of whether a regulation could so diminish the value or usefulness of property as to be tantamount to a taking without formal appropriation of title. Still, harbingers of the modern regulatory takings doctrine appeared in the Fuller era. In an 1891 address Justice Brewer observed that regulation of the use of property might destroy its value and constitute the practical equivalent of outright appropriation. Even more striking were Justice Holmes's comments for the Court in *Hudson Water Co. v. McCarter* (1908). Probing the border between the rights of private property owners and governmental controls, he declared:

> The limits set to property by other public interests present themselves as a branch
> of what is called the police power of the State. The boundary at which the con-

flicting interests balance cannot be determined by any general formula in advance, but points in the line, or helping to establish it, are fixed by decisions that this or that concrete case falls on the nearer or farther side. For instance, the police power may limit the height of buildings, in a city, without compensation. To that extent it cuts down what otherwise would be the rights of property. But if it should attempt to limit the height so far as to make an ordinary building lot wholly useless the rights of property would prevail over the other public interest, and the public power would fail. To set such a limit would need compensation and the power of eminent domain. (*Hudson Water Co.*, 355)

This language was dictum (i.e., not essential to the ruling) in an opinion concerned with unrelated issues, yet Holmes clearly recognized that there were limits to the police-power justification for economic regulations. Moreover, he indicated that a regulation that destroyed the value of property would necessitate the payment of compensation. Holmes thus anticipated the emergence of the regulatory takings doctrine, which achieved constitutional status in the landmark decision of *Pennsylvania Coal Co. v. Mahon* (1922). However tentatively, the Fuller Court perceived that the impact of governmental action upon the owner, not the means employed, should determine the existence of a compensable taking.

Another contested topic in takings law is the requirement that private property be taken for "public use." It was generally agreed in the nineteenth century that eminent domain could only be utilized to acquire property for public benefit. Accordingly, the Fuller Court explained in *Fallbrook Irrigation District v. Bradley* (1896, 161): "The use for which private property is to be taken must be a public use." In one important case, *Missouri Pacific Railway Co. v. Nebraska* (1896), the justices put some teeth into the public-use requirement. At issue was a state commission order compelling a railroad to grant private parties a location on its land for the purpose of building grain elevators. The order was a response to agitation by farm groups seeking to control the price of grain storage by establishing competing facilities. Noting that there was no claimed public use, the Fuller Court characterized this proceeding as "in essence and effect a taking of private property of the railroad corporation for the private use of the petitioners" (*Missouri Pacific*, 417). The Court struck down the measure, reasoning that the taking of the property of one party by a state for the private use of another violated the Due Process Clause of the Fourteenth Amendment even though compensation was paid. The decision seemingly closed the door on the use of eminent domain to acquire property for the benefit of private parties.

The promise of *Missouri Pacific* as a curb on the freewheeling use of eminent domain, however, was not realized. In practice neither the Fuller Court nor later justices treated the public use limitation as a significant restraint on the exercise of eminent domain power. In a line of decisions Fuller and his colleagues upheld the use of eminent domain by the states in a variety of situations, even when the taking was primarily for private advantage and only incidentally for public benefit. For instance, the Fuller Court adopted a loose standard for determining public use in *Fallbrook Irrigation District v. Bradley* (1896). "It is not essential," Justice Peckham wrote for the Court, "that the entire community or even any considerable portion thereof should directly enjoy or participate in an improvement in order to constitute a public use" (*Fallbrook Irrigation*, 161–162). He proceeded to reject an attack on California's irrigation laws on grounds that the water procured was not for public use but only aided certain landowners. Likewise, in *Clark v. Nash* (1905) the Court sustained laws, prevalent in the western states, that conferred eminent domain power upon private persons to obtain rights-of-way across the land of others for mining or irrigation. The Court was evidently convinced that such schemes created an overall resource benefit for the public.

Although not hesitant to employ other legal doctrines to defend property owners against governmental infringement, the Fuller Court was disinclined to read the public use requirement strictly. Fuller and his colleagues repeatedly deferred to state legislative declarations of what amounted to public use. The justices expressly recognized that there was a wide diversity of local conditions and needs across the United States. This willingness to permit the states considerable latitude in the exercise of eminent domain was consistent with the Fuller Court's commitment to federalism and state autonomy and, for all practical purposes, sanctioned the transfer of property from one owner to another. Thus, the Fuller Court, contrary to its image as a champion of property rights, contributed to the process by which the public use limitation was eventually drained of any meaning at the federal level.

The third key element of takings jurisprudence is the mandate of "just compensation" when property is taken by the government. The compensation principle provides a check against inordinate use of eminent domain by requiring the public to pay, and it vindicates the constitutional policy safeguarding individuals against confiscation of their property for public benefit. Conversely, inadequate compensation subverts the protective function of the Takings Clause. The Fuller Court wrestled with the just compensation question in a number of cases and laid the basis for later doctrinal developments.

In the groundbreaking decision of *Monongahela Navigation Co. v. United States* (1893), Fuller and his colleagues gave an expansive reading to the right of compensation. The federal government appropriated a lock and dam as part of a navigation improvement scheme. Under a franchise granted by the state the company was authorized to collect tolls for use of its lock. The only issue was the amount of compensation, with the government arguing that the owner was entitled to simply the value of the tangible property and not to an award for the loss of the franchise to collect tolls. Justice Brewer established an important principle, insisting that the determination of the amount of compensation was a judicial not a legislative function. "It does not rest with the public," he observed, "taking the property, through Congress or the legislature, its representative, to say what compensation shall be paid, or even what shall be the rule of compensation. The Constitution has declared that just compensation shall be paid, and the ascertainment of that is a judicial inquiry" (*Monongahela*, 327). Thus, courts must scrutinize legislative efforts to limit the measure of compensation for a taking to ensure that the compensation satisfies the constitutional standard. Brewer defined just compensation as "a full and perfect equivalent for the property taken" and ruled that the value of property was determined by its profitableness. It followed, therefore, that just compensation mandated payment for the loss of the tolls under the franchise as well as for the physical property taken. *Monongahela Navigation* stands for the proposition that the market value of appropriated property encompasses its income-producing potential.

The Court under Fuller emphasized that the test of just compensation was the loss suffered by the owner. In *Boston Chamber of Commerce v. Boston* (1910) the justices reviewed an assessment of damages for the construction of a street over part of a tract owned by the local chamber of commerce. Since the land in question was encumbered by an easement of way, light, and air in favor of a third party, the city contended that the market value of the land was severely reduced by the servitude. Speaking for a unanimous Court, Justice Holmes held that the condition of the title was relevant in determining compensation. An owner, in other words, could not recover full market value for an unencumbered lot when the parcel taken was subject to an easement that diminished its value. The owner could only recover the value of the land with its use restricted. In often-quoted language, Holmes declared: "[The Constitution] merely requires that an owner of property taken should be paid for what is taken from him. And the question is what the owner has lost not what the taker gained" (*Boston Chamber*, 195).

This formulation is important on two counts. Holmes underscored the character of the Takings Clause as a protection not of objects but for individuals who own property. He also made clear that damages should properly be calculated on the basis of the loss sustained by the owner, not the gain to the government. This cardinal tenet of takings jurisprudence has been repeatedly invoked, if sometimes honored more in the breach than the observance.

Perhaps the most important contribution of the Fuller Court to takings jurisprudence was the extension of the just compensation requirement to the states. This step both signaled the high standing of the constitutional rights of property owners to the Court and marked the initial acceptance of the view that the Due Process Clause of the Fourteenth Amendment made certain fundamental provisions of the Bill of Rights applicable to state and local government.

The seminal case of *Chicago, Burlington, and Quincy Railroad Co. v. Chicago* (1897) arose when the city of Chicago utilized eminent domain to open a street across part of a railroad right of way. The jury in the condemnation proceeding fixed the amount of $1 as the compensation due to the railroad for the land taken. After this judgment was affirmed by the Illinois Supreme Court, the railroad appealed to the U.S. Supreme Court, arguing that the Illinois proceeding had deprived it of property without due process of law in violation of the Fourteenth Amendment. The city responded that the amount of compensation to be awarded for land taken was a matter of local law that posed no federal constitutional question. Recall that the Bill of Rights was originally understood as restraining the federal government, not the states.

Speaking for the Court, Justice John Marshall Harlan rejected the city's argument and ruled that payment of just compensation when private property was taken for public use was an essential element of due process. He observed that the mere form of a proceeding did not satisfy due process if the owner was deprived of property without compensation. In this path-breaking decision the Court read the Due Process Clause as imposing a substantive restraint on state exercise of eminent domain. Consequently, the just compensation norm became in effect the first provision of the Bill of Rights to be applied to the states. Moreover, the decision was a harbinger of later cases that found that other provisions of the Bill of Rights were incorporated into the Fourteenth Amendment and protected against abridgement by the states.

The takings jurisprudence of the Supreme Court under Fuller was shaped by the transformation of American society at the end of the nineteenth century as well as fresh economic and intellectual currents. As with other areas of constitutional law, the justices were called upon to adapt the Takings Clause to the demands of a new age.

Fuller and his colleagues proceeded in an incremental manner to fashion a muscular Takings Clause that reaffirmed the central place of property rights in the constitutional order. The Fuller Court did not apply the Takings Clause without a share of uncertainty as well as respect for state autonomy regarding the need to exercise eminent domain, but the main thrust of its decisions was clear. The Court shared the conviction of the Framers that preservation of individual liberty was closely associated with respect for the rights of property owners. A more vigorous application of the Takings Clause was consistent with the broader solicitude for economic freedom that characterized the Fuller era.

Taxation

The power of taxation has obvious implications for the security of property ownership. As a general proposition, the Fuller Court sustained a variety of federal and state levies and made no systematic attempt to shield wealth from taxation. This record, however, is overshadowed by the fierce controversy over the Court's invalidation of the 1894 income tax.

Although the Constitution conferred upon Congress broad power to levy taxes, this authority was not unfettered. Among other restrictions, article 1, section 9 of the Constitution provides: "No Capitation, or other direct, Tax shall be laid, unless in Proportion to the Census. . . ." Article 1, section 2 similarly declares that direct taxes "shall be apportioned among the several States" according to population. The apportionment rule therefore links direct taxes to a state's share of the national population. The Framers of the Constitution certainly recognized the need for Congress to raise an adequate revenue, but they were also mindful that the taxing power could be abused. They anticipated that most federal revenue would be produced by indirect levies, such as import duties and excise taxes. Resort to direct taxation, such as levies on land, was seen as likely to meet only extraordinary revenue needs. Direct taxes were especially contentious because they fell on individuals rather than commodities. Moreover, the imposition of direct taxes at the federal level could erode sources of state revenue and thereby threaten the role of the states in the constitutional scheme. As a result of these concerns, the Constitution constrained the power of Congress to levy direct taxes by means of the apportionment rule. In effect the apportionment requirement limited the taxing power by rendering impractical any direct tax that could not be readily apportioned.

The Direct Tax Clause raised difficult interpretation problems that centered upon the meaning of "direct taxes." In *Hylton v. United States* (1796) the Supreme Court sustained the constitutionality of an unapportioned carriage tax, holding that the levy was not direct. In so doing, several justices in seriatim (individual) opinions indicated that only capitation and land taxes were "direct" within the meaning of the Constitution. Although this conclusion had no clear grounding in either the Constitution or the infrequent comments of the framers on the subject, the *Hylton* dictum was repeatedly cited by subsequent decisions as narrowly defining "direct taxes." No other type of taxation was found to be direct.

In 1862 Congress enacted an unprecedented tax on earned income to help pay for the Civil War. The income tax grew increasingly unpopular after the war, and eastern and business interests complained that they paid a disproportionate amount of it. There was, moreover, no longer an emergency need for revenue. Congress twice reduced the rates and then allowed the income tax to expire in 1872. Subsequently the Supreme Court in *Springer v. United States* (1881) sustained the levy as applied to professional earnings against the argument that it was a direct tax that had to be apportioned among the states. Curiously, the Court described the Civil War income tax as an excise tax.

During the 1890s there was agitation to revive the income tax. Southern and western states took the initiative in calling for a levy on incomes. The Populists proposed a graduated income tax in the presidential election of 1892. Proponents of the income tax hoped that an alternative source of revenue would facilitate reductions of the high tariff. In addition, they stressed redistributionist objectives. It was widely believed that wealth was increasingly concentrated in a few hands, and supporters saw the levy as a means of shifting the national tax burden from consumption to wealth. They insisted that the wealthy should pay a larger share of the burdens of government. The depression of 1893 added to the pressure for increased taxes on the rich. After bitter debate Congress, under Democratic Party control, enacted the first peacetime income tax in 1894 as part of the Wilson-Gorman Tariff Act. The measure placed a tax, at a flat rate of 2 percent, on individual income above $4,000 per year and on corporate profits. It was estimated that the levy would affect less than 1 percent of the population, with most living in the industrial Northeast and in California. The tax rate was modest by modern standards, but there was of course no guarantee that it would not be raised in the future. Ironically, the Wilson-Gorman Act did not significantly reduce the tariff, and thus it undercut the claim that an income tax was needed to recapture lost tariff revenue.

Public debate over the income tax laid bare political, sectional, and class divisions in American society. Republicans in Congress uniformly opposed the tax on incomes. Opponents charged that southern and western support for the income tax was dictated by the fact that few individuals in those regions would have to pay it. They pictured the tax as a spiteful attack on eastern capital and as a step toward socialism. The income tax was also suspect because it constituted class legislation. By burdening only one segment of society, the income tax breached the widely accepted constitutional maxim enjoining equality of rights and duties. More significant for understanding the role of the Fuller Court, some opponents also charged that a levy on income was a direct tax and therefore unconstitutional unless apportioned.

In the famous case of *Pollock v. Farmers' Loan and Trust Co.* (1895) a stockholder sued a corporation in which he held stock to prevent the company from paying the income tax. At issue in *Pollock*, as Owen M. Fiss aptly notes, was a fundamental question about "the permissibility of using federal power to alter the market distribution of wealth" (Fiss 1993, 77). Fuller, speaking for the Court majority in two opinions, struck down the levy on income as a direct tax that had to be apportioned among the states. Commentators have vied with each other to condemn Fuller's decisions in often harsh terms. In a nutshell, the standard critique proceeds as follows: The Fuller Court in *Pollock* disregarded established precedent and frustrated popular support for an income tax with a class-oriented decision that safeguarded the interests of the wealthy by narrowly construing the taxing power of Congress. There is good reason, however, to question every aspect of this conventional wisdom.

A full account of the complex *Pollock* litigation is beyond the scope of this work. The case was argued twice before the Supreme Court. Prominent attorneys appeared for both sides. In April 1895 Fuller, speaking for a 6–2 majority, took the position that a tax on income from land was the equivalent of a tax on land. He reasoned that either tax reduced the value of land and that consequently both were direct taxes requiring apportionment. Fuller distinguished the earlier *Springer* decision by emphasizing that *Springer* involved personal earnings, not income from real estate. Relying upon a historical analysis, Fuller maintained that the Framers anticipated that direct taxes would be imposed only in unusual circumstances. In that connection, he suggested that a peacetime tax was different than a levy during war. Fuller explained that the apportionment requirement was "manifestly designed to operate to restrain the power of direct taxation to extraordinary emergencies, and to prevent an attack upon accumulated property by mere force of numbers." If this "rule of protection" was undermined, he cautioned, "one of the great landmarks defining the boundary between the Nation and the States of which it is composed, would have disappeared, and with it one of the bulwarks of private rights and private property" (*Pollock* I, 583). Thus, Fuller saw the direct tax provision as part of a constitutional design to protect the role of the states and the owners of property by limiting federal taxing authority.

In addition to striking down the tax on income from land, the Fuller Court unanimously ruled that the tax upon state and municipal bonds was unconstitutional. Such a levy, Fuller insisted, breached the doctrine of intergovernmental tax immunity. The justices, however, were unable to resolve the validity of the income tax as applied to income from personal property as well as from personal earnings. With Justice Howell Jackson absent for reasons of health, the Court appeared equally divided on the matter. Hence, the case was reargued in May before the full bench.

Two weeks later Fuller delivered his second *Pollock* opinion, voiding the entire income tax. Writing on this occasion for a 5–4 majority, he concluded that taxes on income from personal property, such as stocks and bonds, should be treated in the same manner as income from land. As Fiss points out, "in a constitutional context defined by the desire to prevent abuses of the power of taxation, it would have seemed anomalous to draw a line between the income from real property and the income from personal property" (Fiss 1993, 89). Since the tax on property was crucial to the overall tax scheme, Fuller held that the entire measure, including the tax on earned income, was constitutionally infirm. He disclaimed any judicial policy making and stressed that the Court "was not concerned with the question whether an income tax be or not be desirable." Indeed, Fuller observed that the Constitution could be amended to confer income tax authority and that the amendment process would allow time "for the sober second through of every part of country to be asserted" (*Pollock* II, 634–635). Additionally, he stated that states were free to levy income taxes.

There were four strongly expressed dissents. Justice Edward D. White, who as a senator had helped to draft the Wilson-Gorman Act, emphasized the binding force of stare decisis and accused the majority of judicially amending the Constitution to deny Congress a vital power of taxation. He contended that the majority opinion "takes invested wealth and reads it into the Constitution as a favored and protected class of property" (*Pollock* II, 712). Justice Harlan characterized taxation of income as a "just and equitable" means of sharing the cost of government. He added that the effect of the decision was "to give certain kinds of property a position of favoritism and advantage inconsistent with the fundamental principles of our social organization" (*Pollock* II, 676, 685).

The income tax controversy generated intense feeling across the country, and the Court's decisions captured great public interest. The justices could not escape these divisive popular sentiments. Although Fuller focused squarely on the direct tax issue in his two opinions, other members of the Court had broader fears about the constitutional order. Concurring in the first *Pollock* decision, Justice Stephen J. Field darkly warned: "The present assault upon capital is but the beginning. It will be but the stepping-stone to others, larger and more sweeping, till our political contests will become a war of the poor against the rich" (*Pollock* I, 607). The dissenters were even more impassioned. An agitated Justice Harlan made an almost personal attack on the majority justices and pounded his fist to add emphasis. Even more striking were the comments of Justice Henry Billings Brown, who had voted with the majority in the first *Pollock* decision. Now seeing the matter in conspiratorial terms, he decried the result as "nothing less than a surrender of the taxing power to the moneyed class," and he expressed hope that "it may not prove the first step toward the submergence of the liberties of the people in a sordid despotism of wealth" (*Pollock* II, 695).

Many commentators, then as now, reflecting the views of Populists and Progressives, have presented a class-based interpretation of *Pollock* and accused the Fuller Court of usurping the role of Congress by ignoring long accepted law. A more recent body of literature, however, challenges this stereotype and suggests that *Pollock* may well have correctly read the Direct Tax Clause. The oft-repeated notion that Fuller overturned precedent in deciding *Pollock* has been sharply questioned. In fact, most of the statements narrowly defining direct taxes as levies on capitation and land were just dicta in cases addressing unrelated issues. Further, on a more fundamental level, there was ample authority restricting the power of government to redistribute wealth. Morton J. Horwitz, for example, has declared that "far from marking a sharp break with the past, the decision in *Pollock* instead exemplified the crystallization and culmination of ideas that had been gathering strength in American constitutional thought for over fifty years" (Horwitz 1992, 19). He maintained that the outcome in *Pollock* should not have been a surprise. Even more telling, Fuller based his analysis on the Constitution itself and gave little weight to arguably mistaken earlier interpretations. As this suggests, the Fuller Court was no blind follower of precedent. This approach was congruent with modern jurisprudence, which has hardly been characterized by adherence to stare decisis. The New Deal Court and the Warren Court overturned precedent on a massive scale, to the acclaim of many scholars. Considering this record, it is simply unprincipled to condemn Fuller for not following precedent and for examining the Direct Tax Clause anew.

In short, Fuller returned to the basic premise of the direct tax provision as a constraint on federal taxing authority. Erik M. Jensen has cogently observed: "An income tax is nothing like the classic forms of indirect taxation, and the Supreme Court therefore got the result right in the *Income Tax Cases* of 1895: an income tax is a direct tax as that term was originally understood" (Jensen 2001, 1079).

Several other aspects of the *Pollock* litigation warrant consideration. No appraisal of the Fuller Court's handling of *Pollock* can ignore the pronounced sectional dimensions of the income tax controversy. The division of the justices corresponded closely with voting on the levy in Congress. The justices who voted to strike down the income tax—Fuller, Field, Brewer, Horace Gray, George Shiras Jr.—came from states with high per capita wealth. In contrast, three of the dissenters—Harlan, White, and Howell E. Jackson—were from southern states with low per capita wealth. This was not lost on contemporary observers, who pointed out that most of the dissenting justices were from the South.

Finally, it is arguable that the *Pollock* decision was in accord with public opinion in the late nineteenth century. Scholars have rather casually assumed that the ruling was unpopular. To be sure, the Court's action ignited a firestorm. Populists and many Democrats, as well as newspapers in the West and South, denounced the Court. Yet eastern political figures and newspapers hailed the outcome and vigorously defended the majority justices. Public attitudes on the income tax were directly tested in the presidential election of 1896. The Democratic Party platform blasted *Pollock*, and William Jennings Bryan called for the decision to be reversed by revamping the Supreme Court or through constitutional amendment. The victory of Republican William McKinley, however, doomed the income tax for nearly twenty years. As one noted historian has remarked, the *Pollock* decision "may not have been too far from the actual desires of the public" (Beth 1971, 42). By 1904 even the Democrats dropped their demand for an income tax. Not until public opinion changed markedly during the Progressive era would the Sixteenth Amendment effectively overrule *Pollock* and open the door for a tax on income.

Allegations that the Fuller Court was simply a partisan of the wealthy are contradicted by a glance at its decisions in other taxation cases. The justices readily sustained both state and federal inheritance taxes. In *Magoun v. Illinois Trust and Savings Bank* (1898) the Court stressed that states had long levied taxes on property passing at death, and it held that an inheritance tax was not a levy on property but on the privilege to transmit property. Similarly, it ruled in *Knowlton v. Moore* (1900) that a federal inheritance tax, enacted to help finance the Spanish-American War, was not a direct tax and was therefore valid. The burden of inheritance taxes would inevitably fall most heavily on the wealthy, but Fuller and his associates were not prepared to enlarge application of the Direct Tax Clauses beyond income taxation. The Fuller Court also affirmed the validity of a variety of other federal levies, such as stamp taxes on stock transactions, over the complaint that they were direct but unapportioned.

In addition, the Fuller Court repeatedly upheld a broad exercise of state authority to tax business corporations. Hence, the Court validated state franchise taxes on companies that conducted business in many states for the privilege of doing business within the taxing jurisdiction. Since the overall record of the Fuller Court was supportive of state and federal taxing power, the *Pollock* decision cannot fairly be depicted as a move to shield wealth from contributing toward the burdens of government. Instead, the record strongly suggests that the Fuller Court majority was giving real meaning to the Direct Tax Clauses as a restraint on congressional taxing authority.

Contract Clause

Article I, section 10 of the Constitution provides: "No State shall . . . pass any Law impairing the Obligation of Contracts." The Supreme Court, under Chief Justice John Marshall, fashioned the Contract Clause into a significant limitation on state power to interfere with contractual arrangements and to regulate the economy. The Contract Clause occupied a prominent place in constitutional litigation throughout the nineteenth century. Justice Shiras aptly commented in 1896: "No provision of the Constitution of the United States has received more frequent consideration by this Court than that which provides that no State shall pass any law impairing the obligation of contracts" (*Barnitz*, 121). Although the Fuller Court heard numerous Contract Clause cases and invoked the clause at least twenty-eight times to invalidate state laws, the provision nonetheless declined in importance while Fuller was chief.

To be sure, the Contract Clause retained a degree of vitality. In *Barnitz v. Beverly* (1896) and *Bradley v. Lightcap* (1904), for example, the Fuller Court relied on the clause to void state debtor-relief laws that infringed private contractual obligations. In so doing, it followed in the path of previous courts by carefully scrutinizing statutes affecting debtor-creditor relationships.

The Fuller Court also invoked the Contract Clause to prevent states and municipalities from evading their financial commitments. During the Gilded Age, many southern states and western communities enacted a host of legislation designed to reduce the amount of bonded debt or the rate of interest owed, as well as to limit the remedies of bondholders. Much of the ensuing litigation was heard by the Waite Court, but Fuller and his associates grappled with aspects of this complex controversy and generally sided with creditors. The protracted battle over bond repudiation was a fertile source of lawsuits. Anxious to undercut tax-receivable coupons attached to state bonds, Virginia legislators required production of the bond from which the tendered coupons were removed. In *McGahey v. Virginia* (1890) the Fuller Court unanimously held that this duty was so burdensome as to practically destroy the value of the coupons and thus impaired the obligation of contract. The Court likewise looked skeptically at legislative schemes to limit the taxing power of local governments in ways that prevented them from meeting contractual requirements. Thus, in *Hubert v. New Orleans* (1909) the justices held that state laws withdrawing municipal power of taxation and leaving creditors unpaid violated the Contract Clause.

Grants of tax exemption to business enterprise gave rise to another cluster of Contract Clause cases. Such tax immunities were common in the nineteenth century as a means of encouraging economic growth. The Fuller Court insisted that tax exemptions must be unequivocally expressed, and it resolved ambiguous language in favor of the state taxing authority. Still, as illustrated by *Mobile and Ohio Railroad Co. v. Tennessee* (1894), the Court in several cases sustained exemptions against subsequent attempts at taxation. Writing for a 5–4 majority, Justice Jackson ruled that a state levy of taxes on the railroad ran afoul of the Contract Clause. He explained that the purpose of the tax immunity grant "was to invite and encourage the investment of private capital in the enterprise of building the road" (*Mobile and Ohio Railroad*, 501). The majority reached a result in line with one of the main themes of Fuller Court jurisprudence: the protection of investment capital. Interestingly, Fuller and Brewer dissented on grounds that the grant language was unclear and did not amount to an exemption from taxation. Their dissent again demonstrates that members of the Fuller Court did not always follow predictable voting patterns.

Notwithstanding these decisions that curtailed state abridgement of contractual arrangements, the Contract Clause played just a secondary role in protecting economic interests during Fuller's tenure. Several factors explain the declining importance of the Contract Clause. By its terms the clause applied only to the states and afforded no guarantee against federal regulation of contracts. Moreover, as we have seen, the Fuller Court maintained that contracts must be strictly construed. Consequently, the justices often found that the contract under consideration conferred few rights.

Besides strict construction of contracts, the Fuller Court limited the reach of the Contract Clause in two respects. First, in *Illinois Central Railroad v. Illinois* (1892), a case involving a move by Illinois to reclaim submerged land along the Chicago waterfront previously granted to the railroad, a sharply divided Court held that a state could not irrevocably alienate land under navigable waters. Speaking for the majority, Justice Field made a novel application of the public trust doctrine and ruled that any grant of submerged land was necessarily revocable because such land was held in trust for the public. The upshot of *Illinois Central* was to weaken the Contract Clause by encouraging states to rely on an expanded public trust doctrine as a basis to rescind land grants. Second, the Fuller Court restricted the scope of the

Contract Clause by affirming a broad police-power exception. The Waite Court had earlier determined that a state legislature could not bargain away its police power over public health, safety, and morals. This notion of an inalienable police power gave states latitude to modify or revoke public contracts to which the state was a party. In *Manigault v. Springs* (1905) the Fuller Court extended the police-power exception to private contracts, holding that the police power "was paramount to any rights under contracts between individuals" (*Manigault*, 480).

As these developments suggest, the Fuller Court ceased to read the Contract Clause creatively and diluted the protection given contractual arrangements by this provision. During the Fuller years, therefore, the Contract Clause was gradually eclipsed by the Due Process and Takings Clauses as vehicles to safeguard economic rights.

Interstate Commerce Act

In addition to invoking constitutional law doctrines to limit the role of government in economic life, the Fuller Court interpreted regulatory legislation in light of its commitment to economic liberty. This was especially evident in cases dealing with the regulation of railroads under the Interstate Commerce Act of 1887. A compromise measure, the act was calculated more to placate antirailroad agitation than to establish strict control over the rail industry. It declared that charges for interstate railroad transportation should be reasonable and just, but it did not define such a rate. The act also outlawed rate-fixing arrangements and rebates to favored shippers. It further banned rate discrimination against short-haul shippers for transportation "under substantially similar circumstances and conditions." To administer this act Congress created the Interstate Commerce Commission (ICC), a rather feeble regulatory body with few express powers.

The Supreme Court under Fuller took a consistently narrow view of the ICC's authority. In fact, between 1897 and 1906 the ICC won only a single major case out of sixteen argued before Fuller and his colleagues. Two prominent decisions exemplify this trend. In *ICC v. Cincinnati, New Orleans, and Texas Pacific Railway Co.* (1897) Justice Brewer, writing for the Court, ruled that the act conferred no power on the ICC to fix railroad charges. The commission could simply review the reasonableness of rates set by carriers but not set new rates. Equally significant was the famous case of *ICC v. Alabama Midland Railway Co.* (1897), which involved the long haul–short haul clause of the act. The justices concluded that the existence of competition must be considered when applying the "under substantially similar circumstances and conditions" proviso. The practical consequence of *Alabama Midland* was to render the long haul–short haul clause ineffectual. Indeed, Justice Harlan, dissenting alone, complained that the ruling "goes far to make that commission a useless body for all practical purposes" (*Alabama Midland*, 176). It should be noted, however, that *Alabama Midland* reflected the economic realities of the rail industry and underscored the importance of competition in determining prices.

The Fuller Court's construction of the Interstate Commerce Act shows a decided preference for minimizing federal government controls in favor of market competition and retention of rate-making in private hands. The results comported with the Court's constitutional outlook, particularly with its use of the due process norm to curtail state regulatory authority.

Critics have long accused the Fuller Court of undercutting the ICC. Unquestionably the Court's skepticism about economic regulations informed its handling of the ICC cases. But the basic problems with the act were the responsibility of Congress. Since the legislation itself was a jumble of shadowy and contradictory provisions, it is difficult to persuasively argue that the Fuller Court frustrated any clear design of Congress regarding the railroads. Revealingly, Congress was not disturbed by Court decisions adverse to the ICC and made no move to strengthen the commission until the early twentieth century.

After 1900 the Progressive movement called for greater public supervision of railroads. In 1906 Congress enacted the Hepburn Act, which markedly changed railroad regulatory policy. Congress enlarged the ICC's authority, expressly empowered the ICC to fix rates, and curtailed judicial review of ICC orders. The Fuller Court did not resist this effort by Congress to revitalize the ICC, and generally it upheld the enhanced authority of the commission. In *ICC v. Illinois Central Railroad Co.* (1910), decided late in Fuller's tenure, the Court adopted a more deferential posture toward the ICC. Declaring that it would not "under the guise of exerting judicial power, usurp merely administrative functions by setting aside a lawful administrative order upon our conception as to whether the administrative power has been wisely exercised," the Fuller Court upheld a number of ICC orders dealing with rail service and freight charges. Thus, the justices signaled a reduced role for the judiciary in the railroad regulatory process.

Commerce among the States

Article 1, section 8 of the Constitution empowers Congress to "regulate Commerce with foreign Nations, and among the several States, and with the Indian tribes." The scope of congressional authority over economic life has long been one of the most contentious issues in American constitutionalism. It was a commonplace of nineteenth-century law that the power of Congress reached only travel and trade between the states. Neither commentators nor judges understood that federal commerce power extended to virtually every type of economic activity. It was generally recognized that there was a distinction between the production of goods, through industry or agriculture, and trade in those goods between states. Production was under state control, whereas Congress could regulate trade and transportation across state lines. In *Kidd v. Pearson* (1888), decided just after Fuller became chief justice, the Supreme Court stressed the difference between production and commerce. It declared: "The buying and selling and the transportation incidental thereto constitute commerce; and the regulation of commerce in the constitutional sense embraces the regulation at least of such transportation." The Court insisted that Congress was not empowered to regulate manufacturing, agriculture, or "every branch of human industry" (*Kidd*, 20–21).

This reading of the Commerce Clause was consistent with the original constitutional design of a limited federal government. Implicit in cases determining the reach of congressional power over commerce were considerations of federalism. Courts were in effect striking a balance between national and state spheres of government by defining the concept of commerce.

Until the late nineteenth century Congress only sparingly exercised its authority to affirmatively regulate interstate commerce. Hence, there were few opportunities for the Supreme Court to pass upon the extent of federal authority. But a fundamental purpose of the Commerce Clause was to keep the states from interfering with the free flow of goods within the national market. The Supreme Court early established the principle that the Commerce Clause, by its own force, invalidated state laws that unduly burdened interstate commerce. Before 1900 the Court largely focused on this negative, or dormant, impact of the Commerce Clause on state laws.

Fuller's tenure marked a watershed in the interpretation of the Commerce Clause. With the Interstate Commerce Act of 1887 and the Sherman Anti-Trust Act of 1890 Congress began to actively assert its authority over commerce. Congress also started to rely on the commerce power to regulate public morals and health, matters traditionally left to the states under their police power. At the same time, increased state regulatory and tax initiatives threatened to hamper trade across state lines. During the Fuller era, therefore, the Supreme Court was called upon for the first time to address in a sustained way the boundaries of the commerce power. Given its commitment to a limited federal government and the preservation of a vital role for the states, it is hardly surprising that the Fuller Court sought to cabin congressional power under the Commerce Clause. Still, the Court also gingerly upheld novel applications of the commerce power. In short, the Fuller Court wrestled conscientiously to apply long-standing principles to questions raised by the new industrial order.

Sherman Anti-Trust Act

A striking feature of rapid industrialization in the late nineteenth century was the growth of large-scale corporate enterprise that carried on business in several states.

Hoping to stabilize volatile markets, many businesses turned to devices such as mergers, trust arrangements, and holding companies to set prices and control distribution of goods. These developments were seen as reducing economic competition and thus aroused latent antimonopoly sentiment among the public. There was much debate about the legitimacy of large business combinations. Many worried that concentrated economic power in private hands threatened political liberty as well as economic opportunity. There was broad popular support for some type of legislation to rein in these large corporations and preserve competition.

Congress reacted by near-unanimous passage of the Sherman Anti-Trust Act in 1890. The act was predicated upon the common law principle that conspiracies in restraint of trade are against public policy. Rather than create an administrative agency to implement the act, Congress relied upon enforcement through government and private litigation. By prohibiting unlawful practices lawmakers hoped to preserve competition as a means of setting prices and governing economic activity. Aside from an affirmation of the ideal of free markets, however, there was little consensus as to what the Sherman Act was expected to achieve.

Phrased in ambiguous language, the act outlawed "every contract, combination in the form of trust or otherwise, or conspiracy, in restraint of trade or commerce among the several states or with foreign nations." The measure also made it a crime "to monopolize or attempt to monopolize, or combine or conspire . . . to monopolize any part of trade or commerce among the several states." This vague language virtually invited the Supreme Court to give meaning to the act and play a role in formulating antitrust policy. The Fuller Court heard a number of cases involving the Sherman Act and addressed two related issues: the scope of the commerce power, and the construction of the act. Today antitrust cases raise largely technical issues, which arouse little public interest, but in Fuller's era such cases were highly visible.

In *United States v. E. C. Knight Co.* (1895), the first case under the Sherman Act to reach the Supreme Court, the justices accepted the constitutionality of the measure but restricted congressional power to prevent manufacturing monopolies. The case involved an action against the American Sugar Refining Company, which controlled more than 90 percent of all sugar refining in the country. The government argued that the contracts that secured this monopoly constituted combinations in restraint of trade and enabled the company to charge higher prices. The Court rejected this contention in an opinion that circumscribed federal antitrust enforcement. Writing for a majority of eight justices, Fuller adhered to the established precedents that manufacturing was local in nature and subject only to state control. "Commerce succeeds to manufacture," he famously declared, "and is not part of it" (*E. C. Knight*, 12). Because the refining of sugar was manufacturing rather than commerce, such activity could not be governed by Congress. Fuller further differentiated between "direct" and "indirect" effects on interstate commerce and asserted that combinations to control manufacturing or agriculture constituted only an indirect restraint on trade. He conceded that contracts to sell goods among the states were part of interstate trade and could be regulated by Congress, but he distinguished between manufacturing and sales in interstate markets.

Alarmed about the power of "gigantic monopolies" that recognized "none of the restraints of moral obligations controlling the action of individuals," Justice Harlan dissented alone (*E. C. Knight*, 19, 44). He forcefully insisted that the challenged merger was devised to control both the refining and the selling of sugar throughout the country. Harlan felt that Congress was able to regulate production when such production negatively impacted the buying and selling of goods in interstate commerce. Charging that the majority opinion defeated the main object for which the Sherman Act was passed, Harlan concluded that only federal regulation could protect freedom of commerce from monopolistic combinations.

The *E. C. Knight* decision restricted application of the Sherman Act and hampered enforcement of antitrust law. Much of historical scholarship, strongly influenced by the New Deal's expansive conception of the federal commerce power, has derided Fuller's opinion as an illegitimate effort to shield big business from federal controls. This once fashionable interpretation is highly problematic.

It bears emphasis that the prime consideration for Fuller in *E. C. Knight* was the maintenance of the existing balance between federal and state authority over the economy. He declared that respect for the reserved power of the states was "essential to the preservation of the autonomy of the States as required by our dual form of government." Fuller added: "Slight reflection will show that if the national power extends to all contracts and combinations in manufacture, agriculture, mining, and other productive industries, whose ultimate result may affect external commerce, comparatively little of business operations and affairs would be left for state control" (*E. C. Knight*, 13, 16). He correctly realized that enlarging the reach of federal commerce power to encompass all economic activity would be antithetical to the very notion of a federal government of enumerated powers. Moreover, Fuller pointed out that the states could regulate manufacturing and take steps to curb monopolistic business practices. This was no idle suggestion. In fact, at the end of the nineteenth century the states were active in checking corporate aggregations and played a role in formulating antitrust policy. Rather than attempting to prevent regulation of business, therefore, Fuller was looking to states as the appropriate source of control.

This is not to deny that to modern eyes there is an air of unreality about *E. C. Knight*. The distinction drawn between production and commerce seemed to ignore the growing interdependence of economic activities. To Fuller, however, a deep commitment to federalism and limited government transcended economic considerations. In his view the prospect of unlimited federal authority over economic life was more threatening to the constitutional system than the dangers posed by business consolidations. Howard Gillman has persuasively concluded that Fuller's *E. C. Knight* decision "represents, not the abdication of an inherited tradition in pursuit of a fanatical commitment to laissez faire, but rather an attempt to maintain the efficacy of a traditional distinction in commerce clause jurisprudence at a time when changes in the structure of the economy were making this distinction increasingly untenable" (Gillman 1996, 431).

Indeed, Fuller and his colleagues vigorously enforced the antitrust laws in areas where the authority of Congress was clear, such as interstate transportation. In *United States v. Trans-Missouri Freight Association* (1897) and *United States v. Joint Traffic Association* (1898) the Court, by a vote of 5–4, invalidated price-fixing arrangements among a number of railroad companies. Writing for the majority, Justice Peckham brushed aside the argument that the scheme was a reasonable response to ruinous rate wars, and he adopted a literal interpretation of the Sherman Act that allowed no room for price-fixing agreements whatever their rationale. Expressing concern that powerful combinations could drive "small dealers and worthy men" out of business, he declared in *Trans-Missouri* that the Sherman Act abrogated any contracts that interfered with market competition (*Trans-Missouri*, 323). Understood in this way, the Sherman Act was consistent with the Fuller Court's dedication to economic liberty.

Strongly dissenting, Justice White articulated what came to be known as the *rule of reason*. The Sherman Act, he insisted, should be interpreted in light of the common law standard that banned only unreasonable restraints of trade. According to White, the Supreme Court should inquire whether the rate-fixing arrangements at issue were a reasonable effort to halt ruinous competition caused by secretly undercutting rates. White's dissent spotlighted a key issue of statutory construction that was not resolved until after Fuller's death. Later decisions vindicated White's approach. In 1911 the Supreme Court adopted the rule of reason as a guide for interpreting the Sherman Act, a move that gave the judiciary broad discretion to ascertain which restraints of competition were reasonable.

In *Addyston Pipe and Steel Co. v. United States* (1899) the Fuller Court again demonstrated its willingness to enforce antitrust laws when the particular transaction was within the scope of congressional authority under the Commerce Clause. The case involved an agreement among cast-iron pipe manufacturers to fix prices and divide markets. The Fuller Court, in a unanimous opinion by Justice Peckham, held that combinations to control prices that directly impacted sales across state lines were illegal under the Sherman Act. He sweepingly observed that "the power of Congress to regulate interstate commerce comprises the right to enact a law prohibiting the citizen from entering into those private contracts which directly and substantially, and not merely indirectly, remotely, incidentally, and collaterally, regulate to a greater or less degree commerce among the states" (*Addyston Pipe*, 229). By 1900, then, the

Fuller Court had established that Congress was empowered to preserve competition in interstate transportation and in the sale of goods in national markets.

In the early twentieth century President Theodore Roosevelt launched his so-called trust-busting program. He instituted several well-publicized antitrust suits and prevailed in two important cases. In *Northern Securities Co. v. United States* (1904) the government sought to dissolve the Northern Securities Company, a railroad holding company that controlled the stock of competing rail lines in the Pacific Northwest. This arrangement clearly eliminated competition in the region. Yet the case presented complicated legal issues and fragmented the Fuller Court. By a margin of 5–4 the justices held that the company was an illegal combination under the Sherman Act, but it could not agree on a majority opinion. Justice Harlan, speaking for only four justices, gave full vent to his antimonopoly leanings. He lectured that "it is the history of monopolies . . . that predictions of ruin are habitually made by them when it is attempted, by legislation, to restrain their operations and to protect the public against their exactions" (*Northern Securities*, 351). To Harlan's mind the company was simply a façade for an anticompetitive price-fixing scheme among interstate railroads. He reiterated his earlier position that the Sherman Act proscribed all restraints of trade, not just those deemed unreasonable. Justice Brewer concurred on the grounds that the holding company represented an unreasonable restraint of trade. Worried that monopoly power threatened the economic liberty of individuals, he argued that the substance of the arrangement amounted to a combination to destroy competition.

Four justices—White, Fuller, Holmes, and Peckham—joined the two dissenting opinions authored by White and Holmes. Echoing the decision in *E. C. Knight*, White maintained that the formation of a holding company was governed by state law and was not within the scope of the Commerce Clause. He characterized the central issue as one concerning stock transactions and the right to acquire property in the form of stock shares. Holmes, not an enthusiast for the Sherman Act, denied that the purpose of the measure was to preserve competition. He further asserted that Congress could not control economic activity without some direct effect on interstate commerce. Finding that the Northern Securities Company was not a combination in restraint in trade as defined by the act, Holmes passionately assailed Harlan's plurality opinion:

> I am happy to know that only a minority of my brethren adopt an interpretation of the law which in my opinion would make eternal the *bellum omnium contra omnes* and disintegrate society so far as it could into individual atoms. If that were its intent I should regarding calling such a law a regulation of commerce as a mere pretense. It would be an attempt to reconstruct society. I am not concerned with the wisdom of such an attempt, but I believe that Congress was not entrusted by the Constitution with the power to make it and I am deeply persuaded that it has not tried. (*Northern Securities*, 411)

The four dissenters saw the crucial question as the appropriate division of state and federal authority and sought to place some limits on congressional power over commerce.

The *Northern Securities* case sharply divided the Fuller Court, but a year later it unanimously ruled in *Swift and Co. v. United States* (1905) that the Sherman Act could be applied to local enterprises that were part of a wider stream of commerce. At issue were the collusive practices of Illinois stockyards in buying cattle and selling meat. Justice Holmes, speaking for the Court, observed that "commerce among the States is not a technical legal conception, but a practical one, drawn from the course of business" (*Swift*, 399). The outcome in *Swift* foreshadowed a broader reading of the federal commerce power but did not upset the line between production and commerce articulated in *E. C. Knight*.

As this record makes plain, the Fuller Court was not adverse to federal antitrust enforcement. In fact, the Court sustained application of the Sherman Act to a variety of situations involving interstate transportation and trade. Still, the Fuller Court insisted that congressional power over commerce did not encompass manufacturing or production. Born of a genuine conviction that plenary federal control over economic life was fundamentally at odds with the constitutional system of a limited federal government, *E. C. Knight's* definition of commerce as trade governed Commerce Clause jurisprudence until the New Deal era and the so-called constitutional revolution of 1937. Thereafter, the Supreme Court greatly enlarged the power of Congress to regulate every aspect of the economy.

Labor Relations

Labor law evolved slowly in the nineteenth century and was initially the province of state courts and legislatures. A series of strikes and boycotts against railroads, however, interrupted rail service and hampered interstate transportation. During the Gilded Age federal courts were drawn into labor disputes. Federal judges started to enjoin work stoppages on railroads in order to protect the carriers as instruments of interstate commerce. Injunctions were powerful weapons because failure to comply with a court order was punishable as contempt of court without a jury trial.

The use of injunctions in labor disputes was tested in the famous case of *In re Debs* (1895). Angered by an imposed wage reduction, the employees of Pullman Palace Car Company went on strike during May 1894. The American Railway Union, under the leadership of Eugene V. Debs, backed the strikers by organizing a secondary boycott and refusing to handle trains with Pullman cars. The strikers forcibly obstructed rail operations and the movement of mail through Chicago, the nation's rail hub. The resulting paralysis of the rail network halted the shipment of supplies and rapidly assumed crisis proportions. President Grover Cleveland's administration obtained a sweeping injunction from a federal court in Chicago. Predicated on the Sherman Anti-Trust Act, the Pullman injunction ordered union officials and all persons conspiring with them to cease interfering with trains operating in interstate commerce or carrying the mail. When the strikers ignored the injunction, President Cleveland sent federal troops into Chicago. This triggered an outbreak of mob violence and the widespread destruction of railroad property. Military intervention restored order and broke the strike. Debs and other union leaders were convicted of criminal contempt of court for disobeying the injunction. Imprisoned for six months, they sought a writ of habeas corpus from the Supreme Court.

Speaking for a unanimous Court, Justice Brewer denied the writ and forcefully sustained federal authority "to brush away all obstructions to the freedom of interstate commerce or the transportation of the mails" (*Debs*, 582). He took the position that the federal courts had jurisdiction to protect the free flow of commerce among the states by issuing injunctions, even without specific statutory authorization. To buttress this conclusion Brewer invoked the traditional power of equity courts to abate a public nuisance and eliminate obstructions to public highways. In contrast to the trial court, Brewer did not base his opinion on the Sherman Act. He also pointedly observed that the federal government could call upon military force to carry out the laws and commended the government for seeking judicial relief instead. Although Brewer was careful to note that the *Debs* injunction was confined to forcible obstructions and did not ban all strikes, he nonetheless opened the door for the growing use of labor injunctions in labor disputes.

Coming during the same term as the *E. C. Knight* and *Pollock* decisions, the *Debs* ruling prompted complaints that the Fuller Court was prejudiced in favor of propertied classes. Critics maintained that the justices construed federal power broadly when it served to safeguard economic rights and strictly when federal legislation threatened business interests. These views have often been repeated by historians. Yet *Debs* cannot be persuasively explained as a result-oriented probusiness result. The crucial legal issue in *Debs* was quite different from those presented in *E. C. Knight* and *Pollock*. The latter two cases turned upon the disputed scope of congressional authority over commerce and taxation, whereas *Debs* involved the role of the judiciary with regard to railroading, an activity clearly within the reach of interstate commerce. As Fiss has emphasized: "There was . . . ample basis in prevailing doctrine for distinguishing the exertion of federal power in *Debs* (over transportation) from the denial of federal power in *E. C. Knight* (over manufacturing)" (Fiss 1993, 113). The Fuller Court, moreover, made clear in many cases its resolve to safeguard interstate commerce from interference. It was entirely consistent with the Court's constitutional outlook that the justices acted firmly in *Debs* to defend the movement of goods and mail in the face of a national crisis.

In addition to fashioning labor injunctions, the federal courts in the 1890s began to apply the Sherman Anti-Trust Act to union activities. Although union leaders argued that Congress did not intend unions to be covered by the act, the evidence indicates that Congress expected it to reach all combinations, business or labor, that restrained trade. In *Loewe v. Lawlor* (1908) the Fuller Court, according to Herbert Hovenkamp, "adopted the consensus view and applied the Sherman Act to a labor union" (Hovenkamp 1991, 229). As part of its campaign to organize the employees of a small Connecticut hat factory, the hatters' union instituted a nationwide drive to urge merchants and the public not to buy Loewe's hats. Loewe brought suit for a conspiracy in restraint of trade under the Sherman Act and requested treble damages. Speaking for a unanimous Court, Fuller held that "the Act prohibits any combination whatever to secure action which essentially obstructs the free flow of commerce between the States, or restricts, in that regard, the liberty of a trader to engage in business" (*Loewe*, 293). Hence, a secondary boycott aimed at compelling third parties not to engage in trade might constitute a direct restraint of interstate commerce. Having established jurisdiction under the Sherman Act, Fuller remanded the case for a trial on the merits. Subsequently, the Court upheld a sizeable monetary award in favor of Loewe. The *Loewe* decision invited greater judicial scrutiny of the coercive power of unions as being in possible violation of the antitrust laws.

After Fuller's death Congress half-heartedly tried to curtail application of the antitrust laws to unions. The Clayton Anti-Trust Act of 1914 provided that "the labor of a human being is not a commodity or article of commerce." Section 20 of the act added that no injunctions should be granted by federal courts in labor disputes "unless necessary to prevent irreparable injury to property, or to a property right." However, this vague language did not serve to overturn the principle established in *Loewe*. Distinguishing between strikes and boycotts, the Supreme Court found in 1921 that the Clayton Act labor exemption did not protect secondary boycotts from judicial supervision.

Although Fuller and his colleagues acknowledged broad federal authority over transportation across state lines, they balked at novel congressional legislation creating new standards of liability governing injury to railroad workers. The Employers' Liability Act of 1906 imposed liability on common carriers for the injury or death of any employee caused by negligence and abolished the fellow-servant rule as a defense. Hoping to better protect railroad workers, Congress in effect established a federal statutory negligence action.

In the *Employers' Liability Cases* (1908) the justices of the Fuller Court agreed that the power of Congress was confined to employees engaged in interstate commerce at the time of the accident, but they split three ways as to the validity of the statute. Announcing the judgment, Justice White rebuffed the argument that a business engaged in interstate commerce opened its entire operation to regulation by Congress. Such a position, he insisted "would extend the power of Congress to every conceivable subject, however inherently local, would obliterate all the limitations of power imposed by the Constitution, and would destroy the authority of the States" (*Employers' Liability Cases*, 502). Speaking for himself, Fuller, and Brewer, Justice Peckham expressed doubt that Congress was empowered to govern employment relationships. The four dissenting justices were in accord with the proposition that Congress could not regulate intrastate commerce, but they maintained that the measure should be interpreted to limit its application to those employees engaged in interstate commerce at the time of the injury. In the wake of this decision Congress passed a second Employers' Liability Act that applied only to injuries resulting from activities in interstate commerce.

Federal Police Power

It was a widely acknowledged constitutional norm in the nineteenth century that the federal government did not possess a police power to regulate public health, safety, and morals. Such authority was reserved to the states. At the turn of the twentieth century, however, Congress began to make unprecedented use of the Commerce Clause to control indirectly matters not within its enumerated powers. Notwithstanding the line of cases that restrained the federal commerce power by distinguishing between commerce and production, the majority of justices on the Fuller Court were surprisingly receptive to the novel exercises of congressional authority that infringed traditional state police powers.

This was exemplified by *Champion v. Ames* (1903), in which the Court, by a vote of 5–4, held that Congress could prohibit the transportation of lottery tickets from state to state. The obvious purpose of the statute was to suppress lotteries, not to protect the interstate market. The case presented vexing issues and had to be argued three times. Writing for the majority, Justice Harlan found that lottery tickets were subjects of commerce and that Congress could ban items from interstate commerce. Harlan was usually inclined to an expansive conception of the federal commerce power as well as a broad scope for governmental authority to safeguard public morals. His opinion in *Champion* reflected his intense dislike of lotteries. Harlan pointed to congressional concern that "commerce shall not be polluted by the carrying of lottery tickets" and to "the mischiefs of the lottery business" (*Champion*, 356–357).

Fuller, in dissent, asserted that Congress was in effect seeking to exercise a police power to promote public morals. According to Fuller, the majority opinion was inconsistent with the intention of the Framers of the Constitution and threatened to upset the constitutional balance between the national and state governments. "To hold that Congress has general police power," Fuller asserted, "would be to hold that it may accomplish objects not entrusted to the General Government, and to defeat the operation of the Tenth Amendment" (*Champion*, 365).

As Fuller correctly perceived, the practical result of *Champion* was to sanction a federal police power through the device of professing to regulate interstate commerce. The outcome was in sharp contrast to the doctrine of delegated powers and demonstrates that the Fuller Court found it difficult to cabin the exercise of congressional commerce power. Congress, influenced by the Progressive movement, promptly enacted social reform legislation based on the commerce power. For instance, the Pure Food and Drug Act of 1906 excluded adulterated and misbranded foods from interstate commerce. In 1910 Congress passed the Mann Act, outlawing the transportation of women from state to state for immoral purposes. The Supreme Court relied upon the doctrine established in *Champion* to uphold both statutes after Fuller's death.

The Fuller Court likewise approved the use of taxation to regulate or prohibit economic activity that could not be reached directly by Congress under the Commerce Clause. In *McCray v. United States* (1904) the Court, divided 6–3, upheld the imposition of a prohibitory tax on yellow oleomargarine. The government sued McCray, a margarine dealer, for a statutory penalty because he purchased colored oleomargarine without the required revenue stamps. McCray challenged the levy as an inappropriate use of the taxing power for regulatory purposes. Although the evident intent of this tax was not to raise revenue but to assist the dairy industry by prohibiting oleomargarine, the majority declined to consider the motivation of Congress in passing the levy. Justice White, who delivered the opinion for the Court, declared that "the taxing power conferred by the Constitution knows no limit except those expressly stated in that instrument" (*McCray*, 59). Because the taxing power was not restricted to interstate commerce, the *McCray* decision seemingly opened the door for Congress to regulate indirectly all aspects of the economy. This generous understanding of taxing power established an additional basis for a federal police power. It was clearly at odds with *E. C. Knight*; not surprisingly, Fuller dissented.

The *Champion* and *McCray* decisions made clear that the Fuller Court did not consistently define congressional power over commerce in narrow terms. These cases indicate that the justices sometimes worked at cross-purposes in fashioning Commerce Clause jurisprudence, heeding the political economic currents toward centralization while simultaneously trying to maintain the dual form of government implicit in the federal system.

Dormant Commerce Power

Recognized by the Supreme Court long before Fuller became chief justice, the dormant commerce power foreclosed state laws that unduly hampered commerce among the states. Dormant commerce jurisprudence promoted an efficient national market. It reflected fears that state economic protectionism would negatively impact trade across state lines. Yet the states were the principal focus of regulatory authority through the nineteenth century. State police-power regulations dealing with public health, safety, or morals frequently had an incidental effect on interstate commerce. Courts, therefore, grappled with the extent to which particular state regulations impinged upon the congressional commerce power.

The Fuller Court heard many appeals in which state laws were assailed as violative of the dormant commerce power. "It is curious to note the fact," Justice Brewer commented in 1895, "that in a large proportion of the cases in respect to interstate commerce brought to this court the question presented was of the validity of state legislation in its bearing upon interstate commerce" (*Debs*, 581). In these cases Fuller and his associates balanced the interests of the state in imposing economic or social regulations against the barrier to interstate commerce and the needs of the national market. Since dormant commerce cases typically turned upon specific factual situations, the Fuller Court experienced difficulty in drawing precise lines between acceptable state regulations and invasions of federal authority. Despite its tendency to uphold state autonomy, the Court under Fuller wielded the dormant commerce power forcefully to eliminate state-imposed obstacles to commerce among the states. In effect the Commerce Clause provided another vehicle by which the Fuller Court could review and invalidate state economic legislation. Since there was a large volume of dormant commerce litigation, only a few representative cases are examined here.

The Fuller Court looked skeptically at local regulations that denied equality in the marketplace to products from other states. Relying on the Commerce Clause, the justices began to restrict the authority of the states to inspect goods shipped in interstate commerce. In several cases the Court took the position that a state could not, under the pretense of inspection laws, impede the import of food products from other jurisdictions. The problem posed by state inspection laws was illustrated in *Minnesota v. Barber* (1890). At issue was a statute requiring the inspection of cattle within Minnesota twenty-four hours before slaughter. Ostensibly a health measure to ensure purity, the effect of the law was to exclude out-of-state meat from markets in Minnesota. Reasoning that the inspection requirement constituted discrimination in favor of home products, Fuller and his associates unanimously struck down the statute as an unreasonable burden on commerce. Similarly, in *Voight v. Wright* (1891) the Court declared unconstitutional a Virginia law mandating an inspection of flour from other states when no such inspection was required of flour manufactured in Virginia. But the Fuller Court did sustain inspection laws for which there was a compelling justification. In *Reid v. Colorado* (1902) it upheld a state statute banning the transportation of cattle or horses into the state without a certificate that the animals were free from contagious diseases.

As would be expected, state regulation of railroad operations was the source of frequent complaints on Commerce Clause grounds. The Fuller Court generally allowed states broad leeway to protect the safety of passengers and the public. For example, in *New York, New Haven, and Hartford Railroad Co. v. New York* (1897) the Court unanimously validated a New York state law that outlawed the heating of passenger cars by means of a stove in each car. A railroad incorporated in Connecticut contended that this law would necessitate stopping trains from Boston at the New York line and thus interfere with rapid transportation. Stressing the danger of fire, the Court held that possible inconvenience to interstate rail travel did not prevent the states from enacting reasonable safety regulations.

State laws forbidding the operation of freight trains on Sundays had an obvious implication for travel across state lines. The constitutionality of Sunday laws, as applied to interstate rail transportation, came before the Fuller Court in *Hennington v. Georgia* (1896). Writing for a majority of six, Justice Harlan ruled that the measure was within the state police power to protect public health and morals by designating a day of rest. He insisted that any effect on interstate commerce was limited. Fuller, dissenting, took the position that "trade between the States by means of railroads passing through several states, is a matter national in its character and admitting of uniform regulation" (*Hennington*, 318). He persuasively maintained that state laws halting interstate commerce for one day a week interfered with freedom of commerce.

Another vexing Commerce Clause issue related to efforts by states to compel the stoppage of interstate passenger trains at designated points. Designed to meet the needs of local passengers, such laws caused delays for interstate passengers and inconvenience for railroad companies. The Fuller Court was repeatedly asked to strike down state stoppage laws as a burden on interstate commerce. The controversy over such laws higlighted the growing tension between traditional state regulations and the emerging national economic system. The Supreme Court explained in *Cleveland, Cincinnati, Chicago and St. Louis Railway Company v. Illinois* (1900) that stoppage statutes "have been approved or disapproved as they have seemed reasonable or unreasonable, or bore more or less heavily upon the power of railways to regulate their trains in the respective and sometimes conflicting interest of local and through traffic" (*Cleveland, Cincinnati*, 518).

To assess the validity of stoppage laws the Court considered several factors. Among them were the adequacy of existing rail service, the size of the community, and the competitive pressures on railroad companies to capture passenger business. As this suggests, judicial review of state stoppage laws was heavily fact dependent, and the cases are not easily reconciled. In *Illinois Central Railroad Co. v. Illinois* (1896), for instance, the justices invalidated a state law requiring all passenger trains to stop at every county seat, even if this entailed a detour out of their route, as a hindrance to interstate transportation. In contrast, the Fuller Court in *Lake Shore and Michigan Southern Railway Co. v. Ohio* (1899) upheld a statute directing railroads to stop three passenger trains daily each way at villages of more than 3,000 inhabitants.

State laws that outlawed the shipment of certain commodities from one jurisdiction to another also raised nettlesome problems for Fuller and his colleagues. Such bans were ostensibly grounded on the state police power to guard residents against harmful or deceptive products. During Fuller's tenure state laws were often aimed at the interstate shipment of alcoholic beverages, cigarettes, and oleomargarine. As with other cases involving the dormant commerce power, the Fuller Court was called upon to balance the exercise of state police power with the need to guard the national market.

The prohibition movement gained strength after 1880, and a number of states made it illegal to manufacture or sell liquor within their borders. In order to make state prohibition laws effective, however, it was necessary to halt the transportation of liquor into dry jurisdictions. State laws forbidding the shipment of alcoholic beverages from other states triggered a prolonged constitutional controversy at the end of the nineteenth century. The Fuller Court tended to insist that liquor was a legitimate article of interstate trade protected by the dormant commerce clause.

At issue in the important case of *Leisy v. Hardin* (1890) was application of an Iowa prohibition law to beer imported from another state and still in the original packages. Fuller, speaking for a majority of six, held that interstate liquor shipments were a subject requiring commercial uniformity among the states. Drawing upon the original-package doctrine formulated by Chief Justice John Marshall in *Brown v. Maryland* (1827), a case dealing with state taxing authority, Fuller insisted that no state could prevent the sale of imported liquor in the original package. As Fiss pointed out, "the *Leisy* Court simply completed a program of economic nationalism that had in roots in the ideas of John Marshall" (Fiss 1993, 274). As a practical matter, of course, the *Leisy* decision significantly impaired the ability of states to enforce their prohibition laws. Justice Gray, joined by Harlan and Brewer, dissented on grounds that the sale of liquor did not require uniform regulation.

Yet in the *Leisy* opinion Fuller virtually invited Congress to enlarge the power of the states to ban imported liquor. He suggested that Congress could "remove the restriction upon the State in dealing with imported articles of trade within its limits, which have not been mingled with the common mass of property therein, if in its judgment the end secured justifies and requires such action" (*Leisy*, 123–124). Congress quickly responded to Fuller's suggestion by passing the Wilson Act of 1890. This measure sought to restore control of liquor to the states by providing that imported alcoholic beverages were subject "upon arrival" to state laws to the same extent as if they had been produced in the state. Not surprisingly, the Supreme Court upheld the constitutionality of the Wilson Act in *In re Rohrer* (1891). Writing again for the Court, Fuller stressed the importance of freedom of commerce among the states but held that Congress could define the point at which imported liquor lost its interstate character. This problematic decision strengthened the power of the dry states to halt out-of-state liquor, but it was inconsistent with the notion of a national market frequently espoused by the Fuller Court.

In short order, however, the Fuller Court's dedication to free trade in liquor reappeared. In a line of cases, Fuller and his colleagues narrowly construed the scope of the Wilson Act. This trend culminated in *Rhodes v. Iowa* (1898), in which the Court, by a vote of 6–3, ruled that the statutory phrase "upon arrival" did not mean physical arrival in the state but rather delivery to the consignee. Thus, the right of individuals to import liquor was affirmed. Justice White, who wrote the majority opinion, maintained that under the Wilson Act states could interfere with the sale of imported liquor only after its arrival. The effect of *Rhodes* was to undercut state prohibition laws by allowing mail-order shipments of alcoholic beverages directly to consignees.

The Fuller Court's defense of the interstate liquor business continued throughout the first decade of the twentieth century. Frustrated prohibitionists turned once more to Congress for assistance. The Webb-Kenyon Act of 1913, passed after Fuller's death, broadly prohibited the shipment in interstate commerce of liquor to be used in violation of state law. With this measure Congress clearly rejected the notion of free trade in alcoholic beverages and took a big step toward the Eighteenth Amendment and national prohibition.

The interstate shipment of cigarettes also tested the Fuller Court's dormant commerce jurisprudence. Motivated by health concerns as well as the objective of protecting the valuable cigar trade, a number of states in the 1890s banned the sale and use of cigarettes. In *Austin v. Tennessee* (1900) the Court grappled with the contention that such laws interfered with interstate commerce. The justices regarded tobacco products as legitimate articles of commerce and refused to take judicial notice that cigarettes were harmful to health. But they divided 5–4 over whether the original-package doctrine applied in this situation. The majority concluded that a ten-cigarette parcel was not the original package for purposes of protection under the Commerce Clause against state interference. Instead, they maintained that the original-package doctrine contemplated large shipping containers. The upshot was that states could halt the import of cigarettes in small boxes. Speaking for the dissenters, Justice Brewer complained that the majority was defining the size of original packages in such a way as to undercut commerce among the states. He declared that "the whole framework of commercial unity created by the Constitution" was threatened if states could determine what articles could be imported into their jurisdictions.

Besides liquor and cigarettes, many states in the 1880s attempted to block shipments of oleomargarine. Pressured by the dairy lobby, which wished to eliminate competition from margarine, states either outlawed or severely regulated sales of the substance. These prohibitory laws were avowedly grounded upon a state's power to prevent the distribution of harmful or deceptive products.

The Fuller Court heard a series of appeals attacking such legislation as an infringement upon interstate commerce. In *Plumley v. Massachusetts* (1894) the Court, by a vote of 6–3, ruled that a law barring the sale of yellow oleomargarine could be applied to block the sale of such product imported from other states. Writing for the Court, Justice Harlan concluded that a state could exclude yellow margarine as a deceptive product that might mislead the public into purchasing margarine instead of butter. He rejected the contention that the statute conflicted with federal control of interstate trade. The *Plumley* decision was out of harmony with the main current of the Fuller Court's Commerce Clause cases. "I deny," Fuller stressed for the dissenters, "that a state may exclude from commerce legitimate objects of commercial dealings because of the possibility that their appearance may deceive purchasers in regard to their qualities" (*Plumley*, 481). Subsequent margarine decisions moved toward Fuller's position. In *Schollenberger v. Pennsylvania* (1898), for example, the Court struck down a state statute totally outlawing the sale of margarine. It reasoned that a state could not infringe the right of an importer, under the Commerce Clause, to ship and sell a lawful article of commerce in original packages. Moreover, the Court invalidated in *Collins v. New Hampshire* (1898) a law banning the sale of margarine unless it was colored pink. In response to lobbying by dairy interests, Congress reacted to these judicial developments by passing the Oleomargarine Act of 1902 to bolster state control over margarine.

As the record makes clear, the Fuller Court usually protected the sale of articles in the channels of commerce. Unfortunately, the Court was not so stalwart in defense of the interstate recruitment and transportation of workers. In the late nineteenth century, agents, often representing northern business interests, began to recruit impoverished black agricultural workers in the rural South for jobs outside the region. Their efforts endangered the ability of white planters to control local labor markets and hold down labor costs. In reaction to this threat, southern states enacted emigrant-agent laws that required such agents to pay huge taxes to obtain licenses. The obvious purpose of the emigrant-agent laws was to stifle the large-scale migration of black workers and to undercut labor mobility.

Yet in *Williams v. Fears* (1900) the Fuller Court turned a deaf ear to a Commerce Clause challenge to Georgia's emigrant-agent tax. Treating the law as just a matter of routine occupational licensing, Fuller, speaking for eight justices, dubiously ruled that the emigrant agents were not engaged in interstate commerce. He reasoned:

> These labor contracts were not in themselves subjects of traffic between the States, nor was the business of hiring laborers so immediately connected with interstate transportation or interstate traffic that it could be correctly said that those who follow it were engaged in interstate commerce, or that the tax on that occupation constituted a burden on such commerce. (*Williams*, 278)

Justice Harlan dissented without opinion. David E. Bernstein has fairly charged that "Fuller's opinion neglected the reality of the situation before him" and demonstrated a "wooden understanding of the emigrant agent license fee" (Bernstein 1998, 817). It should be noted, however, that the racial implications of the emigrant-agent laws were not forcefully raised before the Supreme Court.

Although the Supreme Court under Fuller sustained the emigrant-agent laws, it did affirm that all citizens had a right to travel from state to state. Fuller declared that "the right to remove from one place to another . . ., is an attribute of personal liberty, and the right . . . of free transit from or through" any state was protected by the Fourteenth Amendment (*Williams*, 274). Thus, the *Williams* decision effectively prevented southern states from passing laws to flatly ban black migration. Individuals were able to leave on their own initiative to pursue better economic opportunities.

Civil Liberties and Racial Discrimination

Although the Fuller Court gave heightened protection to the rights of property owners and the operation of the national market, it was generally unconcerned with guarding other asserted rights from government regulation. Hence the Supreme Court during Fuller's tenure displayed little sympathy for the claims of racial minorities, women, criminal defendants, dissidents, or individuals who breached accepted codes of moral behavior. Several factors help to explain this aloof judicial attitude. One root cause was the Fuller Court's profound commitment to federalism. With the important exception of the just compensation requirement, the justices steadfastly insisted that the guarantees of the Bill of Rights did not apply to the states. Despite adoption of the Fourteenth Amendment, the Court continued to see the states as the primary protectors of individual rights. Moreover, the Fuller Court's treatment of minorities and criminal defendants reflected the larger societal currents of the era. The justices shared the dominant public understanding with respect to personal status, race relations, and crime control. Consequently, they were disinclined to interfere with local autonomy in these areas.

As a result, the Fuller Court's record on civil liberties issues seems bleak in terms of modern constitutional liberalism. It has often been taken to task for inadequately safeguarding noneconomic liberties. Although this criticism is justified to some extent, it can be overdrawn. Any assessment of the performance by Fuller and his colleagues must weigh the political constraints that limited the range of effective judicial behavior. Moreover, one must bear in mind that the justices upheld many restrictions on private economic activity. It was hardly remarkable, therefore, that the Court would similarly sustain broad governmental authority to control other types of individual conduct. Lastly, in a few cases the Supreme Court under Fuller gave a generous reading to provisions of the Bill of Rights and cautiously pointed toward a more expansive judicial role in protecting the noneconomic rights of individuals.

Public Morals and Health

The time-honored American inclination to regulate public morals found new expression in the late nineteenth century. The social disruptions of the age fueled the passage of state laws to control individual behavior. Justified as an exercise of the police power to protect the interests of society, such regulations often clashed with minority values and claimed individual liberties. Yet Americans of the late nineteenth century placed little premium on the supposed right of individuals to live according to their personal notions of morality. Instead, as Michael Les Benedict has aptly pointed out, they thought that society "had a legitimate interest in promoting morality, suppressing immoral behavior, and fostering those institutions that inculcated moral virtue" (Benedict 1992, 104).

In line with this sentiment, Fuller and his colleagues consistently repulsed attacks against morals and health laws and allowed states wide discretion to control individual behavior. For instance, in *Petit v. Minnesota* (1900) the justices unanimously upheld a state law prohibiting most work on Sundays as an appropriate exercise of police power. Accepting the contention that the statute was designed to ensure workers a day of rest, Fuller, speaking for the Court, held that the legislature could compel the closing of barbershops on Sunday. The Court also permitted the states to control prostitution. This was established in *L'Hote v. New Orleans* (1900), in which Justice Brewer declared that New Orleans could establish a red-light district even if such a step indirectly caused the value of land within the district to depreciate in value.

Public health regulations could also clash with claims of individual rights. At issue in *Jacobson v. Massachusetts* (1905) was a state's compulsory smallpox vaccination statute. Brushing aside the contention that this measure infringed individual liberty, the Fuller Court, by a margin of 7–2, declared that a community could adopt health regulations to guard against an outbreak of contagious disease.

Religious Liberty

It was generally understood in the nineteenth century that the religion clauses of the First Amendment did not constrain state authority. The federal courts ordinarily had no jurisdiction over religious subjects. Consequently, the Supreme Court during Fuller's tenure had few opportunities to consider the First Amendment's guarantee of religious freedom. Legislative efforts to supervise public morals, however, sometimes implicated the free exercise of religion. The Mormon practice of polygamy deeply offended the moral sensibilities of most Americans. In *Davis v. Beason* (1890) the Fuller Court heard a challenge to an Idaho territorial law that denied the ballot to any person who was a polygamist or a member of any association that encouraged polygamy. Justice Field, speaking for a unanimous bench, condemned bigamy and polygamy in harsh terms. "They tend," he observed, "to destroy the purity of the marriage relation, to disturb the peace of families, to degrade woman and to debase man. Few crimes are more pernicious to the best interests of society and receive more general or deserved punishment" (*Davis*, 341). The critical point of Field's opinion was the settled constitutional doctrine that distinguished between religious belief and action. An individual was free to adopt any religious doctrine, but the Free Exercise Clause of the First Amendment did not preclude punishment for practices harmful to the good order and morals of society. It followed that, since polygamy was a crime, the suffrage restriction was valid.

Congress was also anxious to suppress polygamy. The Edmunds-Tucker Act of 1887 abrogated the corporate charter of the Mormon Church and ordered legal proceedings to confiscate the church's property in order to support public education in the Utah Territory. By a vote of 6–3 the Fuller Court in *Late Corporation of the Church of Jesus Christ of Latter-Day Saints v. United States* (1890) upheld the legislation and broadly defined congressional power over the territories. The majority, in an opinion by Justice Joseph Bradley, compared polygamy to barbarism and summarily dismissed assertions of religious freedom. Bradley justified the confiscation of Mormon Church property by pointing to common law rules allowing the government substantial control over charitable gifts. Given the Fuller Court's defense of property rights in other contexts, the majority's lack of attention to the economic interests of the Mormon Church is striking. In one of his most forceful dissenting opinions, Fuller protested the seizure of Mormon property and maintained that Congress could exercise in the territories only those powers expressly conferred in the Constitution. He agreed that the government could prosecute polygamy but insisted that Congress was not authorized to confiscate property. Animated more by concerns over separation of powers than by the plight of the Mormons, Fuller maintained that the courts, not Congress, were empowered to distribute the assets of dissolved corporations. Characterized by his biographer as "one of the greatest glories of Fuller's career," the chief's dissent was soon vindicated (King 1950, 147). Congress returned most of the confiscated property to the Mormons in the 1890s.

Fuller and his colleagues gave only cursory consideration to the Establishment Clause of the First Amendment. In *Davis* the justices commented that the clause bars "legislation for the support of any religious tenets, or the modes of worship of any sect" (*Davis*, 342). This observation suggests that legislators could not provide special favors to religious organizations. In *Church of the Holy Trinity v. United States*

(1892), however, the Court seemingly pointed toward a different understanding of church-state relations. The case involved a federal statute that prohibited the importation of aliens to perform contract labor. The Church of the Holy Trinity violated the literal terms of this measure when it contracted for the services of an English minister. Justice Brewer, writing for a unanimous Court, reasonably interpreted the statute as not intended to cover religious bodies. To support this conclusion he engaged in an expansive discussion of the place of religion in American life. Brewer declared that "no purpose of action against religion can be imputed to any legislation" (*Holy Trinity*, 465). He famously added that the United States "is a Christian Nation" (*Holy Trinity*, 471) and enumerated various ways in which Christianity pervaded public life. Brewer's stress on the link between religious faith and legal thought reflected both his deep personal convictions and the informal establishment of Protestant Christianity that prevailed throughout the nineteenth century. Brewer's language has sometimes been taken out of context. The case, after all, turned upon a question of statutory interpretation. Still, the reference to "a Christian Nation" evokes a closer affinity between church and state than modern First Amendment jurisprudence allows. The Fuller Court, in any event, never had a chance to consider the Establishment Clause squarely and thus never explored the implications of *Holy Trinity*.

Free Speech

At the start of the twentieth century few Americans saw freedom of speech as inviolate. The Fuller Court heard only a handful of cases involving free speech, and it demonstrated no interest in a robust reading of the First Amendment. In line with dominant public opinion, Fuller and his colleagues were indifferent toward free speech claims and consistently voted to sustain governmental authority.

Often the Court virtually ignored the free speech implications of cases. For example, in *In re Rapier* (1892) a unanimous Court, in an opinion by Fuller, ruled that Congress could ban from the mails matters seen as harmful to public morals. Denying that freedom of communication was abridged, Fuller declared that Congress was empowered to exclude advertisements relating to lotteries despite the fact that it had no express authority to supervise public morals. Moreover, in *Davis v. Massachusetts* (1897) the Court found that Boston could prevent public speeches in city parks without a permit from the mayor. Analogizing public parks to private property, the justices viewed the case in terms of property rights and paid no heed to the argument that the permit requirement could facilitate censorship. The Fuller Court also sustained obscenity prosecutions under the Comstock Act of 1873.

Fuller and his associates directly addressed free speech claims in only two cases. The assassination of President William McKinley by a self-proclaimed anarchist aroused widespread fear of anarchism. As part of a drive to suppress the movement, Congress sought to shut the door on European anarchists. The Immigration Act of 1903 authorized the deportation of alien anarchists. At issue in *Turner v. Williams* (1904) was an order to deport John Turner, an English labor organizer and anarchist. Writing for the Court, Fuller upheld the constitutionality of the provision regarding the exclusion of anarchists. He stressed the power of Congress to exclude unwanted aliens through immigration laws. Fuller confessed that he was "at a loss" to understand how the act infringed the First Amendment right of free speech. Instead, he emphasized the discretion in Congress to determine what political views were "so dangerous to the public weal that aliens who hold and advocate them would be undesirable additions to our population" (*Turner*, 294). Turner's status as an alien may well have been sufficient to defeat any free speech claim in Fuller's mind. He finished his opinion by declaring: "We are not to be understood as depreciating the vital importance of freedom of speech and of the press, or as suggesting limitations on the spirit of liberty, in itself unconquerable, but this case does not involve those considerations" (*Turner*, 294). Concurring, Justice Brewer appeared willing to enlarge the scope of protected speech by distinguishing between anarchism defined as seeking the violent overthrow of all government and a mere philosophical commitment to anarchism. But he failed to develop this point, and he voted to deport Turner.

The other important free speech case of the Fuller era was *Patterson v. Colorado* (1907). A newspaper published a series of articles critical of decisions by the Colorado Supreme Court and suggesting that the judges had been influenced by partisan considerations. The state attorney general instituted criminal contempt proceedings against the publisher, Thomas M. Patterson. Found guilty of contempt by the Colorado court, Patterson was fined. An appeal to the Supreme Court followed. The justices upheld the contempt conviction by a margin of 7–2. The majority opinion was authored by Holmes, who had joined Fuller's opinion in *Turner*. Although he acknowledged that "courts are subject to the same criticism as other people" (*Patterson*, 463), Holmes adopted a narrow understanding of the First Amendment's free speech guarantee. He first maintained that the First Amendment was limited to preventing prior restraints upon publications and that it did not bar "the subsequent punishment of such as may be deemed contrary to the public welfare" (*Patterson*, 462). Thus, Holmes appeared to adopt the restrictive common law view of freedom of speech, a position sharply at odds with the more expansive interpretation that he espoused after World War I. Holmes next declined to decide whether the Fourteenth Amendment embodied a protection of speech and press against the states similar to the safeguards of the First Amendment. Expressing fear that criticism impugning the motives of judges might obstruct the administration of justice, he insisted that state courts had broad power to determine what constituted contempt. In *Patterson* Holmes displayed the same skepticism about the right of free speech that informed his reluctance to defend contractual freedom in *Lochner.*

There were two dissenting opinions. Justice Harlan argued that "the rights of free speech and of a free press are, in their essence, attributes of national citizenship" protected against state abridgement by the Fourteenth Amendment. He questioned why the Court was prepared to invoke the Fourteenth Amendment to safeguard economic liberties but would not extend the same protection to freedom of speech. In a brief opinion Justice Brewer maintained that Patterson's claim of a federally protected right should have been addressed rather than casually dismissed.

With the *Patterson* decision the Fuller Court affirmed the restrictive common law understanding of free speech. According to Fiss, "The Fuller Court was deeply committed to liberty of contract but had no taste whatsoever for freedom of speech or for any of the political liberties we usually associate with that idea" (Fiss 1993, 323). It remains to consider, therefore, why the Fuller Court downplayed free speech claims, a position in marked contrast to the more extensive judicial concern with freedom of speech that gradually emerged after World War I.

Several factors coalesced to explain the attitude of the Fuller Court toward expressive freedom. As we have seen, Fuller and his colleagues were dedicated to the preservation of individual liberty. They sought to achieve this goal by restraining the substantive power of government rather than assigning a special status to free speech as a means of curbing government abuses. Moreover, there was no well-developed theory of free speech in Fuller's day. On the other hand, the rights of property owners had long been a central concern of constitutional thought. The Fuller Court could draw upon recognized constitutional norms in defending economic liberties. Further, it was a bedrock principle dating to *Barron v. Baltimore* (1833) that the Bill of Rights did not bind the states. Consistent with its high regard for the place of the states in the federal system, Fuller and his colleagues generally adhered to this view. Only the just compensation norm of the Fifth Amendment was applied to the states as part of the Fourteenth Amendment's guarantee of due process. As the Holmes opinion in *Patterson* made clear, the Fuller Court was not prepared to extend free speech protection to the states. Consequently, the justices had no basis on which to review state and local government actions that allegedly infringed free speech.

Although the Fuller Court as a body did little to extend expressive rights, it is important to note that several justices, notably Brewer, exemplified the now largely forgotten conservation libertarian tradition. As Mark A. Graber has explained, conservative libertarians "claimed that the liberty of speech was the same sort of right as the liberty of contract and, indeed, that the system of free expression could only function if the government also protected private property" (Graber 1991, 21).

Several members of the Fuller Court recognized the relationship between freedom of speech and the press and popular government. In extrajudicial remarks, for instance, Justice Brown stressed the vital importance of freedom of the press. "The right of every man to express his opinions in speech or print," he declared in an address in 1900, "is justly esteemed as one of the most sacred prerogatives of a free people." Brown added, somewhat optimistically: "No clause of the Constitution has been more sacredly cherished, and none more carefully upheld by the judicial power" (Brown 1900, 321). Although he expressed concern about the tendency of some newspapers of the day to engage in excessive personal attacks upon individuals, Brown cautioned that "censorship is not to be thought of in a free country" (Brown 1900, 337). A harbinger of future developments to strengthen expressive freedom, Brown's remarks also indicate that public sentiment sustained a free press in the absence of strong judicial support. Additionally, in *Downes v. Bidwell* (1901), one of the Insular Cases discussed below, Brown sustained the power of Congress to govern Puerto Rico. He insisted, however, that "certain natural rights," including the freedom of speech and press as well as private property, were constitutionally protected against abridgement by Congress (*Downes*, 282).

Racial Segregation

The emergence of the modern civil rights movement in the middle of the twentieth century caused scholars to reevaluate the history of race relations in the United States. Indeed, issues of equality and status became prime concerns of American constitutionalism following *Brown v. Board of Education* (1954). In this climate it became easy to castigate the Fuller Court as indifferent to the plight of blacks in the segregated South. Yet such criticism fails to take account of the prevailing social climate in the late nineteenth century and the political realities that constrained the courts in dealing with race relations.

The Fuller Court was a product of its times. Racist assumptions permeated both popular attitudes and scientific opinion in Gilded Age America. Reconstruction was generally viewed as a political disaster and a constitutional mistake. Policymakers stressed sectional reconciliation between the North and South and were anxious not to disturb regional harmony. The president and Congress showed no interest in attacking segregation in the southern states, and so any judicial move in this direction would lack political support. Imperialism at the turn of the twentieth century helped to undercut any criticism of the white South by reinforcing the belief that whites should dominate at home as well as abroad. Moreover, under Fuller's predecessor, Chief Justice Morrison R. Waite, the Supreme Court had already severely limited the potential of the Fourteenth Amendment as a safeguard for the rights of blacks. Regulation of civil rights was therefore left largely to the states. John Braeman has cogently observed that the "Fuller Court's acquiescence in the relegation of the Negro to second-class citizenship represented accommodation to the facts of life in turn-of-the-century America" (Braeman 1988, 121).

Fuller himself doubtless shared the racial views of the age. It will be remembered that he was a supporter of Stephen A. Douglas and had assailed the Emancipation Proclamation as unconstitutional. On issues other than property rights and interstate trade, Fuller generally adopted a position favoring states' rights. He was neither emotionally nor intellectually disposed to assault racial segregation, a step that would have reopened sectional wounds and posed great difficulties in securing enforcement of judicial orders.

Racial segregation on railroad passenger cars evolved gradually in the late nineteenth century. By the late 1880s states in the South started to require separate accommodations for black passengers. There was little pretense that in practice segregated facilities were equivalent to the accommodations afforded white passengers. Railroad companies often opposed the enactment of these separate-car laws because of the additional expense involved and the practical difficulty of enforcing them. The railroads, however, were reluctant to openly disregard community sentiment.

At issue in *Louisville, New Orleans and Texas Railway Company v. Mississippi* (1890), the first segregation case to reach the Fuller Court, was a state law requiring railroad companies to provide separate cars for white and black passengers on trains within Mississippi. The defendant railroad was convicted and fined for failure to comply with the statute. The railroad company argued that the law impeded interstate commerce because it in effect required the addition of another passenger car at the state line. Rejecting this contention, the Mississippi Supreme Court ruled that the statute applied only to transportation within the state and had no bearing on interstate passengers.

The Fuller Court, by a 7–2 vote, agreed that the state law did not abridge congressional power over interstate commerce. Justice Brewer, speaking for the Court, emphasized that the issue was just the authority of the state to compel the railroad to provide separate cars, not the power to assign passengers according to race. He found that the "extra expense" imposed on carriers did not interfere with commerce among the states. Indeed, Brewer compared the separate car law to state statutes requiring certain depot accommodations and compelling trains to stop at specific points. In this narrow opinion Brewer treated the Mississippi law as a regulation of railroad facilities, and strongly intimated that application of state segregation laws to interstate passengers would run afoul of the commerce clause. Following the *Louisville, New Orleans* decision, commentators and judges generally took the position that state segregation laws could not be applied to interstate passengers. The Fuller Court seemingly affirmed this understanding in *Chesapeake and Ohio Railway Company v. Kentucky* (1900). Left unresolved, however, was the validity of a railroad company policy, as distinct from a state law, mandating the segregation of interstate passengers. That issue would be addressed in a later case.

In the famous case of *Plessy v. Ferguson* (1896) the Fuller Court rejected a challenge to railroad segregation based on the Thirteenth Amendment and the Equal Protection Clause of the Fourteenth Amendment. Homer A. Plessy, in an arranged test case, sought to invalidate Louisiana's separate-car law, which imposed criminal penalties on passengers who went into a coach other than the one to which they were assigned on account of race. The Supreme Court sustained the Louisiana law, by a vote of 7–1, with Justice Brewer not participating. Justice Henry Billings Brown, who wrote the majority opinion, gave little attention to the Thirteenth Amendment argument. He simply maintained that a distinction based on race "has no tendency to destroy the legal equality of the two races, or reestablish a state of involuntary servitude" (*Plessy*, 543). Brown conceded that the purpose of the Fourteenth Amendment "was to enforce the absolute equality of the two races before the law" (*Plessy*, 544). But he emphasized that laws requiring racial separation were widely seen as within the state police power. To support this conclusion Brown specifically noted the practice of separate schooling as well as laws forbidding racial intermarriage. Articulating a reasonableness test, Brown asserted that the Louisiana legislature was free "to act with reference to the established usages, customs and traditions of the people" in order to promote social harmony. He then sharply questioned the premise that legislation could overcome deeply rooted racial distinctions:

> We consider the underlying fallacy of the plaintiff's argument to consist in the assumption that the enforced separation of the two races stamps the colored race with a badge of inferiority. If this be so, it is not by reason of anything found in the act, but solely because the colored race chooses to put that construction upon it. . . . The argument also assumes that social prejudices may be overcome by legislation, and that equal rights cannot be secured to the negro except by an enforced commingling of the two races. We cannot accept this proposition. . . . Legislation is powerless to eradicate racial instincts or to abolish distinctions based upon physical differences, and the attempt to do so can only result in accentuating the difficulties of the present situation. If the civil and political rights of both races be equal, one cannot be inferior to the other civilly or politically. If one race be inferior to the other socially, the Constitution of the United States cannot put them upon the same plane. (*Plessy*, 551)

Brown's opinion was predicated on the assumption that equal facilities were available to both blacks and whites. The result of *Plessy* was judicial affirmation that separate-but-supposedly-equal facilities passed constitutional muster.

In an impassioned dissent, Justice Harlan assailed the Louisiana statute and vigorously contended that the Reconstruction amendments banned racial discrimination. Endorsing the ideal of equal rights, Harlan insisted that the Thirteenth and Fourteenth Amendments "removed the race line from our governmental systems." Declaring the majority opinion to be as "pernicious" as the *Dred Scott* case, he broadly observed:

> Our Constitution is color-blind, and neither knows nor tolerates classes among cit-
> izens. In respect of civil rights, all citizens are equal before the law. The humblest
> is the peer of the most powerful. The law regards man as man, and takes no
> account of his surroundings or of his color when his civil rights as guaranteed by
> the supreme law of the land are involved. (*Plessy*, 559)

Harlan's invocation of the ideal of a color-blind Constitution was not congruent with the reigning racial sentiments and was largely ignored for decades. Moreover, it bears emphasis that Harlan's dissenting opinion was influenced by the special obligation of common carriers to transport all persons on equal terms. He did not mention public schooling in connection with his color-blind reading of the Fourteenth Amendment.

Although a source of later controversy, the *Plessy* decision received little attention at the time because it embodied widely held beliefs. Few observers really expected any other outcome. *Plessy* did not create the racial caste system in the South. State law mandating separate educational and travel facilities predated *Plessy*. Still, the ruling constituted a watershed in race relations. It validated segregation laws and opened the road to more extensive state control of racial minorities. Furthermore, *Plessy* signaled the Supreme Court's abandonment of efforts to uphold racial equality.

Realistically, there was probably little that the Fuller Court could have done to check the spread of segregation. But Fuller and his colleagues failed even to enforce the separate-but-equal norm. The case of *Cumming v. Richmond County Board of Education* (1899) was the first Supreme Court decision dealing with the issue of racial segregation in public schools. It arose when a Georgia county school board, pointing to an economic downturn, decided to close the high school for black students and convert the facility into a primary school. The board continued to support the high school education of white students. Alleging a violation of the equal protection of the law, the black plaintiffs requested an injunction to prevent the board from spending taxpayer money on a high school for whites while denying such educational opportunity to black pupils. They evidently hoped that the board would react to an injunction by reopening the black high school rather than closing the white facility. In other words, the plaintiffs did not directly challenge segregated schools.

Justice Harlan, speaking for a unanimous Court, denied the requested relief and refused to enjoin the use of public funds for the white high school. He seemed to treat school segregation as an established practice and accepted at face value the board's argument that it acted for economic reasons and not to discriminate against blacks. Harlan also maintained that public education was primarily a state responsibility and that federal courts should not intervene absent clear evidence of a constitutional violation. Given Harlan's dissent in *Plessy* and his civil rights record as a whole, the *Cumming* opinion appears to be something of an anomaly. Historians have debated how to best explain *Cumming* in light of Harlan's earlier call for a color-blind Constitution. Some have contended that the opinion raises troublesome questions about the depth of Harlan's dedication to civil rights. Others have pointed to the curious framing of the issue—a negative demand to withhold support from the white high school—as presenting an inadequate basis for a decision squarely addressing school segregation. Linda Przybyszewski has astutely postulated that Harlan may well have viewed public accommodations and public schools quite differently because he harbored reservations about more intimate racial associations. Whatever the explanation for Harlan's behavior in *Cumming*, the upshot of the opinion was that public agencies could provide a disproportionate share of benefits to whites as long as they could give some rationale other than race.

More surprising than the Fuller Court's affirmation of segregated public facilities was its refusal to safeguard the right of a private school to offer interracial education. Founded in 1855, privately supported Berea College in Kentucky instructed both white and black students. In 1904 the Kentucky legislature passed a statute that made it illegal for any person or corporation to operate a school in which students of both races were taught together. The Kentucky Court of Appeals brushed aside the college's arguments based on the right of private property owners and the right of voluntary association, and it sustained the law as a valid exercise of the police power to compel racial separation. On appeal, the college cited *Lochner* and other decisions curbing the power of government to control private businesses.

Justice Brewer, speaking for the Court in *Berea College v. Kentucky* (1908), sidestepped the broad constitutional issues. He focused instead on the authority of a state over corporations it had chartered. Brewer treated the law as an amendment to the Berea College charter and thus within the reserved power of the state to control corporations. The corporate charter rationale advanced by Brewer was not compelling, and it seemed at odds with his defense of economic rights in other contexts. It is noteworthy that Brewer did not endorse the frankly racist views of the Kentucky courts. This has lead some scholars to assert that Brewer's narrow opinion suggested an underlying sympathy with the position of the college. Justice Holmes concurred in the judgment. Dissenting, Justice Harlan denied that the central issue involved state power to amend corporate charters. Since in his mind the right to offer instruction was both a property and a liberty interest, it followed that the state law was "an arbitrary invasion of the rights of liberty and property guaranteed by the Fourteenth Amendment against hostile state action" (*Berea*, 67). Justice William R. Day also dissented, but without opinion.

Similarly, the Fuller Court did not resist the growing movement in the South to disenfranchise blacks. Southern legislatures employed numerous devices, including the literacy and understanding tests and the poll tax, to restrict black political participation. Yet any exclusionary device that superficially appeared even-handed was sustained by the Supreme Court despite evidence of discriminatory administration. In

Williams v. Mississippi (1898), for instance, the Court unanimously approved Mississippi's literacy test on grounds that the requirement applied to both white and black voters. Looking only at the text of the statute, the justices declined to examine the actual operation of the literacy test. Another challenge to the disfranchisement policy was presented in *Giles v. Harris* (1903). An Alabama black complained that he was denied registration because of his race and requested a federal court to order his registration. Speaking for a 6–3 majority, Justice Holmes declined to grant relief for technical reasons. Significantly, he acknowledged judicial impotence to deal with systematic racial disfranchisement. If "the great mass of the white population intends to keep the blacks from voting," Holmes wrote, "placing the plaintiff's name on a piece of paper will not defeat them." Relief from such a political wrong by a state, he continued, "must be given by the legislative and political department of the government of the United States" (*Giles*, 488). Holmes never demonstrated much interest in the claims of blacks for equal rights, and the tone of the *Giles* opinion exuded resignation in the face of political forces denying blacks the right to vote. Justices Brewer and Harlan authored brief dissenting opinions that maintained that the federal courts could grant relief in voting rights cases and that the case should have been tried on the merits. Justice Brown dissented as well, but wrote no opinion.

Nor did Fuller and his colleagues raise any objection to the exclusion of black citizens from jury service in the South. A line of such cases culminated in *Thomas v. Texas* (1909). At issue was an allegation by a black defendant convicted of murder that blacks had been intentionally left off the list of trial jurors. Fuller, in a brief opinion, declared that the issue of racial discrimination in the selection of jurors was a question of fact for the state courts to resolve. He added that a violation of the Constitution "cannot be presumed" and that nothing in the record established discrimination (*Thomas*, 282). As this indicates, the Fuller Court was disinclined to examine the actual workings of the jury selection process in order to guard against exclusion based on race.

The Court's indifference to the plight of black citizens continued through Fuller's tenure. As separate-car laws spread, many railroads, for the sake of convenience, adopted their own regulations to segregate both interstate and local travelers. In fact, the line between interstate and intrastate passengers was unclear as they often rode side-by-side, and so railroads racially separated all passengers. In *Chiles v. Chesapeake and Ohio Railway Co.* (1910) Justice Joseph McKenna, speaking for the Court, validated a carrier's policy of segregating interstate passengers. He reasoned that the failure of Congress to legislate in this area amounted to a declaration that railroads could separate white and black passengers in interstate commerce. Justice Harlan dissented alone without opinion.

In the early twentieth century the federal government instituted criminal prosecutions to strike at peonage. Akin to slavery, peonage was a system whereby debtors were bound to work for their creditors until their obligations were paid. Peonage was another means by which white landowners in the South could oppress black laborers. The Fuller Court gave modest encouragement to peonage prosecutions. In *Clyatt v. United States* (1905) Justice Brewer, writing for the Court, sustained the constitutionality of the federal statutes outlawing peonage. He concluded that compulsory service based on indebtedness amounted to involuntary servitude prohibited by the Thirteenth Amendment. But Brewer undercut the impact of *Clyatt* by reversing the conviction of the defendant on procedural grounds. Moreover, in *Hodges v. United States* (1906) the Court limited the reach of the peonage laws by stressing that they did not encompass the actions of private persons who used threats to have black workers fired from their jobs at an Arkansas lumber mill. Although Brewer, again speaking for the Court, had often stressed the vital importance of freedom of contract and the right to pursue a calling, he was not willing to protect these rights from mob action. Instead, Brewer adhered to a narrow definition of peonage as forced labor to pay debts, and he felt that private discriminatory behavior was a matter for the states. Brewer tellingly declared that in the long run blacks would be best served by "taking their chances with other citizens in the States where they should make their homes" (*Hodges*, 20). Dissenting, Justices Harlan and Day argued that a combination to prevent black citizens from making employment contracts was in violation of the freedom established by the Thirteenth Amendment.

Beyond segregation laws and disfranchisement of black voters, a resort to violence in order to maintain the racial caste system was common in the South. A dramatic outbreak of lynching swept across the region at the turn of the twentieth century. Most victims were black, and few lynchers were punished because local officials frequently colluded with the mobs.

In this ugly climate the Fuller Court instituted a unique contempt proceeding for willful disregard of its order staying the execution of a prisoner pending appeal. The case arose from a 1906 lynching of a black defendant convicted of rape in Chattanooga. It was alleged that Sheriff John F. Shipp and his deputies aided and abetted the lynch mob. Fuller was outraged by the murder and promptly called the justices to his home for an emergency meeting. The Court requested that the U.S. attorney general investigate the incident. Attorney General William H. Moody filed an information charging contempt of the Supreme Court. Brushing aside arguments that the Court lacked jurisdiction, Justice Holmes, for a unanimous bench in *United States v. Shipp* (1906), ruled that it had the authority to preserve the existing conditions until the appeal was resolved. The Court then appointed a commissioner who heard testimony concerning the contempt charges during 1907 and 1908.

Writing for a majority of five in *United States v. Shipp* (1909), Fuller found the sheriff, one of his deputies, and four members of the mob guilty of contempt of the Supreme Court. He stated that once the Court granted a stay of execution it became the duty of the sheriff to protect the defendant. Fuller unsparingly condemned the lynching. "It is apparent," he observed, "that a dangerous portion of the community was seized with the awful thirst for blood which only killing can quench, and that considerations of law and order were swept away in the overwhelming flood." He concluded that "this lamentable riot was the direct result of opposition to the administration of the law by this Court" (*Shipp*, 414, 425). The dissenters—Justices Peckham, White, and McKenna—were of the view that there was inadequate evidence to support contempt findings against the sheriff and the deputy. Mindful of his role in instigating the contempt proceedings, newly appointed Justice Moody did not participate in the Court's deliberations. Holmes felt that Shipp deserved imprisonment for one year, but his recommendation did not prevail. Shipp and his deputy were sentenced to ninety days in the District of Columbia jail, and the other defendants received lesser sentences. These punishments seem trivial to modern eyes. But Fuller and his colleagues were making an extraordinary use of the contempt power of the federal judiciary to reach offenses that were otherwise outside normal legal proceedings. Although it was prompted in large part by a desire to vindicate the authority of the Court, Fuller's firm stand helped to publicize the unsavory practice of lynching at a time when many government bodies looked the other way. As one recent study has concluded:

> The Court's courage in taking punitive action against a politically popular Southern sheriff was a significant step in the maturity of jurisprudence in America. This case occurred at a time when lynch law dominated the entire South. . . . the contempt proceeding against Shipp was the only proactive step the U.S. Supreme Court has ever taken to combat mob rule directly and demand that the public respect its authority and the authority of the written law. (Curriden and Phillips 1999, 347–348)

American Indians

During the late nineteenth century the exceptional legal status of Native Americans perplexed policymakers. In 1887 Congress halted the practice of entering into treaties with Indian nations and asserted direct control of Indian territory by statutes. Rejecting the reservation approach, Congress attempted to compel eventual assimilation of Indians into society at large with the Dawes Act of 1887. The act sought to break up reservations by allocating land to individual Indians. It was hoped that Indians would in time adjust to the notion of individual property ownership rather than cling to traditional communal arrangements. Surplus reservation land, not selected by individual Indians, was made available to non-Indian settlers. Yet the view persisted that Native Americans constituted a distinct cultural group that could not be readily integrated.

The Fuller Court did not play a significant role in determining Indian affairs. Fuller and his colleagues consistently stressed the dependent condition of Native Americans and the plenary authority of Congress over them. They adhered to the view that Indians were neither aliens nor citizens but members of distinct political communities. The attitude of the Fuller Court toward the legal status of Indians was best exemplified by the leading case of *Lone Wolf v. Hitchcock* (1903). At issue was the federal government's disposal of vast acreage of "surplus" tribal lands in what is now Oklahoma. Tribal leaders charged that the government's action both violated treaty provisions requiring tribal approval before the disposition of any land and amounted to a deprivation of property protected by the Due Process Clause of the Fifth Amendment. Brushing aside these contentions, Justice White denied that the treaty created any property rights. On the contrary, he insisted: "Plenary authority over the tribal relations of the Indians has been exercised by Congress from the beginning, and the power has always been deemed a political one, not subject to be controlled by the judicial department of the government" (*Lone Wolf*, 565). White ruled that Congress could abrogate treaty provisions and exercise unfettered control of Indian lands. The Court, he further announced, would presume good faith on the part of Congress in dealing with Indians. White suggested that Indians should address any complaints to Congress. Although Justice Harlan felt that Indians had been badly treated by the government, he agreed that they had become in effect wards of the United States. Accordingly, he concurred without opinion in *Lone Wolf*.

The *Lone Wolf* decision helped to inaugurate an era of near-total congressional power over Indian affairs. It allowed the government to appropriate Indian lands without tribal consent. The government could then ignore treaty provisions and convey such land to non-Indians. The ruling in *Lone Wolf* strengthened the allotment program as the basis of federal Indian policy. Unlike other Fuller Court opinions concerning racial minorities, *Lone Wolf* has retained a good deal of vitality. Congressional authority over Indian matters has been narrowed somewhat, but the federal government maintains pervasive control to the present.

Although Fuller and his colleagues declined to review congressional Indian policy, they were willing to interpret particular treaties in a manner supportive of Indian claims. There was frequent litigation before the Court calling for an interpretation of treaties with Indian tribes. In *Jones v. Meehan* (1899) the justices held that property rights of individual Indians specifically conferred by treaty could not be subsequently divested by Congress. Justice Horace Gray, writing for the Court, mirrored the ethnocentric outlook of the era. He declared that Indians "are a weak and dependent people, who have no written language and are wholly unfamiliar with all the forms of legal expression" (*Jones* 1899, 11). Because the Indians were at a disadvantage in negotiations with the government, Gray insisted that "the treaty must therefore be construed, not according to the technical meaning of its words to learned lawyers, but in the sense in which they would naturally be understood by the Indians" (*Jones*, 11). This ruling helped to establish the principle that ambiguous treaty provisions should be resolved liberally in favor of Indians.

Chinese Immigrants

Chinese immigrants were another minority group that did not fare well before the Fuller Court. In a series of cases the justices broadly affirmed the authority of Congress over immigration policy and the status of aliens. Lured by the prospect of employment in mining and railroad construction, many Chinese laborers arrived on the West Coast in the mid-nineteenth century. But in time fear of competition for jobs and concern about the assimilation of immigrants from China fueled virulent anti-Chinese sentiment in the western states. In 1882 Congress suspended the immigration of Chinese laborers for ten years. Supplementary legislation in 1888 prevented Chinese laborers who left the United States from returning, even if they had certificates of identity entitling them to reenter the country. The 1888 act directly contravened treaty provisions between the United States and China.

In the *Chinese Exclusion Case* (1889) a detained Chinese laborer sought a writ of habeas corpus. He assailed the 1888 act as a violation of existing treaties and statutory provisions and asserted that he had a vested right to return. Rejecting this argument, the justices unanimously decided that Congress had the power to abrogate treaty stipulations by enacting inconsistent legislation. Justice Field, who wrote for the Court, explained that the restrictions on Chinese immigration "have been caused by a well-founded apprehension—from the experience of years—that a limitation to the immigration of certain classes from China was essential to the peace of the community on the Pacific Coast, and possibly to the preservation of our civilization there" (*Exclusion Case*, 594). Field also stated that the power to exclude foreigners was inherent in national sovereignty. He suggested that returning Chinese laborers could seek redress from the political arms of government.

Congress further tightened the prohibition on Chinese immigrants with an 1892 act mandating that Chinese laborers living in the United States register and obtain a certificate of residence from federal treasury officials. Administrators were given broad discretion to determine whether an applicant was eligible for a certificate. Chinese laborers who failed to secure such a certificate were subject to summary deportation by a federal judge. By a 6–3 vote the Court in *Fong Yue Ting v. United States* (1893) insisted that aliens resided in the country under the absolute authority of Congress to expel them whenever it deemed their removal necessary. Justice Gray, who often spoke for the Court in the Chinese immigration cases of the 1890s, wrote the majority opinion. Fuller, Brewer, and Field, writing separate opinions, strongly dissented. They argued that resident aliens were protected by the

Constitution against deportation without due process of law. Fuller eloquently declared,

> No euphemism can disguise the character of the act in this regard. It directs the performance of a judicial function in a particular way, and inflicts punishment without a judicial trial. It is, in effect, a legislative sentence of banishment, and, as such, absolutely void. Moreover, it contains within it the germs of the assertion of an unlimited and arbitrary power, in general, incompatible with the immutable principles of justice, inconsistent with the nature of our government, and in conflict with the written Constitution by which that government was created and those principles secured. (*Fong Yue Ting*, 763)

As these dissents made clear, the concerns of Fuller, Brewer, and Field for protecting liberty were not confined to economic rights. Still, the majority in *Fong Yue Ting* rejected the due process claims of Chinese immigrants and endorsed the exclusionary policy of Congress.

The citizenship of children born to Chinese aliens living in the United States also became a contentious issue. Congress had previously declared that Chinese immigrants were ineligible to become citizens by naturalization. The application of the Citizenship Clause of the Fourteenth Amendment to the children of Chinese parents who were excluded from naturalization came before the Fuller Court in *United States v. Wong Kim Ark* (1898). A majority of six, in an opinion by Justice Gray, determined that all persons born in the United States of parents of Chinese descent became citizens at birth. It followed that no act of Congress could abridge citizenship acquired as a birthright under the Fourteenth Amendment. The path-breaking *Wong Kim Ark* decision demonstrated that there were limits to the Supreme Court's deference to the will of Congress concerning the status of Chinese aliens. For the first time it was recognized that some persons of Chinese ancestry were citizens.

In a lengthy dissenting opinion Fuller, joined by Harlan, argued that citizenship was not acquired simply by birth within the geographic limits of the country. He contended that the children of aliens who owed allegiance to their native countries were not "subject to the jurisdiction" of the United States within the meaning of the Fourteenth Amendment.

The voting pattern of two key members of the Fuller Court in Chinese immigration cases warrants comment. Contrary to his historical image as a defender of civil rights, Justice Harlan never showed much sympathy for the constitutional claims of Chinese immigrants. He personally doubted that the Chinese could be assimilated into American society and consistently sustained the power of Congress to exclude them. Justice Brewer, in contrast, was favorably disposed toward equal treatment of blacks but felt constrained in expressing such views from the bench. He emerged, however, as the most stalwart champion of the rights of Chinese immigrants on the

Fuller Court. J. Gordon Hylton has explained: "The roots of Brewer's sympathetic attitude toward the Chinese probably lay in his missionary heritage and in his long-standing concern for world peace and the fear that the United States immigration policy might severely damage its relationship with China" (Hylton 1991, 349, n. 129). Dissenting in *United States v. Sing Tuck* (1904), Brewer soberly warned:

> Finally, let me say that the time has been when many young men from China came to our educational institutions to pursue their studies, when her commerce sought our shores, and her people came to build our railroads, and when China looked upon this country as her best friend. If all this be reversed and the most populous nation on earth becomes the great antagonist of this republic, the careful student of history will recall the words of Scripture, "they have sown the wind, and they shall reap the whirlwind," and for the cause of such antagonism need look no further than the treatment accorded during the last twenty years by this country to the people of that nation. (*Sing Tuck*, 182)

Criminal Justice

The administration of criminal justice did not occupy a prominent spot in the jurisprudence of the Fuller Court. The most salient reason for this was the Court's commitment to federalism. The justices steadfastly refused to extend the procedural guarantees of the Bill of Rights to the states, and they permitted states tremendous autonomy over the criminal process. Consequently, state courts remained the main agencies of criminal justice and the primary protectors of the rights of the accused. These states' rights doctrines rested on interpretations of the Constitution established before Fuller became chief, and the Court under his direction continued in a path marked by its predecessors. Yet in federal prosecutions Fuller and his colleagues often placed a broad construction on provisions in the Bill of Rights. By the late nineteenth century there were in effect two distinct systems of criminal justice operating in the United States. It is therefore instructive to treat separately the Fuller Court's review of state and federal criminal proceedings.

State Criminal Process

Criminal defendants frequently argued that the Privileges and Immunities Clause or the Due Process Clause of the Fourteenth Amendment embraced at least some of the guarantees of the Bill of Rights. Throughout Fuller's tenure, however, the majority of the justices resisted nationalization of the Bill of Rights and respected state sovereignty over the criminal justice system. As a result, the states were at liberty to modify traditional criminal procedures, experiment with different methods of prosecution, and institute new modes of punishment. This deferential attitude was reflected in *O'Neil v. Vermont* (1892), in which the Fuller Court, over dissents by Justices Field, Harlan, and Brewer, made clear that the prohibition against cruel and unusual punishments contained in the Eighth Amendment did not apply to the states. It upheld a severe sentence imposed on John O'Neil, a New York liquor dealer, for selling alcoholic beverages to customers in Vermont in violation of that state's prohibition laws. The dissenters, however, argued that by virtue of the Fourteenth Amendment citizens were protected against state imposition of cruel and unusual punishments.

Attempts by the states to revamp cumbersome criminal proceedings gave rise to allegations that procedural innovations violated the Bill of Rights. For instance, in *Maxwell v. Dow* (1900) a defendant attacked his conviction for robbery because it was based upon a proceeding by information rather than indictment by a grand jury and because he was tried by a jury of eight members rather than the common law jury of twelve. Dismissing these objections, the Court upheld the conviction by a vote of 8–1. Justice Peckham, who spoke for the Court, adhered to the established view that the Privileges and Immunities Clause of the Fourteenth Amendment did not necessarily include all the rights protected by the Bill of Rights against the federal government. Accordingly, neither a conviction based on information nor a trial before a jury of only eight members abridged the defendant's privileges and immunities. Peckham also took the position that trial by jury was not a requisite element of due process of law. Rather, states could decide for themselves the form of procedure in criminal trials. Showing his confidence in state administration of criminal justice, Peckham declared that "there can be no just fear that the liberties of the citizen will not be carefully protected by the States respectively. It is a case of self-protection, and the people can be trusted to look out and care for themselves" (*Maxwell*, 605).

Likewise, the Supreme Court held in *West v. Louisiana* (1904) that the Sixth Amendment right to confront witnesses did not apply to proceedings in state courts. The justices pointed out that the states could control criminal trials subject only to the general constitutional prohibition against depriving a defendant of liberty without due process of law. The Court found that the due process requirement did not encompass the right of an accused in state court to confront the witnesses against him.

The strong deference accorded state criminal process extended to the punishment of crime. Writing for a unanimous Court in *In re Kemmler* (1890), Fuller upheld New York's switch from hanging to electrocution as the mode of execution. Rejecting a due process argument almost out of hand, the chief justice observed: "Punishments are cruel when they involve torture or a lingering death; but the punishment of death is not cruel, within the meaning of that word as used in the Constitution. It implies there is something inhuman and barbarous, something more than the mere extinguishment of life" (*Kemmler*, 447). Since the state legislature determined that electrocution was not a cruel punishment, Fuller could find no deprivation of due process of law. Moreover, in *McElvaine v. Brush* (1891) the justices sustained a law mandating that persons awaiting execution be held in solitary confinement until death was inflicted. Likewise, the Fuller Court in *Moore v. Missouri* (1895) validated habitual offender laws under which states imposed a more severe punishment on persons previously convicted of an offense.

Fuller and his colleagues put a stamp of approval on state immunity statutes that compelled witnesses to give possibly incriminating testimony under a grant of immunity from prosecution. In *Jack v. Kansas* (1905) the Court voted 7–2 to uphold a contempt conviction for failure to answer questions propounded as part of a state antitrust investigation. Brushing aside as a remote possibility the defendant's objection that an answer might incriminate him as a violator of federal law, the majority saw no deprivation of liberty without due process.

To be sure, the Fuller Court insisted that state authority over criminal procedure was not final. The justices reiterated the principle, initially set forth in *Hurtado v. California* (1884), that under the Due Process Clause no state could interfere with "those fundamental principles of liberty and justice which lie at the base of all our civil and political institutions" (*Hurtado*, 535). This formula left open the question of which of the rights enumerated in the Bill of Rights were deemed fundamental principles. But experience demonstrated that Fuller and his associates were reluctant to conclude that any of the provisions of the Bill of Rights were binding on state criminal process.

Only Justice Harlan consistently maintained that the purpose of the Due Process Clause of the Fourteenth Amendment was to impose on the states the restrictions in the Bill of Rights. Dissenting in case after case, Harlan called for nationalization of the rights of the accused. He tellingly highlighted a seeming inconsistency in the Court's interpretation of the Due Process Clause. Harlan asked how the majority could reconcile the holding in *Chicago, Burlington, and Quincy Railroad Co. v. Chicago* (1897) that just compensation for property taken was guaranteed by due process with the line of decisions that due process did not include the procedural protections in the Bill of Rights. He complained that "it would seem that the protection of private property is of more consequence than the protection of the life and liberty of the citizen" (*Maxwell*, 614). In short, the Fuller Court was more inclined to see the security of property ownership, not the rights of criminal defendants, as a fundamental principle of justice protected by due process.

Late in Fuller's tenure, however, the Supreme Court gingerly intimated that some provisions of the Bill of Rights might be effective against the states. At issue in *Twining v. New Jersey* (1908) was a state trial judge's negative comment on a defendant's failure to testify in a criminal trial. The Supreme Court, by an 8–1 margin, ruled that the Fifth Amendment's privilege of immunity against self-incrimination was not an essential principle of liberty encompassed in the concept of due process. In reaching this conclusion, the justices rejected a historical understanding of the Due Process Clause. Such an approach, Justice William H. Moody worried, would fasten ancient common law procedures "upon the American jurisprudence like a straight-jacket" (*Twining*, 101). Again indicating the priorities of the Fuller Court, he commented that the privilege against self-incrimination "cannot be ranked with . . . the inviolability of private property" (*Twining*, 113). Yet Moody ambiguously suggested that "it is possible that some of the personal rights safeguarded against National action may also be safeguarded against state action, because a denial of them would be a denial of due process of law" (*Twining*, 99). The Court, he said, would determine what rights were included in the notion of due process in the course of its future decisions. The implications of *Twining* would not be realized until long after Fuller's death, but the case raised the possibility that the Due Process Clause could be read to encompass some of the provisions of the Bill of Rights. Consistent with his view that the Fourteenth Amendment nationalized the Bill of Rights, Justice Harlan dissented. The *Twining* decision was reversed in *Malloy v. Hogan* (1964), in which the Warren Court ruled that the states were bound by the Fifth Amendment's privilege against self-incrimination.

Federal Criminal Process

Contrary to their hands-off attitude toward state criminal process, the justices gave defendants in federal prosecutions the full protection of the Bill of Rights. Before Fuller's tenure the Supreme Court had little opportunity to interpret the scope of procedural guarantees of the Bill of Rights. Until the late nineteenth century the Supreme Court had no general appellate jurisdiction over federal criminal cases. When in 1889 and 1891 Congress enlarged the right of criminal defendants in federal cases to appeal to the Supreme Court, the justices began for the first time to systematically address criminal procedure guarantees. Alert to safeguarding individual liberties against the federal government, Fuller and his colleagues generally adopted a generous understanding of the rights afforded criminal defendants. The Court may have been influenced in this direction by the fact that some of the leading cases under review grew out of investigations into business practices.

This tendency can be seen in *Counselman v. Hitchcock* (1892), in which the Supreme Court broadly construed the Fifth Amendment privilege against self-incrimination. The case arose when a witness called to testify in a grand jury investigation into alleged violations of the Interstate Commerce Act declined to answer questions and invoked the Fifth Amendment. Justice Blatchford delivered a unanimous opinion holding that the purpose of the self-incrimination provision was to "insure that a person should not be compelled, when acting as a witness in any investigation, to give testimony which might show that he himself had committed a crime" (*Counselman*,

562). Blatchford emphasized that the Fifth Amendment privilege applied not only to criminal trials but to any official proceeding. Nor was the Court impressed by the government's reliance on a federal immunity statute. Finding that the statute afforded no protection from the use of compelled testimony to locate other evidence of a crime, Blatchford declared that a valid immunity statute must offer "absolute immunity against future prosecution for the offence to which the question relates" (*Counselman*, 586).

Although the decision was an important victory for civil liberty, the practical effect of *Counselman* was to hamper federal investigations of illegal business activity. A year later Congress enacted a new and more comprehensive immunity statute covering Interstate Commerce Commission inquiries. In *Brown v. Walker* (1896) the Fuller Court voted 5–4 to sustain contempt convictions for failure to answer questions under the new law. The majority, in an opinion by Justice Brown, brushed aside the objection that the witness was imperfectly protected because he might by virtue of his disclosure be subject to prosecution in state courts. Insisting that Congress could not by statute divest a person of his constitutional right not to be a witness against himself, the dissenters, in opinions by Justices Shiras and Field, were skeptical that the immunity legislation was an adequate substitute for the Fifth Amendment guarantee. Following *Brown*, federal as well as state statutes granting immunity to witnesses would become common.

The Fuller Court again contended with the privilege against self-incrimination in *Hale v. Henkel* (1906). Speaking for the majority, Justice Brown ruled that the Fifth Amendment provision was limited to natural persons and did not extend to corporations. It followed that a federal grand jury could compel a corporate official to produce business documents relating to possible antitrust violations and that the official could not raise the criminality of the corporations as a defense to a subpoena.

Moreover, in *Hale* the Court established a second important principle of law. Drawing a distinction between the Fourth and Fifth Amendments, the justices ruled that corporations were entitled to protection under the Fourth Amendment against unreasonable searches and seizures. In so doing they stressed the vital place of corporate enterprise in American life: "Corporations are a necessary feature of modern business activity, and their aggregated capital has become the source of nearly all great enterprises" (*Hale*, 76). The Court then concluded that the subpoena at issue was too sweeping to be regarded as reasonable. Justices Brewer and Fuller, in dissent, insisted that corporations were protected by both amendments. The different conclusion with respect to the applicability of the Fourth and Fifth Amendments to corporations is not readily explainable. Indeed, the justices offered no rationale for their position. One may speculate that the Court's reading of the Fourth Amendment was prompted in part by a desire to safeguard corporate property rights. But this consideration would have also pertained to the self-incrimination rights of corporations.

Perhaps the *Hale* opinion reflects an unspoken balance between the needs of law enforcement and the legitimate interests of corporations in protecting their records against overly broad subpoenas. In any event, the Fuller Court's line between the Fourth and Fifth Amendment rights of corporations, however unsatisfactory, has proved to be an enduring feature of constitutional jurisprudence.

In other areas as well the Fuller Court moved to protect criminal defendants by giving an expanded meaning to the Bill of Rights. The justices dealt with the Eighth Amendment's ban on cruel and unusual punishments in *Weems v. United States* (1910), a case that originated in the Philippine Islands. Convicted of falsifying public documents, the defendant was sentenced under Philippine law to a heavy fine, fifteen years in prison at hard labor in chains, and perpetual loss of civil liberties. This draconian punishment, derived from the Spanish penal code, remained in effect following acquisition of the Philippines by the United States. The central issue for the Court was whether the prohibition against cruel and unusual punishments applied to the severity of the penalty in relation to the offense. Justice McKenna, who delivered the opinion for a plurality of the Court consisting of Fuller, Harlan, and William R. Day, adopted as a precept of constitutional law that "punishment for crime should be graduated and proportioned to [the] offense" (*Weems*, 367). Rejecting a historical interpretation of the Eighth Amendment, McKenna asserted that the ban on cruel punishments "is not fastened to the obsolete but may acquire meaning as public opinion becomes enlightened by a humane justice" (*Weems*, 378). Justices White and Holmes, dissenting, complained that the majority was limiting legislative authority to define and punish crime. The case had been argued before only seven justices, and Justice Brewer died before the matter was decided.

Between 1893 and 1896 the Fuller Court heard a series of appeals arising from frequent imposition of the death penalty by Issac C. Parker, a federal district court judge. Judge Parker had jurisdiction over crimes committed in the Indian Territory (now Oklahoma), unquestionably a turbulent region. He sentenced eighty-eight defendants to be executed, more than any other judge in American history. The Fuller Court, troubled by Parker's proprosecution sympathies and zeal for the death penalty, reversed a high percentage of his capital sentences that it reviewed. Many of these cases involved claims of self-defense. The Court not only affirmed this right but took the position that there was no absolute duty to retreat before using force in self-defense. The frustration that Fuller and his colleagues felt about Judge Parker was manifest in *Allison v. United States* (1906). Writing for a unanimous bench, Fuller found that Parker's jury charge regarding self-defense was erroneous, and he pointedly condemned Parker's "animated argument" and "forensic ardor," which left the jury "without proper instructions" (*Allison*, 217).

The Fuller Court's dealings with Judge Parker produced another important legacy, the so-called *Allen*, or dynamite, charge given to deadlocked juries. In *Allen v.*

United States (1896) the justices unanimously sustained a jury instruction by Parker that jurors in the minority should doubt the reasonableness of their judgment since the majority disagreed. The *Allen* charge, then, urges minority jurors to reconsider their position in light of the fact that the majority had reached the opposite conclusion. Although the *Allen* charge has been criticized as inherently coercive and calculated to encourage convictions, many trial courts still rely on it to motivate a divided jury to reach a verdict.

The respective functions of judge and jury in criminal cases were a matter of dispute during the nineteenth century. In some jurisdictions the jury had the right to determine the law as well as the facts. But in *Sparf and Hansen v. United States* (1895) the Fuller Court emphatically rejected this approach and stressed that juries in federal criminal trials must follow the judge's instructions as to the law. The jury was just to apply the law, as declared by the trial court, to the facts. "Public and private safety alike would be in peril," Justice Harlan reasoned, "if the principle be established that juries in criminal cases may, of right, disregard the law as expounded to them by the court and become a law unto themselves" (*Sparf and Hansen*, 101).

Foreign Affairs

Foreign relations occupied an increasingly significant place in American public life following the Spanish-American War of 1898, and the resulting acquisition of overseas territories raised contentious political and legal issues. Consequently, the Supreme Court under Fuller was called upon to resolve numerous disputes pertaining to foreign policy. These rulings tended to strengthen the authority of the executive branch and Congress over relations with foreign nations.

This inclination was demonstrated by *Geofroy v. Riggs* (1890), in which a unanimous Court gave a muscular reading to the treaty power. The case involved the right of French citizens to inherit land in the District of Columbia. Justice Field, for the Court, construed a treaty with France as modifying the common law doctrine that prevented aliens from inheriting land. He broadly declared that the treaty power "extends to all proper subjects of negotiation between our government and the governments of other nations" (*Geofroy*, 266). Field intimated that Congress might by treaty provision accomplish results that it could not achieve directly through legislation. The outcome in *Geofroy* set the stage for expansion of the treaty power following Fuller's tenure.

Fuller and his associates also confronted a group of prize cases arising from the Spanish-American War. In most instances the justices upheld the maritime seizure of Spanish vessels as prizes of war. But in the leading case of *The Paquete Habana* (1900) the Supreme Court ruled that the federal government was bound by the rules of international law that exempted coastal fishing ships from seizure. Writing for a majority of six, Justice Gray formulated a much quoted proposition:

> International law is part of our law, and must be ascertained and administered by the courts of justice of appropriate jurisdiction, as often as questions of right depending upon it are duly presented for their determination. For this purpose, where there is no treaty, and no controlling executive or legislative act or judicial decision, resort must be had to the customs and usages of civilized nations. (*Pacquete Habana*, 700)

He qualified the binding effect of customary international law, however, by stating that courts should apply international law in the absence of any federal statute that mandated a different result. Fuller, writing for the dissent, denied that there was "any such established rule" exempting fishing vessels and called for deference to the president's decisions in carrying on war. Notwithstanding Fuller's protest, the *Paquete Habana* decision was a milestone in the recognition of customary international law as part of the law of the United States.

The acquisition of Puerto Rico and the Philippines following the war with Spain sparked an intense but short-lived debate concerning the emergence of the United States as an imperial power. Previous territorial acquisitions had been made with the implicit understanding that they would eventually become states. But the new possessions were not contiguous to the United States and were already populated by persons with racial and cultural backgrounds different from those of most Americans. Imperialists espoused the position that the United States was simply fulfilling its destiny as a great nation and that the federal government had ample authority to dominate and govern overseas territories. In contrast, anti-imperialists condemned the idea that the United States could legitimately hold overseas possessions as colonies. They pictured colonial rule as a betrayal of the principles of the Declaration of Independence and insisted that "the Constitution follows the flag." The status of the new possessions therefore raised basic questions about the nature of American constitutionalism.

Congressional legislation establishing governments for Puerto Rico and the Philippines gave rise to a group of some fourteen decisions, known as the *Insular Cases*, in which the Supreme Court wrestled with the constitutional relationship of these territories to the United States. The *Insular Cases* presented three core issues: (1) whether the United States could acquire new possessions by treaty; (2) whether Congress could govern the new territories as it saw fit; and (3) whether the Bill of Rights applied to the inhabitants of these territories. Decided between 1901 and 1904, the *Insular Cases* highlighted the sharp divisions that characterized both popular and judicial attitudes. These cases also marked a disappointment for Fuller because he was unable to persuade a majority of the Court to adopt his views.

In *DeLima v. Bidwell* (1901) the Court concluded, in an opinion by Justice Brown, that the United States had the authority to acquire new lands. The justices experienced more difficulty in deciding whether goods brought into the United States from Puerto Rico after ratification of the peace treaty were subject to import duties. Resolution of this issue turned upon whether Puerto Rico was a foreign country for purposes of tariff laws. By a 5–4 vote the Court determined that when the United States established control over Puerto Rico the island ceased to be a foreign country. The sharp division among the justices on this point foreshadowed continuing controversy over the legal status of the overseas territories.

The Fuller Court again tackled this question in *Downes v. Bidwell* (1901), the most important of the *Insular Cases*. At issue was the constitutionality of the Foraker Act of 1900, which established a civil government for Puerto Rico and levied a duty on imports from the island. The measure was challenged as a violation of the constitutional requirement that duties be "uniform throughout the United States." A majority of five sustained the statute, but they differed widely in the reasoning that led to their conclusion. Describing Puerto Rico as "a territory appurtenant and belonging to the United States" but not part of the United States for revenue purposes, Justice Brown delivered the judgment of the Court but spoke only for himself. He ruled that Congress had broad power to determine the status of annexed possessions. "The Constitution," Brown emphasized, "was created by the people of the *United States*, as a union of *States*, to be governed solely by representatives of the *States*" (*Downes*, 287, 251). Reflecting the influence of the imperialistic spirit, Brown spoke in terms of "alien races" and "Anglo-Saxon principles." Still, he stopped short of allowing Congress unfettered authority over the overseas territories. Brown indicated that "certain natural rights enforced in the Constitution," including religious freedom, "the right to personal liberty and individual property," and freedom of speech, restrained the power of Congress in dealing with territorial inhabitants (*Downes*, 282).

Justice White rejected Brown's analysis and, in his influential concurring opinion, joined by Justices Shiras and McKenna, provided a separate justification for sustaining congressional authority. After a lengthy review of history, White asserted that constitutional protections applied to a territory only after the territory had been "incorporated" by Congress into the United States. White was unclear as to how incorporation was to be achieved, but he maintained that it did not occur "until in the wisdom of Congress it is deemed that the acquired territory had reached that state where it is proper that it should enter into and form a part of the American family" (*Downes*, 339). Since no congressional action appeared to incorporate Puerto Rico, he felt that the political status of the inhabitants was a matter for Congress. Justice Gray concurred separately. According to the fragmented majority, then, the Constitution did not necessarily extend by its own force to the newly acquired possessions.

The residents of these territories were left in a sort of constitutional limbo, largely subject to the control of Congress.

Speaking for the four dissenters—Justices Brewer, Peckham, Harlan, and himself—Fuller stressed that under the Constitution Congress possessed only enumerated powers. In Fuller's view Congress had no authority to govern territories according to different rules from those pertaining in the United States. He justifiably derided Justice White's concept of incorporation "as if possessed of some occult meaning" and argued that in any event, by passing the Foraker Act, Congress had accepted Puerto Rico as part of the United States (*Downes*, 373). The dissenters concluded that the Foraker Act's import levy was unconstitutional as a violation of the Uniformity Clause. Fuller's dissent was consistent with his propensity to construe strictly the powers of Congress, as well as his distrust of unrestricted legislative authority. In addition, as a Democrat, he was no doubt influenced by that party's anti-imperialist stance.

Notwithstanding the opinion of the chief justice, a majority of his colleagues adopted White's incorporation theory as law in *Dorr v. United States* (1904). Fred Dorr was convicted of libel in the Philippines after a trial without a jury. He challenged his conviction on grounds that the Sixth Amendment guarantee of trial by jury was applicable to the Philippines. Dismissing this argument, Justice Day, speaking for the majority, declared that territories were governed by Congress until they were incorporated into the United States. Reflecting the prevalent imperialist attitude, Day maintained that Congress was not constitutionally required to provide trial by jury:

> If the right to trial by jury were a fundamental right which goes wherever the jurisdiction of the United States extends, or if Congress, in framing laws for outlying territory belonging to the United States, was obliged to establish that system by affirmative legislation, it would follow that, no matter what the needs or capacities of the people, trial by jury, and in no other way, must be forthwith established, although the result may be to work injustice and provoke disturbance rather than to aid the orderly administration of justice. If the United States, impelled by its duty or advantage, shall acquire territory peopled by savages, and of which it may dispose or not hold for ultimate admission to Statehood, if this doctrine is sound, it must establish there the trial by jury. To state such a proposition demonstrates the impossibility of carrying it into practice. (*Dorr*, 148)

Three justices, including Fuller, concurred in result but again declined to accept the incorporation theory. Only Justice Harlan insisted that the right to a jury trial was fundamental in nature and was guaranteed by the Constitution to all inhabitants of the newly acquired possessions.

In the spate of *Insular Cases* the Supreme Court placed its imprimatur on the imperialist policy of overseas expansion. Although they were plagued by division and cloudy analysis, the justices moved in step with dominant public opinion and confirmed congressional authority over the annexed territories. In 1900 the voters had overwhelmingly rejected the anti-imperialist appeal of the Democrats. As the fictional humorist Mr. Dooley, created by journalist Finley Peter Dunne, colorfully observed, "No matter whether th' constitution follows th' flag or not, th' supreme court follows th' illection returns." Aside from these political considerations, the debate over the application of the Bill of Rights to the overseas territories paralleled similar questions about extending federally guaranteed rights to the states.

The Fuller Court also upheld the power of Congress to construct the Panama Canal. In *Wilson v. Shaw* (1907) a taxpayer sought to enjoin the secretary of the treasury from disbursing money for canal purposes. The case had marked political overtones because it called into question the actions of the president and Congress in acquiring the Canal Zone. Fuller and his associates had no difficulty in unanimously dismissing the action. Justice Brewer, writing for the Court, noted that under the Commerce Clause Congress was empowered to build highways and canals within ceded territory. He insisted that the Court had "no supervising control over the political branch of the Government in its action within the limits of the Constitution" (*Wilson*, 32).

Constitutional Polity

By the late nineteenth century the needs of a changing and more complex society posed novel challenges to established modes of governance. As the federal government slowly expanded in size and function, the Supreme Court was called upon to adjudicate the constitutional boundaries of the political branches and police the separation of powers. In addition, the notion of divided sovereignty inherent in federalism produced recurring clashes between claims of states' rights and federal authority. Under Fuller's leadership the Supreme Court began to take a more active role in determining structural developments and defining governmental power. In addressing these matters the justices engaged in a searching examination of constitutional procedures and institutions. There was often intense conflict between traditional values and the perceived needs of the emerging social order. Pulled by contrary forces, the Fuller Court found it difficult to formulate tidy solutions to perplexing governmental and jurisdictional issues. Although they were committed to federalism and respect for state autonomy, Fuller and his associates strengthened the power of the federal judiciary to review state legislation.

Separation of Powers

The Constitution vests all legislative authority in Congress. By the late nineteenth century, however, Congress began increasingly to delegate discretionary power to the executive branch. Obviously neither Congress nor the courts could provide detailed oversight, which necessitated a host of small decisions. The Supreme Court under Fuller recognized that legislators could not anticipate every contingency and in two early administrative law cases sustained the delegation of legislative power. In so doing, it facilitated the rise of the administrative state in which substantial lawmaking authority is exercised by the president and administrative agencies.

The willingness of Congress to grant the executive branch discretion to make regulations came before the Fuller Court in *Field v. Clark* (1892). The case involved a challenge to the reciprocity provision of the 1890 tariff, which empowered the president to suspend the free importation of certain goods from any country if he deemed the duties imposed by that nation on American products to be unreasonable. The retaliatory tariff was to be in effect as long as the president thought just. The Court, in an opinion by Justice Harlan, sustained the measure by a vote of 7–2. Paying lip service to the separation of powers doctrine, the majority declared: "That Congress cannot delegate legislative power to the President is a principle universally recognized as vital to the integrity and maintenance of the system of government ordained by the Constitution" (*Field*, 692). But the Court denied that the president was making law. Instead, the majority asserted that he was "the mere agent of the law-making department to ascertain the existence of specific facts and act in obedience to congressional directive" (*Field*, 693). This fiction opened the door for broader delegations of the lawmaking function. In their dissent, Justice Lucius Q. C. Lamar and Chief Justice Fuller charged that Congress had improperly delegated to the president the power to impose duties upon his own discretion. The decision in *Field* became the foundation for subsequent rulings upholding statutes that conferred wide regulatory authority upon executive departments.

A more comprehensive transfer of legislative power to the executive branch was sustained in *Butterfield v. Stranahan* (1904). Under the Tea Inspection Act of 1897, a board appointed by the secretary of the treasury was authorized to establish quality standards for imported teas. An importer attacked the constitutionality of the statute on grounds that, as a practical matter, it vested legislative power to make law in the executive. A unanimous Court concluded that Congress determined to exclude unwholesome tea and merely delegated to the secretary an executive duty to carry out the policy declared in the statute. "Congress legislated on the subject as far as was reasonably practicable," Justice White remarked for the Court, "and from the necessities of the case was compelled to leave the executive officials the duty of bringing about the result pointed out by the statute" (*Butterfield*, 496). By the end of Fuller's term, therefore, the justices had accepted the delegation of a large amount of discretionary authority to the executive. This approach weakened the separation of powers doctrine and enlarged the scope of presidential power. It also helped to set the stage for a vast expansion of the administrative state later in the twentieth century.

Federalism

Considerations of federalism permeated the jurisprudence of the Fuller Court. As we have seen, federalism figured prominently in the Court's handling of economic issues, race relations, and criminal justice. Fuller and his colleagues also wrestled with the allocation of power between the federal government and the states in a variety of other contexts. Many of these cases dealt directly with the extent of federal judicial power over the states.

Embodying states' rights sentiment, the Eleventh Amendment was framed to protect state authority from the national courts. The amendment deprives the federal courts of jurisdiction over suits against a state by residents of other states. Since its adoption in 1798 this amendment has given rise to a large amount of litigation and has spawned a baffling set of rules. The Eleventh Amendment posed thorny questions for Fuller and his colleagues.

One cluster of issues concerned suits by creditors in federal courts to recover debts owed by state and local governments. Following the Reconstruction era southern states made a concerted effort to repudiate their bonded debt. The Waite Court, anxious to avoid a direct confrontation with the South, construed the Eleventh Amendment to bar federal judicial relief in suits by nonresident creditors. This line of decisions blocked most efforts to force the southern states to honor their obligations.

At the start of Fuller's tenure the Supreme Court expansively interpreted the Eleventh Amendment to preclude suits against a state by a citizen of that state without its consent. The leading case of *Hans v. Louisiana* (1890) involved a suit in federal court by a resident of Louisiana against his own state for bond interest. He charged that Louisiana was impairing the obligation of contract in violation of the Constitution. Going well beyond the language of the amendment, a unanimous Fuller Court, speaking through Justice Joseph P. Bradley, virtually rewrote it. According to Bradley, the Eleventh Amendment conferred sovereign immunity on the states, thereby preventing residents from suing their own states in federal court. Although cast in jurisdictional terms, the *Hans* decision in effect deprived another group of disappointed creditors from seeking a federal court remedy.

The broad reading of the Eleventh Amendment by the Fuller Court in *Hans* has long been controversial, and some have urged that the decision be reassessed. There are reasons to conclude, however, that *Hans* was a sound ruling at the time when it was rendered. Recall that the Eleventh Amendment had already been interpreted to prevent federal court suits against states by nonresidents. It would have been a curious anomaly if the decision in *Hans* had recognized a federal judicial remedy for residents that nonresidents did not possess. Moreover, *Hans* was a prudential ruling given the political reality that any attempt to coerce the states to pay their debts would likely prove unenforceable. Finally, the Fuller Court clearly expressed its disapproval of contract repudiation by the states. Justice Bradley declared that state legislatures were "called upon by the highest demands of natural and political law . . . to hold inviolate the public obligations," and he warned that any departure from this rule "never fails in the end to incur the odium of the world, and to bring lasting injury upon the state itself" (*Hans*, 21). In short, a state repudiating its debt might well suffer a loss of reputation in credit markets, but there was no remedy for creditors available in the federal courts.

Notwithstanding *Hans*, in other respects the Fuller Court narrowed the reach of the Eleventh Amendment and enlarged the suability of localities and states in federal court. For example, the Court unanimously held in *Lincoln County v. Luning* (1890) that the Eleventh Amendment applied only to suits against states and did not protect political subdivisions from being sued in federal court. Justice Brewer, writing for the Court, directed the defaulting county to honor its bonded obligations. Since, as the Court acknowledged, municipalities and counties are creations of the states, the rationale for the decision in *Lincoln County* is not readily apparent. Yet the ruling can be easily understood in political terms. Judicial pressure on defaulting local governments, many of which were located in sparsely settled western states, did not present the same threat to federal judicial authority as that posed by united southern opposition to the payment of state bonds. The distinction between states and localities for purposes of the Eleventh Amendment has proved durable, if not logical. In addition, the Fuller Court's firm stand on fiscal probity by local government enhanced the credit rating of municipal and county bonds.

In the same spirit, the Fuller Court found the Eleventh Amendment no barrier to a suit by Virginia seeking to allocate one-third of its pre–Civil War debt to West Virginia. After decades of fruitless negotiations Virginia instituted an original action in the Supreme Court to obtain an accounting between the states. West Virginia denied the Supreme Court's jurisdiction to hear the complaint. Speaking for a unanimous Court in *Virginia v. West Virginia* (1907), Fuller observed that the Eleventh Amendment did not comprehend controversies between states. He held that the Supreme Court had jurisdiction over the suit and expressed his confidence that the West Virginia legislature would make adequate provision to satisfy any decree. Fuller did not consider the merits of Virginia's claim, and in 1908 the Court referred the case to a special master. The result was eminently sensible since the Supreme Court was the only tribunal capable of resolving such controversies between states. This was the first in a series of cases between these states concerning allocation of fiscal responsibilities, and the matter was finally resolved after Fuller's death when the Supreme Court coerced payment of West Virginia's share of the debt.

Although Fuller and his associates applied the Eleventh Amendment to monetary suits against states and localities in an uneven fashion, they dramatically strengthened the authority of federal courts to issue injunctions against state officials. After 1890 there was a steady increase of suits instituted in federal courts to prevent state officers from carrying out state laws that allegedly violated the Constitution. The Eleventh Amendment seemingly barred such actions, but the Fuller Court revived an earlier doctrine holding that suits against state officials were not suits against the state. This trend became evident in *Pennoyer v. McConnaughy* (1891), in which the plaintiff sought to enjoin Oregon's land commissioners from conveying certain real property to which the plaintiff claimed title based on prior contractual rights. The defendant commissions asserted that the suit was, in effect, against the state within the meaning of the Eleventh Amendment. Rejecting this contention, the justices, in an opinion by Justice Lamar, unanimously ruled that "an officer of a State may be enjoined from executing a statute of the State which is in conflict with the Constitution of the United States, when such execution would violate and destroy the rights and privileges of the complainant" (*Pennoyer*, 11). The Court also pointed out that the plaintiff was not seeking any affirmative relief against the state. Finding a violation of the Contract Clause, the justices upheld an injunction preventing the defendant officials from selling the land.

Railroad companies promptly took advantage of this jurisdictional development by obtaining federal court injunctions in several cases to restrain enforcement of rates fixed by state commissions on grounds the rate schedules were so low as to be confiscatory. This was a less hazardous means of challenging the constitutionality of statutes than violating laws and running the risk of stiff penalties. The Supreme Court's willingness to entertain injunction suits against state officers was therefore closely linked with the emergence of due process review of rate regulations.

This line of decisions culminated in the landmark case of *Ex Parte Young* (1908). It originated as part of the long struggle over state legislation regulating railroads. A 1907 Minnesota law mandated reductions in passenger and commodity rates and imposed enormous fines and severe criminal penalties on railroads and their agents for violations of the act. The evident purpose of the penalties was to intimidate the railroads and their officers from disregarding the imposed rate schedule and turning to the courts to test the validity of the law. Arguing that the reduced rates were confiscatory and hence infringed the Due Process Clause of the Fourteenth Amendment, railroad stockholders obtained a temporary injunction from the federal trial court prohibiting Edward T. Young, the Minnesota attorney general, from enforcing the act. Young disregarded the injunction by attempting to enforce the new rates in state court. Found guilty of contempt, Young was fined, directed to dismiss the state court proceedings, and jailed until he obeyed the federal court order. Young petitioned the Supreme Court for a writ of habeas corpus. He asserted that the suit was in reality an action against the state in contravention of the Eleventh Amendment.

Speaking for the majority of eight, Justice Peckham found the penalty provisions unconstitutional on their face because they effectively denied resort to the courts. He viewed the severity of the sanction as a deprivation of due process calculated to prevent railroads from violating the law in order to challenge the imposed rates. Peckham then rejected the Eleventh Amendment defense and maintained that a state could not impart to an official any immunity from the paramount authority of the United States. He declared that when a state officer sought to enforce an unconstitutional act "he is in that case stripped of his official or representative character and is subjected in his person to the consequences of his individual conduct" (*Young*, 159–160). The Court's distinction between suits against states and suits against state officers alleged to be acting unconstitutionally rested on a convenient legal fiction that facilitated circumvention of the Eleventh Amendment. Justice Harlan emphasized this point in his solitary dissent. Discarding his usual nationalist stance, Harlan warned that the majority opinion "would work a radical change in our governmental system" and "place the States of the Union in a condition of inferiority" (*Young*, 175). He complained that the decision had practically obliterated the Eleventh Amendment. Harlan's dissent is difficult to square with his earlier Eleventh Amendment opinions and is doubly ironic because in *Smyth v. Ames* (1898) he had articulated the right of fair return for regulated industries that *Ex Parte Young* was intended to protect.

The *Young* case was a milestone in the Fuller Court's transformation of federal judicial power. It provided the jurisdictional counterpart to the Court's oversight of economic legislation. The justices were strongly influenced by their suspicion of state railroad regulation and their desire to safeguard property rights. Justice Peckham explained that a company should not be required to risk heavy fines in order to obtain judicial review of regulatory legislation. Protection of investment capital was a recurring theme for Fuller and his associates. "Over eleven million dollars, it is estimated, are invested in railroad property, owned by many thousands of people who are scattered over the whole country from ocean to ocean," Peckham pointedly observed, "and they are entitled to equal protection from the laws and from the courts, with the owners of all other kinds of property, no more, no less" (*Young*, 165).

Although the *Young* decision aroused a storm of protest from Progressives and champions of states' rights, Congress largely accepted the Court's activist role. To placate critics, in 1910 Congress mandated that injunctions preventing state officials from enforcing allegedly unconstitutional state laws be issued by a three-judge court, but it did not curtail the authority of the Supreme Court. Federal judicial power was fundamentally unchanged. Thus, *Young* established a basic precept of modern Eleventh Amendment law. Indeed, in time the three-judge panels proved cumbersome, and Congress repealed the requirement in 1976. Despite detractors, *Ex Parte Young* has survived because the power to enjoin state officials from violating the Constitution proved essential to maintaining the federal system and safeguarding individual rights.

Besides threading its way through the intricacies of Eleventh Amendment doctrine, the Fuller Court had a variety of other opportunities to delineate the balance between state and federal authority. In an unusual case, *In re Neagle* (1890), the Court expansively construed its power to grant a writ of habeas corpus to a federal marshal arrested under state law. This case arose from a colorful episode in which Justice Field was personally involved. There was long-standing animosity between Field and David S. Terry, Field's former colleague on the California Supreme Court, growing out of Field's handling of a celebrated divorce action concerning a prior marriage of Terry's wife. Because Terry had threatened to kill Field, the attorney general assigned special deputies to protect the justice when he performed circuit-court duty in California in 1889. When Terry attacked Field in a restaurant, deputy David Neagle shot and killed Terry. Neagle was arrested for murder by the California authorities. The federal court promptly granted a writ of habeas corpus releasing Neagle from state custody.

Field recused himself from hearing the appeal, but his strong backing for Neagle was no secret to his fellow justices. Public sentiment also leaned heavily toward Neagle. At issue on the appeal was whether the federal court was authorized to interfere with the state's administration of criminal justice in these circumstances. A federal statute provided that the courts could issue a writ of habeas corpus when a prisoner was detained for an act done "in pursuance of a law of the United States." Although no statute expressly empowered the federal government to protect judicial officers from violence, Justice Samuel F. Miller, writing for a majority of six, interpreted the term *law* to encompass the actions of a federal marshal within the scope of his duties. He emphasized the need to safeguard judges from the malice of disgruntled litigants. Since Neagle was acting under the authority of the United States, Miller declared that he was innocent of any crime against California and could not be tried in the state courts. Justice Lucius Q. C. Lamar, joined by Fuller, dissented. Insisting that the word *law* as used in the habeas corpus act referred only to federal statutes, they complained that the Court was invading state criminal jurisdiction. The dissenters expressed confidence that California courts would have acquitted Neagle. To the majority, however, the power of the federal government to protect its officials outweighed deference to state autonomy.

Fuller and his colleagues also had occasion to pass upon the Compact Clause of the Constitution, which provides that no state shall without the consent of Congress "enter into any agreement or compact" with another state. The important case of *Virginia v. Tennessee* (1893) grew out of a conflict between the two states concerning their boundary. Invoking the original jurisdiction of the Supreme Court, Virginia asked the justices to set aside an 1803 survey accepted by both parties for many years. Virginia asserted that the arrangement was void because it had not been approved by Congress. Justice Field, for a unanimous Court, rejected Virginia's position. He reasoned that the Compact Clause did not apply to every agreement between states. Instead, Congress need approve only those compacts that tended to increase the power of the states and thus to encroach upon federal authority. Field added that approval by Congress did not require formal action but could be implied from subsequent legislation. Because the determination of a boundary had no effect upon political influence, he ruled that the boundary settlement at issue did not require the consent of Congress. Although it did not fit comfortably with the language of the Compact Clause, Field's opinion had two virtues. It harmonized with the Fuller Court's persistent attempts to preserve state autonomy within the federal union, and it relieved Congress of the burden of reviewing every agreement between the states. This pragmatic decision still governs interstate compacts.

The Fuller Court reviewed several other cases under its original jurisdiction that raised far-reaching questions about the constitutional order. In *Kansas v. Colorado* (1907) Kansas sought to enjoin Colorado from diverting water from the Arkansas River for the purpose of reclaiming arid land. Kansas contended that under common law it was entitled to the continuous flow of the water, while Colorado asserted that it had a right to diminish the flow of water for irrigation. The United States intervened in the lawsuit, arguing that the states were subject to the superior right of the federal government to control the reclamation of arid land. The government urged the Court to recognize congressional authority to direct water distribution. Speaking for the Court, Justice Brewer emphasized the limited nature of federal power under the Constitution. He dismissed the contention of the United States on grounds that it contradicted the basic design for a government of enumerated powers. Brewer pointed to the Tenth Amendment as a check on the unwarranted exercise of federal power and observed that the Tenth Amendment should "be considered fairly and liberally so as to give effect to its scope and meaning" (*Kansas* 90–91). It followed that the federal government could not interfere with the allocation of water within a state. Although acknowledging the rights of each state to allocate water internally, Brewer nonetheless refused to apply the water law of either Colorado or Kansas. Rather, he declared that the dispute must be resolved by an application of "interstate common law" to be fashioned by the Court. Noting that the advantages of irrigation in Colorado outweighed the harm to southwestern Kansas, Brewer declined on equitable principles to disturb the existing division of water. The result was a qualified victory for Colorado. However, Brewer warned that greater diversion of water by Colorado might destroy the equitable apportionment between the states and require judicial correction. *Kansas v. Colorado* established that federal common law governed water disputes between states. The opinion had broad implications because the justices effectively elevated the power of the federal courts to handle interstate controversies above congressional authority.

During the same term, the Fuller Court heard another case that had an important bearing on the power of the states to control pollution across state lines. Georgia filed an original action in the Supreme Court seeking to enjoin a corporation located in Tennessee from discharging noxious fumes over Georgia territory. Georgia charged that the air pollution was causing wholesale destruction to forests and crops. There was little dispute about the extent of the damage, so the case turned upon the standing of Georgia to maintain the action. Although the state owned little of the affected land, Justice Holmes, speaking for the Court in *Georgia v. Tennessee Copper Co.* (1907), proclaimed that Georgia had "an interest independent of and behind the titles of its citizens, in all the earth and air within its domain" (*Georgia*, 237). Holmes held that the state in its capacity as quasisovereign had standing to sue on behalf of its citizens, and he ordered that an injunction should be issued. This early environmental case demonstrated again that Fuller and his colleagues were not blind champions of business and that they were prepared to deal with the negative consequences of industrial growth.

Private Litigation

Any analysis of the Fuller Court must take into account the nature of its docket. Unlike the modern Supreme Court, which focuses almost entirely on constitutional questions and the interpretation of federal statutes, the Court during Fuller's era heard a heavy volume of private law disputes involving torts, contracts, property, and corporations. Most of this litigation arose under diversity of citizenship jurisdiction. Another category of private controversies emanated from congressional legislation dealing with railroad safety, bankruptcy, patents, and copyrights. The resolution of these private law cases by Fuller and his colleagues had a direct bearing on the growth of the national economy. Accordingly, a brief study of the Fuller Court's private law decisions is vital in providing a full picture of its work in encouraging economic development and strengthening federal judicial power.

Diversity of Citizenship

Under article III of the Constitution federal judicial power extends to suits between citizens of different states or foreign nations. Reflecting worry about local bias against out-of-state claimants, this jurisdiction was designed to provide a neutral forum for the adjudication of interstate private lawsuits. Thus, diversity jurisdiction gave nonresidents a federal alternative to the state courts. But states' rights advocates were uneasy that a broad federal diversity jurisdiction would overshadow state tribunals. Therefore, the Judiciary Act of 1789 sought to restrain the exercise of diversity jurisdiction. Section 34 of the act required federal courts to follow state laws in cases in which they applied. The Supreme Court did not formulate a definitive interpretation of section 34 until the landmark decision in *Swift v. Tyson* (1842).

There the justices held that the term *laws* referred only to state statutes and that the federal courts, in dealing with contracts and commercial instruments, were free to resolve cases in accord with general principles of commercial law in the absence of a relevant state statute. This opened the door for federal judges to render judgments independent of state judge-made common law as to the substantive rules governing commercial transactions. In effect, the federal courts began to formulate a federal common law for diversity cases. Responding to changes in technology and the emergence of a national market for goods, the Supreme Court soon extended the *Swift* principle into other fields of law. By the late nineteenth century multistate business corporations regularly invoked diversity jurisdiction to escape local antipathy and the uncertainty of state laws. Corporate defendants also took advantage of the Removal Act of 1875 to remove cases that were brought against them in state tribunals to federal court. As this suggests, the exercise of diversity jurisdiction was closely tied to the growth of interstate business enterprise.

Business interests gained both substantive and tactical advantages from recourse to federal diversity jurisdiction. The extent to which federal judges consciously fashioned legal doctrine favorable to corporations has been overstated, but federal judges were generally sympathetic to the emerging national economy and less likely than state tribunals to favor local interests. Aside from fear of local prejudice, corporate defendants had other compelling reasons to distrust state courts. Corporations conducting business across state lines faced a bewildering morass of antiquated, diverse, and unsettled legal rules at the state level. The resulting confusion placed a considerable burden on the growing interstate commercial economy. Multistate businesses understandably preferred the unifying application of federal common law based on the *Swift* principle to the uncertainties of state laws. In an age with little national economic regulation, diversity jurisdiction served the crucial purpose of providing an impartial and consistent application of law involving interstate transactions. Additionally, corporate attorneys, more conversant with federal procedures and appellate practice than local counsel, could frequently utilize access to the federal courts as a means of engineering favorable settlements of disputes. By the late nineteenth century railroads and insurance companies were the primary beneficiaries of diversity jurisdiction.

The ever-widening exercise of diversity jurisdiction triggered an attack on federal judicial power. Critics charged that such authority aided corporate interests, gave unfair advantages to out-of-state companies, and undercut state courts as separate law-making authorities. Proposals to limit diversity jurisdiction were debated in Congress but failed to win passage. As with the income tax and bankruptcy legislation, the controversy over diversity jurisdiction laid bare marked sectional differences. Southerners and westerners generally sought to narrow federal judicial power, while eastern investors defended the federal courts as guarantors of credit and capital investment.

During Fuller's tenure the *Swift* principle was applied to numerous areas of law, including negotiable instruments, torts, corporations, real property, and insurance. In resolving diversity issues the Fuller Court was guided for the most part by an instrumentalist conception of law. A study of representative cases demonstrates how the justices molded a body of private law to facilitate commercial transactions and encourage economic growth. It also makes evident that Fuller and his associates did not automatically decide every case in favor of business enterprise. With the conspicuous exception of cases involving the fellow-servant rule, they were engaged in a search for the most appropriate and commercially reasonable rules of law. This is not to deny that many substantive issues were resolved in a manner helpful to business. Since much of the nation's economic activity was conducted by corporations, the Court's efforts to formulate a uniform commercial jurisprudence inevitably assisted multistate business enterprise. In a real sense, then, the Supreme Court under Fuller became the leading commercial tribunal in the United States. Only a few representative diversity cases can be examined here.

The Court, for example, adopted a modern approach to the extent of the powers of a corporation under its charter. In *Jacksonville, Mayport, Pablo Railway and Navigation Co. v. Hooper* (1896) the defendant railroad leased a hotel situated on a beach at the terminus of its line for the use of passengers. At issue was a suit by the landowner for back rent and losses suffered when the hotel was destroyed by fire. The railroad relied on a defense of ultra vires, contending that the lease was void because it was not within the contractual powers of a railroad company. Rejecting this argument, the Supreme Court unanimously held that a railroad had the power to conduct transactions incidental to its main business and could operate a hotel. By softening a strict application of the ultra vires rule, the Court recognized broad corporate authority to engage in business and encouraged corporations to make vertical acquisitions. But the decision was also an example of reliance on general federal law to defeat the interests of a particular corporate defendant when they were inconsistent with wider commercial interests.

Perhaps the most contentious subject of diversity litigation concerned the tort liability of corporations. The federal courts heard numerous actions in which individual plaintiffs sued railroads or manufacturing concerns for personal injuries caused by negligence. Since railroading was an especially hazardous occupation, the docket of the Fuller Court was full of suits against railroads by injured employees. A crucial issue in such litigation was application of the fellow-servant rule. According to this common law doctrine, an employer was not liable for an injury to one employee caused by a fellow employee engaged in common service. Liability therefore often turned upon the test of what constituted common service. In an effort to ameliorate the harsh results of the fellow-servant rule, courts formulated the vice principal exception. This exception held that a superior official represented the company as a vice principal and was not a fellow servant with subordinate employees. It followed that the employer was responsible for the negligence of a vice principal.

The leading case of *Baltimore and Ohio Railroad Co. v. Baugh* (1893) involved a fireman injured by the negligence of an engineer who drove a locomotive over a section of track without following established safety procedures. Justice Brewer, writing for the Court, asserted that the liability of railroads to their employees was a matter of general law and that the decisions of state courts were not authoritative. Noting that railroads were "the main channels through which this interstate commerce passes," he emphasized the need for uniform rules governing the obligations of carriers (*Baugh*, 378). Brewer defined "common service" in sweeping terms and severely limited the vice principal exception. He then determined that the engineer and fireman were fellow servants and that the fireman could not recover from the railroad for injuries due to the engineer's negligence. The adoption of a federal rule of decision in *Baugh* rested on the implicit premise that tort rules had a direct impact on interstate commerce. Justice Field, in an impassioned dissent, insisted that state law should control. Seemingly attacking the very basis of the *Swift* principle, he stated that the general law "is often little less than what the judge advancing the doctrine thinks at the time should be the general law on a particular subject" (*Baugh*, 401). This argument was out of character for Field, who generally supported reliance on federal common law in diversity cases. But it can be understood as an expression of Field's long-standing dislike of the fellow-servant rule. He pointedly remarked that the Court should adopt a rule of law "in accordance with justice and humanity to the servants of a corporation" (*Baugh*, 411). Fuller dissented separately on grounds that the employees were not fellow servants and that the majority ruling unreasonably increased an employer's freedom from liability for employee injuries.

The Supreme Court adhered to an expansive fellow-servant rule throughout Fuller's chief justiceship notwithstanding the steps by some states to abolish or modify this defense. As a result, the fellow-servant rule was applied differently in federal diversity cases from the manner in which it was administered in some state courts. Rigorous application of the fellow-servant rule contributed to the public's perception of a federal forum that favored corporate interests over injured workers. The Supreme Court's dogged dedication to the fellow-servant rule helped to bring the notion of a federal common law of torts into disrepute. Fuller was uncomfortable with the Court's strict application of the fellow-servant rule. He never wrote an opinion that invoked the rule, and he attempted to curtail its operation as much as possible. Fuller seemed to realize instinctively that the fellow-servant rule originated in an earlier era and was not a suitable vehicle through which to determine liability for workplace injuries in a modern industrial society. His dislike of the rule was vindicated when Congress abolished it for railroad employees in 1908 as part of the second Employers' Liability Act. Likewise, states began to enact workers' compensation laws early in the twentieth century, thus initiating a new scheme for compensating injured employees and gradually displacing the federal common law of industrial accidents.

A preoccupation by scholars with fellow-servant cases, however, has produced an unduly bleak assessment of the Fuller Court's handling of industrial accidents. The justices often proved sympathetic to tort claimants. Significantly, the Court imposed a nondelegable obligation on employers to provide safe tools and a safe workplace. In a line of decisions, the justices found railroads liable for injuries arising from faulty roadbeds or defective machinery. "The general rule," Fuller insisted in *Union Pacific Railway Co. v. O'Brien* (1896, 457), "undoubtedly is that a railroad company is bound to provide suitable and safe materials and structures in the construction of its roads and appurtenances." Fuller and his colleagues also adopted several procedural rules favorable to injured parties. In *Union Pacific Railway Co. v. Botsford* (1891), for instance, the Court, in an opinion by Justice Gray, held that personal injury claimants in federal diversity cases need not submit to a physical examination by a doctor selected by the defendant. Gray was influenced by privacy considerations, especially for women. In contrast, most state courts compelled such physical examinations in personal injury cases. These rulings contradict the image of federal diversity jurisdiction as a forum consistently supportive of corporate defendants at the expense of injured parties.

By the end of the Fuller era in 1910 the exercise of federal court diversity jurisdiction had become increasingly controversial. Critics charged that the Supreme Court disregarded state law and rendered decisions unduly sympathetic to business interests. While on the Court Holmes, reflecting a positivist understanding of law, attacked the notion of a federal common law and asserted that state law should be the source of legal authority in federal diversity cases. Progressives resolved to curb federal diversity jurisdiction by requiring federal judges to follow state law in diversity matters. This campaign bore fruit long after Fuller's death when the Supreme Court in *Erie Railroad Co. v. Tompkins* (1938) overruled *Swift*.

Three points about the Fuller Court's handling of diversity of citizenship cases bear emphasis. First, there was a close affinity between the Court's comprehensive diversity jurisdiction and its constitutional jurisprudence. Invocation of federal common law in diversity cases paralleled the Court's far-reaching review of state regulatory legislation under the Due Process Clause and the dormant commerce power as well as its insistence that federal judges were empowered to enjoin the enforcement of unconstitutional state laws. Broadly speaking, Fuller and his colleagues attempted to bring economic activity within the protective orbit of the federal courts. It was, of course, this use of federal diversity jurisdiction that aroused the ire of Progressives early in the twentieth century. Second, the Fuller Court perceptively recognized that the development of a national market necessitated national laws. Interstate commercial transactions could simply no longer be effectively governed by a patchwork of different state laws. In the Fuller era the Supreme Court relied on federal common law in diversity cases as a means of encouraging predictable and uniform rules and of freeing multistate enterprise from aberrational local laws. Third, reliance on federal common law enhanced the power of the federal courts at the same time that Fuller and his colleagues sometimes reigned in the power of Congress over the national economy.

Equity Receiverships

The Fuller Court demonstrated anew its instrumentalist approach to law by approving a pioneering use of equity receiverships. The receivership issue stemmed from the chaotic financial conditions in the railroad industry during the late nineteenth century. Because there was no bankruptcy law in force in the 1880s, financially troubled railroads turned to the federal courts and sought the appointment of a receiver. Despite lack of statutory authority, federal judges relied on their general equity powers to establish receiverships. Historically, courts of equity had named an outside person to collect the assets of an insolvent business for the limited purpose of distributing property among creditors. In 1884 the receivership of the Wabash, St. Louis, and Pacific Railway Company proved innovative in several respects. This was the first occasion that a receiver had been named on motion of a railroad rather than that of its creditors. In addition, the U.S. circuit court picked the managers of the Wabash as receivers. Last, the receivers were expected to operate the railroad, conserve its assets, defer payments of debt, and reorganize the carrier on a financially viable basis.

This unprecedented resort to equity receivership was grounded on important policy considerations. Unlike many other types of property, a railroad was an economic unit and could realistically be disposed of only as a going concern. Public interest, moreover, dictated that transportation services be maintained if at all possible. It followed that the contractual rights of creditors and bondholders had to be subordinated to preservation of the line. The result of this reasoning was a greatly enlarged conception of receivership in which the federal courts were drawn into the business of supervising railroads.

Despite outspoken criticism of equity railroad receiverships, a unanimous Supreme Court, in an opinion by Fuller, had no difficulty sustaining the practice. Although they recognized the extraordinary nature of these receiverships, the justices upheld the Wabash appointment in *Quincy, Missouri, and Pacific Railroad Co. v. Humphreys* (1892). Fuller explained that the relief sought "was obviously framed upon the theory that an insolvent railroad corporation has a standing in a court of equity to surrender its property into the custody of the court, to be preserved and disposed of according to the rights of its various creditors, and, in the meantime, operated in the public interest" (*Quincy, Missouri*, 95). The Wabash precedent soon became the model for many railroad receiverships during the 1890s. Viewed in its most positive light, railroad receivership administration showed the ingenuity of the federal courts in devising a means to balance competing economic interests while keeping an insolvent carrier in operation.

The widespread use of railroad receivers soon engendered a heated political conflict with the forces of economic localism. Federal judges sometimes instructed receivers, as officers of the court, to disregard state laws regulating or taxing railroads. Attempts by state officials to enforce state laws against lines under receivership were treated as contempt of court. Such actions aroused bitter attacks in the South, where political leaders charged that railroad receivers favored northern creditors rather than local interests. Feelings were exacerbated by the fact that many insolvent railroads remained under receivership for years. In 1894 the South Carolina legislature adopted a petition to Congress bitterly protesting that the federal courts were usurping authority to control railroads and thus were invading state autonomy.

Yet in economic terms the equity receivership was a highly successful legal mechanism. It helped many railroads weather the depression of the 1890s. Congress incorporated the equity receivership into the bankruptcy laws in 1933 and thus provided a statutory basis for the reorganization of insolvent lines. With equity receiverships the Fuller Court embraced a bold innovation that, on the whole, served the nation well. Indeed, current reorganization law under the Bankruptcy Act is a direct descendant of this novel device.

Safety Appliance Act

As the number of railroad accidents mounted in the late nineteenth century, Congress took steps to ensure the safety of employees and travelers by passing the Safety Appliance Act in 1893. This measure required railroads to equip their engines with power brakes and their cars with automatic couplers. It also stated that an employee injured by any train operating in violation of the statute was deemed not to have assumed the risk of unsafe conditions.

The Fuller Court was called upon to interpret the Safety Appliance Act in *Johnson v. Southern Pacific Co.* (1904). The plaintiff, a brakeman, was hurt while coupling an engine and a dining car. Although both vehicles were equipped with automatic couplers, they were of different types and were not compatible upon impact. Fuller, for a unanimous bench, gave a generous reading to the statute and ordered a new trial for the plaintiff. As he perceptively remarked:

> The object was to protect the lives and limbs of railroad employees by rendering it unnecessary for a man operating the couplers to go between the ends of the cars, and that object would be defeated, not necessarily by the use of automatic couplers

of different kinds, but if those different kinds would not automatically couple with each other. The point was that the railroad companies should be compelled, respectively, to adopt devices, whatever they were, which would act so far uniformly as to eliminate the danger consequent on men going between cars. (*Johnson*, 16)

More significantly, Fuller stressed that the act was remedial in nature and should be broadly construed "to promote the public welfare by securing the safety of employees and travelers" (*Johnson*, 17). Fuller's opinion constituted a milestone in statutory construction because it rejected strict textualism in favor of an approach that determined statutory meaning in light of legislative purpose. The *Johnson* decision invigorated enforcement of the Safety Appliance Act and again demonstrated that Fuller and his colleagues did not always take the side of corporate defendants in tort litigation. It also demonstrated the Supreme Court's readiness to accept legislative overhaul of the common law of industrial accidents.

Bankruptcy and Intellectual Property

The Constitution vests power in Congress "to establish . . . uniform laws on the subject of bankruptcies throughout the United States." Following years of acrimonious debate, much of it sectional in nature, Congress finally enacted an enduring bankruptcy law in 1898. This measure sought to balance the competing interests of debtors and creditors and to achieve an equitable distribution of a bankrupt's property. A national bankruptcy system was closely tied to federal control of interstate commerce and to the maturing national credit market, both matters of vital concern to the Fuller Court.

The Fuller Court repeatedly affirmed far-reaching congressional authority over bankruptcy and, in so doing, helped lay the foundations of modern bankruptcy practice. In the leading case of *Hanover National Bank v. Moyses* (1902) Fuller, for a unanimous Court, sustained the constitutionality of the 1898 act against several challenges. He articulated three basic propositions. First, he adopted a broad view of the class of persons subject to the bankruptcy power. Rejecting the English practice of applying bankruptcy legislation only to traders, Fuller determined that the authority of Congress was not defined by English law in force when the Constitution was adopted. Rather, he concluded, Congress had plenary power over the whole subject of bankruptcies and could provide that individuals other than traders might be adjudged bankrupts. Second, Fuller upheld the authority of Congress to authorize the retroactive impairment of contracts. "The subject of 'bankruptcies,'" Fuller observed, "includes the power to discharge the debtor from his contracts and legal liabilities, as well as to distribute his property. The grant to Congress involves the power to impair the obligation of contracts, and this the States were forbidden to do" (*Hanover*

National Bank, 188). Third, he considered the uniformity requirement of the bankruptcy clause. Fuller held that uniformity was geographic, not personal, and therefore Congress could give effect to exemptions prescribed by state laws even though this produced different results for debtors in different states.

Creation of a permanent bankruptcy system reflected the push by wholesale distributors in the late nineteenth century for a systematic and national method of providing relief for insolvent debtors while safeguarding the interests of creditors. It was hoped that a uniform law would eliminate the confusion caused by inconsistent state insolvency laws and generate economic benefits by increasing the availability of credit. Not surprisingly, Fuller and his associates gave strong support to the new bankruptcy regime. Their decisions provided the building blocks for subsequent developments in bankruptcy law.

The Constitution also confers on Congress power to award an "exclusive right" to inventors and to grant authors the sole right to their writings. In 1790 Congress enacted patent and copyright laws. Recognition of rights in intellectual property was grounded on the premise that grants of limited monopoly protection served the public interest by encouraging mechanical innovation and literary production. Such thinking, however, ran counter to a long-standing dislike of monopoly and the faith in competition as the best means of intellectual stimulus.

The late nineteenth century witnessed an extraordinary outpouring of inventive activity. The number of patents granted by the U.S. Patent Office mounted dramatically. There was as yet no specialized court to handle patent matters. As a result, Fuller and his colleagues heard a steady stream of cases in which inventors alleged infringement of their patents. In line with its aversion to state-conferred monopoly and its preference for competition, the Fuller Court tended to construe strictly patent requirements and to invalidate a number of claimed patents. Still, the justices upheld some patents. In *The Barbed Wire Patent* (1892), for example, they validated a wire fence patent. The patent jurisprudence of the Fuller Court reflected the unresolved tension between exclusive privilege for inventors and the public interest in access to new devices. As patents became an increasingly important aspect of national economic life, the Fuller Court was caught up in the tension between the need to stimulate creativity and the desire to protect the public from unwarranted special privilege. Although the justices broke little new ground concerning patent jurisprudence, they wrestled with difficult issues that remain in dispute to the present day.

Copyright claims posed similar issues, and the Fuller Court tried to balance the rights of authors with the public interest in free access to information. The case of *Holmes v. Hurst* (1899) illustrates the Court's concerns. This case presented the question whether serial publication of a book in a monthly magazine before securing a copyright vitiated the author's rights. The Court affirmed the long-standing rule that copyright protection was entirely statutory and rested upon compliance with certain statutory formalities, not upon common law principles. Hence, the author's rights in the subsequent book were lost by virtue of its prior publication in the form of magazine articles.

References

Arkes, Hadley. "*Lochner v. New York* and the Cast of Our Laws." In Robert P. George, ed., *Great Cases in Constitutional Law.* Princeton, NJ: Princeton University Press, 2000.

Benedict, Michael Les. "Victorian Moralism and Civil Liberty." In Donald G. Nieman, ed., *The Constitution, Law, and American Life: Critical Aspects of the Nineteenth-Century Experience.* Athens: University of Georgia Press, 1992.

Bernstein, David E. "*Plessy* versus *Lochner:* The Berea College Case." *Journal of Supreme Court History* 25 (2000): 93–111.

———. "The Law and Economics of Post–Civil War Restrictions on Interstate Migration by African-Americans." *Texas Law Review* 76 (1998): 781–847.

Beth, Loren P. *The Development of the American Constitution, 1877–1917.* New York: Harper and Row, 1971.

Braeman, John. *Before the Civil Rights Revolution: The Old Court and Individual Rights.* Westport, CT: Greenwood Press, 1988.

Brown, Henry Billings. "The Liberty of the Press." *American Law Review* 34 (1900): 321–341.

Curriden, Mark, and Leroy Phillips Jr. *Contempt of Court: The Turn-of-the-Century Lynching that Launched 100 Years of Federalism.* New York: Faber and Faber, 1999.

Ely, James W. Jr. *The Chief Justiceship of Melville W. Fuller, 1888–1910.* Columbia: University of South Carolina Press, 1995.

———. "The Fuller Court and Takings Jurisprudence." *Journal of Supreme Court History* 2 (1996): 120–135.

Epstein, Richard A. "The Proper Scope of the Commerce Power." *Virginia Law Review* 73 (1987): 1387–1455.

Fiss, Owen M. *History of the Supreme Court of the United States, Volume 8: Troubled Beginnings of the Modern State, 1888–1910.* New York: Macmillan, 1993.

Freyer, Tony A. *Forums of Order: The Federal Courts and Business in American History.* Greenwich, CT: JAI Press, 1979.

Gillman, Howard. *The Constitution Besieged: The Rise and Demise of Lochner Era Police Power Jurisprudence.* Durham, NC: Duke University Press, 1993.

———. "More on the Origins of the Fuller Court's Jurisprudence: Reexamining the Scope of Federal Power Over Commerce and Manufacturing in Nineteenth-Century Constitutional Law." *Political Research Quarterly* 49 (1996): 415–437.

Gordon, James W. "Religion and the First Justice Harlan: A Case Study in Late Nineteenth Century Presbyterian Constitutionalism." *Marquette Law Review* 85 (2001): 317–422.

Gordon, Sarah Barringer. *The Mormon Question: Polygamy and Constitutional Conflict in Nineteenth Century America.* Chapel Hill: University of North Carolina Press, 2002.

Graber, Mark A. *Transforming Free Speech: The Ambiguous Legacy of Civil Libertarianism.* Berkeley: University of California Press, 1991.

Hamm, Richard F. *Shaping the Eighteenth Amendment: Temperance Reform, Legal Culture, and the Polity, 1880–1920.* Chapel Hill: University of North Carolina Press, 1995.

Horwitz, Morton J. *The Transformation of American Law, 1870–1960.* New York: Oxford University Press, 1992.

Hovenkamp, Herbert. *Enterprise and American Law, 1836–1937.* Cambridge, MA: Harvard University Press, 1991.

Hurst, James Willard. *Law and the Conditions of Freedom in the Nineteenth-Century United States.* Madison: University of Wisconsin Press, 1956.

Hylton, J. Gordon. "The Judge Who Abstained in *Plessy v. Ferguson:* Justice David Brewer and the Problem of Race." *Mississippi Law Journal* 61 (1991): 315–364.

Jensen, Erik M. "The Taxing Power, the Sixteenth Amendment, and the Meaning of 'Incomes.'" *Arizona State Law Journal* 33 (2001): 1057–1158.

Kens, Paul. *Judicial Power and Reform Politics: The Anatomy of Lochner v. New York.* Lawrence: University Press of Kansas, 1997.

Kerr, James Edward. *The Insular Cases: The Role of the Judiciary in American Expansionism.* Port Washington, NY: Kennikat Press, 1982.

King, Willard L. *Melville Weston Fuller: Chief Justice of United States, 1888–1910.* New York: Macmillan, 1950; rpt. Chicago: University of Chicago Press, 1967.

Phillips, Michael J. *The Lochner Court, Myth, and Reality: Substantive Due Process from the 1890s to the 1930s.* Westport, CT: Praeger, 2001.

Przybyszewski, Linda. *The Republic According to John Marshall Harlan.* Chapel Hill: University of North Carolina Press, 1999.

———. "The Religion of a Jurist: Justice David J. Brewer and the Christian Nation." *Journal of Supreme Court History* 25 (2000): 228–242.

Purcell, Edward A. Jr. *Litigation and Inequality: Federal Diversity Jurisdiction in Industrial America, 1870–1958.* New York: Oxford University Press, 1992.

Ross, William G. *A Muted Fury: Populists, Progressives, and Labor Unions Confront the Courts, 1890–1937.* Princeton, NJ: Princeton University Press, 1994.

White, G. Edward. *The Constitution and the New Deal.* Cambridge, MA: Harvard University Press, 2000.

4

Legacy and Impact

T he Fuller era was one of the most controversial in the history of the Supreme Court. By and large scholars have not been kind to Fuller and his colleagues. For decades critics have been all too prone to echo the views of Progressives and New Dealers, who pictured the Fuller Court as a partisan of big business and hostile to workers and minorities. Articulating the conventional wisdom, Owen M. Fiss declared: "By all accounts, the Court over which Melville Weston Fuller presided, from 1888 to 1910, ranks among the worst" (Fiss 1993, 3).

A rising tide of revisionist scholarship, however, has called into question this account of late-nineteenth-century jurisprudence. New literature has done much to dispel the entrenched mythology that has long distorted our understanding of the Fuller Court. What has emerged is a more balanced portrait of the Supreme Court under Fuller.

Fuller and his colleagues built upon a constitutional tradition that assigned a high value to property rights, private economic ordering, and limited government. Recall that protection of property rights had been a central concern of the Court under Chief Justice John Marshall (1801–1835). Closer to Fuller's era, the Supreme Court under Chief Justice Morrison R. Waite, in cases such as *Munn v. Illinois* (1877), was inclined to affirm state economic regulations. Yet the Waite Court also manifested its willingness to uphold the rights of property owners. In a line of cases, the Waite Court sustained the validity of local bonds despite efforts by local governments to repudiate their obligations. Moreover, the Waite Court cautioned that states could not impose confiscatory rates upon railroads and moved toward the position that the Due Process Clause of the Fourteenth Amendment guaranteed substantive rights. Waite and his colleagues also narrowly construed the protection afforded racial minorities by the Fourteenth Amendment, ruling in the *Civil Rights Cases* (1883) that the amendment did not ban private discrimination.

The Fuller Court, therefore, represented not a sharp break with the past but a flowering of time-honored themes of constitutionalism. As Morton J. Horwitz has aptly pointed out, "by seeking to stigmatize the *Lochner* era, Progressive historians lost sight of the basic continuity in American constitutional history before the New

Deal" (Horwitz 1992, 7). Similarly, Howard Gillman persuasively asserted that the Supreme Court of the late nineteenth century remained "loyal to the historically defined conception of political legitimacy" forged by the Framers. He cautioned that we should not "overlook the continuities in nineteenth-century in American political culture and the extent to which the justices of the late nineteenth century interpreted the social turmoil of the 1880s and 1890s through an ideological prism developed" by the framers of the Constitution (Gillman 1993, 199).

An essential element of Fuller Court jurisprudence was the traditional Anglo-American premise that the law should safeguard private property in the name of liberty. For Fuller and his colleagues property and liberty were inseparable, and both were closely related to freedom of contract and private economic ordering. Like most Americans of the age, the justices of the Fuller Court tended to define liberty primarily in economic terms. Justice David J. Brewer revealingly declared in 1892: "The utmost possible liberty to the individual, and the fullest possible protection to him and his property is both the limitation and duty of government" (*Budd v. New York* [1892], 551). The Fuller Court championed private property and contractual freedom in order to limit the reach of government and thereby protect liberty. As Fiss recognized: "Liberty was the guiding ideal of the Fuller Court, the notion that gave unity and coherence to its many endeavors" (Fiss 1993, 389).

The Fuller Court's solicitude for the rights of property owners stemmed from utilitarian considerations as well as philosophical imperatives. Investment capital was vital to finance economic development. Associating the security of private property with industrial growth, Fuller and his colleagues persistently sought to protect capital formation. In the railroad rate cases, for instance, the justices emphasized the importance of private capital and voiced concern that stringent state controls would produce such a meager return as to discourage investment. Excessive rate regulation would therefore not only impair the value of existing property but also inhibit new investment essential for development. With respect to late nineteenth judicial behavior, historian Morton Keller perceptively noted that "an old concern for private rights and individual freedom coexisted with the desire to foster the development of a national economy" (Keller 1977, 370).

Although prepared to afford heightened protection to the rights of property owners, the Fuller Court's pattern of decisionmaking was complex and gave weight to other constitutional values as well. Foremost among these was a strong commitment to the federal system. Consistent with its dedication to a limited federal government, the Court was anxious to preserve the traditional distribution of power between the national and state governments. Consequently, Fuller and his colleagues tended to defer to state governance of criminal justice, race relations, and public morals. This belief in federalism also led the justices to reject an expansive application of the Bill of Rights to the states.

Even in the economic area the Fuller Court saw a major role for the states. Not only were most state business regulations upheld, but the justices hoped to maintain a balance between federal and state authority over the economy. The states' rights theme was prominent in such leading decisions as *United States v. E. C. Knight Co.* (1895) and *Pollock v. Farmers' Loan and Trust Co.* (1895), in which the Court restrained congressional power. In short, the Fuller Court was leery of legislation that seemed to portend a fundamental alteration of federal-state relations.

Of course, there was a degree of tension between the Fuller Court's defense of property rights and its high regard for state autonomy. In the late nineteenth century state legislatures, acting under their police power to advance public health, safety, and morals, took the initiative in seeking to harness the new economic forces transforming America. Such exercises of state authority often impinged the prerogatives of property owners and employers, stimulating a stream of legal challenges. The quandary inherent in protecting property owners while simultaneously vindicating states' rights was strikingly evident in the Fuller Court's handling of state-imposed railroad rates and state regulations that burdened interstate commerce. The Court acknowledged that states could control the intrastate charges of railroads but fashioned the fair-value rule in *Smyth v. Ames* (1898) to restrain state rate-making authority. Likewise, Fuller and his colleagues steadfastly championed the national market for goods and free trade among the states. To this end, the Fuller Court carefully scrutinized state laws that hampered the shipment of products across state lines. The commitment to the United States as a free trade zone caused the justices to wield forcefully the dormant commerce power to eliminate state obstacles to national economic life.

The conflicting pull of support for private property rights and respect for federalism also informed the Fuller Court's takings jurisprudence. In a number of important rulings it strengthened the Takings Cause as a guarantee of individual rights against arbitrary governmental power. Some of these decisions curbed state power over private property. In *Chicago, Burlington, and Quincy Railroad Co. v. Chicago* (1897), for example, the Court insisted that the Due Process Clause of the Fourteenth Amendment imposed the just compensation principle on the states, thereby limiting the exercise of eminent domain. But Fuller and his associates regularly allowed states broad latitude to determine what should be considered public use for the purpose of acquiring private property. Thus, emerging takings jurisprudence reflected the efforts of the Fuller Court to balance national constitutional norms and state autonomy.

Place in History

In most areas of public law, ranging from criminal justice to control of immigration, the Fuller Court upheld state and congressional legislation. Consequently, the historical reputation of the Court is closely tied with its vigorous record in defense of rights associated with property and commerce. Populists, Progressives, and later historians who reflect their views have cast the work of the Supreme Court under Fuller in a harsh light. Unable to believe in the libertarian foundation of the Fuller Court decisions, scholars raised in the intellectual wake of the New Deal dismissed the Court's rhetoric about liberty as camouflage for rulings that frustrated the popular will to secure a more equitable social order. The justices of the Fuller Court were accused of reading their economic predictions into the Constitution. Rather than accept the work of the Court at face value, historians developed a variety of hypotheses to explain the jurisprudence of the Fuller era. Although increasingly challenged by revisionist scholarship, these interpretations held sway for decades. They therefore warrant brief treatment.

One line of criticism posits that the major goal of the Fuller Court was protection of the business community. A number of studies charge that Court under Fuller favored business enterprise and the wealthy at the expense of workers and the poor. The protection-of-business thesis echoes the fierce attacks of the Populists and Progressives upon the Supreme Court in Fuller's day. This thesis, however, is problematic. It oversimplifies a more knotty story, downplays contrary evidence, and impugns the integrity of Fuller and his colleagues. As a study of its decisions makes clear, the Fuller Court was far from a consistent champion of business enterprise. The justices upheld quite a few restrictions and tax levies on business. Thus, the Fuller Court applied the Sherman Anti-Trust Act to railroads and stockyards, broadly interpreted the Safety Appliance Act, sustained a wide variety of state regulatory measures, and validated both state and federal inheritance taxes. Such decisions fly in the face of the breezy assertion that the Supreme Court under Fuller was dedicated to laissez-faire in the service of enterprise.

Another thesis emphasizes the supposed impact of social Darwinism on the work of the Court. Derived from the evolutionary theory of Charles Darwin, social Darwinism endeavored to apply Darwin's insights to society at large. Social Darwinists argued that competition and survival of the fittest would improve overall economic productivity. Government could therefore do little to achieve social progress and should play only a minimal role in managing the economy. For years it was an article of faith among many historians that the Fuller Court was strongly influenced by social Darwinism. They invariably pointed to Justice Oliver Wendell Holmes Jr.'s dissenting opinion in *Lochner v. New York* (1905), in which he implicitly accused the majority of having adopted Darwinist assumptions about the role of government. A single dissenting opinion, of course, is slender evidence for a generalization about the work of a group of justices over twenty-two years.

Despite some lingering influence, the social Darwinist thesis has been largely discredited. In fact, the Supreme Court under Fuller never endorsed or even cited the views of leading Darwinists. Deeply religious justices, such as Brewer and John M. Harlan, were unlikely to share the outlook of Darwinism. Indeed, the only member of the Fuller Court who can be identified with Darwinism was, ironically, Holmes himself. There is simply no credible evidence that Fuller and his colleagues wrote social Darwinism into the Constitution. On the contrary, as Herbert Hovenkamp has concluded, "The degree to which Darwinism and Social Darwinism *failed* to permeate the thinking of the Supreme Court in any way is most amazing" (Hovenkamp 1991, 99–100).

Still another interpretation paints the Fuller Court as apprehensive about radicalism in the 1890s. It has been argued that the justices, responding to the crisis atmosphere generated by the 1893 depression, enlarged judicial power to defend the rights of property owners from threatened spoliation by the majority. Unquestionably the justices were aware of heightened social tensions in late-nineteenth-century America and that criticism of private property had increased. Both Justices Brewer and Henry Billings Brown felt the need to deliver major public addresses in the 1890s defending private property. Still, the depiction of the Fuller Court as driven by fear is wide of the mark. "It is, in fact, too simple-minded," Lawrence M. Friedman noted, "to portray the justices as frightened, reactionary men, defending a dying social order" (Friedman 2002, 23). Most justices of the Fuller era avoided alarmist rhetoric and were confident about the long-range stability of society. They recognized that the United States was passing through a period of change, but they were optimistic about the future.

More recently, Cass Sunstein has theorized that the judiciary of the late nineteenth and early twentieth centuries, encompassing the Fuller era, treated common law norms as a constitutional baseline and was reluctant to sanction any deviation by legislators from this model. The result, according to Sunstein, was to freeze the existing distribution of wealth under the façade of seemingly neutral common law principles. Although the Sunstein thesis has gained popularity, it is beset with difficulties. First, Sunstein grounds his proposition on just a handful of cases. Second, and more troublesome, he overlooks a host of Fuller Court decisions that upheld legislation designed to alter common law rules to meet new situations. Fuller and his colleagues, for instance, sustained laws abolishing the fellow-servant rule, limiting the hours of work for miners and women, and banning the payment of employees in script. Likewise, they allowed lawmakers to impose new burdens on landowners. The justices validated tenement reform measures and laws placing height restrictions on buildings in urban areas. In all of these situations the Fuller Court accepted changes in common law rights. In fact, the Court repeatedly noted the mutability of common law rules. This record flies in the face of any notion that the Court was dedicated to preserving the status quo by strict adherence to the common law.

Given the weakness of these theories, attention should be paid to a number of factors that facilitate a better appreciation of Fuller Court jurisprudence and its devotion to individual liberty. In the first place, one should view the work of the Court in broad perspective. It bears emphasis that the justices under Fuller sustained far more regulations than they struck down. They demonstrated considerable tolerance for legislation protecting public safety and welfare against harmful activities, as well as for laws enhancing public morals. Although generally sympathetic to the market system, Fuller and his colleagues were far from doctrinaire and never sought to impose anything remotely resembling a laissez-faire economy. It is simply historical nonsense to suggest that the Fuller Court blocked all reform efforts.

Second, one must be careful not to attribute an elaborate judicial philosophy to the Fuller Court. Virtually all members of the Court shared to some degree the core values of limited government and private property, but they were primarily practical men, not academic theorists. Writing about the early twentieth century, Friedman has cogently observed: "In short, the justices and judges in general, were cautious and incremental. They did not consistently adhere to any economic philosophy. They simply reacted in the way that respectable, moderate conservatives of their day would naturally react" (Friedman 2002, 24). The Fuller Court, then, allowed a good deal of room for moderate reform when justified by the circumstances. But the justices were instinctively unprepared for novel laws that appeared to redistribute wealth or enlarge federal control of the economy. Such measures threatened liberty as they understood it.

Third, the Fuller Court operated within the contours of dominant public opinion. Put another way, Fuller and his colleagues championed values—limited government, respect for the states, private property, contractual freedom—that were widely shared by turn-of-the-century Americans. President Grover Cleveland, Fuller's good friend, gave a classic articulation of this view in 1887: "The lesson should be constantly enforced that though the people support the Government, the Government should not support the people" (Veto Message, "Distribution of Seeds," February 16, 1887, quoted in Ely 1998, 45). The fact that the Fuller Court was in accord with prevailing political ideology was made clear by the pivotal presidential election of 1896. William Jennings Bryan, the nominee of the Democratic Party, assailed the Fuller Court, urged wealth redistribution through an income tax, and called for increased governmental intervention in the economy. Americans decisively rejected this Populist program in 1896 and again in 1900. It is entirely fanciful to postulate that the general public in Fuller's day was yearning for big government and vast social welfare schemes.

As this indicates, the Fuller Court, despite its activist bent, generally mirrored the social and economic attitudes of American society as a whole. As one scholar has perceptively observed, "*Lochner* era jurists realized the importance of public opinion in the evolution of constitutional law. In propounding laissez-faire constitutionalism, they believed public opinion was on their side" (Siegel 1991, 108). Fuller and his colleagues tended to ratify majoritarian preferences in most areas of law. Like other

Americans of the age, for example, the justices displayed little sympathy for the claims of racial minorities or unionists. Even when the Court struck down legislation, it acted in accord with what it perceived to be public sentiment. The Fuller Court, in short, spoke for the conservative political alliance that dominated American public life at the end of the nineteenth century.

Finally, scholars would do well to look with a skeptical eye at the Progressive legislative program. Too often the issue of property rights at the turn of the twentieth century has been presented within the simplistic context of a conflict between the public interest and a judiciary devoted to big business. But it unfairly loads the historical deck to presume the benign purpose and effect of so-called reform legislation. The actual picture is much less tidy. There is room to doubt the efficacy of many of the regulations promoted by the Populists and Progressives. For example, the Progressive faith in management of the economy by experts along scientific lines seems naive and almost quaint to modern eyes. Moreover, a good deal of regulatory legislation, although couched in terms of general benefit, was enacted at the behest of special interest groups. It is certainly arguable that the Fuller Court's doubt about regulatory solutions and dedication to economic liberty may well have served the long-term public interest.

The White Court and Beyond

Chief Justice Fuller died on July 4, 1910, at his summer home in Maine. He had served as chief for twenty-two years, a period longer than that of any other chief justice except John Marshall and Roger B. Taney. President William Howard Taft, who earnestly desired the center chair for himself, selected Associate Justice Edward D. White to succeed Fuller as chief justice. This marked the first time that a sitting justice had been elevated to the position of chief.

The White Court continued to wrestle with the extent of governmental power to regulate the economy. On this key constitutional issue the White Court pursued a somewhat erratic course. The Court under White was generally disinclined to apply constitutional doctrines developed under Fuller, such as the liberty of contract principle, to new situations. It was also willing to affirm greater regulation of land use and workplace conditions. In *Hadacheck v. Sebastian* (1915), for instance, the justices sustained an ordinance that banned the operation of a brickyard in a residential neighborhood and caused a severe economic loss to the owner. Similarly, in *Bunting v. Oregon* (1917), decided only twelve years after *Lochner*, they upheld a state law establishing a ten-hour day for factory employees. Moreover, in *Wilson v. New* (1917), a divided White Court affirmed the validity of the Adamson Act of 1916, which fixed an eight-hour workday and a temporary wage scale for railroad operating employees.

This decision opened the door for broader congressional authority to regulate labor relations in the rail industry.

The White Court also began to haltingly move away from the Fuller Court's record in the field of civil rights, rendering several decisions that improved the legal position of blacks. Particularly noteworthy was *Guinn v. United States* (1915), which invalidated the grandfather clause in Oklahoma's literacy test for voting. The Court found this clause an unconstitutional attempt to evade the Fifteenth Amendment's ban on racial discrimination in suffrage qualifications.

Not surprisingly, the White Court consistently voted to back the growth of federal power during World War I. It upheld the Selective Service Act in the *Selective Draft Law Cases* (1918). It supported the suppression of wartime dissent by sustaining convictions under the Espionage Act in *Schenck v. United States* (1919) and other cases. The Court under White also looked favorably on extension of governmental authority over the wartime economy. The justices endorsed congressional legislation authorizing the president to operate the nation's railroads during the war. In response to a wartime housing shortage, some localities imposed rent controls. Over a forceful dissent by White, the Court in *Block v. Hirsh* (1921) concluded that housing conditions in the District of Columbia warranted temporary regulation of rent and that such controls did not constitute an unconstitutional taking of property.

On occasion, however, themes from the Fuller era were articulated by the White Court. Building on precedent from the Fuller Court, White and his colleagues in *Bailey v. Alabama* (1911) struck down a peonage statute under which an employee could be forced to work to pay a debt. The justices ruled that the statute imposed involuntary servitude in violation of the Thirteenth Amendment. In the landmark decision of *Buchanan v. Warley* (1917), moreover, the White Court stressed the fundamental importance of property rights in striking down residential segregation ordinances as a deprivation of property without due process of law. The *Buchanan* decision highlighted the link between property and liberty and constituted the most significant judicial victory for civil rights during the early twentieth century. Similarly, in *Coppage v. Kansas* (1915) the White Court invalidated a state law prohibiting yellow dog contracts as a violation of the liberty of contract.

The power of Congress in effect to promote public morals by professing to regulate interstate commerce vexed the Supreme Court during White's tenure. In *Champion v. Ames* (1903), it will be remembered, the Fuller Court determined that Congress could exclude lottery tickets from interstate commerce. Relying on this precedent, the White Court in *Hoke v. United States* (1913) sustained the Mann Act, which made it a crime to transport women across state lines for immoral purposes. Yet in *Hammer v. Dagenhart* (1918) the Court ruled that a federal statute outlawing shipments in interstate commerce of goods produced by child labor exceeded the power of Congress under the Commerce Clause. It distinguished between a prohibition of trade in inherently harmful goods and a ban of goods, harmless in themselves, produced by child labor. In *Hammer* the White Court again adhered to the line between manufacturing and commerce drawn by the Fuller Court.

Following White's death in May 1921, and other changes in the composition of the bench, the 1920s and early 1930s saw a resurgence of constitutional thought associated with the Fuller era. The Supreme Court under Chief Justice William Howard Taft (1921–1930) and Charles Evans Hughes (1930–1941) employed Fuller-period doctrines to safeguard both economic and noneconomic rights. In essence, the Court continued to see its role as preserving individual liberty by reining in governmental power. These developments will only be sketched briefly here.

The liberty of contract doctrine was reasserted in *Adkins v. Children's Hospital* (1923), which invalidated a minimum wage for women. Justice George Sutherland, writing for the Court, declared that "freedom of contract is . . . the general rule and restraint the exception" (*Adkins*, 546). The protection afforded landowners under the Takings Clause was broadened when the Court in *Pennsylvania Coal Co. v. Mahon* (1922) held that a land-use regulation might be so severe as to constitute an effective taking of property. The origins of the regulatory takings doctrine can be traced to the Fuller era. In *Meyer v. Nebraska* (1923), moreover, the justices enlarged the range of fundamental rights protected by due process beyond economic liberties to encompass the right of parents to educate their children. The *Meyer* decision opened the way for due process to safeguard a variety of substantive personal rights, including privacy. Also noteworthy was the ruling by the Hughes Court in *New State Ice Co. v. Liebmann* (1932). There the justices invalidated as a violation of due process a state law that in effect conferred a de facto monopoly on existing ice businesses. The right of individuals to engage in ordinary businesses was, of course, a major theme of Fuller-era jurisprudence. Here the doctrine was applied in a way to preserve economic opportunity.

The Great Depression and the election of Franklin D. Roosevelt as president in 1932 marked a watershed in American political history. His New Deal program was based on the premise that government should manage the national economy and promote general social welfare. The New Deal legislative program directly challenged the insistence on limited government, marketplace competition, and respect for private property that were the hallmarks of constitutional thought well before the Fuller era. The upshot was a lacerating battle between the Supreme Court and the New Dealers. In 1935 and 1936 the justices struck down a series of New Deal regulatory measures. A particular sticking point was the Court's adherence to the long-established distinction between production and interstate commerce, a position that doomed congressional attempts to control the national economy. As a practical matter, however, it is very difficult for the judiciary to move counter to public opinion for a prolonged period. Faced with President Roosevelt's sweeping reelection in 1936 and his subsequent Court-packing plan, the conservative majority of the Supreme

Court was politically isolated. Under intense pressure in a drastically changed political environment, the Court abruptly changed course and began to sustain federal and state economic regulations.

This shift, known as the constitutional revolution of 1937, resulted in a wholesale reversal of constitutional doctrine. The Supreme Court effectively repudiated the liberty of contract doctrine and adopted a broad reading of the Commerce Clause that gave Congress authority to reach virtually any economic activity. Likewise, in *Federal Power Commission v. Hope Natural Gas Co.* (1944) the justices abandoned the fair-value standard of *Smyth v. Ames* (1898). This step allowed the states greater latitude in setting utility charges. The cornerstone of the emerging liberal constitutionalism was a dichotomy between property rights and personal liberties. In *United States v. Carolene Products Co.* (1938) the Court indicated that economic regulations would henceforth receive only minimum judicial scrutiny while a preferred category of personal rights would receive greater judicial protection. Although it is difficult to reconcile the subordination of property rights with either the views of the Framers or the text of the Constitution, the constitutional double standard formulated in *Carolene Products* became the new orthodoxy. For decades thereafter the Supreme Court was preoccupied with civil liberties and civil rights and gave only perfunctory attention to property rights issues. The Court became increasingly active in promoting liberal social policies and defending racial minorities while allowing legislators almost carte blanche to fashion economic controls.

For a generation scholars writing in the New Deal tradition of pervasive government found it hard to comprehend, much less share, the constitutional values of the Fuller era. The libertarian heritage that linked individual liberty and respect for the rights of property owners was foreign to their thinking. Little wonder, then, that it was easy to denigrate the Fuller Court and assign its decisions to a sort of legal dead-letter box.

Lasting Significance

It remains to consider the legacy of the Fuller Court. Any assessment of segments of Supreme Court history is a hazardous enterprise. One must recognize that evaluations of judges and courts are inevitably somewhat subjective. They rest in the last analysis upon individual value preferences. Many rankings of Supreme Court justices, for instance, are marred by both a presentist and a liberal political bias. Moreover, Supreme Court decisions on high-visibility issues open a dialogue between the justices and the public. To have a lasting impact, decisions must be in harmony with the march of history. The legacy of Fuller and his colleagues turns upon how one understands the verdict of history.

Unquestionably time has erased many of the achievements of the Fuller Court. We as a nation have traveled far from a constitutional order grounded on the principles of limited government, state autonomy, and regard for the rights of property owners. Fuller's efforts to confine congressional taxation and regulatory powers were ultimately unsuccessful. Indeed, judicial and scholarly opinion has embraced a greatly expanded role for government in American life. Property rights—the cornerstone of the Fuller Court's libertarian jurisprudence—were seen by later justices and commentators as an obstacle to establishing governmental authority over the economy. For decades following the New Deal era the claims of property owners were commonly ignored or belittled, in sharp contrast to judicial solicitude for an expanding number of noneconomic rights. In addition, the renewed civil rights movement following World War II has discredited the Fuller Court's acceptance of the policy of racial segregation in the South. An egalitarian stress on the problems of outsiders has eclipsed the Fuller Court's dedication to economic liberty. One might well be inclined to dismiss the Fuller Court as a relic of another day.

From another perspective, however, the jurisprudence of the Fuller years can be viewed as pointing toward modern American society. Fuller and his colleagues were more receptive to the new realities of American economic life than many of their critics, whose values were often rooted in a preindustrial world. The justices envisioned a future based on capitalist enterprise and sought to promote the new industrial order by safeguarding investment capital and the national market for goods. In so doing, the Fuller Court was swimming with the tide of history.

Furthermore, each generation forges a fresh perspective about history. The New Deal consensus on the role of government, which dominated American political life for decades, has dissipated. Changing political and legal currents have opened the window to a new appreciation of the past. As thinking about the regulatory state has altered, legislation once seen as a triumph of Progressive reform now appears in a different light. Consider the question of railroad rate regulation, which frequently appeared on the docket of the Fuller Court. As Friedman has explained:

> The Supreme Court was crucified in its day because the justices refused to let the states, or state agencies, regulate railroad and utility rates, at least in some cases; but today, in an age of free markets, and a kind of capitalist triumphalism, rate regulation has gone completely out of fashion. Indeed, to many economists (and ordinary people) rate regulation seems like a bad historical joke. (Friedman 2002, 23)

Viewed in this context, the Fuller Court's skepticism about rate controls seems forward-looking and modern.

Other themes of the Fuller era also resonate in the contemporary legal culture. Current deregulation and tax-cutting initiatives reflect continuing interest in free-market ordering. Recently, the Supreme Court has even gingerly reaffirmed the traditional view that Congress does not possess plenary lawmaking authority under the Commerce Clause. More striking has been the reemergence of property rights on the constitutional agenda. The Supreme Court under Chief Justice William H. Rehnquist has been more sympathetic to property owners than any Court since the 1930s. This attitude has been most strikingly manifest in a line of cases strengthening the protection afforded property owners under the Takings Clause of the Fifth Amendment. Writing for the Court in *Dolan v. City of Tigard* (1994), Rehnquist pointedly observed that the Takings Clause is an integral part of the Bill of Rights that should not "be relegated to the status of a poor relation" (*Dolan*, 392). In language reminiscent of the Fuller era, jurists and scholars have rekindled a wide-ranging debate about the relationship between property ownership and individual liberty.

Indeed, it has been argued that the Supreme Court under Rehnquist's leadership is reviving a number of constitutional tenets associated with the Fuller era. Fiss, for instance, has asserted:

> Like the Fuller Court before it, the present Court has posited the priority of liberty over equality, treated liberty as little more than a promise of limited government, and as indicated most dramatically in its decisions on state action, has separated state and society into two spheres and treated the social sphere, largely defined by market exchange, as natural and just. (Fiss 1993, 394–395)

This assessment may well overstate the similarity between the Fuller and Rehnquist Courts, but clearly recent developments have demonstrated that a reconsideration of the continuing legacy of the Fuller Court to constitutional thought is in order.

Aside from jurisprudence, the work of the Fuller Court has a lasting importance for another reason: It established the Supreme Court as a key participant in the polity. Fuller and his colleagues strengthened the power of the federal courts to enforce the Constitution. On a broad range of issues the Court showed vitality as a policymaker. It did much to establish federal courts as the primary protectors of constitutional rights. Expansive use of federal judicial power in the late twentieth century was build upon precedents, such as *Ex Parte Young* (1908), from the Fuller era.

Fuller's tenure as chief justice left a lasting imprint on the Supreme Court and American law. This is not to claim that Fuller and his colleagues were uniquely talented or invariably reached meritorious conclusions. But the members of the Court were conscientious individuals who dealt with nettlesome challenges in a period of rapid and unsettling change. Willing to innovate in many areas of law and accommodate a degree of change, the justices never lost sight of the historic tie between property rights and individual liberty. The Fuller Court, like the Framers of the Constitution and the Bill of Rights, considered the right to acquire and use property as an element of individual liberty. Its historical reputation will always be closely linked to the place of economic freedom in America's constitutional and political culture.

References

Ely, James W. Jr. *The Chief Justiceship of Melville W. Fuller, 1888–1910*. Columbia: University of South Carolina Press, 1995.

———. *The Guardian of Every Other Right: A Constitutional History of Property Rights*. 2nd ed. New York: Oxford University Press, 1998.

———. "Melville W. Fuller Reconsidered." *Journal of Supreme Court History* 1 (1998): 35–49.

Fiss, Owen M. *History of the Supreme Court of the United Sates, Volume 8: Troubled Beginnings of the Modern State, 1888–1910*. New York: Macmillan, 1993.

Friedman, Lawrence M. *American Law in the Twentieth Century*. New Haven, CT: Yale University Press, 2002.

Gillman, Howard. *The Constitution Besieged: The Rise and Demise of Lochner Era Police Powers Jurisprudence*. Durham, NC: Duke University Press, 1993.

Horwitz, Morton J. *The Transformation of American Law, 1870–1937*. New York: Oxford University Press, 1992.

Hovenkamp, Herbert. *Enterprise and American Law, 1836–1960*. Cambridge, MA: Harvard University Press, 1991.

Keller, Morton. *Affairs of State: Public Life in Late Nineteenth Century America*. Cambridge, MA: Harvard University Press, 1977.

Siegel, Stephen A. "*Lochner* Era Jurisprudence and the American Constitutional Tradition." *North Carolina Law Review* 70 (1991): 1–111.

Sunstein, Cass R. "Lochner's Legacy." *Columbia Law Review* 87 (1987): 873–919.

PART TWO

Reference Materials

Key People, Laws, and Events

Bankruptcy Act of 1898

Although the Constitution empowered Congress to establish "uniform Laws on the subject of Bankruptcies throughout the United States," the bankruptcy laws of 1800, 1841, and 1867 were unpopular and short-lived. Throughout much of the nineteenth century, in the absence of a national law, the states were free to enact their own insolvency systems but could not discharge interstate debts. With the growth of a national credit market after the Civil War, debtor-creditor relationships became less personal. Wholesale merchants were increasingly frustrated with the ineffective, inconsistent, and often vague state laws governing insolvency. Seeking a more stable economic environment, they generated a renewed push for a national debt relief law. This drive for a national bankruptcy law was, therefore, closely linked to the desire of the business community to promote the national economy and provide greater safeguards for creditors. Congress repeatedly debated a bankruptcy bill in the 1890s but had difficulty reaching agreement. Members of Congress from southern and western states, representing rural constituents, preferred to rely on state debt relief laws, and some bitterly assailed the pending national legislation as a harsh measure aimed at unfortunate debtors.

Finally, in 1898 Congress adopted what became a permanent national bankruptcy law. The act authorized any insolvent debtor to obtain the benefits of voluntary bankruptcy. Creditors could also force insolvent debtors into involuntary bankruptcy. The new law created priorities for the equitable distribution of the assets of a bankrupt, and it banned the practice of debtors granting preferences among their creditors. It also allowed the states to exempt certain assets from bankruptcy proceedings. By virtue of the act insolvent debtors could obtain a discharge from their obligations and thus gain a fresh start. Administration of the bankruptcy act was vested in the federal district courts, which in turn delegated power to separate bankruptcy referees.

The Fuller Court sustained broad congressional power over bankruptcy in *Hanover National Bank v. Moyses* (1902). Decisions by the Fuller Court laid the basis for later developments in the bankruptcy field. Eventually the 1898 act became outmoded for modern business conditions. Congress revised bankruptcy provisions during the Great Depression with the Chandler Act. More recently, in the Bankruptcy Reform Act of 1978 Congress significantly overhauled the bankruptcy system established by the 1898 act.

Bryan, William Jennings

William Jennings Bryan (1860–1925) was a major force in shaping the political climate of the late nineteenth century. Born in Illinois, Bryan studied law in Chicago and began a routine legal practice in Jacksonville. Moving to Lincoln, Nebraska, Bryan formed a law partnership but devoted much of his energy to Democratic Party politics. Stressing the need for tariff reform, he was elected to Congress in 1890. Increasingly attracted to the coinage of silver as a means of inflating the currency, Bryan broke with President Grover Cleveland over Cleveland's hard money policy. Bryan became a leading spokesman for the silver movement, and his name was mentioned as a possible presidential candidate in 1896. Bryan's eloquent and famous "Cross of Gold" speech at the Democratic Convention helped him win the party's nomination. Since Bryan backed a number of Populist principles, he was also nominated by the People's Party. During the campaign Bryan urged tariff reform, demanded free coinage of silver, and criticized the use of court injunctions in labor disputes. He urged an income tax but was reluctant to forcefully criticize the Fuller Court decisions in *Pollock v. Farmers' Loan and Trust Co.* (1895) invalidating such a levy. In the election, however, the voters decisively chose Republican William McKinley over Bryan.

After his defeat Bryan returned to the practice of law. He unsuccessfully argued before the Fuller Court in support of Nebraska's railroad rate regulations in *Smyth v. Ames* (1898). Remaining politically active, Bryan was again nominated for the presidency by the Democrats in 1900. The silver issue had lost much of its public appeal, and so Bryan criticized the policy of imperialism that followed the Spanish-American War. Although defeated once more by McKinley, Bryan had a loyal following and called for programs that would gradually be adopted during the Progressive era. He envisioned a more active role for government in the economy and thus challenged the tenets of limited government and contractual freedom espoused by Fuller and his colleagues.

Bryan's later career was also noteworthy. He was defeated for the presidency for the third and last time in 1908. Thereafter Bryan served as secretary of state under President Woodrow Wilson until he resigned in 1915 in protest over the drift toward American intervention in World War I. He spoke widely on political and religious topics and was drawn into the antievolution movement. Alert to the conservative social implications of Darwinian theory, Bryan stressed his Christian convictions and battled the teaching of evolution in public schools. In 1925 he ended his long career as a special prosecutor in the well-known Scopes trial in Dayton, Tennessee, dying only a few days after the close of the trial.

Chinese Exclusion Act of 1882

In the late nineteenth century, Chinese immigrants became a cheap source of labor on the West Coast and were targeted by labor unions who complained that whites were losing the competition for jobs. Congress responded by enacting the Chinese Exclusion Act of 1882.

In 1848 gold was discovered in California. Large numbers of laborers from different countries, including China, flocked to the United States. At first these Chinese laborers were welcomed as domestic servants and outdoor workers. Many Chinese laborers helped build the transcontinental railroad. The Burlingame Treaty of 1868 between China and the United States gave citizens of each country who traveled or resided in the other country the "privileges, immunities, and exemptions" enjoyed by the citizens of that nation. But as more laborers came from China, they began to take more skilled jobs and were therefore in competition with white laborers, particularly since they would work for cheaper wages. This caused growing resentment in western states. In 1878 the California constitutional convention declared that the immigration of Chinese laborers was a "menace to our civilization" and asked Congress to put a stop to future immigration.

In addition to the competition over employment, perceived racial differences were a growing problem. Voicing a common fear, Justice Stephen J. Field declared in 1889 that Chinese immigrants remained "strangers in the land" and that there was a "great danger that at no distant day that [western] portion of our country would be overrun by them unless prompt action was taken to restrict their immigration" (*Chinese Exclusion Case*, 595).

Congress was concerned that by excluding Chinese immigrants it would violate the Burlingame Treaty. In 1880 a supplementary treaty was ratified that gave the United States the right to limit the immigration of Chinese laborers if the government felt that these workers threatened the interests of the United States.

In May 1882 Congress passed the Chinese Exclusion Act, which essentially carried the supplemental treaty into effect. The act suspended the immigration of Chinese laborers for ten years. The act did not apply to laborers who were already in the United States. The Chinese Exclusion Act was amended in 1884 and 1888 to make it more difficult for Chinese laborers to prove that they were in the country before the passage of the 1882 act and were therefore eligible to stay in the United States. The Supreme Court upheld the Act in the *Chinese Exclusion Case* (1889). The Court ruled that the power to exclude foreigners was an inherent part of national sovereignty and that Congress could abrogate treaty stipulations by enacting inconsistent laws. In

1892 Congress extended the Chinese Exclusion Act for another decade, and in 1902 it halted Chinese immigration indefinitely.

Choate, Joseph Hodges

Joseph Hodges Choate (1832–1917) was a leading appellate advocate who frequently appeared before the Supreme Court and many state courts during the late nineteenth century. Born in Massachusetts, Choate was educated at Harvard College and Harvard Law School. He soon moved to New York City, where he practiced for the rest of his career at the bar. A versatile and skillful attorney, Choate handled cases spanning a wide range of law. He also served as president of the American Bar Association and as president of the New York State constitutional convention of 1894.

Choate is best remembered for the important cases he argued before the Supreme Court. The most significant of these was *Pollock v. Farmers' Loan and Trust Co.* (1895), in which Choate successfully contended that the 1894 income tax was an unconstitutional direct tax. Describing the tax as "communistic in its purpose and tendencies," Choate made clear his strong belief in the rights of property owners and the duty of government to protect those rights. In another famous case, *Mugler v. Kansas* (1887), Choate argued that Iowa's prohibition law deprived his client, a brewer, of property without due process of law. Although the Supreme Court sustained the statute as a valid exercise of state police power, the justices stressed that they had the authority to scrutinize the purpose behind state regulations as well as the means employed to achieve the ostensible ends of the legislation. This was a key step toward the Supreme Court's later use of substantive due process to safeguard private property rights. Choate commonly represented propertied interests, but he sometimes appeared before the Supreme Court on behalf of underdogs. In *Fong Yue Ting v. United States*(1893), for instance, he defended to no avail a Chinese alien in an attack on a Chinese expulsion law.

In 1899 President William McKinley named Choate as ambassador to Great Britain, and he served in that position until 1905. Choate's legal skills served him well as ambassador. He was instrumental in the creation of a tribunal that resolved the disputed boundary between Alaska and Canada.

Cleveland, Grover

Grover Cleveland (1837–1908) was the only Democrat elected to the presidency between the Civil War and 1912. He was also the only president to serve two nonconsecutive terms. Cleveland studied law by apprenticeship with a Buffalo, New York, firm and was admitted to the New York bar in 1859. He furnished a substitute rather than fight in the Civil War. Active in Democratic Party affairs, Cleveland began a rapid rise in the political world when he was elected mayor of Buffalo in 1881. A year later Cleveland was elected governor of New York. In 1884 the Democrats nominated Cleveland for President. Stressing civil service reform and the evil of the spoils system, Cleveland narrowly prevailed over Republican James G. Blaine in a colorful campaign.

During his first term Cleveland attacked the spoils system. He vetoed numerous special pension bills and carefully observed the newly enacted civil service law with its emphasis on merit hiring. Cleveland also supported the creation of the Interstate Commerce Commission in 1887 to impose federal regulation on railroads. He urged a reduced tariff on imported goods. Cleveland envisioned a limited role for the federal government and resisted the paternalistic notion that the government should relieve individual distress. In April 1888 Cleveland nominated Melville W. Fuller to be chief justice of the Supreme Court. Later that year, however, Republican Benjamin Harrison defeated Cleveland in a close contest.

Cleveland practiced law in New York City until he was again nominated by the Democrats as a candidate for president. In 1892 Cleveland handily triumphed over Harrison. Cleveland's second administration was vexed by the sharp economic downturn that dominated the mid-1890s. An adherent of the gold standard and sound money, Cleveland successfully urged repeal of the Sherman Silver Purchase Act as a means to bolster the currency and halt the depression. Cleveland allowed the Wilson-Gorman Tariff Act of 1894, which modestly reduced tariffs and imposed the first peacetime income tax, to become law without his signature. When the Pullman strike of 1894 resulted in the blockage of mail trains and destruction of railroad property, the Cleveland administration obtained a court injunction against interference with trains and dispatched federal troops to Chicago to maintain order. During his second term Cleveland appointed property-minded conservative Democrats, Edward D. White and Rufus W. Peckham, to the Supreme Court. Under Cleveland's leadership the United States intervened in the boundary dispute between Great Britain and Venezuela and engineered a solution through international arbitration. Cleveland's conservative economic politics, particularly his antisilver stance, split the Democratic Party. Cleveland was succeeded in 1897 by Republican William McKinley. Cleveland retired to Princeton, New Jersey, and later became a trustee of Princeton University.

Cooley, Thomas McIntyre

Thomas McIntyre Cooley (1824–1898) was a leading treatise writer and jurist in the late nineteenth century. During the 1860s Cooley served as a law professor at the University of Michigan. Cooley became a member of the Michigan Supreme Court in 1865 and remained on the bench until 1885. As a judge he relied heavily on precedent and the common law in rendering decisions. During these years he also served as a railroad receiver and became an authority on railroad issues.

In 1868, Cooley published his influential and widely cited treatise *The Constitutional Limitations Which Rest Upon the Legislative Power of the States of the American Union*. Much of Cooley's historical reputation is based upon this significant work. Cooley's primary goal was to fashion limits on arbitrary legislative action. He tied the Jacksonian principles of equal rights and hostility to special economic privilege with due process protection of property rights. Cooley embraced a broad reading of the due process norm as a substantive restraint on legislative power. He defined liberty as encompassing the right to make contracts and hold property. Moreover, he assailed class legislation, laws that aided one segment of society at the expense of others. Cooley's work provided much of the intellectual underpinnings for judicial moves to fashion the Due Process Clause of the Fourteenth Amendment into a formidable safeguard for economic rights in the late nineteenth century.

It is important to note that Cooley was equally concerned about the growth of monopoly and concentration of economic power. He opposed the use of public resources to subsidize private enterprises, insisting that taxation could be imposed only for a public purpose. Cooley's defense of individual rights was not limited to economic matters. He saw no dichotomy between property rights and other individual liberties. For example, he was supportive of freedom of expression and religious liberty.

Cooley made other contributions to American law. He wrote treatises dealing with the law of taxation and torts, as well as numerous articles. In 1887 President Grover Cleveland named Cooley to the new Interstate Commerce Commission. Cooley generally pursued a conservative course as chairman of the commission and received high marks for his efforts to make the agency effective in eliminating railroad abuses while respecting the interests of all parties.

Dawes Act

Westward expansion of the United States throughout the nineteenth century repeatedly raised important questions about the legal status of Indian tribes. The original policy of treating Indian tribes as foreign nations gradually eroded. By the late nineteenth century many observers felt that the reservation system had reduced Indians to helpless wards of the government. Congress stopped making treaties with Indian tribes and eventually adopted a plan of assimilation under which the federal government sought to integrate Indians into the dominant social order. The cornerstone of this new policy was the Dawes Act of 1887. Sponsored by Senator Henry L. Dawes of Massachusetts, the act provided for the breakup of communal landholding by tribes and the allotment of reserved tribal lands to Indians on an individual basis. Each head of a family was to receive 160 acres, the title to which was to be held by the government in trust for twenty-five years. The act also granted American citizenship to Indians who received allotments, but it excluded from citizenship those remaining in tribes. It rested on the premise that the private ownership of land was an essential step in the process of acculturating Indians into white society. The goal was for Indians to become independent family farmers. Although many supporters of the Dawes Act were sincerely concerned about the deteriorating situation of the Indians, others saw allotment as a means of breaking down reservations and opening surplus land on reservations to white settlement.

Whatever the motives behind the Dawes Act, the administration of the law proved disastrous for most Indians. Although Indians were not all of one mind, many opposed allotment and preferred their traditional tribal system. The allotment of tribal lands proceeded swiftly, and tracts not used for allotments were sold to non-Indian owners. Moreover, much of the land allocated to individual Indians was not suitable for agriculture, and there was no realistic prospect that the owners would become self-sufficient. Indian cultural patterns also ran counter to the hopes behind the allotment system. Congress amended the Dawes Act several times, but the net result was increased demoralization and economic distress. In the twentieth century Congress abandoned the policy of forced assimilation and upheld tribal autonomy.

Debs, Eugene V.

Born in Terre Haute, Indiana, Eugene V. Debs (1855–1926) quit school at an early age and went to work for a railroad. He became active in the Brotherhood of Locomotive Firemen and in Democratic Party politics in Indiana. In the late 1880s Debs began to move away from traditional craft unionism, and in 1893 he became the president of the newly formed American Railway Union. Membership in this organization was open to all railroad workers regardless of their particular job. The American Railway Union grew rapidly and pursued a confrontational policy with management. Debs became one of the most prominent labor leaders in the country.

In May 1894 the employees of the Pullman Palace Car Company, which manufactured sleeping cars for lease to railroads, went on strike to protest wage cuts and the refusal of the company to reduce rents for company housing. A number of the Pullman employees were members of the American Railway Union, and in June the union voted to refuse to handle any trains with Pullman cars. The strike and boycott hindered rail traffic through Chicago, paralyzing much of the national rail system. Debs sought to prevent violence but could not control events. National newspapers turned strongly against Debs and accused him of encouraging anarchy. In July Debs and other union officials were enjoined by a federal court from inducing railroad employees to cease work. Subsequently, Debs was convicted of contempt of court for violating the injunction and was ordered to jail for six months. The Fuller Court upheld the injunction and the Debs conviction in *In re Debs* (1895).

The Pullman strike further radicalized Debs and sharpened his critique of capitalism. He disbanded the American Railway Union and helped to organize the Socialist Party. The socialists nominated Debs as their candidate for president five times. He was never a serious contender, but he did capture 6 percent of the national vote in 1912. Debs was imprisoned in 1918 for violating the Espionage Act by his vocal opposition to American involvement in World War I. He was released from prison in 1921 by President Warren Harding. Neither an intellectual nor a skillful politician, Debs was widely admired for his sincerity and dedication to his principles.

Erdman Act

In the aftermath of the bitter Pullman strike of 1894, President Grover Cleveland appointed a commission to investigate the causes of the unrest. The commission condemned the intransigence of the Pullman Palace Car Company, stressed the huge financial cost of the disorders, and recommended arbitration as a means of resolving railroad labor disputes. In addition, a number of railroad managers came to recognize that labor organizations might stabilize the workforce. After lengthy consideration, Congress passed the Erdman Act in 1898, the first step in fashioning a new framework for securing labor peace in the rail industry.

The Erdman Act created a mechanism for the mediation of disputes on interstate railroads at the request of either management or labor. The act also provided for voluntary arbitration of any controversy by a special board. In a bid to encourage the growth of rail unions, Congress outlawed the practice of requiring employees to enter into so-called yellow dog contracts in which they agreed not to join any labor organization. It further prohibited railroads from discriminating against employees because of union membership. Sponsors of the Erdman Act hoped that responsible organized labor in the rail industry would exert a restraining influence and help prevent work stoppages.

The limitations of the Erdman Act soon became apparent. The voluntary arbitration mechanism was virtually ignored for years, although after 1906 a number of disputes were settled by procedures under the act. Moreover, in *Adair v. United States* (1908) the Fuller Court invalidated the portion of the act that prevented railroads from discharging an employee because of union membership. The Court determined that there was no connection between the encouragement of labor organizations and interstate commerce. This provision, therefore, exceeded congressional authority under the Commerce Clause and infringed the liberty of contract as guaranteed by the Fifth Amendment. For all its shortcomings, however, the Erdman Act did represent a watershed of sorts. By seeking to extend legal protection to railroad workers, Congress implicitly recognized that the suppression of strikes by force was not a long-term solution to labor unrest in the rail industry.

Evarts Act

The Evarts Act of 1891, also know as the Circuit Court of Appeals Act, was the culmination of years of agitation for a reorganization of the federal judiciary. It was the first significant overhaul of the federal court system since the original Judiciary Act of 1798.

By the late nineteenth century problems abounded with the increasingly antiquated federal court structure. One problem was the drain on the time and energy of the Supreme Court justices. In addition to attending sessions of the Supreme Court, justices were required to hold circuit court in their respective regional circuits. This onerous duty necessitated lengthy travel to conduct trials in the circuit courts. A second problem was the lack of intermediate courts of appeals. Cases appealed from the circuit courts went directly to the Supreme Court as a matter of right. Consequently, the Supreme Court's docket ballooned beyond control. Relatively routine private law cases consumed a good deal of time. An overworked Court faced a growing backlog in the disposition of cases.

Senator William M. Evarts of New York led the fight to modify the federal court structure. Chief Justice Melville W. Fuller also actively encouraged the reform movement. Although retaining much of the existing court arrangements, the Evarts Act gave substantial relief to the Supreme Court. The measure created new intermediate circuit courts of appeal and curtailed appeals to the Supreme Court. Decisions of the circuit courts of appeal arising under diversity of citizenship jurisdiction or involving patent or admiralty law were reviewable only by a writ of certiorari. Hence, the Supreme Court could decline to hear appeals not deemed to be of sufficient importance. The Evarts Act, however, did not abolish the existing circuit courts and enlarged the right of appeal to the Supreme Court in federal criminal cases. Nonetheless, under the Evarts Act the justices gained greater control of their docket, and the number of new cases dropped sharply. Moreover, the act hastened the Supreme Court's shift toward focusing on public law issues by reducing the frequency of cases involving private law.

Federal Employers' Liability Act (FELA)

By the late nineteenth century industrial accidents were killing or injuring thousands of employees annually. Railroads in particular were a dangerous place to work. There were increased demands for legislation to overhaul the common law rules governing industrial accidents, many of which had been forged in a preindustrial era.

Mounting dissatisfaction over the resolution of frequent injuries to employees on railroads induced Congress to enact the Federal Employers' Liability Act in 1906. FELA in effect created a federal statutory negligence action for injured railroad workers. It modified the common law system by abolishing the fellow-servant and contributory negligence defenses utilized by employers. It also invalidated any contractual release of liability when employees accepted benefits from private relief associations. Congress hoped not only to better protect railroad workers and their dependents but also to motivate companies to become more safety-conscious by raising the cost of accidents.

In the *Employers' Liability Cases* (1908) a badly splintered Fuller Court held that the act was unconstitutional because it embraced subjects outside of the power of Congress to regulate commerce. Specifically, the Court found the act invalid because it covered railroad employees engaged in intrastate as well as interstate commerce. Congress promptly responded with a second Federal Liability Act, which applied only to workers engaged in interstate commerce at the time of the accident. This subsequent measure was sustained by the Supreme Court after the close of the Fuller era. The *Employers' Liability Cases* demonstrated that the Fuller Court remained reluctant to extend the power of Congress to all aspects of the economy.

Although FELA marked a significant improvement in the law governing liability for railroad accidents, it was no panacea. The act did not make carriers the insurers of workers' safety. Instead, liability was still predicated on a showing of negligence by the employer. Moreover, it was necessary to decide whether a particular activity by an employee took place within the scope of interstate commerce in order for the act to apply. As a consequence, FELA has produced a steady volume of litigation to the present day. Yet FELA has proved an enduring remedy despite periodic calls to replace the act with a workers' compensation scheme.

Harrison, Benjamin

Benjamin Harrison (1833–1901), a Republican, was elected president in 1888, defeating the incumbent Democrat Grover Cleveland. Harrison, however, decisively lost a rematch with Cleveland in 1892, making Harrison the only president to serve in office between the nonconsecutive terms of another. A graduate of Miami University of Ohio, Harrison practiced law in Indianapolis and became active in Republican politics. He joined the Union Army in 1862 and gained the rank of brigadier general. Harrison was elected to the U.S. Senate in 1881 and served a single term. Although Cleveland garnered a slight majority in the popular vote in 1888, Harrison won the most electoral votes and became president.

Harrison favored a protective tariff, a sound currency, and benefits for Union veterans. He generally supported conservative economic policies and was disinclined to pursue an activist role with respect to domestic affairs. Nonetheless, Congress enacted a number of important measures during the Harrison administration. The most significant was the Sherman Anti-Trust Act of 1890, which Harrison signed but did not seek to enforce. Harrison repeatedly urged Congress to mandate improved safety devices for railroads to reduce employee accidents, and he engineered passage of the Safety Appliance Act of 1893. He unsuccessfully called for federal supervision of congressional elections to protect black voters in the South. Harrison supported the creation of a "new" Navy of steel warships. In addition, he worked for the annexation of Hawaii, a process that would be completed later in the 1890s.

Although president for just one term, Harrison had a profound impact on the Supreme Court. He made four appointments to the Court: David J. Brewer, Henry Billings Brown, George Shiras, Jr., and Howell E. Jackson. All were generally conservative in outlook, and Brewer soon emerged as an intellectual force on the Fuller Court. Furthermore, Harrison recommended to Congress the formation of intermediate courts of appeal in order to reduce the backlog of the Supreme Court, and he helped to secure passage of the Evarts Act of 1891. The last Civil War general to serve as president, Harrison devoted much of his time after leaving the White House to representing Venezuela in the boundary dispute with British Guiana.

Hepburn Act

In the early years of the twentieth century political figures associated with the Progressive movement sought to address the imbalance of economic power associated with the emerging industrial order. They took particular aim at the dominant position of railroads in American economic life, and they demanded increased public accountability. The feeble Interstate Commerce Commission (ICC), created by Congress in 1887, had brought about no basic change in the operations of the rail industry. The Progressives therefore championed laws to strengthen the ICC.

After several years of prodding by President Theodore Roosevelt, Congress enacted the Hepburn Act in 1906, a development that marked a watershed in railroad regulatory history. The most important feature of the Hepburn Act was the conferral upon the ICC of power to set railroad charges. The ICC was authorized, upon receipt of a complaint, to review railroad charges and to determine "the just and reasonable rate." Railroads were still free to set rates in the first instance, however, and the ICC could not initiate a new rate on its own. The act also restricted the scope of judicial review of agency decisions and provided that ICC orders were binding when issued. In addition, the Hepburn Act banned the issuance of most free passes and gave the ICC power to require uniform accounting techniques. The commodities clause of the act attempted to divorce transportation from production and manufacturing. In a provision aimed largely at the control of anthracite coal mines in Pennsylvania by several railroads, the commodities clause barred railroads from carrying in interstate commerce any materials produced by companies controlled by the carriers. So strong was antirailroad sentiment by 1906 that the Hepburn Act passed both houses of Congress by overwhelming margins. Enactment of this measure marked the first step in the railroad industry's loss of control over the rate-making process.

Although often skeptical about economic regulations, the Supreme Court under Chief Justice Melville W. Fuller generally sustained the enlarged power of the ICC. It upheld a number of rate-setting orders despite railroads' objections. The Hepburn Act set the stage for additional regulatory measures, until Congress gave the ICC sweeping authority over the industry in the Transportation Act of 1920. After World War II, however, critics increasingly argued that heavy-handed controls contributed to the decline of railroading, and in 1980 Congress largely abandoned rate regulation as part of a deregulation policy.

Interstate Commerce Commission (ICC)

In the decades following the Civil War there was mounting political pressure to impose public controls on railroads. State legislatures initially took the initiative by establishing railroad commissions and attempting to fix maximum rates for transportation. It became apparent, however, that the states could not meaningfully supervise the emerging network of interstate railroads. Moreover, in 1886 the Supreme Court held that state regulation of interstate railroad rates invaded federal authority under the Commerce Clause because it threatened to negatively impact trade among the states. This decision provided the catalyst for Congress to pass the Interstate Commerce Act in 1887.

A compromise measure, the act outlawed preferential treatment for any shipper, banned the pooling of revenue among carriers, and required that rates be "reasonable and just." It created the Interstate Commerce Commission with power to conduct hearings and halt practices in violation of the statute. But the act did not define reasonable rates or confer ratemaking authority on the ICC. A series of decisions by the Fuller Court in the 1890s narrowly construed the power of the ICC, and the commission was largely ineffective until the early twentieth century. Still, the ICC was important as the first tentative step by Congress toward administrative control of economic activity.

During the Progressive era there was renewed clamor for more stringent controls of railroads. Several statutes, the most important of which was the Hepburn Act of 1906, greatly expanded ICC authority and gave it the power to determine rail charges. The courts generally upheld the enhanced power of the ICC over rates and even allowed the ICC to control intrastate rates that discriminated against interstate commerce, but they occasionally overturned ICC orders. In the Transportation Act of

1920 Congress further enlarged the power of the ICC and authorized the agency to approve the merger of rail lines notwithstanding possible antitrust concerns. Despite the hopes of reformers, the ICC proved reluctant to take the lead in formulating rail policy. In fact, the ICC, a supposedly independent body, was often subject to enormous political pressure to set rates favorable to different sections of the country. Following World War II, railroads entered a long period of decline. The ICC tended to oppose competition among railroads, trucks, and barges. Criticism of the ICC as a stand-pat and sluggish agency, which aided neither carriers nor consumers, grew steadily. Many blamed suffocating regulations for the stagnation of the rail industry, and in 1980 Congress embraced the policy of deregulation, eliminating most of the ICC's control over rates. Finally, in 1995 Congress abolished the ICC, the nation's oldest regulatory body. The ICC's remaining functions were transferred to the newly created Surface Transportation Board.

McKinley, William

William McKinley (1843–1901), a Republican, was elected president in the pivotal election of 1896, defeating William Jennings Bryan. Born in Ohio, McKinley briefly attended Allegheny College. He served with distinction in the Union Army during the Civil War and was promoted to the rank of major. After the Civil War McKinley studied law privately and at Albany Law School. He established a successful legal practice in Canton, Ohio, and became active in the Republican Party. Elected to the House of Representatives in 1876, he served in that body, with some interruptions, until 1891. McKinley was named chairman of the House Ways and Means Committee in 1889, and his name was linked with the protective tariff of 1890. He was elected governor of Ohio in 1891 and was reelected two years later. During these years McKinley formed a close friendship with Mark Hanna, an Ohio businessman and a shrewd political figure.

Nominated as a presidential candidate by the Republicans in 1896, McKinley ran on a platform promising a protective tariff and a gold standard for money. The campaign against Bryan was dominated by the monetary issue and Bryan's call for the coinage of silver. Winning decisively, McKinley swept the northeastern states and cemented Republican Party hegemony in national politics for decades. He was easily reelected in 1900.

A skillful administrator, McKinley generally pursued a conservative course as president. The tariff on imported goods was revised upward. Although unenthusiastic about conflict with Spain in 1898, McKinley did not resist the popular clamor for war. Yet he favored commercial expansion overseas and supported American retention of the former Spanish colonies after the war. Likewise, McKinley backed the annexation of Hawaii. He also sent a U.S. contingent to join the international army that suppressed the Boxer Rebellion in China in 1900. McKinley named Joseph McKenna to the Supreme Court in 1897. In September 1901 McKinley was assassinated by an anarchist in Buffalo; he was succeeded by Vice President Theodore Roosevelt.

Olney, Richard

Richard Olney (1835–1917) graduated from Brown University and Harvard Law School and became a prominent corporation lawyer in Boston. He represented a number of railroads, helping to facilitate mergers and working to protect railroads from regulation. Aside from advising his corporate clients, Olney primarily practiced before appellate courts and regulatory bodies. A blunt and pugnacious man, Olney was a longtime Democrat despite his generally conservative political views.

President Grover Cleveland named Olney U.S. attorney general at the start of his second term in 1893. In this capacity Olney participated in some of the most significant cases before the Fuller Court. Adhering to a restrictive understanding of interstate commerce, Olney had little interest in antitrust prosecutions. The government's position in the sugar trust case, *United States v. E. C. Knight Co.* (1895), was inadequately prepared, and some historians have attributed the outcome in the case to Olney's dislike of the Sherman Act. Olney unsuccessfully defended the 1894 income tax in two arguments before the Supreme Court in *Pollock v. Farmer's Loan and Trust Co.* (1895). He urged federal intervention to break the secondary boycott growing out of the Pullman strike. Olney authorized the application for a court injunction and favored the dispatch of federal troops to Chicago. He skillfully argued the contempt case against strike leaders, *In re Debs* (1895), before the Fuller Court and was vindicated with a unanimous decision upholding his contentions. In addition to judicial appearances, Olney formulated policies to thwart Jacob S. Coxey's "march" of unemployed men to Washington to demand public works projects.

In June 1895 Cleveland nominated Olney as secretary of state. A vigorous champion of U.S. interests abroad, Olney famously asserted the Monroe Doctrine as a justification for American intervention in the boundary dispute between Venezuela and British Guiana. He also dealt with vexing issues created by the revolt in Cuba against Spanish rule. Leaving office in 1897, Olney returned to his business practice in Washington, devoting himself largely to drafting agreements and consultations. He helped to organize the Northern Securities Company, a railroad holding company, and assisted behind the scenes in the unsuccessful defense of the firm against antitrust charges.

Pullman Strike

The Pullman strike of 1894 was a defining moment in American labor history. It was the culmination of decades of conflict between railroads and workers. In response to an imposed wage reduction, employees of the Pullman Palace Car Company went on strike in May. To support the strike, the newly organized American Railway Union, under the leadership of Eugene V. Debs, began a secondary boycott by refusing to handle trains with Pullman cars. The boycott spread rapidly and disrupted much of the national rail transportation system. Strikers placed obstructions on tracks, and the movement of trains through Chicago was blocked. Transportation of the mail was, of course, disrupted. President Grover Cleveland and U.S. Attorney General Richard Olney grew increasingly alarmed, and Olney secured a broad injunction from the federal circuit court against any actions that impeded the movement of trains operating in interstate commerce or carrying mail. Events rapidly spun out of control. When violence continued and even spread westward, Cleveland in early July ordered federal troops to Chicago to maintain order. Perhaps sparked by the arrival of troops, rampaging mobs destroyed a good deal of railroad property. Within a few days, however, the army cleared the tracks and effectively ended the boycott.

Public opinion turned against the strike and held the American Railway Union responsible for the violence. Debs and other union leaders were convicted of contempt of court for violating the injunction and were imprisoned. In 1895 the Fuller Court unanimously upheld the convictions and broadly asserted federal authority to protect interstate commerce. The fledgling American Railway Union was broken. Although a sharp setback for unions, the Pullman strike aroused interest in finding a better means of handling railroad labor disputes. The Erdman Act of 1898 was a turning point because it encouraged the use of mediation and arbitration.

Pure Food and Drug Act of 1906

During the nineteenth century there were efforts in Congress to pass legislation aimed at regulating food and drugs, but most of these laws were directed toward imposing taxes and protecting American industries from foreign imports. Eventually, ideas were circulated about the need to protect consumers from fraud that might be inflicted upon the public by domestic producers. As early as 1879 a bill was introduced in Congress that would have outlawed the adulteration of food and drink, but the measure died. Although efforts to pass a national bill proved unsuccessful, various states passed food and drug laws aimed at products. These state laws were upheld under the states' police powers.

In 1906 Upton Sinclair published the book *The Jungle* in which he detailed the conditions in the plants of the Chicago meatpacking industry. This exposé horrified the public with descriptions of the filthy processing plants and the actual ingredients in processed meats. The book provided a final impetus for the passage of the Pure Food and Drug Act of 1906, the first comprehensive federal law excluding adulterated or mislabeled foods and drugs from interstate commerce. Shipment of adulterated food or drugs was made a crime, and such items were subject to confiscation. Congress drafted the law to prohibit interstate shipment because it was concerned that a direct regulation of adulteration or misbranding of food and drugs would be seen as an unconstitutional extension of federal police power into an area of state responsibility. The act was one of a series of social reform laws by Congress in the early twentieth century based on the commerce power.

In *Hipolite Egg Co. v. United States* (1911) the Supreme Court unanimously upheld the constitutionality of the act as within the power of Congress to regulate interstate commerce. Relying in part on *Champion v. Ames* (1903), decided by the Fuller Court, the justices ruled that Congress could prevent trade between the states in adulterated products. Implicit in the *Hipolite* decision was an expansion of federal authority.

Railroad Receivers

A receiver is an officer appointed by a court to receive and preserve property and to dispose of it at the direction of the court. The appointment of a receiver is a well-established equitable remedy utilized by courts when it is no longer thought appropriate that either of the parties to litigation should retain control of certain property. Any interference with property in the hands of a receiver is punishable as contempt of court. Receivers were sometimes appointed to take possession of an insolvent business. The receiver would take control of the enterprise, sell its assets, and pay the creditors under the supervision of the appointing court.

By the late nineteenth century the frequent insolvency of railroads raised novel challenges and helped to enlarge the role of receivers. The continued operation of insolvent lines was deemed important for the public interest. In addition, railroads were worth more as a going concern than if their assets were sold piecemeal. Consequently, in the absence of a bankruptcy law, federal courts fashioned new rules for railroad receivers. They began to authorize receivers to continue the operations of insolvent lines and to borrow additional capital, which would take priority over existing indebtedness.

Courts soon went a step further. They began to appoint receivers at the request of the carrier itself, even when there was no suit yet pending against the company. Federal judges also began to appoint the current managers of the railroad, instead of outside neutral individuals, as receivers. The primary consideration of railroad receivers was the preservation of transportation services. This often entailed a corporate reorganization in which the rights of creditors and bondholders were subordinated. Chief Justice Melville W. Fuller, writing for the Supreme Court, upheld this new type of receivership in *Quincy, Missouri, and Pacific Railroad Co. v. Humphreys* (1892). Soon the standard practice for carriers in financial difficulty was to seek receivership protection. This enlarged understanding of receivership pulled the federal courts heavily into the business of supervising troubled railroads. Moreover, federal judges started to enjoin strikes against railroads in receivership on the grounds that such activity interfered with the receiver's management of the line.

During the 1880s and 1890s hundreds of rail lines went into receivership. The appointment of receivers by federal courts was bitterly resented in southern states because the receivers were viewed as representatives of northern capital interests. Despite this political controversy, the use of equity receiverships to reorganize rail lines proved successful. In 1933 Congress amended the bankruptcy law to expressly permit insolvent railroads to seek reorganization.

Roosevelt, Theodore

When William McKinley was assassinated in September 1901, Vice President Theodore Roosevelt (1858–1919) assumed the duties of the presidency. Born into a prominent New York family and educated at Harvard University, Roosevelt entered political life as a reform-minded Republican in the 1880s. He served as a state legislator and in 1886 failed in his bid to be elected mayor of New York City. Thereafter, Roosevelt was police commissioner of New York City as part of a reform political coalition. In 1898 he was elected governor of New York on the Republican ticket and strengthened the state's franchise tax on public utilities.

Elected vice president under McKinley in 1900, and becoming chief executive only months later upon McKinley's death, Roosevelt helped to transform the presidency into the center of the constitutional system. Espousing a broad view of presidential powers, he forced a settlement of the 1902 coal strike and instituted a well-publicized campaign to enforce the Sherman Anti-Trust Act to check corporate power. Although he prevailed in such dramatic antitrust cases as *Northern Securities Co. v. United States* (1904), Roosevelt believed that some business combinations were inevitable. He also pressured Congress to strengthen railroad regulations by enacting the Hepburn Act of 1906, and he championed conservation. Roosevelt pursued an interventionist foreign policy, climaxing in his support for the construction of the Panama Canal.

Roosevelt was not a lawyer, and he had little reverence for the Supreme Court as an institution. Roosevelt futilely sought to induce Melville W. Fuller to resign as chief justice in order to name his close friend, William Howard Taft, to the post. He appointed three justices—Oliver Wendell Holmes Jr., William R. Day, and William H. Moody—to the Supreme Court. All adopted a somewhat more expansive reading of governmental power than was the norm among members of the Court under Fuller. In 1910, as Roosevelt started a campaign to regain the presidency, he criticized the Supreme Court's record on social legislation and singled out *Lochner v. New York* (1905) as an example of how the court obstructed reform.

A growing schism in the Republican Party provided the impetus for Roosevelt to bolt the party and run unsuccessfully for president in 1912 as the nominee of the Progressive Party. He was defeated by Woodrow Wilson. Roosevelt was a forceful advocate of U.S. intervention in World War I.

Safety Appliance Act

Work on railroads in the late nineteenth century was extremely hazardous. Railroad workers, especially those employees engaged in coupling and uncoupling cars, ran a high risk of death or loss of limbs. The invention of air brakes and automatic couplers after the Civil War promised increased safety for both employees and passengers. Air brakes eliminated the need for a brakeman to climb to the top of moving train cars in order to manually operate the brakes. Automatic couplers replaced the hand-operated link-and-pin method of connecting cars and thus ended the necessity for employees to go between cars for that purpose. Railroad companies generally adopted air brakes and automatic couplers for passenger trains, but they resisted these safety devices for freight cars. They were motivated in part by the expense of converting to this new technology, but they were also concerned that use of inconsistent couplers could complicate the exchange of freight cars between lines.

President Benjamin Harrison called upon Congress to mandate improved safety devices on trains. In 1893 Congress passed the Safety Appliance Act, which required the use of air brakes and automatic couplers by 1898 on carriers engaged in interstate commerce. Congress did not specify any particular type of coupler, leaving selection of a uniform device to the railroad companies. The act also abolished the assumption of the risk defense for injuries arising from a violation of the act.

In a line of cases, the Fuller Court broadly construed and vigorously enforced the Safety Appliance Act in order to vindicate the congressional policy of securing the safety of employees and passengers. It repeatedly ruled that carriers were liable for injuries to workers that occurred when the trains were not equipped with safety devices. The Safety Appliance Act did not immediately reduce the number of accidents. Nonetheless, enactment of this measure marked a significant turning point in the regulation of workplace safety. Congress subsequently enacted a number of measures that set workplace safety standards and overhauled the common law of industrial accidents.

Spanish-American War

The Spanish-American War of 1898 marked the debut of the United States as a power on the world stage, but it also raised awkward questions about whether America could legitimately pursue a policy of imperialism overseas. In the late nineteenth century the emerging "yellow press" vigorously competed for circulation, and journalists often fabricated stories in order to attract readers. The Cuban revolt against Spanish colonial rule in the 1890s provided newspapers with a captivating topic. They described in shocking detail the oppression of Cubans by the Spanish, including stories about Spanish cannibalism, torture, and death camps. These stories provoked the American public to take an interest in war with Spain. The seminal blow came on February 15, 1898, when the U.S. warship *Maine* blew up in Havana Harbor. Although the cause was never determined, the newspapers and the public were convinced that Spain was to blame for the explosion, which killed more than 250 men. The rallying cry "Remember the *Maine!* To hell with Spain!" was heard all over the country. Reluctant to go to war, President William McKinley was faced with an uncontrollable uproar from the public, the press, and Congress. Pressure mounted to take action, and on April 25 the United States declared war against Spain.

The conflict resulted in a swift and decisive victory for the United States. As a result of this so-called short and glorious war, the United States and Spain signed a peace treaty on December 10, 1898. The treaty transferred Cuba to the United States for temporary occupation preceding the island's independence. Spain also gave up Puerto Rico and Guam to the United States and relinquished the Philippines for $20 million. Americans felt that the inhabitants of these islands were culturally, socially, and politically different and did not see these territories as suitable for eventual statehood. The overriding constitutional issue was to determine how to justify governing the overseas territories under the Constitution without moving toward statehood.

American overseas expansion presented unique political and legal questions. Differing views as to what the Constitution meant by "the United States"—whether it referred to just the states themselves or also included any territories—led to competing opinions as to how Congress was to treat the new territories. One of the biggest issues dealt with tariffs. If the territories were part of the United States, then no tariffs could be charged on goods imported from those territories. This issue, and others, rested largely on the distinction between "foreign" and "domestic." Disputes over these questions led to a cluster of Supreme Court cases, commonly called the *Insular Cases.* The leading such case was *Downes v. Bidwell* (1901), in which a divided Fuller Court concluded that the United States could acquire new territory and exercise broad power in determining what rights to grant to its inhabitants. Essentially, the Court said, the full range of constitutional rights and protections did not necessarily extend to the people of overseas territories.

Sherman Anti-Trust Act

The economy of the late nineteenth century was characterized by the growth of large-scale corporate enterprise that conducted multistate business operations. Seeking to stabilize volatile markets, many businesses utilized a variety of devices, such as trust arrangements, mergers, and holding companies, to control the marketing of goods and to set prices. These business consolidations were seen as diminishing competition and thus aroused long-standing antimonopoly sentiment among the public. Many people worried that concentrated economic power in private hands posed a threat to political liberty and economic opportunity. There was an increasing clamor for some type of regulation to restrain these giant corporations and restore competition.

Responding to this sentiment, Congress almost unanimously passed the Sherman Anti-Trust Act in 1890. In some respects this legislation was rather traditional in outlook. It built upon the common law concept that conspiracies in restraint of trade were against public policy. Consequently, the measure outlawed "every contract, combination in the form of trust or otherwise, or conspiracy, in restraint of trade or commerce among the several states or with foreign nations." The statute also made it a crime to "monopolize or attempt to monopolize, or combine or conspire . . . to monopolize any part of the trade or commerce among the several states." Violations were punishable by fines, and injured parties could seek injunctions and treble damages. The Sherman Act was premised on the notion that the prohibition of wrongful practices would allow competition to determine prices and regulate economic activity. It was a symbolic affirmation of the ideal of free markets. But the Sherman Act was vaguely worded, and there was little agreement among proponents of the legislation as to what it was expected to accomplish. Moreover, Congress did not create an administrative agency to enforce the act. Instead, it relied upon judicial interpretation and enforcement through both government and private litigation.

Although a long mainstay of antitrust policy, the Sherman Act has been subject to varying interpretations over time. In *United States v. E. C. Knight Co.* (1895) the Fuller Court narrowly construed the reach of the Sherman Act, differentiating between commerce and manufacturing. Some members of the Fuller Court also articulated a rule of reason standard to govern applications of this measure, an approach that left considerable discretion in the hands of judges. Presidents Theodore Roosevelt and William Howard Taft encouraged vigorous enforcement of the Sherman Act but did not halt the trend toward economic concentration. In recent years the Supreme Court has given added weight to economic perspectives and efficiency concerns in construing antitrust policy. The protection afforded competition under the Sherman Act continues to evolve.

Sixteenth Amendment

The Sixteenth Amendment, ratified in 1913, provides in part that Congress "shall have power to lay and collect taxes on incomes, from whatever source derived, without apportionment among the several states." This amendment was designed to overturn a pair of decisions by the Fuller Court in *Pollock v. Farmers Loan and Trust Co.* (1895) and to pave the way for enactment of a federal income tax.

The income tax remained politically controversial following the *Pollock* rulings. In 1896 the platform of the Democratic Party criticized *Pollock*, and William Jennings Bryan gingerly urged an income tax during his presidential campaign. The defeat of Bryan, however, coupled with the return of prosperity during the presidential administration of William McKinley, stifled agitation for an income tax. The political process seemingly ratified the *Pollock* decisions. Although Congress adopted a modest inheritance tax to help finance the Spanish-American War of 1898, the proposed income tax was no longer a central issue. By 1904 even the Democrats dropped their call for such a levy. Still, as the forces of Progressivism gained strength, public opinion began to change. In 1906 President Theodore Roosevelt recommended taxation of income but did not press the matter. During the 1908 presidential election all the major political parties favored an income tax, and the victorious Republican candidate, William Howard Taft, expressed support for this view.

In 1909, as part of a debate over a new tariff bill, Democrats in Congress proposed the adoption of a new income tax law. President Taft was alarmed that such a move would represent a direct assault on the authority and prestige of the Supreme Court. Consequently, he urged passage of a constitutional amendment authorizing the imposition of a federal income tax. Senator Nelson Aldridge of Rhode Island, a staunch opponent of such a levy, calculated that an income tax amendment would fail to win ratification by the states. Such a failure, he reasoned, would strengthen arguments against the constitutionality of an income tax. With President Taft's support, Senator Aldridge called for the adoption of a constitutional amendment. Both houses of Congress approved the income tax amendment by overwhelming margins. Nonetheless, state ratification of the proposed amendment proceeded slowly. There was considerable opposition in the high-income states of the Northeast. Political victories for the forces of Progressivism in 1910 and 1912 provided the muscle to secure majorities for ratification in a sufficient number of states. The amendment was ratified in the spring of 1913, and that autumn Congress enacted a modest but graduated income tax. The Sixteenth Amendment was the first change to the Constitution since Reconstruction. It opened the door to a number of other proposed amendments, such as the direct election of U.S. senators. It also provided the financial base for a greatly expanded federal government.

Taft, William Howard

William Howard Taft (1857–1930) was the only person to serve both as president and chief justice. Born in Cincinnati into a judicial family, Taft graduated from Yale College in 1878 and attended the University of Cincinnati Law School. After a brief period of private practice, he was named to the Ohio Superior Court in 1887. President Benjamin Harrison named Taft, a loyal Republican, solicitor general in 1890. Two years later Harrison appointed Taft as a federal judge on the U.S. Court of Appeals for the Sixth Circuit. On the circuit bench Taft upheld the right of employees to organize unions and strike, but he frequently enjoined secondary boycotts. He was also strongly supportive of the rights of property owners.

In 1900 President William McKinley appointed Taft president of the Philippines Commission, and he remained in the islands for four years, ultimately serving as civil governor. Taft returned to Washington in 1904 when President Theodore Roosevelt appointed him secretary of war. He developed a close personal friendship with Roosevelt and, in fact, functioned as a kind of executive assistant to the president. Taft had little flair for political life and had long hoped for elevation to the Supreme Court. Nonetheless, with Roosevelt's endorsement Taft was easily elected president in 1908.

Taft's years in the White House were not happy. He was unable to halt a widening split within the Republican Party and eventually broke with his friend Roosevelt. Taft was especially alarmed about Roosevelt's attack on the federal judiciary. Taft was, however, able to shape the Supreme Court. He made five appointments to the high bench, more than any other one-term president. Taft selected Horace H. Lurton, Charles Evans Hughes, Willis Van Devanter, Joseph R. Lamar, and Mahlon Pitney. Only Lurton joined the bench while Melville W. Fuller was chief justice. Upon Fuller's death Taft also elevated a sitting justice, Edward D. White, to the chief justiceship, despite the fact that White was a Democrat. Defeated in the bitter three-way contest for president in 1912, Taft left office with relief and joined the faculty at Yale Law School. Taft's greatest wish finally came true in June of 1921 when President Warren Harding appointed him chief justice. Taft generally pursued a conservative course as chief justice and is perhaps best remembered for his administrative skills. Among other things, Taft persuaded Congress to appropriate funds for the construction of a separate building for the Supreme Court.

Tiedeman, Christopher G.

Christopher G. Tiedeman (1857–1903) was born in Charleston, South Carolina. After graduation from the College of Charleston in 1876, he spent a year and a half studying at universities in Germany. He received a law degree from Columbia Law School in 1879 and practiced for a short time in Charleston and St. Louis. Tiedeman entered academic life in 1881, first as a professor of law at the University of Missouri, then at the University of the City of New York, and ended his career as dean of the law school at the University of Buffalo.

Tiedeman was a prolific writer, authoring a number of treatises and books, including textbooks that were used in many law schools in the United States. He advocated the philosophy of laissez-faire constitutionalism and was a strong believer in constitutional protection of unenumerated constitutional rights. He condemned as unconstitutional laws regulating the hours and wages of workers, usury laws, laws regulating morality, and protective tariffs.

In his *Treatise on the Limitations of Police Power in the United States* (1886), Tiedeman's stated purpose was to demonstrate the constitutional limitations on the police power and to make the public aware of constitutional doctrines that protected private rights against radical social reformers. He stressed that contractual freedom was not generally subject to regulation. In his 1890 treatise *The Unwritten Constitution of the United States*, Tiedeman maintained that judicial review of legislative acts, with regard to both express and unwritten constitutional rights, was necessary to the enduring existence of popular government.

Tiedeman's books and treatises contributed ideas that eventually evolved into the doctrines of substantive due process and liberty of contract. The *Limitations* treatise was a vital reference for lawyers and judges in their attacks upon economic regulations in the late nineteenth century. Tiedeman's works were cited in well over 100 judicial opinions.

Waite, Morrison R.

Morrison R. Waite (1816–1888) graduated from Yale College and studied law by the time-honored apprenticeship system. He practiced law in Toledo, Ohio, and became active in the newly organized Republican Party. Waite gained national attention when he was named one of the American counsel to the Geneva Arbitration Tribunal, and he helped to secure a sizeable award in the settlement of the *Alabama* claims. Thereafter, he was elected president of the Ohio constitutional convention. Early in 1874, after failed efforts to advance other candidates, President Ulysses S. Grant nominated Waite to be chief justice.

Despite initial skepticism from some of the other justices, Waite established himself as a skillful manager of the Supreme Court. A man of high integrity, Waite had a judicial philosophy characterized by respect for precedent and deference to legislative decisionmaking. He generally supported state autonomy with respect to civil rights and economic regulations. Under his leadership, the Supreme Court narrowly construed the protection afforded newly freed slaves and ruled in the *Civil Rights Cases* (1883) that the Fourteenth Amendment banned only state interference with individual rights, not discriminatory private conduct. Likewise, Waite upheld the power of the states to regulate businesses "affected with a public interest" in *Munn v. Illinois* (1877). This doctrine had particular application to railroads. He also sustained in the *Sinking Fund Cases* (1879) congressional authority to revise the charter of the federally incorporated Pacific Railroad.

But in a line of cases, the Waite Court held that the Contract Clause safeguarded the holders of municipal bonds from repudiation. Waite further declared that corporations were persons for the purpose of Fourteenth Amendment guarantees, and he cautioned that the power to regulate would not justify confiscation of private property. Despite its general tendency to sustain economic controls, therefore, the Waite Court helped pave the way for the more property-conscious Fuller Court.

Wilson Act of 1890

In the nineteenth century, many Americans blamed a variety of social evils, including crime and unemployment, on the consumption of liquor. Maine became the first state to pass a prohibition statute in 1851, and a number of other states soon followed suit. Enforcing these laws proved to be nearly impossible, however, largely because liquor was being shipped across state lines.

The battle over prohibition between the "wets" and the "drys" was renewed after the Civil War. In *Mugler v. Kansas* (1887) the Supreme Court upheld the constitutionality of a Kansas prohibition law. *Mugler* dealt primarily with the issue of whether state prohibition laws interfered with property rights in violation of the Fourteenth Amendment's Due Process Clause. The Court held that the production and sale of alcoholic beverages were subject to regulation by the state government under its police power to protect public health and morals. The *Mugler* decision cleared the path for state-by-state regulation of liquor. So the brewers and other wets turned to the Commerce Clause as a means to limit state prohibition laws. In *Leisy v. Hardin* (1890) the Supreme Court, in an opinion by Chief Justice Melville W. Fuller, struck down an Iowa law that banned shipments of liquor into the state without a license as a barrier to interstate commerce.

Congress quickly responded to the Supreme Court's decision by passing the Wilson Act of 1890. This statute provided that alcoholic beverages were subject "upon arrival" to state laws to the same extent as if they had been produced in the state. Essentially, it empowered states to control imported liquor, creating a right that the Supreme Court had previously said states did not possess. The Supreme Court upheld the validity of the Wilson Act in *In re Rahrer* (1891). However, the Wilson Act did not prove to be the panacea that prohibitionists had hoped. Legal issues abounded over the interstate shipment of liquor because of the uncertain boundaries between state and federal jurisdiction. Narrowly construing the Wilson Act, the Supreme Court continued to protect interstate shipments of alcohol, and its rulings undermined state prohibition laws.

For some years after the Wilson Act was passed, it was the basis for the legislative strategy of the prohibitionists as they sought to strengthen state laws by curtailing the shipment of liquor across state lines. Prohibitionists gradually realized, however, that state laws banning the sale and manufacture of alcohol would not achieve their goal of a dry nation. Therefore prohibitionists turned to a constitutional amendment, eventually achieving ratification of the Eighteenth Amendment in 1919.

Wilson-Gorman Tariff Act

Grover Cleveland was reelected president in 1892 with a pledge to reduce the high protective tariff on imported goods. The House of Representatives voted for moderate reductions in tariff duties, but the Senate restored protective schedules on many items. The resulting Wilson-Gorman Tariff Act of 1894 was a disappointment to Cleveland because it fell far short of his hopes for tariff reform. He allowed the measure to become law without his signature.

The House of Representatives attached an income tax provision to the tariff act. This step represented an attempt to shift the tax burden from consumers to the wealthy. It was also thought that the income tax would replace the anticipated revenue loss to the federal government by virtue of lower tariff rates. In fact, the tariff was not significantly reduced, and so this argument lost much of its force. Moreover, in *Pollock v. Farmers' Loan and Trust Co.* (1895) the Fuller Court invalidated the income tax provision of the Wilson-Gorman Tariff Act as an unconstitutional direct tax that was not apportioned among the states according to population.

Appendix: Selected Documents

Address in Commemoration of the Inauguration of George Washington as First President of the United States, December 11, 1889, Melville W. Fuller

Mr. President, Mr. Speaker, and gentlemen of the Senate and House of Representatives: By the terms of that section of the act of Congress under which we have assembled in further commemoration of the historic event of the inauguration of the first President of the United States, George Washington, the 30th of April, A.D. 1889, was declared a national holiday, and in the noble city where that event took place its centennial anniversary has been celebrated with a magnificence of speech and song, of multitudinous assembly, and of naval, military and civic display, accompanied by every manifestation of deep love of country, of profound devotion to its institutions and of intense appreciation of the virtues and services of that illustrious man, whose assumption of the Chief Magistracy gave the assurance of the successful setting in motion of the new Government.

Nothing on the occasion of that celebration could be more full of encouragement and hope than the testimony so overwhelmingly given that Washington still remained first in the hearts of his countrymen, and that the example afforded by his career was still cherished as furnishing that guide of public conduct which had kept and would keep the nation upon the path of glory for itself and of happiness for its people.

The majestic story of that life – whether told in the pages of Marshall or Sparks, of Irving or Bancroft, or through the eloquent utterances of Allies or Webster, or Everett or Winthrop, or the matchless poetry of Lowell or the verse of Byron – never grows old.

We love to hear again what the great Frederick and Napoleon, what Erskine and Fox and Brougham and Talleyrand and Fontanes and Guizot said of him, and how crape enshrouded the standards of France, and the flags upon the victorious ships of England fell fluttering to half-mast at the tidings of his death.

The passage of the century has not in the slightest degree impaired the irresistible charm; and whatever doubts or fears assail us in the turmoil of our impetuous national life, that story comes to console and to strengthen, like the shadow of a great rock in a weary land.

Washington had become first in war, not so much by reason of victories over the enemy, though he had won such, or of success in strategy, though that had been his, as of the triumphs of a constancy which no reverse, no hardship, no incompetency, no treachery could shake or overcome.

And because the people comprehended the greatness of their leader and recognized in him an entire absence of personal ambition, an absolute obedience to convictions of duty, an unaffected love of country, of themselves and of mankind, he had become first in the hearts of his countrymen.

Because thus first, he was to become first in peace, by bringing to the charge of the practical working of the system he had participated in creating, on behalf of the people whose independence he had achieved, the same serene judgment, the same sagacity, the same patience, the same sense of duty, the salve far-sighted comprehension of the end to be attained, that had marked his career from its beginning.

From the time he assumed command, he had given up all idea of accommodation, and believed that there was no middle ground between subjugation and complete independence, and that independence the independence of a nation.

He had demanded national action in respect of the Army; he had urged, but a few weeks after Bunker Hill, the creation of a Federal court with jurisdiction coextensive with the colonies; he had during the war repeatedly pressed home his deep conviction of the indispensability of a strong central government, and particularly at its close, in his circular to the governors of the States and his farewell to his comrades. He had advocated the promotion of commercial intercourse with the rising world of the West, so that its people might be bound to those of the seaboard by a chain that could never be broken. Appreciating the vital importance of territorial influences to the political life of a commonwealth, he had approved the cessions by the landed States, none more significant than that by his own, and had made the profound suggestion – which was acted on – of a line of conduct proper to be observed for the government of the citizens of America in their settlement of the western country which involved the assertion of the sovereign right of eminent domain. He had advised the commissioners of Virginia and Maryland, in consultation at Mount Vernon in relation to the navigation of the Potomac, to recommend a uniform currency and a uniform system of commercial regulations, and this led to the calling of the conference of commissioners of the thirteen States. At the proper moment he had thrown his immense personal influence in favor of the convention and secured the ratification of the Constitution.

It remained for him to crown his labors by demonstrating in their administration the value of the institutions whose establishment had been so long the object of his desire.

"It is already beyond doubt," wrote Count Moustier, in June, 1789, – that in spite of the asserted beauty of the plan which has been adopted, it would have been necessary to renounce its introduction if the same man who presided over its formation had not been placed at, the head of the enterprise. The extreme confidence in his patriotism, his integrity and his intelligence forms today its principal support."

There were obvious difficulties surrounding the first President. Eleven States had ratified, but the assent of some had been secured only after strenuous exertion, considerable delay, and upon close votes.

So slowly did the new Government get under way that the first Wednesday of March, the day designated for the Senate and House to assemble, came and went, and it was not until the 1st of April that the House obtained a quorum, and not until the 6th that the electoral vote was counted in joint convention.

An opposition so intense and bitter as that which had existed to the adoption of the Constitution could not readily die out, and the antagonisms which lay at its base were as old as human nature.

Jealousies existed between the smaller and the larger, between the agricultural and the commercial States, and these were rendered the keener by the rivalries of personal ambition.

Those who admired the theories of the French philosophical school and those who preferred the British model could not readily harmonize their differences, while the enthusiastic believers in the capacity of man for self-government denounced the more conservative for doubting the extent of the reliance which could be placed upon it.

The fear of arbitrary power took particular form in reference to the presidential office, which had been fashioned in view of the personal government of George the Third, rather than on the type of monarchy of the English system as it was in principle, and as it is in fact.

And this fear was indulged notwithstanding the frequency of elections, since no restriction as to re-eligibility was imposed upon the incumbent.

But no fear, no jealousy, could be entertained of him who had indignantly repelled the suggestion of the bestowal of kingly power; who had unsheathed the sword with reluctance and laid it down with joy; who had never sought official position, but accepted public office as a public trust, in deference to so unanimous a demand for his services as to convince him of their necessity; whose patriotism embraced the whole country, the future grandeur of which his prescience foresaw.

Nevertheless, while there could be no personal opposition to the unanimous choice of the people, and while his availability at the crisis was one of those providential blessings which, in other instances, he had so often insisted had been bestowed upon the nation, the fact remained that the situation was full of trial and danger, and demanded the application of the highest order of statesmanship.

Nor are we left to conjecture Washington's feelings in this regard.

Indeed, it may be said that at every period of his public life, though he possessed the talent for silence and did his work generally with closed lips, it is always possible to gather from his remarkable letters the line of his thought upon current affairs, and his inmost hopes, fears and aspirations as to the public weal.

Take for illustration that, in which, on the 9th of January, 1790, little more than eight months after his inauguration, he says:

"The establishment of our new Government seemed to be the last great experiment for promoting human happiness by a reasonable compact in civil society. It was to be, in the first instance, in a considerable degree a government of accommodation as well as a government of laws. Much was to be done by prudence, much by conciliation, much by firmness. Few, who are not philosophical spectators, can realize the difficult and delicate part which a man in my situation had to act. All see and most admire the glare which hovers round the external happiness of elevated office. To me there is nothing in it beyond the lustre which may be reflected from its connection with a power of promoting human felicity. In our progress towards political happiness my station is new, and, if I may use the expression, I walk on untrodden ground. There is scarcely an action the motive of which may not be subject to a double interpretation. There is scarcely any part of my conduct which may not hereafter be drawn into precedent. If, after all my honorable and faithful endeavors to advance the felicity of my country and mankind, I may indulge a hope that my labors have not been altogether without success, it will be the only compensation I can receive in the closing scenes of life."

Here he admits with a certain suppressed sadness that he realizes that private life has ceased to exist for him; and that from his previous participation in public affairs, the exalted character of the new office and the fact that he is the first to fill it, his every act and word thereafter may be referred to in guidance or control of others, and as bearing upon the nature of the Government of which he was the head. It is borne in upon him that in this instance, in a greater degree than ever before, his conduct is to become an historical example. Questions of etiquette, questions pertaining to his daily life, unimportant in themselves, cease to be so under the new conditions, and this interruption of the domestic tenor of his way, to which he was of choice and ardently attached, finds no compensation in the gratification of a morbid hunger and thirst for applause, whether of the few or of the many.

But in the consciousness of having contributed to the advancement of the felicity of his country and of mankind lies the true reward for these renewed labors.

The promotion of human happiness was the key-note of the century within which Washington's life was comprised.

It was the century of Franklin and Turgot; of Montesquieu and Voltaire and Rousseau; of Frederick the Great and Joseph the Second; of Pitt and Fox and Burke and Grattan; of Burns and Cowper and Gray; of Goethe and Kant; of Priestly and

Hume and Adam Smith; of Wesley and Whitefield and Howard, as well as of the long line of statesmen and soldiers, and voyagers over every sea; of poets and artists and essayists and encyclopaedists and romancers, which adorned it.

It was the century of men like Condorcet, who, outlawed and condemned by a revolutionary tribunal, the outcome of popular excesses, calmly sat down, in hiding, to compose his work upon the progress of the human mind.

It was a century instinct with the recognition of the human soul in every human being, and alive with aspirations for universal brotherhood.

With this general longing for the elevation of mankind Washington sympathized, and in expressing a hearty desire for the rooting out of slavery considered this not only essential to the perpetuation of the Union, but desirable on the score of human dignity. Nevertheless, with the calm reason in reference to government, of the race from which he sprang, he regarded the promotion of human happiness as to be best secured by a reasonable compact in civil society, and that established by the Federal Constitution as the last great experiment to that end.

Washington and his colleagues were familiar with prior forms of government and their operation, and with the speculations of the writers upon that subject. They were conversant with the course of the Revolution of 1688, the then triumph of public opinion, and the literature of that period. They accepted the thesis of Locke that, as the true end of government is the mutual preservation of the lives, liberties and estates of the people, a government which invades these rights is guilty of a breach of trust, and can lawfully be set aside; and they were persuaded of the soundness of the views of Montesquieu, that the distribution of powers is necessary to political liberty, which can only exist when power is not abused, and in order that power may not be abused it must be so distributed that power shall check power.

It is only necessary to consult the pages of the Federalist – that incomparable work on the principles of free government – to understand the acquaintance of American statesmen with preceding governmental systems, ancient and modern, and to comprehend that the Constitution was the result, not of a desire for novelty, but of the effort to gather the fruit of that growth which, having its roots in the past, could yield in the present and give promise for the future.

The colonists possessed practically a common nationality, and took by inheritance certain fundamental ideas upon the development of which their growth had proceeded. Self-government by local subdivisions, a legislative body of two houses, an executive head, a distinctive judiciary, constituted the governmental methods.

Magna Charta, the Petition and Declaration of Right, the habeas corpus act, the act of settlement, all the muniments of English liberty, were theirs, and the New England Confederation of 1643, the schemes of union of 1754 and 1765, the revolutionary Congress, the Articles of Confederation, the colonial charters and constitutions furnished a vast treasury of experience upon which they drew.

Their work in relation to what had gone before was in truth but in maintenance of that continuity of which Hooker speaks: "We were then alive in our predecessors and they in their successors do live still." They did not seek to build upon the ruins of older institutions, but to develop from them a nobler, broader and more lasting structure, and in effecting this upon so vast a scale and under conditions so widely different from the past, the immortal instrument was indeed the product of consummate statesmanship.

Of the future greatness of the new nation Washington had no doubt. He saw, as if face to face, that continental domain which glimmered to others as through a glass darkly.

The great West was no sealed book to him, and no one knew better than he that no foreign power could long control the flow of the Father of Waters to the Gulf.

He is said to have lacked imagination, and if the exhilaration of the poet, the mystic, or the seer is meant, this may be true.

His mind was not given to indulgence in dreams of ideal commonwealths like the republic of Plato or of Cicero, the City of God of Augustine, or the Utopia of Sir Thomas More, but it grasped the mighty fact of the empire of the future, and acted in obedience to the heavenly vision.

But the question was, could that empire be realized and controlled by the people within its vast boundaries in the exercise of self-government?

Could the conception of a central government, operating directly upon citizens, who at the same time were subject to the jurisdiction of their several States, be carried into practical working operation so as to reconcile imperial sway with local independence?

Would a scheme work which was partly national and partly federal, and which aimed at unity as well as union?

And could the rule of the majority be subjected with binding force to such restraints through a system by representation, that of a republic rather than that of a pure democracy, that the violence of faction could not operate in the long run to defeat a common government by the many, throughout so immense an area?

Could the restraints essential to the preservation of society, the equilibrium between progress and order, be so guarded as to allow of that sober second thought which would secure their observance, and thus the liberty and happiness of the people and the enduring progress of humanity?

While the general genius of the Government was thoroughly permeated with the ideas of freedom in obedience, yet time was needed to commend the form in which it was for the future to exert itself.

Hence administration in the first instance required accommodation as well as adherence to the letter, and prudence and conciliation as well as firmness.

The Cabinet of the first President illustrates his sense of the nature of the exigency.

All its members were friends and supporters of the Constitution, but possessed of widely different views as to the scope of its powers and the probabilities of its successful operation in the shape it then bore.

Between Jefferson and Hamilton there seemed to be a great gulf fixed, yet a common patriotism bridged it, and a common purpose enabled them for these critical years to act together. And this was rendered possible by the fact that the leadership of Washington afforded a common ground upon which every lover of a united country could stand. And as the first four years were nearing their close, Hamilton and Jefferson severally urged Washington to consent to remain at the helm for four years longer, that the Government might acquire additional firmness and strength before being subjected to the strain of the contention of parties.

Undoubtedly Hamilton desired this also, because of nearer coincidence of thought on some questions involving serious difference of opinion, but both concurred in urging it upon the ground that the confidence of the whole Union was centered in Washington, and his being at the helm would be more than an answer to every argument which could be used to alarm and lead the people in any quarter into violence or secession.

Appointments to the Supreme Bench involved less reason for accommodation, but equal prudence and sagacity.

The great part which that tribunal was to play in the development of our institutions was yet to come, but the importance of that branch of the Government to which was committed the ultimate interpretation of the Constitution was appreciated by Washington, who characterized it as the keystone of the political fabric.

To the headship of the court, Washington called the pure and great-minded Jay of New York, and associated with him John Rutledge of South Carolina, who, from the stamp-act Congress of 1765; had borne a conspicuous part in the history of the country and of his State; James Wilson of Pennsylvania, who, like Rutledge, had been prominent in the Continental Congress and in the Federal convention, a signer of the Declaration of Independence, and one of the most forcible, acute and learned debaters on behalf of the Constitution, as the records of the Federal and his State conventions show; Cushing, chief-justice of Massachusetts, experienced in judicial station, and the only person holding office under the Crown who adhered to his country in the Revolution; Harrison of Maryland, Washington's well-known secretary; Blair of Virginia, a judge of its court of appeals, and one of Washington's fellow-members in the convention; and in place of Rutledge and Harrison, who preferred the highest judicial positions in their own States, Thomas Johnson of Maryland and James Iredell of North Carolina.

It will be perceived that the distribution was made with tact, and the selections with consummate wisdom.

The part the appointees had taken in the cause of the country, and especially in laying the foundations of the political edifice, their eminent qualifications and recognized integrity, commended the court to the confidence of the people, and gave assurance that this great department would be so administered as to effectuate the purposes for which it had been created.

As to appointments generally, he did not recognize the rule of party rewards for party work, although, when party opposition became clearly defined, he wrote Pickering that to "bring a man into any office of consequence knowingly, whose political tenets are adverse to the measures which the General Government is pursuing," would be, in his opinion, "a sort of political suicide." To integrity and capacity, as qualifications for high civil office, he added that of "marked eminence before the country, not only as the more likely to be serviceable, but because the public will more readily trust them." As in appointments, so in the conduct of affairs, prudence, conciliation and accommodation carried the experiment successfully along, while firmness in essentials was equally present, as when, at a later day, the suppression of the whiskey rebellion and the maintenance of neutrality in the war between France and England gave information at home that there existed a central Government strong enough to suppress domestic insurrection, and abroad, that a new and self-reliant power had been born into the family of nations.

The course taken in all matters, whether great or small, was the result of careful consideration and the exercise of deliberate judgment as to the effect of what was done, or forborne to be done, upon the success of the newly constructed fabric. Thus, the regulation of official behavior was deemed a matter of such consequence, that Adams, Jay, Hamilton and Madison were consulted upon it, for although republican simplicity had been substituted for monarchy and titles, and was held inconsistent with concession of superiority by reason of occupancy of official station, yet the transition could not be violently made, and the people were, in any event, entitled to expect their agents to sustain with dignity the high positions to which they had been called.

During the entire Presidency of Washington, upon the details of which it is impracticable here to dwell, time for solidification was the dominant thought. The infant giant could defend himself even in his cradle; but to become the Colossus of Washington's hopes, the gristle must have opportunity to harden.

After more than seven years of devotion to the interests committed to his charge and intense watchfulness over the adjustment and working of the machinery of the new system, having determined upon his own retirement, thereby practically assigning a limit to the period during which the office could with propriety be occupied by his successors, still regarding the problem as not solved, and still anxiously desiring to contribute to the last to the welfare of the constant object of his veneration and love, he gives to his countrymen in the farewell of "an old and affectionate friend," the results of his observations and of his reflections on the operation of the great scheme he had assisted in creating and had so far commended to the people by his administration of its provisions.

Punctilious as he was in official observances, and dear as his home and his own State were to him, this address was one that rose above home, and State, and official place, that brought him near, not simply to the people to whom it was immediately directed, but to that great coming multitude whom no man could number, and towards which he felt the pathetic attachment of a noble and prophetic soul. And so he dates it, not from Mount Vernon nor from his official residence, but from the "United States."

Hamilton, Madison and Jay had, in the series of essays in advocacy of the Constitution, largely aided in bringing about its ratification, and displayed wonderful comprehensiveness of view, depth of wisdom and sagacity of reflection in their treatment of the topics involved. Throughout Washington's administration they had to the utmost assisted in the successful carrying on of the Government, in the Cabinet, in Congress, upon the bench, or in diplomatic station, and to them as tried and true friends and men of a statesmanship as broad as the country, Washington turned at one time and another for advice in the preparation of these closing words.

Notwithstanding that innate modesty which had always induced a certain real diffidence in assuming station, he was conscious of his position as founder of the state; he felt that every utterance in this closing benediction would be cherished by coming generations as disinterested advice, based on experience and knowledge and illuminated by the sincerest affection, and he invited the careful scrutiny of his friends that it might "be handed to the public in an honest, unaffected, simple garb." But his work was his own, as all his work was. The virtue went out of him, even when he used the hand of another.

If we turn to this remarkable document and compare the line of conduct therein recommended with the course of events during the century – the advice given with the results of experience – we are amazed at the wonderful sagacity and precision with which it lays down the general principles through whose application the safety and prosperity of the Republic have been secured. To cherish the public credit and promote religion, morality and education were obvious recommendations. Economy in public expense, vigorous exertion to discharge debt unavoidably occasioned, acquiescence in necessary taxation, and candid construction of governmental action in the selection of its proper objects, were all parts of the first of these. The increase of net ordinary expenditures from three millions to two hundred and sixty-eight millions of dollars, and of net ordinary receipts from four and one-half to three hundred and eighty millions of dollars, renders his practice of economy, as contradistinguished from wastefulness, as commendable today as theory but it must be a judicious economy; for, as Washington said, timely disbursements frequently prevent much larger.

The extinction of the public debt at one time, and the marvelous reduction, within a quarter of a century of its creation, of a later public debt of more than twenty-five hundred millions of dollars, demonstrate practical adherence to the rule laid down. It is true that the great material prosperity which has attended our growth has enabled us to meet an enormous burden of taxation with comparative ease, but it is nevertheless also true that the general judgment has never wavered upon the question of the sacred observance of plighted faith; and if at any moment the removal of the bars designed to imprison the powerful giant of a paper currency seemed to imperil the preservation of the, public honor, the sturdy common sense of the people has checked through their representatives the dangerous tendency before it has gone too far.

Education was one of the two hooks (the other was local self-government) upon which the continuance of republican government was considered absolutely hanging.

The action of the Continental Congress in respect to the western territory was next in importance to that on independence and union. Apart from its political significance we recall the familiar fact that one section out of every township was reserved under the ordinances of 1785 and 1787 for the maintenance of schools, because religion, morality and knowledge were considered essential to good government and the happiness of mankind. The one section has been made two, and many millions of acres have been granted for the endowment of universities, of normal, scientific and mining schools, and institutions for the benefit of agriculture and the mechanic arts, including from three hundred and fifty to four hundred and fifty thousand acres for educational and charitable institutions, to each of the new States recently admitted, by an act appropriately passed into law on the birthday of Washington. A thousand universities, colleges and institutions of learning, twelve millions of children attending two hundred thousand public schools, with three hundred and sixty thousand teachers, at an expenditure of one hundred and twenty-five millions and with property worth two hundred millions, and sixty-two million dollars in private benefactions for education in the decade of the last census, testify that the importance of education is not underestimated in a country whose institutions are dependent upon the intelligence of the people.

Washington insists that national morality cannot prevail in exclusion of religious principle, though the influence of refined education on minds of a peculiar structure may have induced an opposite conclusion.

History accords with this view. Plutarch said, "You may travel over the world and you may find cities without walls, without king, without mint, without theatre or gymnasium, but you will never find a city without God, without prayer, without oracle, without sacrifice;" and the eighteen centuries since his day confirm the truth of his words.

"Take from me," said Bismarck, "my faith in a divine order which has destined this German nation for something good and great, and you take from me my fatherland."

Washington declares that "the mere politician, equally with the pious man, ought to respect and cherish religion and morality as the firmest props of the duties of men and citizens." He did not mean that the value of trust and faith has no relation to the reality of the objects of that trust and faith, nor that those to whom he referred should indulge in religious observances as mere mummeries to deceive, while smiling among themselves, as Cicero with his fellow-augurs, nor that faith should be betrayed by accommodation to superstition, as in the action of the town clerk of Ephesus, but he demanded that they should recognize in fact the indispensability of these supports of political prosperity.

And here again the answer of the century's watchman tells that the night is passing.

Crime, drunkenness, pauperism have steadily decreased in proportion as population has increased, philanthropic agencies have multiplied, moral sensitiveness has become keener, and higher standards of personal and official conduct have come to be required, while at the same time the statistics of religious progress exhibit wonderful and most gratifying results.

Washington had never permitted his public action to be influenced by personal affection or personal hostility, and in urging the avoidance of political connections or personal alliances with any portion of the foreign world, he characteristically, condemned indulgence in an inveterate antipathy towards particular nations and a passionate attachment for others, while observing good faith and justice towards all. No reason existed for becoming implicated in the ordinary vicissitudes of the politics of Europe, or the ordinary combinations and collisions of her friendships or enmities. Intervention meant war, not arbitration; the assumption of obligation meant force, not words. No field was to be opened here for foreign intrigues, and no necessity created here for standing armies and the domination of the civil by the military authority.

So scrupulous was Washington's abstinence from the slightest appearance of interference, that, notwithstanding his tender friendship for LaFayette, he would not make official application for his release from Olmutz. So absolute was his conviction that this country must not become a make-weight in Europe's balances of power, that he sternly held it to neutrality under circumstances which would have rendered it impossible for any other man to do so. Such has been the policy unchangeably pursued, but it has not required the concealment of our sympathy with all who have wished to put American institutional ideas into practical operation, or our confidence in their ultimate prevalence. Nor has the rule prevented the Republic from the declaration that it should take its own course in case of the interference by other nations with the primary interests of America.

In the lapse of years international relations have been constantly assuming larger importance with the growth of the country and the world and the increasing nearness of intercommunication. We are justified in claiming that the delicate and difficult function of government involved has been from the first discharged in so admirable a manner that the solution of the grave questions of the future may be awaited without anxiety.

It is matter of congratulation that the first year of our second century witnesses the representatives of the three Americas engaged in the effort to increase the facilities of commercial intercourse, "consulting the natural course of things, diffusing and diversifying by gentle means the streams of intercourse, but forcing nothing," success in which must knit closer the ties of fraternal friendship, and bring the peoples of the two American continents into harmonious control of the hemisphere.

The course of events has equally shown the profound wisdom of the propositions of the Farewell Address bearing directly on the form of government delineated in the Federal Constitution.

First of these is the necessity of the preservation of the distribution of powers, and of resistance to any encroachment by one department upon another.

The executive power was vested in the President, but he had a voting power in the right to veto, and the power of initiation as to treaties, which became binding with the advice and consent of the Senate.

The interposition of the latter was also permitted by the requisition of assent in the confirmation of appointments, and it could sit in judgment on the President if articles of impeachment were presented. In some particulars, therefore, the two departments approached each other in the exercise of functions appropriate to each.

This made it all the more important that there should be no invasion of the one by the other. No effort to diminish the executive authority or to interfere with the exercise of its legitimate discretion has commanded the support of the public voice, and impeachment has not been considered a proper resort to reconcile differences of judgment, however serious.

The right to initiate and to pass laws having been lodged in Congress, the balance of power was actually there reposed, and the danger of encroachment would naturally present itself from that quarter.

And here the Federal judiciary was interposed as a coordinate department, with power to determine when the limitations of the fundamental law were transgressed. Without an exact precedent, the creation of a tribunal possessed of that power was the natural result of the existence of a written constitution; for to leave to the instrumentalities by which governmental power is exercised the determination of boundaries upon it, would dispense with them altogether.

In England the executive and legislative powers are practically vested in Parliament and exercised by the Cabinet, which amounts to a committee of the Commons, acting with the additional power which secret agreement on a given course imparts. The constitution is what Parliament makes it, and the judicial tribunals only interpret and apply the action of that body, being necessarily destitute of the power to hold such action void by reference to any higher law than its own enactments.

Not so with us. Every act of Congress, every act of the state legislatures, every part of the constitution of any State, if repugnant to the Constitution of the United States, is void, and to be so treated. The Supreme Court, by the decision of cases in which such acts or provisions are drawn in question, and in the exercise of judicial functions, renders the Constitution in reality as well as in name the supreme law of the land.

Its judgments command the assent of Congress and the Executive, the States and the people, alike, and it is this unique arbitrament that has challenged the admiration of the world.

The court cannot be abolished by Congress, but the number of its judges may be increased, or diminished on the occurrence of vacancies, and so, while its jurisdiction cannot be impaired, the exercise of it may be curtailed.

Nevertheless, no legislation to control it in any way has ever been approved by definite public opinion, and the tribunal remains in the complete discharge of the vital and important functions it was created to perform.

Scrupulously abstaining from the decision of strictly political questions and from the performance of other than judicial duties; never grasping an ungranted jurisdiction and never shrinking from the exercise of that conferred upon it, it commands the reverence of a law-abiding people.

Again, Washington urges not only that his countrymen shall steadily discountenance irregular opposition to the acknowledged authority of the Government, and resist with care the spirit of innovation upon its principles, but shall oppose any change in the system except by amendment in the mode provided, particularly warning them, as fearful of objection to the pressure of the Government, that the energy of the scheme must not be impaired, as vigor is not only required to manage the common interests throughout so extensive a country, but is necessary to protect liberty itself.

In no part of the Constitution was greater sagacity displayed than in the provision for its amendment. No State, without its consent, could be deprived of its equal suffrage in the Senate, but otherwise (with an exception now immaterial) the instrument might be amended upon the concurrence of two-thirds of both Houses, and the ratification of the legislatures or conventions of three-fourths of the several States, or through a Federal convention when applied for by the legislatures of two-thirds of the States, and upon like ratification.

It was designed that the ultimate sovereignty thus reposed should not be called into play, except through this slow and deliberate process, which would give time for mere hypothesis and opinion to exhaust themselves, and the conclusion reached to be the result of gravity of thought and judgment, and of the concurrence of substantially every part of the country.

The first ten amendments hardly come within the application of the principle, as they were in substance requested by many of the States at the time of ratification. In the Pennsylvania convention, James Wilson declared that the subject of a bill of rights was not mentioned in the constitutional convention until within three days of its adjournment, and even then no direct motion upon the subject was offered; and that such a bill was entirely unnecessary in a government having none but enumerated powers; but Jefferson urged from Paris that a bill of rights was "what the people are entitled to against every government on earth, general or particular," and that one ought to be added, "providing clearly and without the aid of sophism, for freedom of religion, freedom of the press, protection against standing armies, restriction of monopolies, the eternal and unremitting force of the habeas corpus laws and trials by jury in all matters of fact triable by the laws of the land, and not by the laws of nations." This view prevailed, but in order that the affirmance of certain rights might not disparage others or lead to implications in favor of the possession of other powers, it was added that the enumeration of certain rights should not be construed to deny or disparage others retained by the people, and that the powers not delegated were reserved.

Congress, in the preamble to these amendments, and Washington, in his inaugural, commend their adoption out of regard for the public harmony and a reverence for the characteristic rights of freemen.

The eleventh inhibited the extension by construction, in the particular named, of the Federal judicial power, and the twelfth related to matters of detail in the election of President and Vice-President. No one of the twelve was in restraint of State action.

Sixty years elapsed before the ratification of the thirteenth, fourteenth and fifteenth amendments. These definitively disposed of the subject of slavery, that Serbonian bog 'twixt the extreme views of the two schools of political thought dividing the country—views which, except for the existence of that institution, might never have been pushed to an extreme, but might have continued peacefully to operate in the production of a golden mean between the absorption of power by the central and its diffusion among the local governments. And by the fourteenth an additional guaranty was furnished against the arbitrary exercise by the States of the powers of government, unrestrained by the established principles of private rights and distributive justice.

Undoubtedly the effect of these later amendments was to increase the power of Congress, but there was no revolutionary change. It is as true of the existing government, as it was of the proposed government, that it must stand or fall with the State governments.

Added provisions for the protection of personal rights involved to that extent additional powers, but the essential elements of the structure remained unchanged.

In other words, while certain obstructions to its working have been removed, the clock-work has not been thrown out of gear, but the pendulum continues to swing through its appointed arc and the vast machinery to move noiselessly and easily to and fro, marking the orderly progress of a great people in the achievement of happiness by the exercise of self-government.

But while direct alterations have been few, the fundamental law has been developed in the evolution of national growth, as Washington, indeed, anticipated. "Time and habit," said he, "are at least as necessary to fix the true character of government as of other human institutions;" and "experience is the surest standard by which to fix the real tendency of the existing constitution of a country."

In this he applies the language of Hume, and speaks in spirit of the observation of Bacon, that "rightly is truth called the daughter of time, not of authority."

Time, habit, experience, legislation, usage may have assisted in expanding the Constitution in the quiet, imperceptible manner in which nature adapts itself to new conditions, though remaining still the same.

Yet its chief growth is to be found in the interpretation of its provisions by the tribunal upon which that delicate and responsible duty was imposed. And in that view what "a debt immense of endless gratitude" is owed to those luminous decisions of John Marshall, which placed the principles of the Constitution upon an impregnable basis and rendered an experimental system permanent.

Renowned and venerable name! It was he who liberated the spirit which lived within the Constitution – the mind infused "through every member of the mighty mass" – so that it might "pervade, sustain and actuate the whole."

The fact that the conclusions reached by the court and set forth by the persuasive and logical reasoning of the great Chief-Justice did not at the moment move in the direction of public opinion, but finally met with the entire approval of the matured judgment of the people, furnishes an impressive illustration of the working of our system of government.

Doubtless, in many instances, the Constitution has been subjected to strains which have tested its elasticity without breaking the texture, but the watchfulness of party has aided to keep the balance true, absolute infraction has been deprecated or denied, and a law-loving and law-abiding people has welcomed the rebound which restored the rigid outline and even tenor of its way.

The departing statesman dwells with insistence, on the grounds both of interest and sensibility, upon the paramount importance of the Union and of that unity of government which makes of those who live under it one people and one nation, and will, he hopes, induce all its citizens, whether by birth or choice, to glory in the name "American."

Here, the ideal which influenced his conduct may be read between the lines—the ideal of a powerful and harmonious people, possessed of freedom because capable of self-restraint, and working out the destinies of an ocean-bound republic, whose example should be a message of glad tidings to all the earth.

And the realization of that ideal involved a patriotism not based upon the dictates of interest, but springing from devotion of the heart, and pride in the object of that devotion.

What Washington desired, as Lodge's fine biography makes entirely clear, was, that the people should become saturated with the principles of national unity and love of country, should possess an "American character," should never forget that they were "Americans." Hence he opposed education abroad, lest our youth might contract principles unfriendly to republican government; and discouraged immigration, except of those who, by "all intermixture with our people," could themselves, or their descendants, "get assimilated to our customs, measures and laws; in a word, soon become one people."

To be an American was to be part and parcel of American ideas, institutions, prosperity and progress. It was to be like-minded with the patriotic leaders who have served the cause of their native or adopted land, from Washington to Lincoln. It was to be convinced of the virtues of republican government as the bulwark of the true and genuine liberties of mankind, which would ultimately transmute suffering through ignorance into happiness through light.

Who would not glory in the name American, when it carries with it such illustrative types as Washington, and Franklin, and Samuel Adams, and Jefferson, and such a type as Lincoln, whose very faults were American, as were the virtues of his sad and heroic soul?

As the lust for domination is in perpetual conflict with the longing to be free, so the tendency to concentration struggles perpetually with the tendency to diffuse.

It is in the maintenance of the equilibrium that the largest liberty consistent with the greatest progress has been found. And this is as true between the States and the Federal Government as between the individual and the State.

But while the play of the two forces is a natural one, the gravitation is to the center, with human nature as it is.

The passage of the century, with the vast material development of the country, has brought this strikingly home to us in the increased importance of the Federal Government in prestige and power, as compared with that of the State governments in the time of Washington. Position on the Supreme Bench or Cabinet place might still be declined for personal reasons, but not because of preference for the headship of a State government, or of a State tribunal, and no punctilio would cause the governor of today to hesitate upon a question of official etiquette when the President visits a State capital.

Rapidity and ease of communication by railroad, telegraph and post; the handling of the vast income and expenditure of the Federal Treasury, and the knitting together of the innumerable ties of family, social and business relations, have created a solidarity which demands, ill the regulation of commerce, the management of financial affairs, and the like, the interposition of Federal authority. The National Banking system, the Interstate Commerce Commission, the Agricultural Department, the Labor and Educational Bureaus, the National Board of Health, indicate the drift toward the exertion of the national will, a natural and perhaps inevitable result of that unity which formed the object of Washington's desire.

But what he wished was solidarity without centralization in destruction of local regulation, for it must not be assumed that he did not realize the vital importance of the preservation of local self-government through the States. To realize its great destiny the country must oppose externally a consolidated front and contain, within itself a single people only; but popular government must be preserved, and the doubt was whether a common government of the popular form could embrace so large a sphere.

Hence the earnestness with which Washington invoked the spirit of essential unity through pride and affection to move upon the face of the waters. When the new political world had airly taken form and substance other considerations would resume their due importance. He was profoundly disturbed by the apprehension that different portions of the population might become, through contradictory interests, in effect rival peoples, and the Union be destroyed by the contention for mastery between them. His sagacious mind perceived the danger arising from the social and economic condition produced by an institution with which the framers of the Constitution had found themselves unable to deal, and he deprecated an appeal to the last reason of kings in preservation of one government over our whole domain.

Yet that appeal was fortunately so long delayed that when it came the civil war determined the perpetuity and indissolubility of the Union, without the loss of distinct and individual existence or of the rights of self-government by the States.

This conflict demonstrated that no part of the country was destitute of that old fighting spirit, which rouses at the invocation of force through arms, and which long years of prosperity could not weaken or destroy, and, at the same time, that gigantic armies drawn from the ranks of a citizen soldiery, however skilled they may become in the arts of war, on the cessation of hostilities at once resume the normal cultivation of the arts of peace.

And from an apparent invasion of the carefully constructed scheme to secure popular government, popular government has obtained a wider scope and renewed power, and from an apparent industrial overthrow has come an unexampled industrial development. "Out of the eater came forth meat, and out of the strong came forth sweetness."

The waste of war is always rapidly replaced, and in its effect on institutions time may repair its injuries without weakening its benefits.

Is it possible to conceive of a more searching test of the wisdom and lasting quality of our form of government than that applied by the civil war? Is it possible to conceive of a more convincing demonstration than the reconciliation which has followed the conclusion of the struggle, and the complete reinstatement of the system in harmonious operation over the entire national domain? No conquered provinces perpetuated personal animosities, and by the fact of their existence, through despotic rule over part, changed the government over all. On the contrary, the States, vital parts of the system, and in whose annihilation the system perishes, resumed the relations temporarily suspended, and the continuance of local self-government on its accustomed course prevented the old connection from carrying with it the bitterness of enforced change. It was the triumph of the machinery that its practical working so speedily assumed its normal movement, substantially uninjured by the convulsion that had shaken it.

And as the wheels within the wheels revolve, the aspiration finds a response in every heart: "Come from the four winds, O breath, and breathe upon these slain that they may live" – live with their reunited brethren, one in the hand of God.

Finally, the country is warned against the baleful effects of the spirit of party as the worst enemy of governments of the popular form.

Franklin wrote that all great affairs are carried on by parties, but that as soon as a party has gained its general point each member becomes intent upon his particular interest; that few in public affairs act from a mere view of the good of their country, and fewer still with a view to the good of mankind. But these observations would, in the light of the history of our country, be regarded as too sweeping, although they suggest grounds for the objection of Washington to the domination of party spirit.

Parties based on different opinions as to the principles on which the Government is to be conducted must necessarily exist. To them we look for that activity in the advocacy of opposing views; that watchfulness over the assertion of authority; that keen debate as to the course most conducive to well-being, essential to the successful growth of popular institutions. That voice of the people which, when duly given and properly ascertained, directs the action of the State is largely brought to declare itself through the instrumentality of party. It is this which corrects that general apathy rightly regarded by De Tocqueville as a serious menace to popular government because conducive to its complete surrender to the domination of its agents if they will but relieve responsibility and gratify desire. But if the spirit of party is so extreme that party itself becomes a despotism, or, if government itself becomes nothing but organized party, then the danger apprehended by Washington is upon us.

With the increase of population and wealth and power; with the spoils of office dependent upon the elections; with vast interests affected by legislation, as in the care and disposition of public property, the raising of public revenue, the grant or regulation of corporate powers and monopolistic combinations, the danger is that corruption, always insidious, always aggressive, and always dangerous to popular government, will control party machinery to effect its ends, tempt public men into accepting favors at its hands by taking office purchased by its influence, and flourish in rank luxuriance under the shelter of a system which confounds the honest and the patriotic with the cunning and the profligate. An intelligent public opinion ceases to exist when it cannot assert itself, and great measures and great principles are lost when elections degenerate into the mere registration of the decrees of selfishness and greed.

Whenever party spirit becomes so intense as to compass such results it will have reached the height denounced by Washington, and will realize in the action it dictates the terrible definition of despotic government: "When the savages wish to eat fruit they cut down a tree and pluck the fruit."

However difficult it may be to fully appreciate the influence of great men upon the cause of civilization, it is impossible to overestimate that of Washington, thus exerted through precept as well as by example. In the general recognition of today of the effect of that which he did, that which he said, that which he was, upon the public conscience, is found the justification of the confident claim that popular government under the form prescribed by the fundamental law has ceased to be an experiment. Neither foreign wars, nor attacks upon either of the coordinate departments, nor the irritation of a disputed national election, nor territorial aggrandizement, nor the addition of realm after realm to the empire of States, nor sectional controversies, nor the destruction of a great economical, social and political institution, nor the shock of arms in internecine conflict, have impaired the structure of the Government or subverted the orderly rule of the people.

But the deliverance vouchsafed in time of tribulation is as earnestly to be sought in time of prosperity, when material acquisition may deaden the spiritual sense and impede the progress of human elevation.

In the growth of population; in the expansion of commerce, manufactures and the useful arts; in progress in scientific discovery and invention; in the accumulation of wealth; in material advancement of every kind, the century has indeed been marvelous. Steam, electricity, gas, telegraphy, photography, have multiplied the instrumentalities for the exercise of human power. Science, philosophy, literature and art have moved forward along the lines of prior achievement. But wants have multiplied as civilization has advanced, and with multiplied wants and the increased freedom of the individual have come the antagonisms inevitably incident to inequality of condition, even though there is widely extended improvement upon the whole, and often because of it, and added to them the more serious discontents arising from the existence, notwithstanding the immense results of stimulated production, of privation and distress.

The Declaration asserted political equality and the possession of the inalienable rights of life, liberty and the pursuit of happiness, and the future of the individual was assumed to be secured in securing through government that equality and those rights.

In spite of the violent overthrow of institutions in the French revolution, that great convulsion carried within it the same salutary principles, while a quickening outburst of spiritual energy marked the commencement of the industrial development of England, and all Europe glowed with the fires of sympathy with the wretched and oppressed.

Throughout the hundred years thus introduced, aspiration for the elevation of humanity has not diminished in intensity, and hope of the general attainment of a more exalted plane has gained new strength in the effort to remove or mitigate the ills which have oppressed mankind. The enhanced valuation of human life, the abolition of slavery, the increase of benevolent and charitable institutions, the large public appropriations and private benefactions to the cause of education, the wide diffusion of intelligence, perceptible growth in religion, morality and fraternal kindness, encourage the effort and give solid ground for the hope. And since the protection and regulation of the rights of individuals, as between themselves and as between them and the community, ultimately come to express the will of the latter, it is not unreasonable to contend that the perfectibility of man is bound up in the preservation of republican institutions.

Where the pressure upon the masses has been intense, the drift has been towards increased interference by the State in the attempt to alleviate inequality of condition. So long as that interference is enabling and protective only to enable, and individual effort is not so circumscribed as to destroy the self-reliance of the people, they move onward with accelerated speed in intellectual and moral as well as material progress; but where man allows his beliefs, his family, his property, his labor, each of his acts, to be subjected to the omnipotence of the state, or is unmindful of the fact that it is the duty of the people to support the government and not of the government to support the people, such a surrender of independence involves the cessation of such progress in its largest sense.

The statement that popular outbreaks were often as beneficial in the political world as storms in the physical was defended upon the ground that, although evils, they were productive of good by preventing the degeneracy of government and nourishing that general attention to public affairs, the absence of which would be tantamount to the abdication of self-government.

But while the rights to life, to use one's faculties in all lawful ways, and to acquire and enjoy property are morally fundamental rights antecedent to constitutions, which do not create, but secure and protect them, yet it is within the power of the State to promote the health, peace, morals, education and good order of the people by legislation to that end, and to regulate the use of property in which the public has such an interest as to be entitled to assert control. In this wide field of regulation by law, and in the reformation of laws which are found to promote inequality, as well as in the patient efforts of mutual forbearance which the education of conflict produces, the direction of the rule of the people is steadily towards an amelioration not to be found in the dead level of despotism, nor in the destruction of society proposed by the anarchist.

It is but little more than thirty years since the well-known prophecy was uttered, that with the increase of population and the taking up of the public lands, our institutions then being really put to the test, either some Caesar or Napoleon would seize the reins of government, or our Republic would be plundered and laid waste as the Roman Empire had been, but by Huns and Vandals engendered within our own country and by our own institutions.

The brilliant essayist did not comprehend the character of our fundamental law, the securities carefully devised to prevent facility in changing it, and the provisions which inhibit the subversion of individual freedom, the impairment of the obligation of contracts, and the confiscation of property, nor realize the practical operation of a governmental scheme intended to secure that sober second thought which alone constitutes public opinion in this country, and which makes of government by the people a government strong enough, in the language of the address, to "withstand the enterprises of faction, to confine each member of the society within the limits prescribed by the laws, and to maintain all in the secure and tranquil enjoyment of the rights of person and property," without which "liberty is little else than a name."

Undoubtedly to this people, who from four have become seventy millions in the passage of their first century, to reach by the close of the second, perhaps, seven hundred millions, with resources which can feed and clothe and render happy more than twice that number, the solution of grave problems is committed.

How shall the evils of municipal government, the poverty, the vice, engendered by the disproportionate growth of urban populations, be dealt with as that growth continues? How shall immigration be, regulated so that precious institutions may not be threatened by too large an influx of those lacking in assimilative power and inclination? How shall the full measure of duty towards that other race, to which in God's providence this country has been so long a home, be discharged so that participation in common blessings and in the exercise of common rights may lead to and rest upon equal education and intelligence? How shall monopoly be checked, and the pressure of accumulation yield to that equitable distribution, which shall "undo excess, and each man have enough?" How shall the individual lie held to the recognition of his responsibility for government, and to meet the demand of public obligations? How shall corruption in private and public life be eradicated?

These and like questions must be answered, and they will be by the nation of Washington, which in the exercise of the sagacity and prudence and self-control born of free institutions, and the cultivation of the humanities of Christian civilization will hallow the name, American, by making it the synonym of the highest sense of duty, the highest morality, the highest patriotism, and so become more powerful and more noble than the powerful and noble Roman nation, which stood for centuries the embodiment of law and order and government, but fell when the gods of the fireside fled from hearthstones whose sanctity had been invaded, and its citizens lost the sense of duty in indulgence in pleasure.

And so the new century may be entered upon in the spirit of optimism, the natural result, perhaps, of a self-confidence which has lost nothing in substance by experience, though it has gained in the moderation of its impetuosity; yet an optimism essential to the accomplishment of great ends, not blind to perils, but bold in the fearlessness of a faith whose very consciousness of the limitations of the present asserts the attainability of the untravelled world of a still grander future.

No ship can sail forever over summer seas. The storms that it has weathered test and demonstrate its ability to survive the storms to come, but storms there must be until there shall be no more sea.

But as amid the tempests in which our ship of state was launched, and in the times succeeding, so in the times to come, with every exigency constellations of illustrious men will rise upon the angry skies, to control the whirlwind and dispel the clouds by their potent influences, while from the "clear upper sky" the steady light of the great planet marks out the course the vessel must pursue, and sits shining on the sails as it comes grandly into the haven where it would be.

"The Income Tax Cases and Some Comments Thereon," Address at State University of Iowa, 1898, David J. Brewer

... Before proceeding to any comments on the decision it is well to understand exactly what was decided, and in a general way the reasons therefore. The income tax law levied a tax of two per cent upon all incomes over four thousand dollars derived from any kind of property, rents, interest, dividends, or salaries, or from any profession, trade, employment or vocation, or any other source whatever; and this tax was not apportioned between the states according to their population, but levied directly upon all such incomes by whomsoever or wherever received. The decision was that so far as the law imposed a tax on the rents or income received from real estate or personal property it was in conflict with Section 2 of Article I of the constitution, which provides: "Representatives and direct taxes shall be apportioned among the several states which may be included within this union, according to their respective numbers;" and Section 9 of the same article, which reads: "No capitation, or other direct tax shall be laid, unless in proportion to the census or enumeration hereinbefore directed to be taken;" and that by reason of the impossibility of separating the incomes derived from these sources from those derived from other sources the whole income tax was void. The decision only went to the proposition that rents and income received from real and personal property could not be reached by the federal government for taxation otherwise than through, the system of, apportionment named in the constitution. Incomes obtained from personal labors, professional services, speculation, or in any other way, were not adjudged within the reach of the constitutional limitation. It is, of course, not questioned that enforcing this rule of apportionment will, by reason of the inconveniences attending it, incline the federal government against direct taxation, and will generally induce the collection of federal revenues by duties on imports, by licenses and, by other forms of excises, just as has been the ordinary practice of the government from its commencement to the present time. And yet while that is so it is not true that the rule places beyond the reach of the taxing power of the national government, if ever emergency arises, a single dollar of the tangible property of the country. As every individual in the nation is subject to the call of the government when needed in case of foreign invasion or civil war, so every dollar's worth of property is within the reach of the government when occasion demands.

    * * *

It is not strange that the apportioning of direct taxes among the states was insisted upon as a matter of moment. The struggle of the revolution had been that taxation and representation should go together. The articles of confederation, under which we commenced our existence, provided that all taxes should be collected by the states, and that they should supply the general treasury with all its funds. Each of the states was considered, and so declared by those articles of confederation to retain its "sovereignty, freedom, and independence," and by virtue thereof had absolute control over all taxation within its borders and from its own collections supplied the common treasury. Accustomed as the states were, therefore, to this full control over all taxation, it is not strange that among the things stipulated for were certain limitations upon the power of congress to come into their midst and collect taxes. While in forming the constitution the people contemplated a stronger central government, there never was a thought that the states should be wiped out of existence, or that they should cease to have within certain limits an independent sovereignty. So far as local matters were concerned they retained supreme control, and for the preservation of their own existence they knew that taxation was essential. They fully appreciated that which was so tersely said years thereafter by the great chief justice that the power to tax is the power to destroy, and knew that if an unrestricted power of taxation was granted to the national government, congress would hold every state within its grasp, and that combinations might grievously burden some unpopular section and endanger even the very existence of the states therein. They surrendered to the general government all revenues from imports and exports; they gave to it general power of taxation in licenses and other forms of excise, and they further provided that all tangible property, the real and personal property within the limits of the states, might be reached by a direct tax imposed by Congress. But in order that equality might be maintained between the states, that by no combination should an excessive burden be placed upon one state, they affirmatively and negatively, once and again declared that direct taxes should be apportioned according to population. They meant to establish beyond question that the burdens of direct taxation should be borne by all the states in proportion to their population. An eminent judicial friend of mine, living in Arkansas, said to me jokingly, that the people in his state were all in favor of the income tax because there was no man in it that had an income of $4,000. In other words they were enthusiastically in support of a tax which they did not have to pay. That public spirit was like the patriotism which Artemus Ward possessed when he said that he was willing to have all his wife's relations drafted into the army. But it was against such a public spirit that the fathers intended to guard. They meant to prevent any combination between some of the states to cast all the burdens of direct taxation upon the people of a few. They foresaw that within the discretion given to Congress it might conclude to make all imports and exports free. It might conclude not to levy any license or other taxes but to collect all the revenues by direct taxation upon the tangible property and in such an event, or in any case that the tangible property was sought to be reached, they meant that each state should bear its proportionate share of the burden.

The power of Congress to levy direct taxes under any circumstances was one of the objective points of attack made in the various conventions called to ratify the constitution, and there was strenuous antagonism to it on that ground. Massachusetts in ratifying recommended the adoption of an amendment in these words: "That Congress do not lay direct taxes but when the moneys arising from the impost and excise are insufficient for the public exigencies, nor then until Congress shall have first made a requisition upon the states to assess, levy and pay their respective proportions of such requisition, agreeably to the census fixed in the said constitution in such way and manner as the legislatures of the states shall think best." And in this recommendation South Carolina, New York, New Hampshire and Rhode Island concurred. Notice in this that "direct taxes" are placed over against "impost and excise." Ellsworth, afterwards chief justice of the Supreme Court, and Roger Sherman wrote the governor of Connecticut, on September 26, 1787, ten days after the convention had been signed by the delegates, "the principal branch of revenue will be duties on imports. What may be necessary to be raised by direct taxation is to be apportioned on the several states, according to the number of their inhabitants; and although Congress may raise the money by their own authority, if necessary, yet that authority need not be exercised if each state will furbish its own quota." And declarations of a similar nature were made by the leading men engaged in framing the constitution and in urging its adoption. So that it seems hardly open to doubt, that the general understanding at the time was that the tangible property should be left primarily to the states as the source of their revenues, and should be reached by the national government only by the rule of apportionment.

No one has questioned that a tax levied in the ordinary way upon land is a direct tax within the meaning of the constitution. There has been doubt whether a similar tax upon tangible personal property is also a direct tax, yet it seems very difficult in principle to distinguish between the two and hold one a direct and the other an indirect tax. But the greater contention has been that, conceding that a tax levied upon real and personal property, according to its value in the ordinary method of taxation, is a direct tax, yet a tax upon the income, the rents and profits of such property, is not. It is said that a tax on income does not touch the tangible real and personal property, that the real estate, the farms and town lots, the personalty, the stocks of goods, are all left to the states for taxation and no burden is cast upon them; that the income is something separate and apart from the property itself; that the tangible property is one thing and that which the owner may receive in the way of rents and profits from it another and entirely different thing; and that while a tax upon the tangible property, real or personal, may be a direct tax within the meaning of the constitution, yet a mere charge upon the income, the rents and profits derived from such property, is not. But with all respect to those who entertain such views it seems to me that they make constitutional guaranties a mockery and delusion and sacrifice matters of substance to forms of expression. What is it that makes property something to be desired? Is it the mere holding of the legal title, or is it the profit, the income derived from ownership? Of what good would be a fee simple title to 100,000 acres at the North Pole, or half the area of the moon, land which could never be reached, and from which no gain could ever come? Is not that which gives value to property the fact that you are able to derive income from it? To leave the mere title undisturbed while taking away all benefit flowing from ownership and still say that constitutional guaranties of protection are respected is trifling.

* * *

Another matter: Soon after the decision was announced, I noticed in some magazine or paper an amusing article by Mr. Ingersoll, of Tennessee. He called attention to the fact that all the justices coming from south of Mason and Dixon's line upheld the law, while all who believed that its provisions conflicted with the constitution were from the north, and of New England descent. No one from the north thought the law valid except our good brother, Brown of Michigan, and he agreed with the majority as to the invalidity of the income tax so far as applied to rents from land. It is curious also to note that following the same line of division the chief denunciation has come from that section of the country which fifty years ago, inspired by the teachings of John C. Calhoun, held that the states were of the greater and the nation of the less importance, while the support of the decision both in and out of court has come from those who at the feet of Daniel Webster and John Marshall were taught that the nation was supreme. Perhaps as suggested, the change is explainable on the ground that the latest converts are always the most radical and extreme, especially when the methods of their conversion have been severe and painful.

Lochner v. New York, *198 U.S. 45 (1905)*

MR. JUSTICE PECKHAM delivered the opinion of the court.

The indictment, it will be seen, charges that the plaintiff in error violated the one hundred and tenth section of article 8, chapter 415, of the Laws of 1897, known as the labor law of the State of New York, in that he wrongfully and unlawfully required and permitted an employe working for him to work more than sixty hours in one week. There is nothing in any of the opinions delivered in this case, either in the Supreme Court or the Court of Appeals of the State, which construes the section, in using the word "required," as referring to any physical force being used to obtain the labor of an employe. It is assumed that the word means nothing more than the requirement arising from voluntary contract for such labor in excess of the number of hours specified in the statute. There is no pretense in any of the opinions that the statute was intended to meet a case of involuntary labor in any form. All the opinions assume that there is no real distinction, so far as this question is concerned, between the words "required" and "permitted." The mandate of the statute that "no employe shall be required or permitted to work," is the substantial equivalent of an enactment that "no employe shall contract or agree to work," more than ten hours per day, and as there is no provision for special emergencies the statute is mandatory in all cases. It is not an act merely fixing the number of hours which shall constitute a legal day's work, but an absolute prohibition upon the employer, permitting, under any circumstances, more than ten hours work to be done in his establishment. The employe may desire to earn the extra money, which would arise from his working more than the prescribed time, but this statute forbids the employer from permitting the employe to earn it.

The statute necessarily interferes with the right of contract between the employer and employes, concerning the number of hours in which the latter may labor in the bakery of the employer. The general right to make a contract in relation to his business is part of the liberty of the individual protected by the Fourteenth Amendment of the Federal Constitution. *Allgeyer* v. *Louisiana*, 165 U.S. 578. Under that provision no State can deprive any person of life, liberty or property without due process of law. The right to purchase or to sell labor is part of the liberty protected by this amendment, unless there are circumstances which exclude the right. There are, however, certain powers, existing in the sovereignty of each State in the Union, somewhat vaguely termed police powers, the exact description and limitation of which have not been attempted by the courts. Those powers, broadly stated and without, at present, any attempt at a more specific limitation, relate to the safety, health, morals and general welfare of the public. Both property and liberty are held on such reasonable conditions as may be imposed by the governing power of the State in the exercise of those powers, and with such conditions the Fourteenth Amendment was not designed to interfere. *Mugler* v. *Kansas*, 123 U.S. 623; *In re Kemmler*, 136 U.S. 436; *Crowley* v. *Christensen*, 137 U.S. 86; *In re Converse*, 137 U.S. 624.

The State, therefore, has power to prevent the individual from making certain kinds of contracts, and in regard to them the Federal Constitution offers no protection. If the contract be one which the State, in the legitimate exercise of its police power, has the right to prohibit, it is not prevented from prohibiting it by the Fourteenth Amendment. Contracts in violation of a statute, either of the Federal or state government, or a contract to let one's property for immoral purposes, or to do any other unlawful act, could obtain no protection from the Federal Constitution, as coming under the liberty of person or of free contract. Therefore, when the State, by its legislature, in the assumed exercise of its police powers, has passed an act which seriously limits the right to labor or the right of contract in regard to their means of livelihood between persons who are *sui juris* (both employer and employe), it becomes of great importance to determine which shall prevail—the right of the individual to labor for such time as he may choose, or the right of the State to prevent the individual from laboring or from entering into any contract to labor, beyond a certain time prescribed by the State.

This court has recognized the existence and upheld the exercise of the police powers of the States in many cases which might fairly be considered as border ones, and it has, in the course of its determination of questions regarding the asserted invalidity of such statutes, on the ground of their violation of the rights secured by the Federal Constitution, been guided by rules of a very liberal nature, the application of which has resulted, in numerous instances, in upholding the validity of state statutes thus assailed. Among the later cases where the state law has been upheld by this court is that of *Holden* v. *Hardy*, 169 U.S. 366. A provision in the act of the legislature of Utah was there under consideration, the act limiting the employment of workmen in all underground mines or workings, to eight hours per day, "except in cases of emergency, where life or property is in imminent danger." It also limited the hours of labor in smelting and other institutions for the reduction or refining of ores or metals to eight hours per day, except in like cases of emergency. The act was held to be a valid exercise of the police powers of the State. A review of many of the cases on the subject, decided by this and other courts, is given in the opinion. It was held that the kind of employment, mining, smelting, etc., and the character of the employes in such kinds of labor, were such as to make it reasonable and proper for the State to interfere to prevent the employes from being constrained by the rules laid down by the proprietors in regard to labor. The following citation from the observations of the Supreme Court of Utah in that case was made by the judge writing the opinion of this court, and approved: "The law in question is confined to the protection of that class of people engaged in labor in underground mines, and in smelters and other works wherein ores are reduced and refined. This law applies only to the classes subjected by their employment to the peculiar conditions and effects attending underground mining and work in smelters, and other works for the reduction and refining of ores. Therefore it is not necessary to discuss or decide whether the legislature can fix the hours of labor in other employments."

It will be observed that, even with regard to that class of labor, the Utah statute provided for cases of emergency wherein the provisions of the statute would not apply. The statute now before this court has no emergency clause in it, and, if the statute is valid, there are no circumstances and no emergencies under which the slightest violation of the provisions of the act would be innocent. There is nothing in *Holden* v. *Hardy* which covers the case now before us. Nor does *Atkin* v. *Kansas*, 191 U.S. 207, touch the case at bar. The *Atkin case* was decided upon the right of the State to control its municipal corporations and to prescribe the conditions upon which it will permit work of a public character to be done for a municipality. *Knoxville Iron Co.* v. *Harbison*, 183 U.S. 13, is equally far from an authority for this legislation. The employes in that case were held to be at a disadvantage with the employer in matters of wages, they being miners and coal workers, and the act simply provided for the cashing of coal orders when presented by the miner to the employer.

The latest case decided by this court, involving the police power, is that of *Jacobson* v. *Massachusetts*, decided at this term and reported in 197 U.S. 11. It related to compulsory vaccination, and the law was held valid as a proper exercise of the police powers with reference to the public health. It was stated in the opinion that it was a case "of an adult who, for aught that appears, was himself in perfect health and a fit subject for vaccination, and yet, while remaining in the community, refused to obey the statute and the regulation adopted in execution of its provisions for the protection of the public health and the public safety, confessedly endangered by the presence of a dangerous disease." That case is also far from covering the one now before the court.

Petit v. *Minnesota*, 177 U.S. 164, was upheld as a proper exercise of the police power relating to the observance of Sunday, and the case held that the legislature had the right to declare that, as matter of law, keeping barber shops open on Sunday was not a work of necessity or charity.

It must, of course, be conceded that there is a limit to the valid exercise of the police power by the State. There is no dispute concerning this general proposition. Otherwise the Fourteenth Amendment would have no efficacy and the legislatures of the States would have unbounded power, and it would be enough to say that any piece of legislation was enacted to conserve the morals, the health or the safety of the people; such legislation would be valid, no matter how absolutely without foundation the claim might be. The claim of the police power would be a mere pretext—become another and delusive name for the supreme sovereignty of the State to be exercised free from constitutional restraint. This is not contended for. In every case that comes before this court, therefore, where legislation of this character is concerned and where the protection of the Federal Constitution is sought, the question necessarily arises: Is this a fair, reasonable and appropriate exercise of the police power of the State, or is it an unreasonable, unnecessary and arbitrary interference with the right of the individual to his personal liberty or to enter into those contracts in relation to labor which may seem to him appropriate or necessary for the support of himself and his family? Of course the liberty of contract relating to labor includes both parties to it. The one has as much right to purchase as the other to sell labor.

This is not a question of substituting the judgment of the court for that of the legislature. If the act be within the power of the State it is valid, although the judgment of the court might be totally opposed to the enactment of such a law. But the question would still remain: Is it within the police power of the State? and that question must be answered by the court.

The question whether this act is valid as a labor law, pure and simple, may be dismissed in a few words. There is no reasonable ground for interfering with the liberty of person or the right of free contract, by determining the hours of labor, in the occupation of a baker. There is no contention that bakers as a class are not equal in intelligence and capacity to men in other trades or manual occupations, or that they are not able to assert their rights and care for themselves without the protecting arm of the State, interfering with their independence of judgment and of action. They are in no sense wards of the State. Viewed in the light of a purely labor law, with no reference whatever to the question of health, we think that a law like the one before us involves neither the safety, the morals nor the welfare of the public, and that the interest of the public is not in the slightest degree affected by such an act. The law must be upheld, if at all, as a law pertaining to the health of the individual engaged in the occupation of a baker. It does not affect any other portion of the public than those who are engaged in that occupation. Clean and wholesome bread does not depend upon whether the baker works but ten hours per day or only sixty hours a week. The limitation of the hours of labor does not come within the police power on that ground.

It is a question of which of two powers or rights shall prevail—the power of the State to legislate or the right of the individual to liberty of person and freedom of contract. The mere assertion that the subject relates though but in a remote degree to the public health does not necessarily render the enactment valid. The act must have a more direct relation, as a means to an end, and the end itself must be appropriate and legitimate, before an act can be held to be valid which interferes with the general right of an individual to be free in his person and in his power to contract in relation to his own labor.

This case has caused much diversity of opinion in the state courts. In the Supreme Court two of the five judges composing the Appellate Division dissented from the judgment affirming the validity of the act. In the Court of Appeals three of the seven judges also dissented from the judgment upholding the statute. Although found in what is called a labor law of the State, the Court of Appeals has upheld the act as one relating to the public health—in other words, as a health law. One of the judges of the Court of Appeals, in upholding the law, stated that, in his opinion, the regulation in question could not be sustained unless they were able to say, from common knowledge, that working in a bakery and candy factory was an unhealthy employment. The judge held that, while the evidence was not uniform, it still led him to the conclusion that the occupation of a baker or confectioner was unhealthy and tended to result in diseases of the respiratory organs. Three of the judges dissented from that view, and they thought the occupation of a baker was not to such an extent unhealthy as to warrant the interference of the legislature with the liberty of the individual.

We think the limit of the police power has been reached and passed in this case. There is, in our judgment, no reasonable foundation for holding this to be necessary or appropriate as a health law to safeguard the public health or the health of the individuals who are following the trade of a baker. If this statute be valid, and if, therefore, a proper case is made out in which to deny the right of an individual, *sui juris*, as employer or employe, to make contracts for the labor of the latter under the protection of the provisions of the Federal Constitution, there would seem to be no length to which legislation of this nature might not go. The case differs widely, as we have already stated, from the expressions of this court in regard to laws of this nature, as stated in *Holden* v. *Hardy* and *Jacobson* v. *Massachusetts, supra.*

We think that there can be no fair doubt that the trade of a baker, in and of itself, is not an unhealthy one to that degree which would authorize the legislature to interfere with the right to labor, and with the right of free contract on the part of the individual, either as employer or employe. In looking through statistics regarding all trades and occupations, it may be true that the trade of a baker does not appear to be as healthy as some other trades, and is also vastly more healthy than still others. To the common understanding the trade of a baker has never been regarded as an unhealthy one. Very likely physicians would not recommend the exercise of that or of any other trade as a remedy for ill health. Some occupations are more healthy than others, but we think there are none which might not come under the power of the legislature to supervise and control the hours of working therein, if the mere fact that the occupation is not absolutely and perfectly healthy is to confer that right upon the legislative department of the Government. It might be safely affirmed that almost all occupations more or less affect the health. There must be more than the mere fact of the possible existence of some small amount of unhealthiness to warrant legislative interference with liberty. It is unfortunately true that labor, even in any department, may possibly carry with it the seeds of unhealthiness. But are we all, on that account, at the mercy of legislative majorities? A printer, a tinsmith, a locksmith, a carpenter, a cabinetmaker, a dry goods clerk, a bank's, a lawyer's or a physician's clerk, or a clerk in almost any kind of business, would all come under the power of the legislature, on this assumption. No trade, no occupation, no mode of earning one's living, could escape this all-pervading power, and the acts of the legislature in limiting the hours of labor in all employments would be valid, although such limitation might seriously cripple the ability of the laborer to support himself and his family. In our large cities there are many buildings into which the sun penetrates for but a short time in each day, and these buildings are occupied by people carrying on the business of bankers, brokers, lawyers, real estate, and many other kinds of business, aided by many clerks, messengers, and other employes. Upon the assumption of the validity of this act under review, it is not possible to say that an act, prohibiting lawyers' or bank clerks, or others, from contracting to labor for their employers more than eight hours a day, would be invalid. It might be said that it is unhealthy to work more than that number of hours in an apartment lighted by artificial light during the working hours of the day; that the occupation of the bank clerk, the lawyer's clerk, the real estate clerk, or the broker's clerk in such offices is therefore unhealthy, and the legislature in its paternal wisdom must, therefore, have the right to legislate on the subject of and to limit the hours for such labor, and if it exercises that power and its validity be questioned, it is sufficient to say, it has reference to the public health; it has reference to the health of the employes condemned to labor day after day in buildings where the sun never shines; it is a health law, and therefore it is valid, and cannot be questioned by the courts.

It is also urged, pursuing the same line of argument, that it is to the interest of the State that its population should be strong and robust, and therefore any legislation which may be said to tend to make people healthy must be valid as health laws, enacted under the police power. If this be a valid argument and a justification for this kind of legislation, it follows that the protection of the Federal Constitution from undue interference with liberty of person and freedom of contract is visionary, wherever the law is sought to be justified as a valid exercise of the police power. Scarcely any law but might find shelter under such assumptions, and conduct, properly so called, as well as contract, would come under the restrictive sway of the legislature. Not only the hours of employes, but the hours of employers, could be regulated, and doctors, lawyers, scientists, all professional men, as well as athletes and artisans, could be forbidden to fatigue their brains and bodies by prolonged hours of exercise, lest the fighting strength of the State be impaired. We mention these extreme cases because the contention is extreme. We do not believe in the soundness of the views which uphold this law. On the contrary, we think that such a law as this, although passed in the assumed exercise of the police power, and as relating to the public health, or the health of the employes named, is not within that power, and is invalid. The act is not, within any fair meaning of the term, a health law, but is an illegal interference with the rights of individuals, both employers and employes, to make contracts regarding labor upon such terms as they may think best, or which they may agree upon with the other parties to such contracts. Statutes of the nature of that under review, limiting the hours in which grown and intelligent men may labor to earn their living, are mere meddlesome interferences with the rights of the individual, and they are not saved from condemnation by the claim that they are passed in the exercise of the police power and upon the subject of the health of the individual whose rights are interfered with, unless there be some fair ground, reasonable in and of itself, to say that there is material danger to the public health or to the health of the employes, if the hours of labor are not curtailed. If this be not clearly the case the individuals, whose rights are thus made the subject of legislative interference, are under the protection of the Federal Constitution regarding their liberty of contract as well as of person; and the legislature of the State has no power to limit their right as proposed in this statute. All that it could properly do has been done by it with regard to the conduct of bakeries, as provided for in the other sections of the act, above set forth. These several sections provide for the inspection of the premises where the bakery is carried on, with regard to furnishing proper wash-rooms and water-closets, apart from the bake-room, also with regard to providing proper drainage, plumbing and painting; the sections, in addition, provide for the height of the ceiling, the cementing or tiling of floors, where necessary in the opinion of the factory inspector, and for other things of that nature; alterations are also provided for and are to be made where necessary in the opinion of the inspector, in order to comply with the provisions of the statute. These various sections may be wise and valid regulations, and they certainly go to the full extent of providing for the cleanliness and the healthiness, so far as possible, of the quarters in which bakeries are to be conducted. Adding to all these requirements, a prohibition to enter into any contract of labor in a bakery for more than a certain number of hours a week, is, in our judgment, so wholly beside the matter of a proper, reasonable and fair provision, as to run counter to that liberty of person and of free contract provided for in the Federal Constitution.

It was further urged on the argument that restricting the hours of labor in the case of bakers was valid because it tended to cleanliness on the part of the workers, as a man was more apt to be cleanly when not overworked, and if cleanly then his "output" was also more likely to be so. What has already been said applies with equal force to this contention. We do not admit the reasoning to be sufficient to justify the claimed right of such interference. The State in that case would assume the position of a supervisor, or *pater familias*, over every act of the individual, and its right of governmental interference with his hours of labor, his hours of exercise, the character thereof, and the extent to which it shall be carried would be recognized and upheld. In our judgment it is not possible in fact to discover the connection between the number of hours a baker may work in the bakery and the healthful quality of the bread made by the workman. The connection, if any exists, is too shadowy and thin to build any argument for the interference of the legislature. If the man works ten hours a day it is all right, but if ten and a half or eleven his health is in danger and his bread may be unhealthful, and, therefore, he shall not be permitted to do it. This, we think, is unreasonable and entirely arbitrary. When assertions such as we have adverted to become necessary in order to give, if possible, a plausible foundation for the contention that the law is a "health law," it gives rise to at least a suspicion that there was some other motive dominating the legislature than the purpose to subserve the public health or welfare.

This interference on the part of the legislatures of the several States with the ordinary trades and occupations of the people seems to be on the increase. In the Supreme Court of New York, in the case of *People* v. *Beattie*, Appellate Division, First Department, decided in 1904, 89 N.Y. Supp. 193, a statute regulating the trade of horseshoeing, and requiring the person practicing such trade to be examined and to obtain a certificate from a board of examiners and file the same with the clerk of the county wherein the person proposes to practice such trade, was held invalid, as an arbitrary interference with personal liberty and private property without due process of law. The attempt was made, unsuccessfully, to justify it as a health law.

The same kind of a statute was held invalid (*In re Aubry*) by the Supreme Court of Washington in December, 1904. 78 Pac. Rep. 900. The court held that the act deprived citizens of their liberty and property without due process of law and denied to them the equal protection of the laws. It also held that the trade of a horseshoer is not a subject of regulation under the police power of the State, as a business concerning and directly affecting the health, welfare or comfort of its inhabitants; and that therefore a law which provided for the examination and registration of horseshoers in certain cities was unconstitutional, as an illegitimate exercise of the police power.

The Supreme Court of Illinois in *Bessette* v. *People*, 193 Illinois, 334, also held that a law of the same nature, providing for the regulation and licensing of horseshoers, was unconstitutional as an illegal interference with the liberty of the individual in adopting and pursuing such calling as he may choose, subject only to the restraint necessary to secure the common welfare. See also *Godcharles* v. *Wigeman*, 113 Pa. St. 431, 437; *Low* v. *Rees Printing Co.*, 41 Nebraska, 127, 145. In these cases the courts upheld the right of free contract and the right to purchase and sell labor upon such terms as the parties may agree to.

It is impossible for us to shut our eyes to the fact that many of the laws of this character, while passed under what is claimed to be the police power for the purpose of protecting the public health or welfare, are, in reality, passed from other motives. We are justified in saying so when, from the character of the law and the subject upon which it legislates, it is apparent that the public health or welfare bears but the most remote relation to the law. The purpose of a statute must be determined from the natural and legal effect of the language employed; and whether it is or is not repugnant to the Constitution of the United States must be determined from the natural effect of such statutes when put into operation, and not from their proclaimed purpose. *Minnesota* v. *Barber*, 136 U.S. 313; *Brimmer* v. *Rebman*, 138 U.S. 78. The court looks beyond the mere letter of the law in such cases. *Yick Wo* v. *Hopkins*, 118 U.S. 356.

It is manifest to us that the limitation of the hours of labor as provided for in this section of the statute under which the indictment was found, and the plaintiff in error convicted, has no such direct relation to and no such substantial effect upon the health of the employe, as to justify us in regarding the section as really a health law. It seems to us that the real object and purpose were simply to regulate the hours of labor between the master and his employes (all being men, *sui juris*), in a private business, not dangerous in any degree to morals or in any real and substantial degree, to the health of the employes. Under such circumstances the freedom of master and employe to contract with each other in relation to their employment, and in defining the same, cannot be prohibited or interfered with, without violating the Federal Constitution.

The judgment of the Court of Appeals of New York as well as that of the Supreme Court and of the County Court of Oneida County must be reversed and the case remanded to the County Court for further proceedings not inconsistent with this opinion. *Reversed.*

DISSENT:

MR. JUSTICE HARLAN, with whom MR. JUSTICE WHITE and MR. JUSTICE DAY concurred, dissenting.

While this court has not attempted to mark the precise boundaries of what is called the police power of the State, the existence of the power has been uniformly recognized, both by the Federal and state courts.

All the cases agree that this power extends at least to the protection of the lives, the health and the safety of the public against the injurious exercise by any citizen of his own rights.

In *Patterson* v. *Kentucky*, 97 U.S. 501, after referring to the general principle that rights given by the Constitution cannot be impaired by state legislation of any kind, this court said: "It [this court] has, nevertheless, with marked distinctness and uniformity, recognized the necessity, growing out of the fundamental conditions of civil society, of upholding state police regulations which were enacted in good faith, and had appropriate and direct connection with that protection to life, health, and property which each State owes to her citizen." So in *Barbier* v. *Connolly*, 113 U.S. 27: "But neither the [14th] Amendment—broad and comprehensive as it is—nor any other Amendment was designed to interfere with the power of the State, sometimes termed its police power, to prescribe regulations to promote the health, peace, morals, education, and good order of the people."

Speaking generally, the State in the exercise of its powers may not unduly interfere with the right of the citizen to enter into contracts that may be necessary and essential in the enjoyment of the inherent rights belonging to every one, among which rights is the right "to be free in the enjoyment of all his faculties; to be free to use them in all lawful ways; to live and work where he will; to earn his livelihood by any lawful calling; to pursue any livelihood or avocation." This was declared in *Allgeyer* v. *Louisiana*, 165 U.S. 578, 589. But in the same case it was conceded that the right to contract in relation to persons and property or to do business, within a State, may be "regulated and sometimes prohibited, when the contracts or business conflict with the policy of the State as contained in its statutes" (p. 591).

So, as said in *Holden* v. *Hardy*, 169 U.S. 366, 391: "This right of contract, however, is itself subject to certain limitations which the State may lawfully impose in the exercise of its police powers. While this power is inherent in all governments, it has doubtless been greatly expanded in its application during the past century, owing to an enormous increase in the number of occupations which are dangerous, or so far detrimental to the health of the employes as to demand special precautions for their well-being and protection, or the safety of adjacent property. While this court has held, notably in the cases of *Davidson* v. *New Orleans*, 96 U.S. 97, and *Yick Wo* v. *Hopkins*, 118 U.S; 356, that the police power cannot be put forward as an excuse for oppressive and unjust legislation, it may be lawfully resorted to for the purpose of preserving the public health, safety or morals, or the abatement of public nuisances, and a large discretion 'is necessarily vested in the legislature to determine not only what the interests of the public require, but what measures are necessary for the protection of such interests.' *Lawton* v. *Steele*, 152 U.S. 133, 136." Referring to the limitations placed by the State upon the hours of workmen, the court in the same case said (p. 395): "These employments, when too long pursued, the legislature has judged to be detrimental to the health of the employes, and, so long as there are reasonable grounds for believing that this is so, its decision upon this subject cannot be reviewed by the Federal courts."

Subsequently in *Gundling* v. *Chicago*, 177 U.S. 183, 188, this court said: "Regulations respecting the pursuit of a lawful trade or business are of very frequent occurrence in the various cities of the country, and what such regulations shall be and to what particular trade, business or occupation they shall apply, are questions for the State to determine, and their determination comes within the proper exercise of the police power by the State, and unless the regulations are so utterly unreasonable and extravagant in their nature and purpose that the property and personal rights of the citizen are unnecessarily, and in a manner wholly arbitrary, interfered with or destroyed without due process of law, they do not extend beyond the power of the State to pass, and they form no subject for Federal interference.

"As stated in *Crowley* v. *Christensen*, 137 U.S. 86, 'the possession and enjoyment of all rights are subject to such reasonable conditions as may be deemed by the governing authority of the country essential to the safety, health, peace, good order and morals of the Community.'"

In *St. Louis, Iron Mountain &c. Ry.* v. *Paul*, 173 U.S. 404, 409, and in *Knoxville Iron Co.* v. *Harbison*, 183 U.S. 13, 21, 22, it was distinctly adjudged that the right of contract was not "absolute in respect to every matter, but may be subjected to the restraints demanded by the safety and welfare of the State." Those cases illustrate the extent to which the State may restrict or interfere with the exercise of the right of contracting.

The authorities on the same line are so numerous that further citations are unnecessary.

I take it to be firmly established that what is called the liberty of contract may, within certain limits, be subjected to regulations designed and calculated to promote the general welfare or to guard the public health, the public morals or the public safety. "The liberty secured by the Constitution of the United States to every person within its jurisdiction does not import," this court has recently said, "an absolute right in each person to be, at all times and in all circumstances, wholly freed from restraint. There are manifold restraints to which every person is necessarily subject for the common good." *Jacobson* v. *Massachusetts*, 197 U.S. 11.

Granting then that there is a liberty of contract which cannot be violated even under the sanction of direct legislative enactment, but assuming, as according to settled law we may assume, that such liberty of contract is subject to such regulations as the State may reasonably prescribe for the common good and the well-being of society, what are the conditions under which the judiciary may declare such regulations to be in excess of legislative authority and void? Upon this point there is no room for dispute; for, the rule is universal that a legislative enactment, Federal or state, is never to be disregarded or held invalid unless it be, beyond question, plainly and palpably in excess of legislative power. In *Jacobson* v. *Massachusetts, supra*, we said that the power of the courts to review legislative action in respect of a matter affecting the general welfare exists *only* "when that which the legislature has done comes within the rule that if a statute purporting to have been enacted to protect the public health, the public morals or the public safety, has no real or substantial relation to those objects, or is, beyond all question, a plain, palpable invasion of rights secured by the fundamental law"—citing *Mugler* v. *Kansas*, 123 U.S. 623, 661; *Min-*

nesota v. *Barber*, 136 U.S. 313, 320: *Atkin* v. *Kansas*, 191 U.S. 207, 223. If there be doubt as to the validity of the statute, that doubt must therefore be resolved in favor of its validity, and the courts must keep their hands off, leaving the legislature to meet the responsibility for unwise legislation. If the end which the legislature seeks to accomplish be one to which is power extends, and if the means employed to that end, although not the wisest or best, are yet not plainly and palpably unauthorized by law, then the court cannot interfere. In other words, when the validity of a statute is questioned, the burden of proof, so to speak, is upon those who assert it to be unconstitutional. *McCulloch* v. *Maryland*, 4 Wheat. 316, 421.

Let these principles be applied to the present case. By the statute in question it is provided that, "No employe shall be required or permitted to work in a biscuit, bread or cake bakery or confectionery establishment more than sixty hours in any one week, or more than ten hours in any one day, unless for the purpose of making a shorter work day on the last day of the week; nor more hours in any one week than will make an average of ten hours per day for the number of days during such week in which such employe shall work."

It is plain that this statute was enacted in order to protect the physical well-being of those who work in bakery and confectionery establishments. It may be that the statute had its origin, in part, in the belief that employers and employes in such establishments were not upon an equal footing, and that the necessities of the latter often compelled them to submit to such exactions as unduly taxed their strength. Be this as it may, the statute must be taken as expressing the belief of the people of New York that, as a general rule, and in the case of the average man, labor in excess of sixty hours during a week in such establishments may endanger the health of those who thus labor. Whether or not this be wise legislation it is not the province of the court to inquire. Under our systems of government the courts are not concerned with the wisdom or policy of legislation. So that in determining the question of power to interfere with liberty of contract, the court may inquire whether the means devised by the State are germane to an end which may be lawfully accomplished and have a real or substantial relation to the protection of health, as involved in the daily work of the persons, male and female, engaged in bakery and confectionery establishments. But when this inquiry is entered upon I find it impossible, in view of common experience, to say that there is here no real or substantial relation between the means employed by the State and the end sought to be accomplished by its legislation. *Mugler* v. *Kansas, supra.* Nor can I say that the statute has no appropriate or direct connection with that protection to health which each State owes to her citizens, *Patterson* v. *Kentucky, supra;* or that it is not promotive of the health of the employes in question, *Holden* v. *Hardy, Lawton* v. *Steele, supra;* or that the regulation prescribed by the State is utterly unreasonable and extravagant or wholly arbitrary, *Gundling* v. *Chicago, supra.* Still less can I say that the statute is, beyond question, a plain, palpable invasion of rights secured by the fundamental law. *Jacobson* v. *Massachusetts*, *supra*. Therefore I submit that this court will transcend its functions if it assumes to annul the statute of New York. It must be remembered that this statute does not apply to all kinds of business. It applies only to work in bakery and confectionery establishments, in which, as all know, the air constantly breathed by workmen is not as pure and healthful as that to be found in some other establishments or out of doors.

Professor Hirt in his treatise on the "Diseases of the Workers" has said: "The labor of the bakers is among the hardest and most laborious imaginable, because it has to be performed under conditions injurious to the health of those engaged in it. It is hard, very hard work, not only because it requires a great deal of physical exertion in an overheated workshop and during unreasonably long hours, but more so because of the erratic demands of the public, compelling the baker to perform the greater part of his work at night thus depriving him of an opportunity to enjoy the necessary rest and sleep, a fact which is highly injurious to his health." Another writer says: "The constant inhaling of flour dust causes inflammation of the lungs and of the bronchial tubes. The eyes also suffer through this dust, which is responsible for the many cases of running eyes among the bakers. The long hours of toil to which all bakers are subjected produce rheumatism, cramps and swollen legs. The intense heat in the workshops induces the workers to resort to cooling drinks, which together with their habit of exposing the greater part of their bodies to the change in the atmosphere, is another source of a number of diseases of various organs. Nearly all bakers are pale-faced and of more delicate health than the workers of other crafts, which is chiefly due to their hard work and their irregular and unnatural mode of living, whereby the power of resistance against disease is greatly diminished. The average age of a baker is below that of other workmen; they seldom live over their fiftieth year, most of them dying between the ages of forty and fifty. During periods of epidemic diseases the bakers are generally the first to succumb to the disease, and the number swept away during such periods far exceeds the number of other crafts in comparison to the men employed in the respective industries. When, in 1720, the plague visited the city of Marseilles, France, every baker in the city succumbed to the epidemic, which caused considerable excitement in the neighboring cities and resulted in measures for the sanitary protection of the bakers."

In the Eighteenth Annual Report by the New York Bureau of Statistics of Labor it is stated that among the occupations involving exposure to conditions that interfere with nutrition is that of a baker (p. 52). In that Report it is also stated that "from a social point of view, production will be increased by any change in industrial organization which diminishes the number of idlers, paupers and criminals. Shorter hours of work, by allowing higher standards of comfort and purer family life, promise to enhance the industrial efficiency of the wage-working class—improved health, longer life, more content and greater intelligence and inventiveness" (p. 82).

Statistics show that the average daily working time among workingmen in different countries is, in Australia, 8 hours; in Great Britain, 9; in the United States, 9 3/4; in Denmark, 9 3/4; in Norway, 10; Sweden, France and Switzerland, 10 1/2; Germany, 10 1/4; Belgium, Italy and Austria, 11; and in Russia, 12 hours.

We judicially know that the question of the number of hours during which a workman should continuously labor has been, for a long period, and is yet, a subject of serious consideration among civilized peoples, and by those having special knowledge of the laws of health. Suppose the statute prohibited labor in bakery and confectionery establishments in excess of eighteen hours each day. No one, I take it, could dispute the power of the State to enact such a statute. But the statute before us does not embrace extreme or exceptional cases. It may be said to occupy a middle ground in respect of the hours of labor. What is the true ground for the State to take between legitimate protection, by legislation, of the public health and liberty of contract is not a question easily solved, nor one in respect of which there is or can be absolute certainty. There are very few, if any, questions in political economy about which entire certainty may be predicated. One writer on relation of the State to labor has well said: "The manner, occasion, and degree in which the State may interfere with the industrial freedom of its citizens is one of the most debatable and difficult questions of social science." Jevons, 33.

We also judicially know that the number of hours that should constitute a day's labor in particular occupations involving the physical strength and safety of workmen has been the subject of enactments by Congress and by nearly all of the States. Many, if not most, of those enactments fix eight hours as the proper basis of a day's labor.

I do not stop to consider whether any particular view of this economic question presents the sounder theory. What the precise facts are it may be difficult to say. It is enough for the determination of this case, and it is enough for this court to know, that the question is one about which there is room for debate and for an honest difference of opinion. There are many reasons of a weighty, substantial character, based upon the experience of mankind, in support of the theory that, all things considered, more than ten hours' steady work each day, from week to week, in a bakery or confectionery establishment, may endanger the health, and shorten the lives of the workmen, thereby diminishing their physical and mental capacity to serve the State, and to provide for those dependent upon them.

If such reasons exist that ought to be the end of this case, for the State is not amenable to the judiciary, in respect of its legislative enactments, unless such enactments are plainly, palpably, beyond all question, inconsistent with the Constitution of the United States. We are not to presume that the State of New York has acted in bad faith. Nor can we assume that its legislature acted without due deliberation, or that it did not determine this question upon the fullest attainable information, and for the common good. We cannot say that the State has acted without reason nor ought we to proceed upon the theory that its action is a mere sham. Our duty, I submit, is to sustain the statute as not being in conflict with the Federal Constitution, for the reason—and such is an all-sufficient reason—it is not shown to be plainly and palpably inconsistent with that instrument. Let the State alone in the management of its purely domestic affairs, so long as it does not appear beyond all question that it has violated the Federal Constitution. This view necessarily results from the principle that the health and safety of the people of a State are primarily for the State to guard and protect.

I take leave to say that the New York statute, in the particulars here involved, cannot be held to be in conflict with the Fourteenth Amendment, without enlarging the scope of the Amendment far beyond its original purpose and without bringing under the supervision of this court matters which have been supposed to belong exclusively to the legislative departments of the several States when exerting their conceded power to guard the health and safety of their citizens by such regulations as they in their wisdom deem best. Health laws of every description constitute, said Chief Justice Marshall, a part of that mass of legislation which "embraces everything within the territory of a State, not surrendered to the General Government; all which can be most advantageously exercised by the States themselves." *Gibbons* v. *Ogden*, 9 Wheat. 1, 203. A decision that the New York statute is void under the Fourteenth Amendment will, in my opinion, involve consequences of a far-reaching and mischievous character; for such a decision would seriously cripple the inherent power of the States to care for the lives, health and well-being of their citizens. Those are matters which can be best controlled by the States. The preservation of the just powers of the States is quite as vital as the preservation of the powers of the General Government.

When this court had before it the question of the constitutionality of a statute of Kansas making it a criminal offense for a contractor for public work to permit or require his employes to perform labor upon such work in excess of eight hours each day, it was contended that the statute was in derogation of the liberty both of employes and employer. It was further contended that the Kansas statute was mischievous in its tendencies. This court, while disposing of the question only as it affected public work, held that the Kansas statute was not void under the Fourteenth Amendment. But it took occasion to say what may well be here repeated: "The responsibility therefore rests upon legislators, not upon the courts. No evils arising from such legislation could be more far-reaching than those that might come to our system of government if the judiciary, abandoning the sphere assigned to it by the fundamental law, should enter the domain of legislation, and upon grounds merely of justice or reason or wisdom annul statutes that had received the sanction of the people's representatives. We are reminded by counsel that it is the solemn duty of the courts in cases before them to guard the constitutional rights of the citizen against merely arbitrary power. That is unquestionably true. But it is equally true—indeed, the public interests imperatively demand—that legislative enactments should be recognized and enforced by the courts as embodying the will of the people, unless they are plainly and palpably, beyond all question, in violation of the fundamental law of the Constitution." *Atkin* v. *Kansas*, 191 U.S. 207, 223.

The judgment in my opinion should be affirmed.

MR. JUSTICE HOLMES dissenting.

I regret sincerely that I am unable to agree with the judgment in this case, and that I think it my duty to express my dissent.

This case is decided upon an economic theory which a large part of the country does not entertain. If it were a question whether I agreed with that theory I should desire to study it further and long before making up my mind. But I do not conceive that to be my duty, because I strongly believe that my agreement or disagreement has nothing to do with the right of a majority to embody their opinions in law. It is settled by various decisions of this court that state constitutions and state laws may regulate life in many ways which we as legislators might think as injudicious or if you like as tyrannical as this, and which equally with this interfere with the liberty to contract. Sunday laws and usury laws are ancient examples. A more modern one is the prohibition of lotteries. The liberty of the citizen to do as he likes so long as he does not interfere with the liberty of others to do the same, which has been a shibboleth for some well-known writers, is interfered with by school laws, by the Post Office, by every state or municipal institution which takes his money for purposes thought desirable, whether he likes it or not. The Fourteenth Amendment does not enact Mr. Herbert Spencer's Social Statics. The other day we sustained the Massachusetts vaccination law. *Jacobson* v. *Massachusetts*, 197 U.S. 11. United States and state statutes and decisions cutting down the liberty to contract by way of combination are familiar to this court. *Northern Securities Co.* v. *United States*, 193 U.S. 197. Two years ago we upheld the prohibition of sales of stock on margins or for future delivery in the constitution of California. *Otis* v. *Parker*, 187 U.S. 606. The decision sustaining an eight hour law for miners is still recent. *Holden* v. *Hardy*, 169 U.S. 366. Some of these laws embody convictions or prejudices which judges are likely to share. Some may not. But a constitution is not intended to embody a particular economic theory, whether of paternalism and the organic relation of the citizen to the State or of *laissez faire*. It is made for people of fundamentally differing views, and the accident of our finding certain opinions natural and familiar or novel and even shocking ought not to conclude our judgment upon the question whether statutes embodying them conflict with the Constitution of the United States.

General propositions do not decide concrete cases. The decision will depend on a judgment or intuition more subtle than any articulate major premise. But I think that the proposition just stated, if it is accepted, will carry us far toward the end. Every opinion tends to become a law. I think that the word liberty in the Fourteenth Amendment is perverted when it is held to prevent the natural outcome of a dominant opinion, unless it can be said that a rational and fair man necessarily would admit that the statute proposed would infringe fundamental principles as they have been understood by the traditions of our people and our law. It does not need research to show that no such sweeping condemnation can be passed upon the statute before us. A reasonable man might think it a proper measure on the score of health. Men whom I certainly could not pronounce unreasonable would uphold it as a first installment of a general regulation of the hours of work. Whether in the latter aspect it would be open to the charge of inequality I think it unnecessary to discuss.

Chronology

1888

March 23   Chief Justice Morrison R. Waite dies.

April 30   President Grover Cleveland nominates Melville W. Fuller as chief justice.

July 20   Senate votes to confirm Fuller's appointment.

October 8   Fuller commissioned as Chief Justice of the United States.

November 6   Benjamin Harrison elected president, defeating Cleveland.

1889

March 22   Justice Stanley Matthews dies.

May 13   *Chinese Exclusion Case* (1889) holds that Congress could abrogate existing treaties and exclude Chinese laborers from the United States.

1890

January 6   David J. Brewer replaces Stanley Matthews.

March 24   *Chicago, Milwaukee, and St. Paul Railway Co. v. Minnesota* (1890) holds that state-imposed railroad rates are subject to judicial review under the Due Process Clause of the Fourteenth Amendment.

April 14   *In re Neagle* concludes that the federal courts could grant a writ of habeas corpus to protect actions of a federal marshal within the scope of his duties.

April 28   *Leisy v. Hardin* rules that interstate shipments of liquor into dry states are protected by the Commerce Clause.

1890, *continued*

May 19   *Late Corporation of the Church of Jesus Christ of Latter-Day Saints v. United States* sustains congressional authority to abrogate the charter of the Mormon Church and seize its assets as part of a campaign to eliminate polygamy.

July 2   Sherman Anti-Trust Act outlaws combinations in restraint of trade.

August 8   Wilson Act declares that alcoholic beverages transported into a state shall "upon arrival" be subject to state liquor laws.

October 1   McKinley Tariff Act increases duties on imported goods.

October 13   Justice Samuel F. Miller dies.

1891

January 5   Henry Billings Brown replaces Samuel F. Miller.

March 3   Evarts Act establishes Circuit Courts of Appeals, reducing the appellate burden of the Supreme Court.

May 25   *In re Rahrer* upholds constitutionality of Wilson Act governing interstate shipment of liquor.

May 25   *Voight v. Wright* strikes down state flour inspection as a burden on interstate commerce.

1892

January 11   *Counselman v. Hitchcock* holds that federal statute must afford absolute immunity against future prosecutions before witnesses can be compelled to give incriminating testimony.

January 22   Justice Joseph P. Bradley dies.

February 29   *Church of the Holy Trinity v. United States* declares that federal statute prohibiting foreign contract labor does not apply to religious societies, observing that the United States is "a Christian nation."

February 29   *Budd v. New York* sustains state law regulating maximum charges for elevating grain.

October 10   George Shiras Jr. replaces Joseph P. Bradley.

November 8   Cleveland elected president, defeating Benjamin Harrison.

December 5   *Illinois Central Railroad v. Illinois* applies the public trust doctrine to submerged land and holds that a grant of such land was revocable.

1893

January 23   Justice Lucius Q.C. Lamar dies.

March 2   Safety Appliance Act mandates use of air brakes and automatic couplers on trains operating in interstate commerce.

March 4   Howell E. Jackson replaces Lucius Q.C. Lamar.

March 27   *Monongahela Navigation Co. v. United States* holds that the Just Compensation Clause of the Fifth Amendment should be liberally construed to protect owners whose property is taken for public use.

April 3   *Virginia v. Tennessee* determines that the Compact Clause of the Constitution does not apply to every agreement among states and that Congress need only approve those compacts that threaten to increase the power of the states at the expense of the federal government.

May 1   *Baltimore and Ohio Railroad Co. v. Baugh* applies fellow-servant rule as part of general law in diversity of citizenship cases.

May 15   *Fong Yue Ting v. United States* declares that aliens reside in the United States under the absolute authority of Congress to expel them whenever it feels their removal is necessary.

July 7   Death of Samuel Blatchford.

1894

March 12   Edward D. White replaces Samuel Blatchford.

May 14   *Mobile and Ohio Railroad Co. v. Tennessee* rules that a tax immunity conferred in a corporate charter is protected by the Contract Clause against a later state effort to levy taxes.

1894, *continued*

May 26   *Reagan v. Farmers' Loan and Trust Co.* insists that federal courts will examine the reasonableness of state-imposed railroad rates and invalidates rate schedule at issue as confiscatory.

August 28   Wilson-Gorman Tariff Act fails to significantly reduce tariff duties, but includes first peacetime income tax.

1895

January 21   *United States v. E. C. Knight* narrows the reach of the Sherman Anti-Trust Act by holding that Congress cannot regulate manufacturing under the Commerce Clause.

January 21   *Sparf and Hansen v. United States* concludes that juries in federal criminal trials must follow the judge's instructions.

April 8   *Pollock v. Farmers' Loan and Trust Co.* rules that tax on income from land is direct tax that is unconstitutional because it is not apportioned among the states according to population.

May 20   *Pollock v. Farmers' Loan and Trust Co.* finds that tax on income from personal property is also a direct tax and that consequently the entire 1894 income tax is unconstitutional.

May 27   *In re Debs* sustains an injunction against interference by union officials with trains operating in interstate commerce.

August 8   Justice Howell E. Jackson dies.

1896

January 6   Rufus W. Peckham replaces Howell E. Jackson.

May 18   *Plessy v. Ferguson* upholds state law requiring racial segregation on railroads.

May 18   *Hennington v. Georgia* sustains state law forbidding the operation of freight trains on Sunday despite impact on interstate commerce.

November 3   William McKinley elected president, defeating William Jennings Bryan.

November 16 *Fallbrook Irrigation District v. Bradley* adopts broad definition of "public use" for purposes of taxation and eminent domain.

November 30 *Missouri Pacific Railway Co. v. Nebraska* declares that taking property for the private use of another violates the Due Process Clause even though compensation is paid.

December 14 *Covington and Lexington Turnpike Road Co. v. Sandford* reaffirms principle that courts could inquire whether rates prescribed by state legislature are so unreasonable as to constitute a deprivation of property without due process.

1897

March 1 *Allgeyer v. Louisiana* articulates principle that liberty to enter contracts is protected by Due Process Clause of the Fourteenth Amendment.

March 1 *New York, New Haven, and Hartford Railroad Co. v. New York* upholds state law that banned heating railroad passenger cars by stoves as a safety measure.

March 1 *Chicago, Burlington, and Quincy Railroad Co. v. Chicago* declares that the just compensation requirement when private property is taken for public use is an element of due process applicable to the states by virtue of the Fourteenth Amendment.

March 22 *United States v. Trans-Missouri Freight Association* applies Sherman Anti-Trust Act to railroad pooling arrangement and adopts literal interpretation of the act.

November 8 *Interstate Commerce Commission v. Alabama Midland Railway Co.* construes Interstate Commerce Act to limit power of the Interstate Commerce Commission to ban long haul/short haul rate differential.

December 1 Justice Stephen J. Field resigns.

1898

January 26 Joseph McKenna replaces Stephen J. Field.

February 28 *Holden v. Hardy* sustains constitutionality of state law limiting the hours of work in underground mines.

1898, *continued*

March 7   *Smyth v. Ames* establishes fair-value rule as constitutional norm for determining reasonableness of state-imposed rates in regulated industries.

March 28   *United States v. Wong Kim Ark* concludes that, under the Citizenship Clause of the Fourteenth Amendment, persons born in the United States of Chinese parents become citizens at birth.

April 25   United States declares war on Spain.

April 25   *Williams v. Mississippi* sustains constitutionality of state literacy test despite discriminatory impact on black voters.

June 1   Erdman Act attempts to create new framework governing labor relations for interstate carriers.

July 7   Joint Resolution by Congress provides for the annexation of the Hawaiian Islands to the United States.

December 10   Peace treaty concludes war with Spain.

1899
October 30   *Jones v. Meehan* insists that ambiguous language in treaties with Indian tribes should be construed in favor of the Indians.

December 4   *Addyston Pipe and Steel Co. v. United States* applies Sherman Anti-Trust Act to strike down agreement to divide territorial markets, which directly impacts interstate commerce.

December 18   *Cumming v. Richmond County Board of Education* allows school board to provide high school education for white students but not for black students.

1900
January 8   *The Paquete Habana* asserts that the United States is bound by the rules of customary international law in the absence of a governing treaty or federal law.

February 26   *Maxwell v. Dow* determines that the states are not bound by the procedural guarantees of the Bill of Rights concerning criminal trials and are therefore free to adopt procedural innovations.

May 14   *Knowlton v. Moore* upholds constitutionality of federal inheritance tax.

November 6   William McKinley reelected president, again defeating William Jennings Bryan.

November 19   *Austin v. Tennessee* recognizes tobacco products as legitimate articles of interstate commerce but concludes that state could ban import of cigarettes in small boxes.

December 10   *Williams v. Fears* upholds state laws hampering emigrant agents and thus limiting mobility of black laborers.

1901

May 27   *Downes v. Bidwell*, the most important of the *Insular Cases*, sustains the power of Congress to place a duty on imports from Puerto Rico and rules that the full range of constitutional guarantees does not extend to the overseas territories until Congress acts.

September 14   President McKinley dies one week after being shot; Vice President Theodore Roosevelt becomes chief executive.

October 21   *Knoxville Iron Co. v. Harbison* validates a state law requiring that workers must be paid their wages in money.

1902

June 2   *Hanover National Bank v. Moyses* affirms constitutionality of Bankruptcy Act of 1898.

September 15   Justice Horace Gray dies.

December 1   *Reid v. Colorado* sustains state law prohibiting importation of cattle or horses until the owner obtains certificate that livestock are free from disease.

December 8   Oliver Wendell Holmes Jr. replaces Horace Gray.

1903

January 5   *Lone Wolf v. Hitchcock* declares that Congress has plenary authority over relations with Indians and may exercise unfettered control over tribal lands.

February 23   *Champion v. Ames* holds that Congress could exclude lottery tickets from interstate commerce, in effect recognizing a federal police power to supervise public morals.

February 23   Justice George Shiras Jr. resigns.

March 2   William R. Day replaces George Shiras Jr.

April 27   *Giles v. Harris* dismisses complaint that black voter was denied registration because of race.

1904

February 23   *Butterfield v. Stranahan* upholds delegation by Congress of discretionary authority to an executive agency to make rules that have the effect of laws.

March 14   *Northern Securities Co. v. United States* declares a railroad holding company to be an illegal combination under Sherman Anti-Trust Act.

May 31   *McCray v. United States* sustains prohibitory federal tax on oleomargarine, thereby allowing Congress to regulate the economy indirectly by means of its taxing power.

November 8   Theodore Roosevelt elected president in his own right, defeating Alton B. Parker.

December 19   *Johnson v. Southern Pacific Co.* gives broad reading to Safety Appliance Act in order to protect safety of railroad employees and passengers.

1905

January 30   *Swift and Co. v. United States* holds that Sherman Anti-Trust Act covers activities that are part of a current of commerce among the states.

April 17   *Lochner v. New York*, one of the most important and controversial cases in the history of the Supreme Court, rules that a state law limiting the hours of work in bakeries abridged the freedom of contract protected by the Fourteenth Amendment.

May 15   *Clark v. Nash* sustains state law granting eminent power to private individuals to obtain rights-of-way for mining or irrigation purposes.

December 4   *Manigault v. Springs* weakens Contract Clause by holding that state police power could override private contracts between individuals.

1906

March 12   *Hale v. Henkel* rules that Fifth Amendment privilege against self-incrimination does not apply to corporations but that corporations are protected by the Fourth Amendment against unreasonable searches and seizures.

May 28   Justice Henry Billings Brown resigns.

June 11   Federal Employers' Liability Act creates federal statutory action covering employees injured by accidents on railroads and abolishes certain common law defenses invoked by the carriers.

June 29   Hepburn Act strengthens the power of the Interstate Commerce Commission to regulate railroads.

June 30   Pure Food and Drug Act outlaws shipment of adulterated or mislabeled food and drugs in interstate commerce.

December 17   William H. Moody replaces Henry Billings Brown.

1907

April 15   *Patterson v. Colorado* adopts narrow construction of First Amendment's free speech guarantee as limited to prior restraints.

May 13   *Kansas v. Colorado* fashions interstate common law to govern dispute between two states over the diversion of water from a river.

May 13   *Georgia v. Tennessee Copper Co.* upholds right of a state to maintain nuisance action seeking to halt air pollution caused by manufacturing plant in another state.

1907, *continued*

May 27   *Virginia v. West Virginia* holds that Eleventh Amendment does not bar a suit by Virginia seeking to allocate part of its pre–Civil War debt to West Virginia.

1908

January 6   *Employers' Liability Cases* strike down Federal Employers' Liability Act on grounds that Congress could impose liability on carriers only when employees were engaged in interstate commerce at the time of injury.

January 27   *Adair v. United States* invalidates provision of Erdman Act banning contracts that make it a condition of employment that employees not belong to a labor union.

February 3   *Loewe v. Lawlor* applies Sherman Anti-Trust Act to a secondary boycott organized by a labor union.

February 24   *Muller v. Oregon* sustains state laws limiting working hours for women.

March 23   *Ex Parte Young* holds that states cannot deny resort to the federal courts and that state officials could be enjoined from enforcing unconstitutional act.

April 22   Second Employers' Liability Act governs liability only for railroad workers injured while working in interstate commerce.

November 1   William Howard Taft elected president, defeating William Jennings Bryan.

November 9   *Twining v. New Jersey* rules that the privilege against self-incrimination was not an essential principle of liberty protected by the Due Process Clause of the Fourteenth Amendment against abridgement by the states.

November 9   *Berea College v. Kentucky* upholds application of state law forbidding education of white and black students together to a private college.

1909

January 4   *McLean v. Arkansas* validates state law governing the method of calculating the wages owed to miners.

February 29   *Hubert v. New Orleans* finds that state violated Contract Clause by curtailing municipal powers of taxation, thus leaving creditors unpaid.

May 17   *Welch v. Swasey* sustains regulations limiting the height of buildings.

May 24   *United States v. Shipp* finds sheriff and other officials guilty of contempt of Supreme Court for failure to make reasonable efforts to protect federal prisoner from mob violence.

October 24   Justice Rufus W. Peckham dies.

1910

January 3   Horace H. Lurton replaces Rufus W. Peckham.

January 10   *Interstate Commerce Commission v. Illinois Central Railroad Co.* upholds enlarged powers of the Interstate Commerce Commission under Hepburn Act and signals greater judicial deference toward its decisions.

March 28   Justice David J. Brewer dies.

April 4   *Boston Chamber of Commerce v. Boston* declares that just compensation in eminent domain proceedings should be determined by the value of what the owner has lost.

May 31   *Chiles v. Chesapeake and Ohio Railway Co.* allows railroad companies to adopt regulations segregating white and black passengers in interstate commerce.

July 4   Chief Justice Melville W. Fuller dies.

October 10   Charles Evans Hughes replaces Brewer.

November 20   Justice William M. Moody resigns.

December 19   Justice Edward D. White becomes chief justice, replacing Melville W. Fuller.

Table of Cases

Adair v. United States, 208 U.S. 161 (1908)

Adamson v. California, 332 U.S. 46 (1947)

Addyston Pipe and Steel Company v. United States, 175 U.S. 211 (1899)

Adkins v. Children's Hospital, 261 U.S. 525 (1923)

Allen v. United States, 164 U.S. 492 (1896)

Allgeyer v. Louisiana, 165 U.S. 578 (1897)

Allison v. United States, 160 U.S. 203 (1895)

Austin v. Tennessee, 179 U.S. 343 (1900)

Baltimore and Ohio Railroad Company v. Baugh, 149 U.S. 368 (1893)

Barbed Wire Patent, The, 143 U.S. 275 (1892)

Barnitz v. Beverly, 163 U.S. 118 (1896)

Barron v. Baltimore, 32 U.S. 243 (1833)

Berea College v. Kentucky, 211 U.S. 45 (1908)

Block v. Hirsh, 256 U.S. 135 (1921)

Boston Chamber of Commerce v. Boston, 217 U.S. 189 (1910)

Bowman v. Chicago Northwestern Railway Company, 125 U.S. 465 (1888)

Boyd v. United States, 116 U.S. 616 (1886)

Bradley v. Lightcap, 195 U.S. 1 (1904)

Bradwell v. Illinois, 83 U.S. 130 (1873)

Brass v. North Dakota, 153 U.S. 391 (1894)

Brown v. Board of Education, 347 U.S. 483 (1954)

Brown v. Maryland, 25 U.S. 419 (1827)

Brown v. Walker, 161 U.S. 591 (1896)

Buchanan v. Warley, 245 U.S. 60 (1917)

Budd v. New York, 143 U.S. 517 (1892)

Bunting v. Oregon, 243 U.S. 426 (1917)

Butterfield v. Stranahan, 192 U.S. 470 (1904)

Champion v. Ames, 188 U.S. 321 (1903)

Chesapeake and Ohio Railway Company v. Kentucky, 179 U.S. 388 (1900)

Chicago, Burlington, and Quincy Railroad Company v. Chicago, 166 U.S. 226 (1897)

Chicago, Milwaukee, and St. Paul Railway v. Minnesota, 134 U.S. 418 (1890)

Chiles v. Chesapeake and Ohio Railway Company, 218 U.S. 71 (1910)

Chinese Exclusion Case, 130 U.S. 581 (1889)

Church of the Holy Trinity v. United States, 143 U.S. 457 (1892)

City of Minneapolis v. Minneapolis Street Railway Company, 215 U.S. 417 (1910)

Civil Rights Cases, 109 U.S. 3 (1883)

Clark v. Nash, 198 U.S. 361 (1905)

Clyatt v. United States, 197 U.S. 207 (1905)

Collins v. New Hampshire, 171 U.S. 31 (1898)

Coppage v. Kansas, 236 U.S. 1 (1915)

Counselman v. Hitchcock, 142 U.S. 547 (1892)

Covington and Lexington Turnpike Road Company v. Sandford, 164 U.S. 578 (1896)

Cummings v. Missouri, 71 U.S. 277 (1867)

Cummings v. Richmond County Board of Education, 175 U.S. 528 (1899)

Davis v. Beason, 133 U.S. 333 (1890)

Davis v. Massachusetts, 167 U.S. 43 (1897)

DeLima v. Bidwell, 182 U.S. 1 (1901)

Dolan v. City of Tigard, 512 U.S. 374 (1994)

Dorr v. United States, 195 U.S. 138 (1904)

Downes v. Bidwell, 182 U.S. 244 (1901)

Dred Scott v. Sandford, 60 U.S. 393 (1858)

Employers' Liability Cases, 207 U.S. 463 (1908)

Erie Railroad Company v. Tompkins, 304 U.S. 64 (1938)

Fallbrook Irrigation District v. Bradley, 164 U.S. 112 (1896)

Federal Power Commission v. Hope Natural Gas Company, 320 U.S. 591 (1944)

Field v. Clark, 143 U.S. 649 (1892)

Fong Yue Ting v. United States, 149 U.S. 698 (1893)

Garland, Ex Parte, 71 U.S. 333 (1867)

Geofroy v. Riggs, 133 U.S. 258 (1890)

Georgia v. Tennessee Copper Company, 206 U.S. 230 (1907)

Gibson v. United States, 166 U.S. 269 (1897)

Giles v. Harris, 189 U.S. 475 (1903)

Gladson v. Minnesota, 166 U.S. 427 (1897)

Guinn v. United States, 238 U.S. 347 (1915)

Hadacheck v. Sebastian, 239 U.S. 394 (1915)

Hale v. Henkel, 201 U.S. 43 (1906)

Hammer v. Dagenhart, 247 U.S. 251 (1918)

Hanover National Bank v. Moyses, 186 U.S. 181 (1902)

Hans v. Louisiana, 134 U.S. 1 (1890)

Glossary

Alien A person residing in a country who is not a citizen of that country. In the United States, an alien is generally entitled to the same due process protections of life, liberty, and property that are afforded to citizens. Still, Congress has broad authority over aliens, and they are subject to deportation proceedings.

Certiorari A discretionary writ that an appellate court issues to order a lower court to hand over a case for review. Certiorari is only available where there is no direct appeal and it is appropriate to review and correct decisions of lower courts. In a case of certiorari, the lower court is required to forward a record of its proceedings to the higher court. In the nineteenth century many types of cases could be appealed to the Supreme Court as a matter of right, but in modern practice the writ of certiorari is the primary means of seeking Supreme Court review.

Common law The common law originated in decisions of judges in the royal courts of medieval England. Based on judicial opinions, common law can be contrasted with statutes or express constitutional provisions. During the era of the American Revolution, common law was seen by the colonists as a bulwark of individual rights. Although rooted in tradition, the common law evolved to meet new conditions. Today, the concept of common law embodies both certain substantive rules and a means of analyzing legal disputes.

Decree A court order, or a judgment of a court, generally in equity or admiralty cases. A decree that directs or forbids conduct is called an injunction.

Diversity of citizenship jurisdiction The federal courts have jurisdiction under article III of the U.S. Constitution to hear cases between citizens of different states involving a value in excess of a specific amount set by Congress, currently $75,000. Diversity jurisdiction is thought to allow out-of-state litigants to escape local prejudice and to encourage national economic growth. Diversity cases are typically private law disputes but often have implications for commercial activity.

Dormant commerce power The principle that the commerce clause in the Con-

291

stitution, by its own force, bars states from interfering with interstate commercial activity, even if Congress has not exercised its power to regulate the activity.

Due process   The concept of due process of law, guaranteed in both the Fifth and Fourteenth Amendments, can be traced to the Magna Carta (1215). There are two components to due process: procedural and substantive. Procedural due process is a restriction on how the government can act with respect to individuals. The aim of procedural due process is to prevent arbitrary government by imposing procedural requirements, such as notice and an opportunity to be heard, before an individual is deprived of life, liberty, or property. Substantive due process is a restriction on what the government can do. It is premised on the notion that there are certain fundamental rights that government cannot infringe regardless of what procedures are employed. Historically, substantive due process focused on defending the rights of property owners, but more recently the doctrine has protected rights associated with privacy.

Eminent domain   The government has the inherent power to take private property and convert it to public use. The Fifth Amendment and most state constitutions limit the exercise of eminent domain to "public use" and require the payment of "just compensation."

Equity   Equity evolved in England as a separate body of law that both conflicted with and complemented the common law. Originally grounded in notions of justice as conscience, it developed substantive law doctrines and remedies that differed from common law in many ways. For instance, courts of equity did not utilize trial by jury, issued injunctions, and devised the law of trusts. In modern practice courts of law and equity are substantially merged.

Ex parte   Action taken by or for one party without notice to or challenge by the opposing party. A judicial order can be ex parte if it is granted for the benefit of one party without notice to any person adversely affected.

Federalism   The allocation of power between the federal government and the state governments.

Fellow servant rule   A common law rule that shielded an employer from liability when an employee was injured in the workplace by a negligent coworker. The only recourse of the injured worker was against the fellow servant. The Federal Employers' Liability Act and state workers' compensation laws have generally abolished this rule.

Grandfather clause   A grandfather clause exempted men eligible to vote in 1867 and their descendants from literary and property voting requirements enacted by a number of southern states in the late nineteenth and early twentieth centuries. This was an attempt to preserve the right of poor white illiterates to vote while applying literary and property tests to disfranchise potential black voters.

Habeas corpus　An order issued by a court to bring a person before it, generally to make certain that the person's incarceration or confinement is not unlawful. It is usually used as a postconviction remedy by persons in custody to challenge the legality of their confinement.

Inheritance tax　A tax levied on the property an individual receives by inheritance. The tax is not generally termed a property tax but rather a tax on the right to receive property.

Injunction　A court decree that orders a party to act or to refrain from doing something. To obtain an injunction, the complaint must show that there is no adequate remedy available at law and that an irreparable injury will result unless the relief is granted.

Liberty of contract　Courts generally assume that contracts are freely negotiated and therefore parties should be bound to what they agreed upon and courts should not obstruct the enforcement of contracts. In the late nineteenth century the Supreme Court held that liberty of contract was protected by the Due Process Clause of the Fourteenth Amendment against state abridgement except for legislation to protect public health, safety, or morals.

Natural law　Law that is derived from universal principles of human nature or divine justice, instead of statutes or court rulings. Natural law is based on moral principles that purportedly agree with the nature of man, so that societal peace and happiness depend on the adherence to these principles.

Negligence　The central idea of negligence is that people should exercise reasonable care to guard against harm to other people. When a person fails to exercise that care, their conduct is negligent. Conduct is generally deemed negligent if the harmful consequences could have reasonably been foreseen and prevented by the exercise of reasonable care. Negligence is the heart of modern tort law.

Original jurisdiction　A court has original jurisdiction when that court has the authority to hear a case before any other court can consider the matter. Article III confers original jurisdiction on the Supreme Court over cases involving states as parties. The Court hears few original jurisdiction cases, usually involving a state suing another state.

Peonage　The unlawful and forced servitude of someone who owes a debt in order to satisfy that debt. Peonage was part of the system of forced labor of blacks that continued in the South into the early twentieth century. Forcing debtors to work for creditors at the threat of imprisonment is a federal crime.

Police power   The inherent power of state governments to make laws that protect the public health, morals, welfare, and safety. The extent to which the federal government may exercise a police power remains contested.

Privileges and Immunities Clause   The Fourteenth Amendment to the Constitution prohibits states from making laws that restrain the privileges and immunities of U.S. citizens. The privileges and immunities enjoyed by citizens are generally restricted to those that arise out of the nature of the national government, such as the right to travel between the states.

Prize cases   The admiralty jurisdiction of the federal courts extends to prize cases brought to condemn enemy ships captured in time of war.

Receiver   An unbiased person appointed by the court to protect, collect, or manage property that is the subject or likely to become the subject of litigation.

Regulatory takings   The regulatory takings doctrine holds that a regulation on the use of land may be so severe as to amount to a taking of property by the government for which compensation is required by the Fifth Amendment.

Separation of powers   The separation of powers doctrine, reflected in the Constitution by the creation of three branches of government, was designed not to promote efficiency but to prevent the exercise of arbitrary power by the government. This doctrine guards against too much power being concentrated into one of the branches, and it protects each branch from the overreaching of the other branches. In practice, however, the powers of the branches of the federal government are not entirely distinct, and the emergence of administrative agencies has served to blend legislative and executive authority.

Stay   An order to delay or stop a judicial proceeding or the carrying out of a judgment that resulted from a judicial proceeding. A stay generally maintains the status quo pending the outcome of some defined contingency. A stay is not a dismissal, but it is an injunction that is appealable.

Takings Clause   The Fifth Amendment of the Constitution prohibits the government from taking property from a private owner for public use without the payment of just compensation to the owner. Similar provisions appear in state constitutions.

Tort   A civil, as opposed to a criminal, wrong for which an injured party can obtain a remedy, generally the payment of monetary damages, from the wrongdoer. A tort is a wrong committed in violation of a standard of conduct imposed by law; it is not wrong committed in the breach of a contract. The most frequently litigated torts involve physical injuries to persons.

Treaty power   The authority that article II, section 2 of the U.S. Constitution confers on the president to make treaties, subject to the advice and consent of the Senate. A treaty is a contract or agreement between two or more sovereign nations, and within the United States a treaty is the supreme law of the land.

Ultra vires   Unlawful acts by a corporation beyond the scope of its charter or beyond the powers conferred to it by the laws of the state of incorporation.

Vested right   A right that cannot be taken away from a person because the right wholly and entirely belongs to that person. This right is absolute and cannot be contingent upon the happening of some event.

Workers' compensation   The system in most states for granting benefits to employees who are injured in the workplace. Under this system workers are barred from suing employers for injuries on the job, but they are compensated for such injuries without having to demonstrate that the employer was at fault. Workers compensation statutes thus largely supplant tort law in the context of workplace injuries. The amount of compensation is based on a statutory schedule intended to replace future wages that the employee would have earned had he not been injured.

Writ   A court order that authorizes a person to provide service on a party, to summon a defendant, or otherwise to command the recipient to do or not do certain acts.

Yellow-dog contract   An employment contract that forbids an employee from becoming a member of a labor union and provides for termination if the employee violates the contract and does join a union.

Annotated Bibliography

Abraham, Henry J. *Justices, Presidents, and Senators: A History of U.S. Supreme Court Appointments from Washington to Clinton.* Latham, MD: Rowman and Littlefield, 1999.

> Informative analysis of the selection of Supreme Court justices throughout American history, considering the goals of the appointing president and the process of Senate confirmation.

Alschuler, Albert W. *Law Without Values: The Life, Work, and Legacy of Justice Holmes.* Chicago: University of Chicago Press, 2000.

> A sharply critical examination of the judicial outlook and legacy of Holmes, stressing his profound skepticism and rejection of moral values.

Arkes, Hadley. "*Lochner v. New York* and the Cast of Our Laws." In Robert P. George, ed., *Great Cases in Constitutional Law.* Princeton, NJ: Princeton University Press, 2000.

> A spirited defense of *Lochner* and the liberty of contract doctrine as protective of individual freedom.

Baker, Liva. *The Justice from Beacon Hill: The Life and Times of Oliver Wendell Holmes.* New York: HarperCollins, 1991.

> Comprehensive biography of Holmes, giving extensive attention to his pre–Supreme Court experiences and stressing that he was misunderstood as a liberal.

Barnes, Catherine A. *Journey from Jim Crow: The Desegregation of Southern Transit.* New York: Columbia University Press, 1983.

> Provides a detailed account of the lengthy struggle to end segregated transportation in the South.

Benedict, Michael Les. "Laissez-Faire and Liberty: A Re-Evaluation of the Meaning and Origins of Laissez-Faire Constitutionalism." *Law and History Review* 3 (1985): 293–331.

> Insightful study of nineteenth-century laissez-faire philosophy, demonstrating that conservative judges and scholars were genuinely interested in individual liberty.

————. "Victorian Moralism and Civic Liberty." In Donald G. Nieman, ed., *The Constitution, Law, and American Life: Critical Aspects of the Nineteenth-Century Experience*. Athens: University of Georgia Press, 1992.

> Thoughtful exploration of why judges in the late nineteenth century were willing to guard property rights but allowed legislators broad power to enforce moral values.

Bergan, Francis. "Mr. Justice Brewer: Perspective of a Century." *Albany Law Review* 25 (1961): 191–202.

> Provides good treatment of Brewer's pre-Court education and experience, as well as his extrajudicial efforts to encourage the peaceful settlement of international disputes by arbitration.

Bernstein, David E. *Only One Place of Redress: African Americans, Labor Regulations, and the Courts From Reconstruction to the New Deal*. Durham, NC: Duke University Press, 2001.

> Offers a bold argument that judicial enforcement of freedom of contract assisted racial minorities in the face of the discriminatory impact of labor laws; gives careful consideration to emigrant-agent laws challenged before the Fuller Court.

————. "*Plessy* Versus *Lochner*: The *Berea College* Case." *Journal of Supreme Court History* 25 (2000): 93–111.

> Persuasively argues that the liberty of contract recognized in *Lochner* was at odds with state-imposed segregation and that the Fuller Court evaded this conflict in the *Berea College* opinion.

————. "The Law and Economics of Post–Civil War Restrictions on Interstate Migration by African-Americans." *Texas Law Review* 76 (1998): 781–847.

> A detailed analysis of the legal challenges to emigrant-agent laws in the southern states.

Beth, Loren P. *John Marshall Harlan: The Last Whig Justice*. Lexington: University Press of Kentucky, 1992.

> A helpful biography of Harlan, giving attention to the role of family background and political views in shaping his judicial philosophy.

————. *The Development of the American Constitution, 1877–1917*. New York: Harper and Row, 1971.

> A good overview of constitutional decisionmaking at the turn of the twentieth century.

Braeman, John. *Before the Civil Rights Revolution: The Old Court and Individual Rights*. Westport, CT: Greenwood Press, 1988.

> A rewarding study of the Supreme Court's handling of civil rights and civil liberties issues before 1937, noting that the Court was increasingly active in defending individual rights.

Brodhead, Michael J. *David J. Brewer: The Life of a Supreme Court Justice, 1837–1910.* Carbondale: Southern Illinois University Press, 1994.

> Provides a favorable evaluation of Brewer, an important but often neglected figure of the Fuller era.

Brown, Henry Billings. "The Liberty of the Press." *American Law Review* 34 (1900): 321–341.

> Revealing consideration of freedom of the press by a member of the Fuller Court.

Calvani, Terry. "The Early Professional Career of Howell Jackson." *Vanderbilt Law Review* 30 (1977): 39–72.

> Discussing Jackson's Civil War military service and career at the bar before his appointment to the federal bench.

Clark, Blue. *Lone Wolf v. Hitchcock: Treaty Rights and Indian Law at the End of the Nineteenth Century.* Lincoln: University of Nebraska Press, 1994.

> A study of a seminal decision by the Fuller Court establishing the plenary authority of Congress over Indian affairs notwithstanding treaty provisions.

Curriden, Mark, and Leroy Phillips Jr. *Contempt of Court: The Turn-of-the-Century Lynching That Launched 100 Years of Federalism.* New York: Faber and Faber, 1999.

> Detailed treatment of a 1906 lynching that led to an extraordinary decision by the Fuller Court holding local officials in contempt.

Currie, David P. *The Constitution in the Supreme Court: The Second Century, 1888–1986.* Chicago: University of Chicago Press, 1990.

> This historical overview of the Supreme Court contains several chapters devoted to the Fuller era, stressing the protection of economic rights.

Duker, William F. "Mr. Justice Rufus Peckham: The Police Power and the Individual in a Changing World." *Brigham Young University Law Review* (1980): 47–67.

> Discussing Peckham's activist conception of the judicial role in safeguarding economic liberty.

Ely, James W. Jr. *The Guardian of Every Other Right: A Constitutional History of Property Rights.* 2nd ed. New York: Oxford University Press, 1998.

> Balanced overview of the pivotal place of private property in the American constitutional system.

——. *The Chief Justiceship of Melville W. Fuller, 1888–1910.* Columbia: University of South Carolina Press, 1995.

> Provides a fresh interpretation of the work of the Supreme Court under Fuller's leadership, highlighting the Court's commitment to economic liberty and limited government.

——. *Railroads and American Law.* Lawrence: University Press of Kansas, 2001.

> The first comprehensive legal history of the rail industry, this volume chronicles the impact of railroading on the formation of new legal norms.

————. "Melville W. Fuller." In Melvin I. Urofsky, ed., *The Supreme Court Justices: A Biographical Dictionary*. New York: Garland, 1994, pp. 183–188.

>   Helpful sketch of Fuller as chief justice.

————. "The Fuller Court and Takings Jurisprudence." *Journal of Supreme Court History* 2 (1996): 120–135.

>   The only analysis of the pioneering work of the Fuller Court in developing the jurisprudence of the Takings Clause of the Fifth Amendment.

————. "Melville Fuller Reconsidered." *Journal of Supreme Court History* 1 (1998): 35–49.

>   A concise treatment of the constitutional tenets of the Fuller Court.

————. "'The Railroad System Has Burst through State Limits': Railroads and Interstate Commerce, 1830–1920." *Arkansas Law Review* 55 (2003): 933–980.

>   Examines how the growth of interstate railroading opened the door for a more expansive interpretation of the Commerce Clause, with particular attention to the Fuller era.

Epstein, Richard A. "The Proper Scope of the Commerce Power." *Virginia Law Review* 73 (1987): 1387–1455.

>   Contends that *E. C. Knight* correctly distinguished between manufacturing and commerce and that affirmative power of Congress under Commerce Clause should be limited.

Fairman, Charles. "What Makes a Great Justice? Mr. Justice Bradley and the Supreme Court, 1870–1892." *Boston University Law Review* 30 (1950): 49–102.

>   Provides a positive evaluation of Bradley's tenure on the Supreme Court.

————. *Mr. Justice Miller and the Supreme Court, 1862–1890*. Cambridge, MA: Harvard University Press, 1939.

>   The leading if somewhat dated biography of Miller, this work discusses at length his role in shaping early interpretations of the Fourteenth Amendment.

Faulkner, Harold U. *Politics, Reform, and Expansion: 1890–1900*. New York: Harper and Row, 1959.

>   Provides a comprehensive survey of the economic and political developments of the 1890s.

Fiss, Owen M. *History of the Supreme Court of the United States, Volume 8: Troubled Beginnings of the Modern State, 1888–1910*. New York: Macmillan, 1993.

>   A lengthy exploration of the principal themes of the Fuller era, maintaining that the Court sought to enforce a constitutional ideal of economic liberty.

Freyer, Tony A. *Forums of Order: The Federal Courts and Business in American History*. Greenwich, CT: JAI Press, 1979.

>   A fine analysis of how the federal courts asserted authority over the development of interstate enterprise through diversity jurisdiction.

Friedman, Lawrence M. *American Law in the Twentieth Century*. New Haven, CT: Yale University Press, 2002.

A masterful treatment of the changes in public and private law in the twentieth century, giving some attention to the first decade when Fuller was chief justice.

Fuller, Melville W. "Address in Commemoration of the Inauguration of George Washington as First President," December 11, 1889, reprinted in 132 U.S. 706 (1889).

Furer, Howard B., ed. *The Fuller Court, 1888–1910*. Millwood, NJ: Associated Faculty Press, 1986.

Provides a chronology of the Fuller era, together with excerpts from leading decisions and brief biographical sketches of the justices.

Gamer, Robert, E. "Justice Brewer and Substantive Due Process: A Conservative Court Revisited." *Vanderbilt Law Review* 18 (1965): 615–641.

A balanced portrait of Brewer, noting his distrust of business monopolies.

Gillman, Howard. *The Constitution Besieged: The Rise and Demise of Lochner Era Police Powers Jurisprudence*. Durham, NC: Duke University Press, 1993.

Impressive account of nineteenth-century constitutional doctrines that curtailed legislative power.

———. "More on the Origins of the Fuller Court's Jurisprudence: Reexamining the Scope of Federal Power Over Commerce and Manufacturing in Nineteenth-Century Constitutional Law." *Political Science Quarterly* 49 (1996): 415–437.

Argues that Fuller Court decisions on congressional authority under the Commerce Clause were consistent with original understanding of clause and reflected commitment to federalism.

Glennon, Robert J. Jr. "Justice Henry Billings Brown: Values in Tension." *University of Colorado Law Review* 44 (1973): 553–604.

A helpful analysis of Brown's judicial opinions, noting that he never developed a coherent philosophy but reflected the views of late-nineteenth-century America.

Gordon, James W. "Religion and the First Harlan: A Case Study in Late Nineteenth Century Presbyterian Constitutionalism." *Marquette Law Review* 85 (2001): 317–422.

Thoughtful treatment of the role of religion in fashioning Harlan's judicial outlook.

Gordon, Sarah Barringer. *The Mormon Question: Polygamy and Constitutional Conflict in Nineteenth-Century America*. Chapel Hill: University of North Carolina Press, 2002.

Explores legislative efforts to abolish polygamy and constitutional debate over the scope of religious freedom, giving attention to decisions by the Fuller Court.

Graber, Mark A. *Transforming Free Speech: The Ambiguous Legacy of Civil Libertarianism*. Berkeley: University of California Press, 1991.

Important study that examines the conservative libertarian tradition at the close of the nineteenth century, a body of thought that emphasized the importance of both free speech and private property as security for liberty.

Hall, Kermit L., ed. *The Oxford Companion to the Supreme Court of the United States*. New York: Oxford University Press, 1992.

> Comprehensive volume with helpful essays on the Supreme Court, the justices, and leading decisions.

————. *The Magic Mirror: Law in American History*. New York: Oxford University Press, 1989.

> An outstanding synthesis of the broad themes of American legal history, with a valuable discussion of the judicial response to economic regulations in the late nineteenth century.

Hamm, Richard F. *Shaping the Eighteenth Amendment: Temperance Reform, Legal Culture, and the Polity, 1880–1920*. Chapel Hill: University of North Carolina Press, 1995.

> A fine study of interaction between the prohibition movement and the legal culture, with special attention to the impact of federalism and interstate commerce doctrines on prohibition tactics.

Highsaw, Robert B. *Edward Douglass White: Defender of the Conservative Faith*. Baton Rouge: Louisiana State University Press, 1981.

> A solid judicial biography of White, stressing his dedication to federalism and his role in formulating the rule of reason in antitrust cases.

Horwitz, Morton J. *The Transformation of American Law, 1870–1960*. New York: Oxford University Press, 1992.

> A sweeping account of how the Progressive movement sought to displace traditional views about contractual freedom and property rights.

Hovenkamp, Herbert. *Enterprise and American Law, 1836–1937*. Cambridge, MA: Harvard University Press, 1991.

> This outstanding work charts the interplay between economic theory and the law governing business enterprise.

Howe, Mark de Wolfe. *Justice Oliver Wendell Holmes: The Proving Years, 1870–1882*. Cambridge, MA: Harvard University Press, 1963.

> Classic study of Holmes's legal career and Harvard professorship before he joined the Supreme Judicial Court of Massachusetts.

Hudspeth, Harvey Gresham. "Howell Edmunds Jackson and the Making of Tennessee's First Native-Born Supreme Court Justice, 1893–1895." *Tennessee Historical Quarterly* 58 (1999): 141–155.

> Provides a careful consideration of Jackson's nomination to the Supreme Court.

Hurst, James Willard. *Law and the Conditions of Freedom in the Nineteenth-Century United States*. Madison: University of Wisconsin Press, 1956.

> Pathbreaking exploration of the relationship between law and economic growth in the nineteenth and early twentieth centuries.

Hylton, Joseph Gordon. "David Josiah Brewer: A Conservative Justice Reconsidered." *Journal of Supreme Court History* (1999): 45–64.

> A helpful reconsideration of Brewer's constitutional theories, pointing out that he often upheld business regulations and was not a doctrinaire supporter of the liberty of contract doctrine.

Jensen, Erik M. "The Taxing Power, the Sixteenth Amendment, and the Meaning of 'Incomes.'" *Arizona State Law Journal* 33 (2001): 1057–1158.

> A helpful revisionist analysis of the original understanding of the direct tax cause.

———. "The Apportionment of 'Direct Taxes': Are Consumption Taxes Constitutional?" *Columbia Law Review* 97 (1997): 2334–2419.

> Maintains that *Pollock* decision correctly interpreted Direct Tax Clause.

Keller, Morton. *Affairs of State: Public Life in Late Nineteenth Century America.* Cambridge, MA: Harvard University Press, 1977.

> A comprehensive assessment of the political and economic changes that transformed American society in the Gilded Age, with a fine chapter on the role of the Supreme Court in the polity.

Kens, Paul. *Justice Stephen Field: Shaping Liberty from the Gold Rush to the Gilded Age.* Lawrence: University Press of Kansas, 1997.

> Insightful discussion of Field's judicial career, with special attention to the values on which his judicial philosophy was based and to his political ambitions.

———. *Judicial Power and Reform Politics: The Anatomy of* Lochner v. New York. Lawrence: University Press of Kansas, 1990.

> A rewarding study of one of the most famous decisions of the Fuller Court.

Kerr, James Edward. *The Insular Cases: The Role of the Judiciary in American Expansionism.* Port Washington, NY: Kennikat Press, 1982.

> The most complete discussion of the legal issues arising out of the acquisition of overseas territories following the Spanish-American War.

King, Willard L. *Melville Weston Fuller: Chief Justice of United States, 1888–1910.* New York: Macmillan, 1950; reprint Chicago: University of Chicago Press, 1967.

> Contains a detailed biographical treatment of Fuller but provides little critical analysis of Fuller Court jurisprudence.

Kosma, Montgomery N., and Ross E. Davies. *Fuller and Washington at Centuries' Ends.* Washington, DC: Green Bay Press, 1999.

> Reprints Washington's farewell address and Fuller's 1889 address as vehicles for assessing the changing conditions of law and society in the United States.

Kull, Andrew. *The Color-Blind Constitution.* Cambridge, MA: Harvard University Press, 1992.

> Traces the color-blind principle from the antebellum period to the present, giving particular attention to Harlan's dissenting opinion in *Plessy v. Ferguson.*

Lofgren, Charles A. *The Plessy Case: A Legal-Historical Interpretation*. New York: Oxford University Press, 1987.

>   A meticulous reassessment of a landmark case, this fine study insists that the *Plessy* decision was well-grounded in contemporary constitutional law.

Magrath, C. Peter. *Morrison R. Waite: The Triumph of Character*. New York: MacMillan, 1963.

>   The most authoritative work on Waite, offering insights into his judicial outlook and leadership of the Court as chief justice.

McCurdy, Charles W. "The *Knight* Sugar Decision of 1895 and the Modernization of American Corporate Law, 1869–1903." *Business History Review* 53 (1979): 304–342.

>   Maintains that corporation law became national in reach as federal courts looked skeptically at state regulations.

———. "Justice Field and the Jurisprudence of Government-Business Relations: Some Parameters of Laissez-Faire Constitutionalism, 1863–1897." *Journal of American History* 61 (1975): 970–1005.

>   An excellent reassessment of Field's efforts to separate private economic rights from governmental controls.

McDevitt, Matthew. *Joseph McKenna: Associate Justice of the United States*. Washington, DC: Catholic University of America Press, 1946; reprint New York: DeCapo Press, 1974.

>   Useful but not particularly analytical account of McKenna's tenure on the Supreme Court.

McLean, Joseph E. *William Rufus Day: Supreme Court Justice from Ohio*. Baltimore: Johns Hopkins University Press, 1946.

>   Helpful exploration of Day's pre–Supreme Court background as well as his time on the Court.

Morris, Jeffrey B. "The Era of Melville Weston Fuller." *Supreme Court Historical Society* (*Yearbook 1981*): 37–51.

>   A brief but balanced assessment of Fuller as chief and the work of the Court during his tenure.

Murphy, James B. *L.Q.C. Lamar: Pragmatic Patriot*. Baton Rouge: Louisiana State University Press, 1973.

>   This biography of Lamar examines his political career in detail but offers only a skimpy treatment of his time on the Supreme Court.

Neely, Alfred S. "'A Humbug Based on Economic Ignorance and Incompetence': Antitrust in the Eyes of Justice Holmes." *Utah Law Review* (1993): 1–66.

>   A detailed discussion of the skeptical antitrust views of Holmes and the extent to which his personal opinion impacted his voting record in antitrust cases.

Orth, John V. *The Judicial Power of the United States: The Eleventh Amendment in American History*. New York: Oxford University Press, 1987.

Ably examines state and municipal debt repudiation in the late nineteenth century and concludes that Supreme Court invoked Eleventh Amendment to avoid application of Contract Clause to southern states.

Palmore, Joseph R. "The Not-So-Strange Career of Interstate Jim Crow: Race, Transportation, and the Dormant Commerce Clause, 1878–1946." *Virginia Law Review* 83 (1997): 1773–1817.

A thoughtful analysis of the application of dormant Commerce Clause doctrine to racial segregation on railroads.

Paul, Arnold M. *Conservative Crisis and the Rule of Law: Attitudes of Bar and Bench, 1887–1895.* Ithaca, NY: Cornell University Press, 1960.

Seeks to explain property-conscious decisions by Supreme Court as a response to perceived threats to the social order.

Phillips, Michael J. *The Lochner Court, Myth and Reality: Substantive Due Process from the 1890s to the 1930s.* Westport, CT: Praeger, 2001.

This volume challenges the standard account of the judicial use of the Due Process Clause to uphold economic liberty and maintains that some Supreme Court decisions striking down economic legislation were justified.

Pierce, Carl A. "A Vacancy on the Supreme Court: The Politics of Judicial Appointment 1893–1894." *Tennessee Law Review* 39 (1972): 555–612.

A study of the patronage quarrel between President Cleveland and Senator Hill that led to the 1894 appointment of Edward D. White to the Supreme Court.

Porter, Mary Cornelia. "That Commerce Shall Be Free: A New Look at the Old Laissez-Faire Court." *Supreme Court Review* (1976): 135–159.

This important revisionist piece disputes the older notion that the Supreme Court between 1880 and 1940 was probusiness and asserts that judicial review of utility rates was designed to protect investment as the key to an expanding national economy.

Pratt, Walter F. Jr. *The Supreme Court Under Edward Douglass White, 1910–1921.* Columbia: University of South Carolina Press, 1999.

A helpful chronological approach to the Supreme Court under Chief Justice White, skillfully probing his leadership style as well as changes in the Court's jurisprudence.

———. "Rhetorical Styles on the Fuller Court." *American Journal of Legal History* 24 (1980): 189–220.

An important article pointing out that the justices on the Fuller Court had different perceptions of their role and different styles of judicial decisionmaking.

Przybyszewski, Linda. *The Republic According to John Marshall Harlan.* Chapel Hill: University of North Carolina Press, 1999.

A thoughtful analysis of how notions of paternalism, nationalism, and religious faith influenced Harlan's understanding of constitutional law.

————. "The Religion of a Jurist: Justice David J. Brewer and the Christian Nation." *Journal of Supreme Court History* 25 (2000): 228–242.

> Examines the role Christian doctrine had in shaping Brewer's jurisprudence.

Purcell, Edward A. Jr. *Litigation and Inequality: Federal Diversity Jurisdiction in Industrial America, 1870–1958*. New York: Oxford University Press, 1992.

> A detailed study of both the procedural and substantive law governing diversity
> actions, as well as the litigation strategy of parties in federal court.

Reeder, Robert P. "Chief Justice Fuller." *University of Pennsylvania Law Review* 59 (1910): 1–14.

> Written at the time of Fuller's death, this brief article examines his judicial opin-
> ions and notes the absence of political partisanship on the Fuller Court.

Ross, Michael A. "Cases of Shattered Dreams: Justice Samuel Freeman Miller and the Rise and Fall of a Mississippi River Town." *Annals of Iowa* 57 (1998): 201–239.

> Explains Miller's judicial outlook, and especially his hostility to suits by bond-
> holders, in terms of disappointed economic expectations rather than agrarian
> radicalism.

————. "Justice for Iowa: Samuel Freeman Miller's Appointment to the United States Supreme Court during the Civil War." *Annals of Iowa* 60 (2001): 111–138.

> Discusses the political circumstances that brought about Miller's appointment
> to the Supreme Court.

Ross, William G. *A Muted Fury: Populists, Progressives, and Labor Unions Confront the Courts, 1890–1937*. Princeton, NJ: Princeton University Press, 1994.

> Explains the hostility toward the Supreme Court during the Progressive era and
> considers why the critics were unable to curb judicial power.

Semonche, John E. *Charting the Future: The Supreme Court Responds to a Changing Society, 1890–1920*. Westport, CT: Greenwood Press, 1978.

> Helpful survey of the decisions of the Fuller and White Courts.

Shiras, George III. *Justice George Shiras Jr. of Pittsburgh*. Pittsburgh, PA: University of Pittsburgh Press, 1953.

> The only biography of Shiras, this volume discusses his pre-Court career as well
> as his judicial philosophy and role on the Fuller Court.

Siegel, Stephen A. "Understanding the Lochner Era: Lessons from the Controversy Over Railroad and Utility Rate Regulation." *Virginia Law Review* 70 (1984): 187–263.

> Fine analysis of judicial review of rate regulations.

————. "*Lochner* Era Jurisprudence and the American Constitutional Tradition." *North Carolina Law Review* 70 (1991): 1–111.

> Stresses continuity between *Lochner*-era jurisprudence and earlier constitu-
> tional developments but points out that *Lochner*-era justices saw Constitution
> as evolving.

Spector, Robert M. "Legal Historian on the United States Supreme Court: Justice Horace Gray, Jr., and the Historical Method." *American Journal of Legal History* 12 (1968): 181–210.

> The most thorough assessment of Gray's tenure on the Supreme Court.

Steamer, Robert J. *Chief Justice: Leadership and the Supreme Court.* Columbia: University of South Carolina Press, 1986.

> Evaluates the office of chief justice and the different styles of leadership that chiefs have employed to manage the Court.

Sunstein, Cass R. "Lochner's Legacy." *Columbia Law Review* 87 (1987): 873–919.

> Advances problematic theory, with little historical grounding, to explain *Lochner* era in terms of a common law baseline.

Swisher, Carl Brent. *Stephen J. Field: Craftsman of the Law.* Washington, DC: Brooking Institution, 1930; reprint Chicago: University of Chicago Press, 1969.

> A classic but dated judicial biography of Field.

Twiss, Benjamin R. *Lawyers and the Constitution: How Laissez-Faire Came to the Supreme Court.* Princeton, NJ: Princeton University Press, 1942.

> A study of the role of lawyers in urging laissez-faire views on the Supreme Court, but reflecting the largely discredited position that the Fuller Court was influenced by social Darwinism.

Urofsky, Melvin I., ed. *The Supreme Court Justices: A Biographical Dictionary.* New York: Garland, 1994.

> A valuable collection of essays about each of the justices who have served on the Supreme Court.

Warren, Charles. *The Supreme Court in United States History.* 2 vols. Rev. ed. Boston: Little, Brown, 1926.

> An older but still useful account of the Supreme Court, emphasizing the interplay between jurisprudence and larger political currents but giving little attention to the Fuller era.

Westin, Alan Furman. "The Supreme Court, the Populist Movement, and the Campaign of 1896." *Journal of Politics* 15 (1953): 3–41.

> Discusses impact of the Fuller Court decisions on the Populist movement and the presidential campaign of 1896.

White, G. Edward. *Justice Oliver Wendell Holmes: Law and the Inner Self.* New York: Oxford University Press, 1993.

> An outstanding biography of Holmes, exploring both his personal life and his work on the Supreme Court.

———. *The Constitution and the New Deal.* Cambridge, MA: Harvard University Press, 2000.

> Discusses changes in early-twentieth-century jurisprudence and challenges the standard account of a triumphant New Deal.

———. "John Marshall Harlan I: The Precursor." *American Journal of Legal History* 19 (1975): 1–21.

> Concludes that Harlan had no consistent theory of judging and decided cases based on an individualized sense of justice.

Wright, Benjamin Fletcher. *The Contract Clause of the Constitution.* Cambridge, MA: Harvard University Press, 1938.

> A classic, if somewhat dated, history of the Contract Clause, giving some attention to the Fuller era.

Index

About the Author

James W. Ely, Jr., is Milton R. Underwood Professor of Law and professor of history at Vanderbilt University Law School. He is the author of numerous articles and books dealing with U.S. legal and constitutional history, including *The Chief Justiceship of Melville W. Fuller, 1888–1910* (1995), *The Guardian of Every Other Right: A Constitutional History of Property Rights*, 2nd ed. (1998), and *Railroads and American Law* (2001).